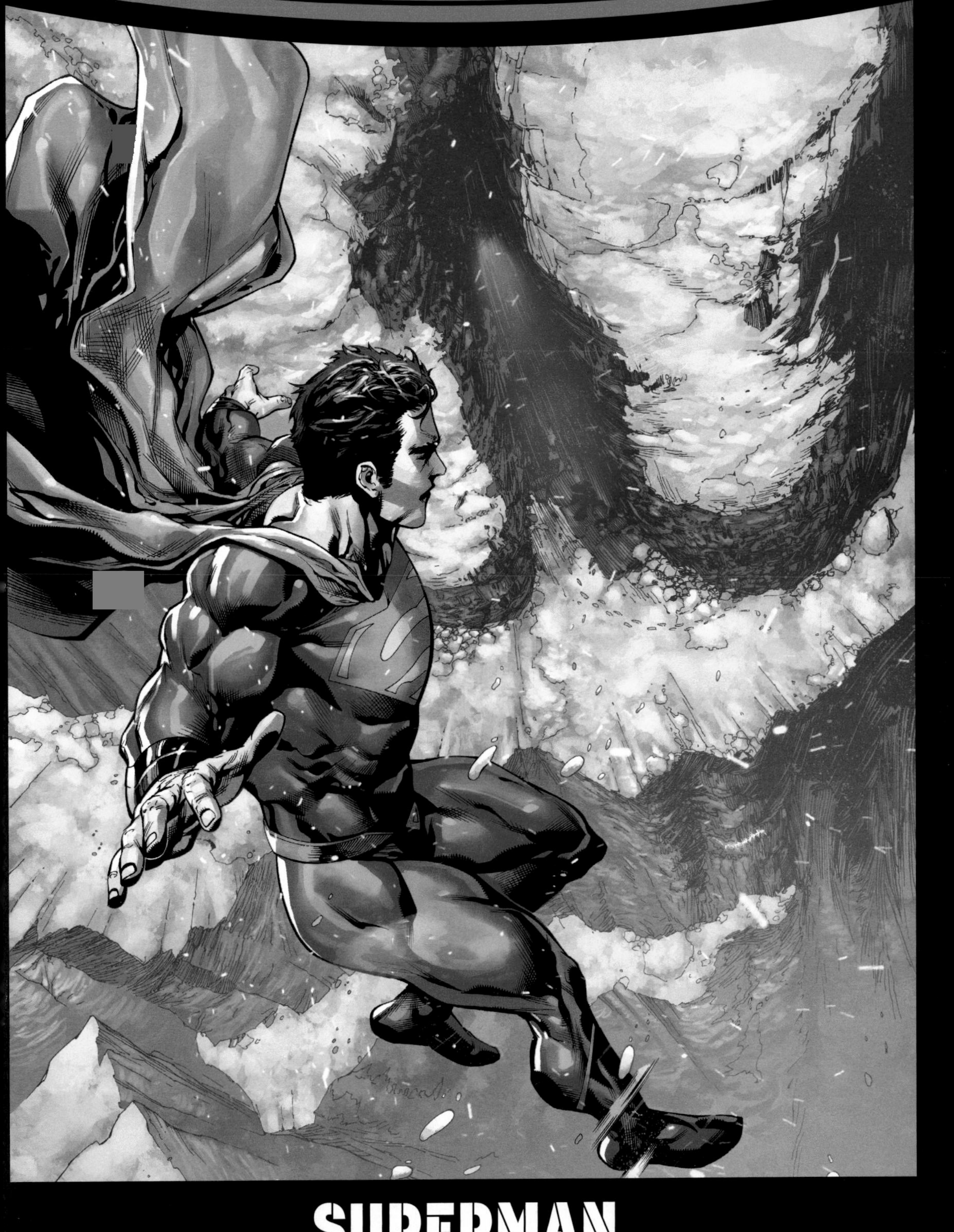

SUPERMAN
REBORN

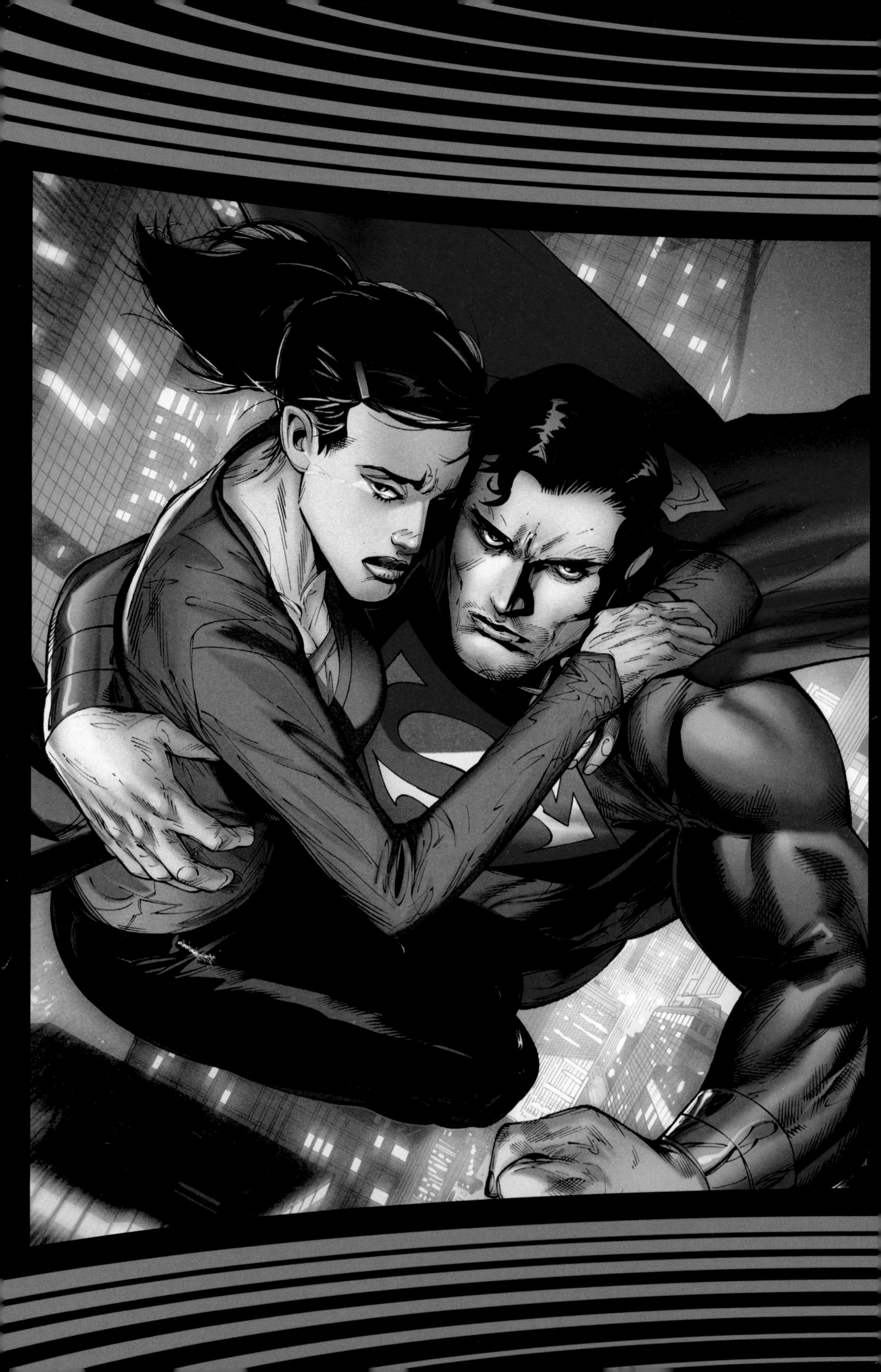

SUPERMAN
REBORN

DAN JURGENS * **PETER J. TOMASI**
PATRICK GLEASON * **PAUL DINI**
writers

DOUG MAHNKE * **JAIME MENDOZA** * **CHRISTIAN ALAMY**
TREVOR SCOTT * **PATRICK GLEASON** * **MICK GRAY** * **IAN CHURCHILL**
PATCH ZIRCHER * **STEPHEN SEGOVIA** * **ART THIBERT**
artists

ARIF PRIANTO * **ULISES ARREOLA** * **WIL QUINTANA**
JOHN KALISZ * **MIKE ALTIYEH**
colorists

ROB LEIGH
letterer

PATRICK GLEASON and JOHN KALISZ
collection cover artists

SUPERMAN CREATED BY JERRY SIEGEL AND JOE SHUSTER.
BY SPECIAL ARRANGEMENT WITH THE JERRY SIEGEL FAMILY.

SUPERBOY CREATED BY JERRY SIEGEL.
BY SPECIAL ARRANGEMENT WITH THE JERRY SIEGEL FAMILY.

MIKE COTTON, EDDIE BERGANZA Editors - Original Series
PAUL KAMINSKI Associate Editor - Original Series ✳ ANDREW MARINO Assistant Editor - Original Series
JEB WOODARD Group Editor - Collected Editions ✳ PAUL SANTOS Editor - Collected Edition
STEVE COOK Design Director - Books ✳ SHANNON STEWART Publication Design

BOB HARRAS Senior VP - Editor-in-Chief, DC Comics

DIANE NELSON President ✳ DAN DiDIO Publisher ✳ JIM LEE Publisher ✳ GEOFF JOHNS President & Chief Creative Officer
AMIT DESAI Executive VP - Business & Marketing Strategy, Direct to Consumer & Global Franchise Management
SAM ADES Senior VP - Direct to Consumer ✳ BOBBIE CHASE VP - Talent Development
MARK CHIARELLO Senior VP - Art, Design & Collected Editions ✳ JOHN CUNNINGHAM Senior VP - Sales & Trade Marketing
ANNE DePIES Senior VP - Business Strategy, Finance & Administration ✳ DON FALLETTI VP - Manufacturing Operations
LAWRENCE GANEM VP - Editorial Administration & Talent Relations ✳ ALISON GILL Senior VP - Manufacturing & Operations
HANK KANALZ Senior VP - Editorial Strategy & Administration ✳ JAY KOGAN VP - Legal Affairs
THOMAS LOFTUS VP - Business Affairs ✳ JACK MAHAN VP - Business Affairs
NICK J. NAPOLITANO VP - Manufacturing Administration ✳ EDDIE SCANNELL VP - Consumer Marketing
COURTNEY SIMMONS Senior VP - Publicity & Communications
JIM (SKI) SOKOLOWSKI VP - Comic Book Specialty Sales & Trade Marketing
NANCY SPEARS VP - Mass, Book, Digital Sales & Trade Marketing

SUPERMAN REBORN

DC Comics, 2900 West Alameda Ave., Burbank, CA 91505
Printed by LSC Communications, Kendallville, IN, USA. 8/11/17. First Printing.
ISBN: 978-1-4012-7358-3

Library of Congress Cataloging-in-Publication Data is available.

PEFC Certified

Printed on paper from
sustainably managed
forests, controlled
sources

PEFC/29-31-337   www.pefc.org

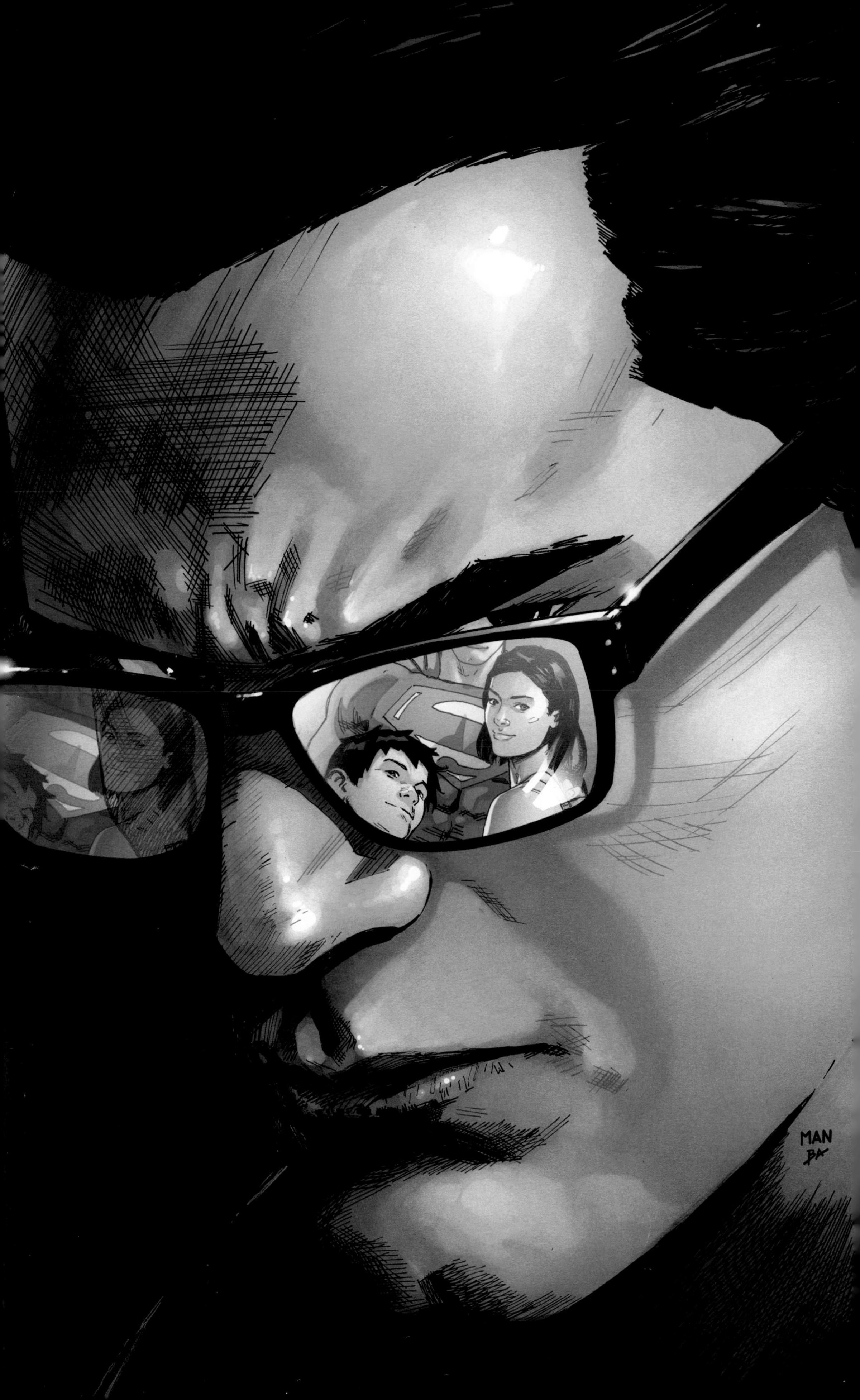
MAN
BA

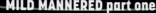

MILD MANNERED part one

DAN JURGENS writer * PATCH ZIRCHER & STEPHEN SEGOVIA pencillers
PATCH ZIRCHER & ART THIBERT inkers * ARIF PRIANTO colorist
CLAY MANN & BRAD ANDERSON cover art

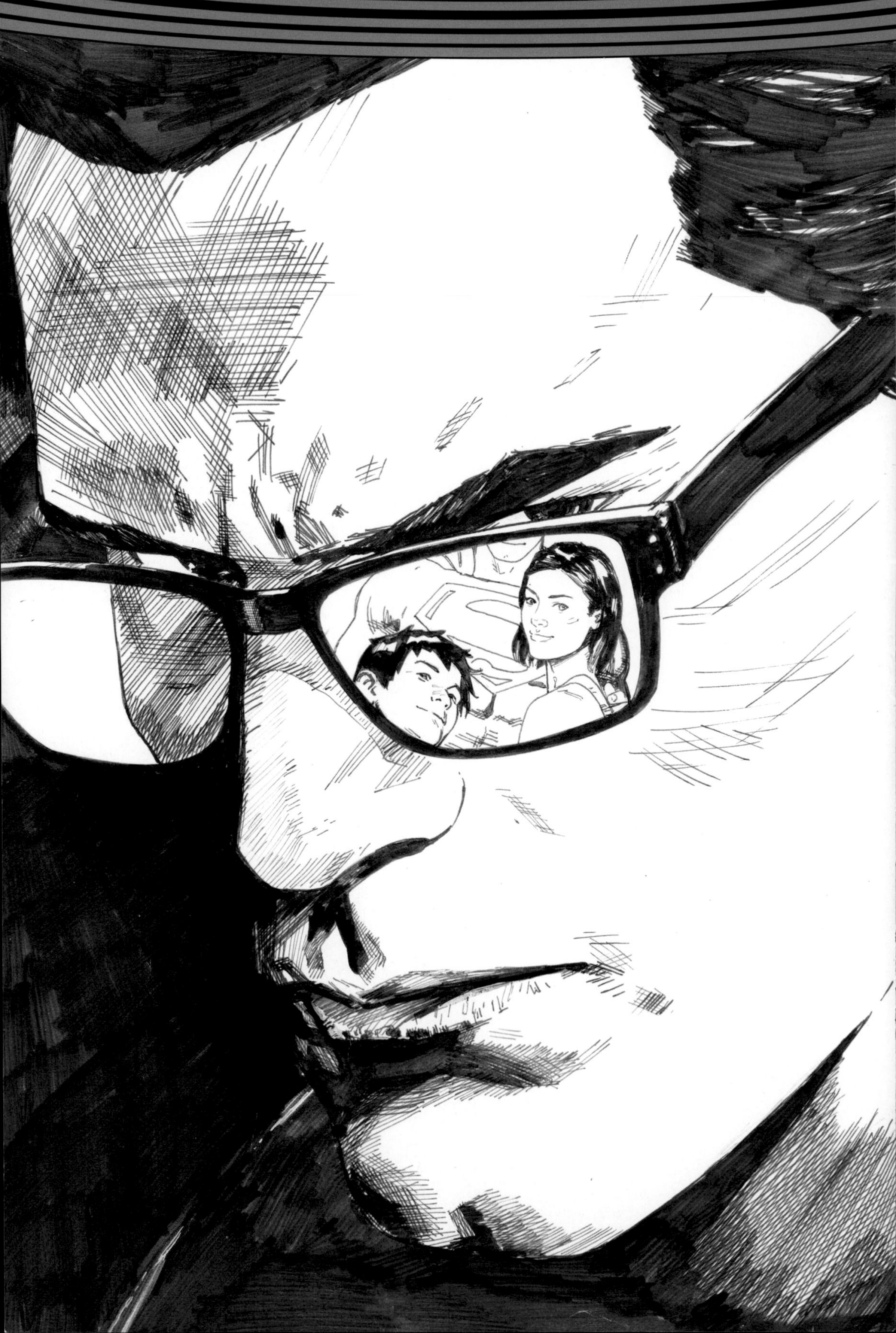

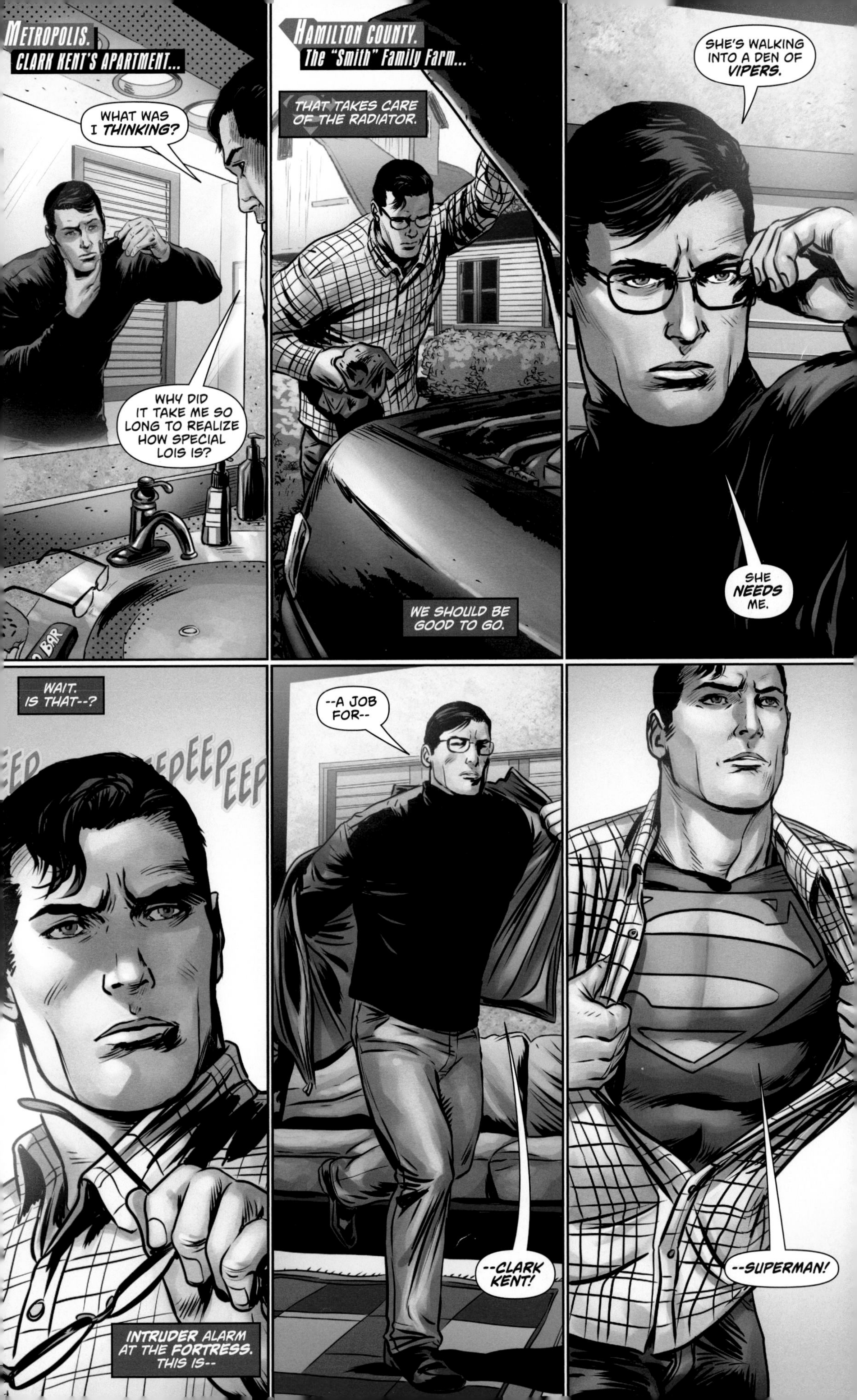
METROPOLIS.
CLARK KENT'S APARTMENT...
WHAT WAS I THINKING?
WHY DID IT TAKE ME SO LONG TO REALIZE HOW SPECIAL LOIS IS?
HAMILTON COUNTY.
The "Smith" Family Farm...
THAT TAKES CARE OF THE RADIATOR.
WE SHOULD BE GOOD TO GO.
SHE'S WALKING INTO A DEN OF VIPERS.
SHE NEEDS ME.
WAIT. IS THAT--?
EEPEEPEEP
INTRUDER ALARM AT THE FORTRESS. THIS IS--
--A JOB FOR--
--CLARK KENT!
--SUPERMAN!

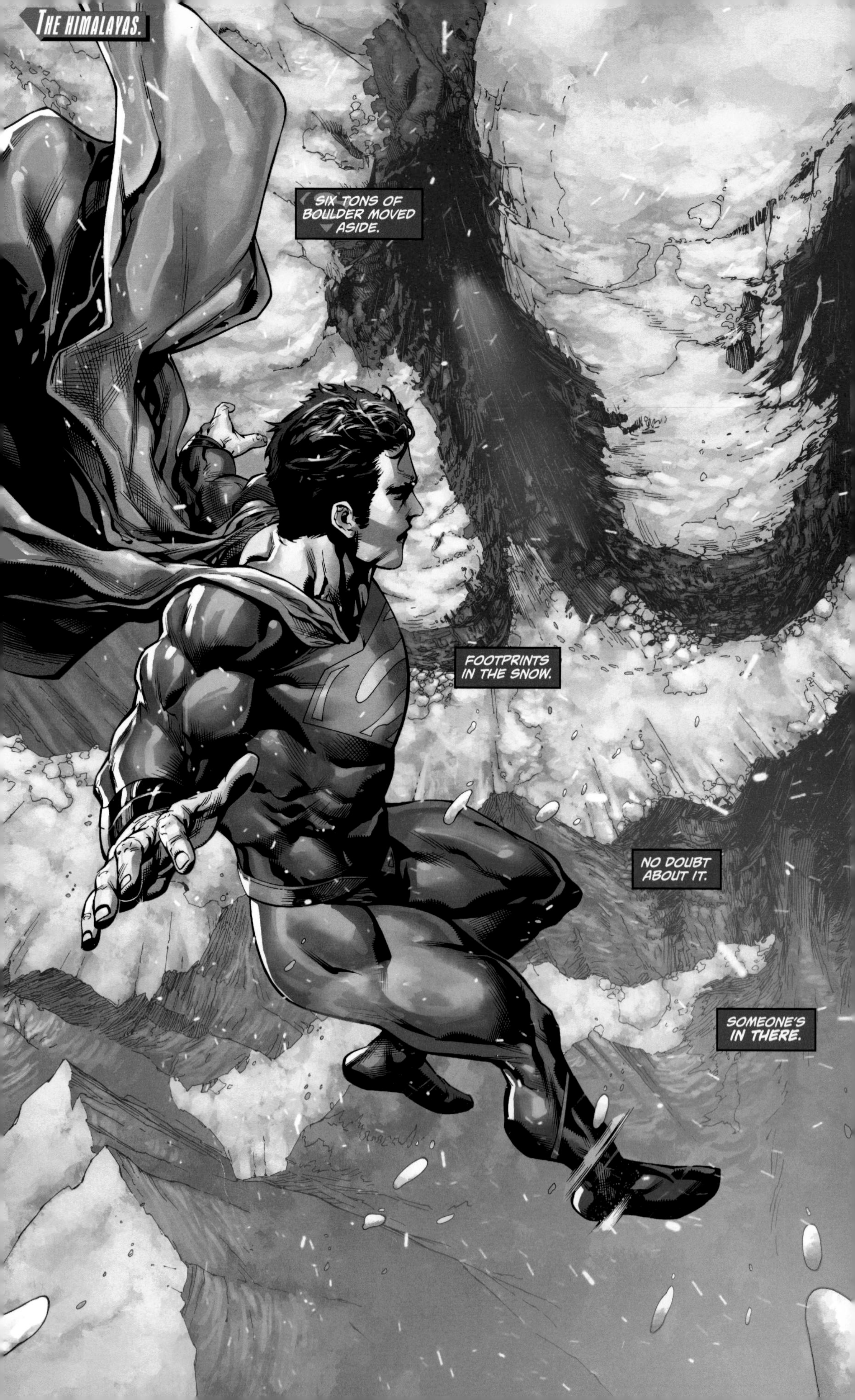
THE HIMALAYAS.
SIX TONS OF BOULDER MOVED ASIDE.
FOOTPRINTS IN THE SNOW.
NO DOUBT ABOUT IT.
SOMEONE'S IN THERE.

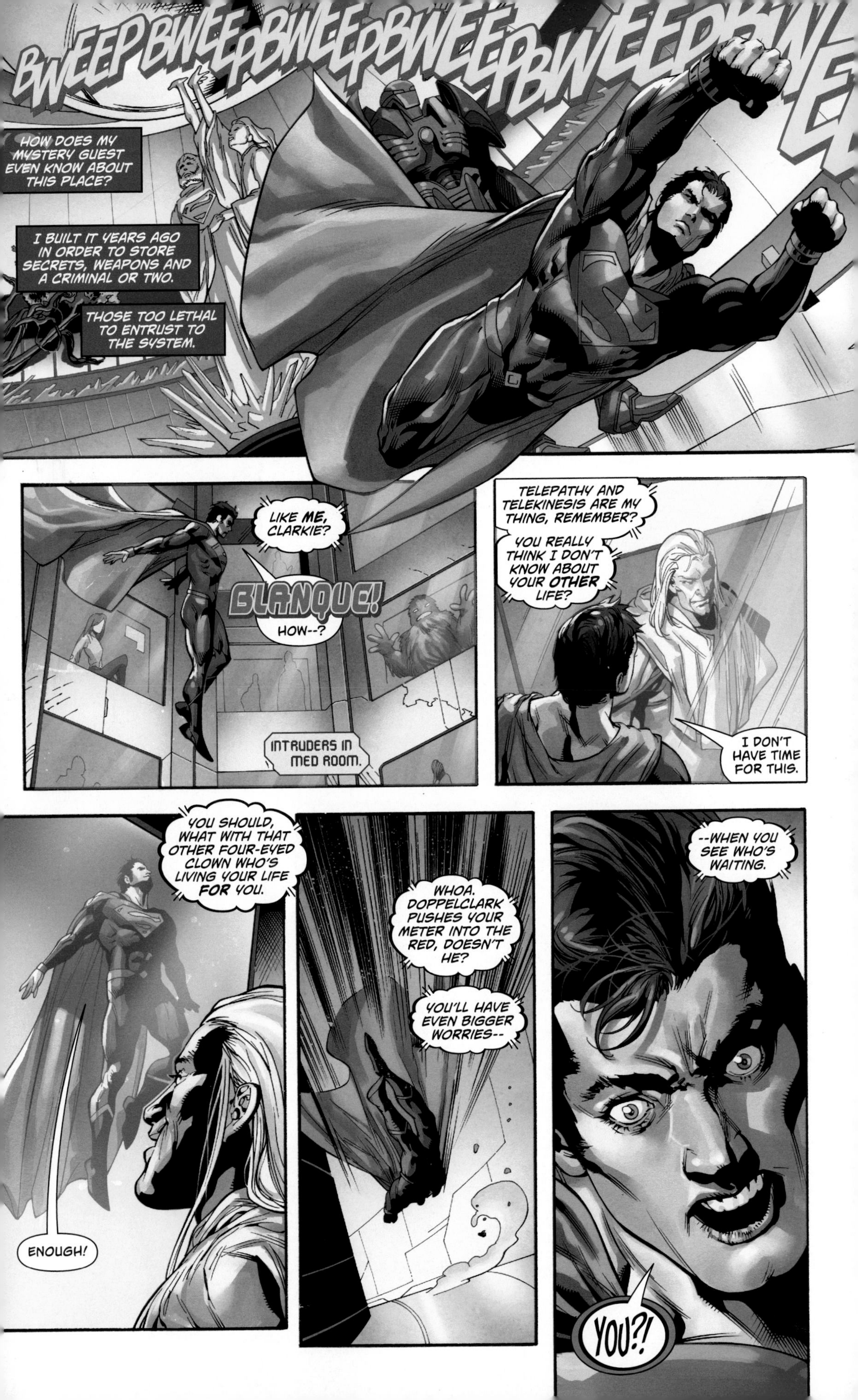

BWEEPBWEEPBWEEPBWEEPBWEEPBWEE
HOW DOES MY MYSTERY GUEST EVEN KNOW ABOUT THIS PLACE?
I BUILT IT YEARS AGO IN ORDER TO STORE SECRETS, WEAPONS AND A CRIMINAL OR TWO.
THOSE TOO LETHAL TO ENTRUST TO THE SYSTEM.
LIKE ME, CLARKIE?
BLANQUE!
HOW--?
INTRUDERS IN MED ROOM.
TELEPATHY AND TELEKINESIS ARE MY THING, REMEMBER?
YOU REALLY THINK I DON'T KNOW ABOUT YOUR OTHER LIFE?
I DON'T HAVE TIME FOR THIS.
YOU SHOULD, WHAT WITH THAT OTHER FOUR-EYED CLOWN WHO'S LIVING YOUR LIFE FOR YOU.
ENOUGH!
WHOA. DOPPELCLARK PUSHES YOUR METER INTO THE RED, DOESN'T HE?
YOU'LL HAVE EVEN BIGGER WORRIES--
--WHEN YOU SEE WHO'S WAITING.
YOU?!

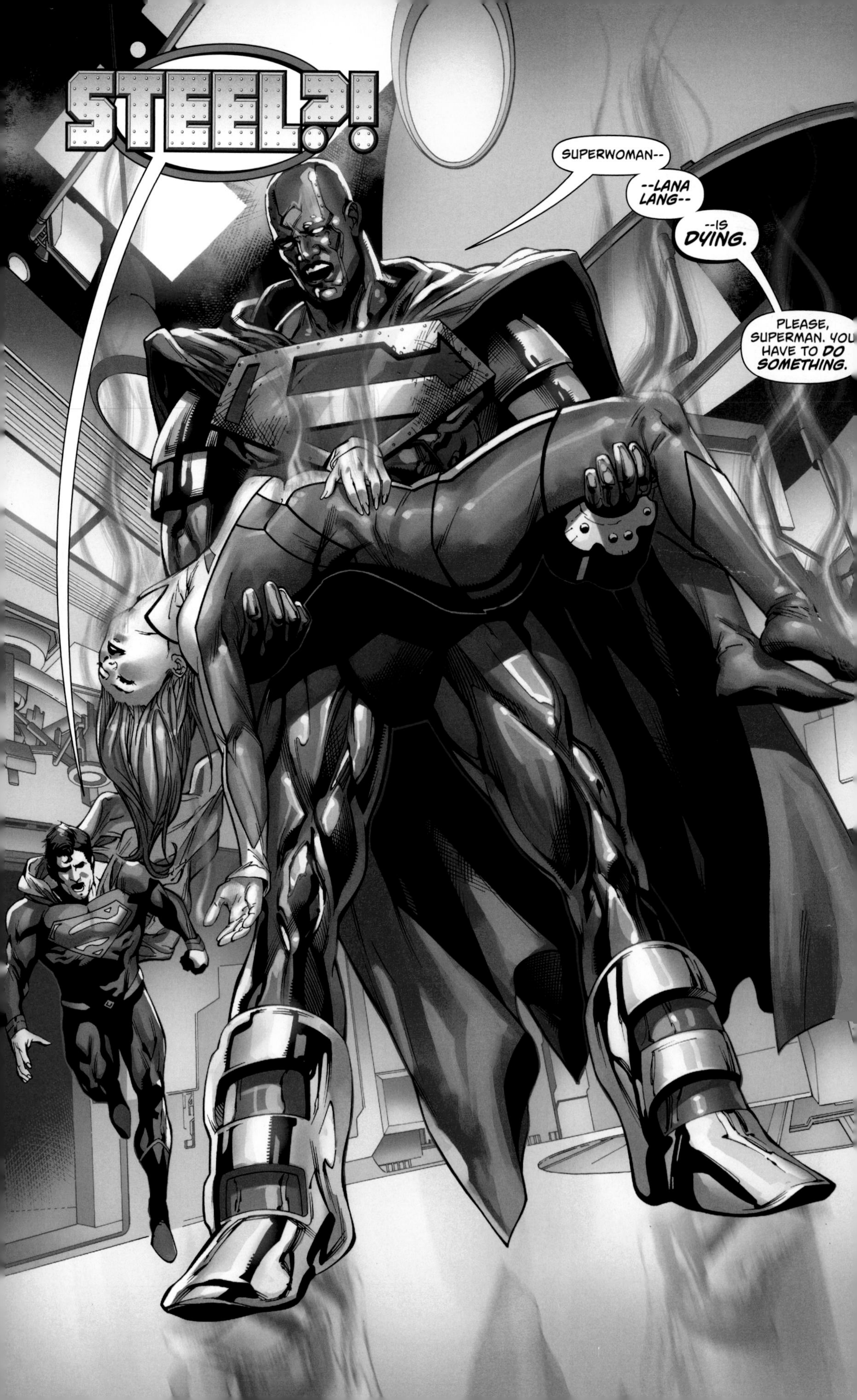
STEEL?!
SUPERWOMAN--
--LANA LANG--
--IS DYING.
PLEASE, SUPERMAN. YOU HAVE TO DO SOMETHING.

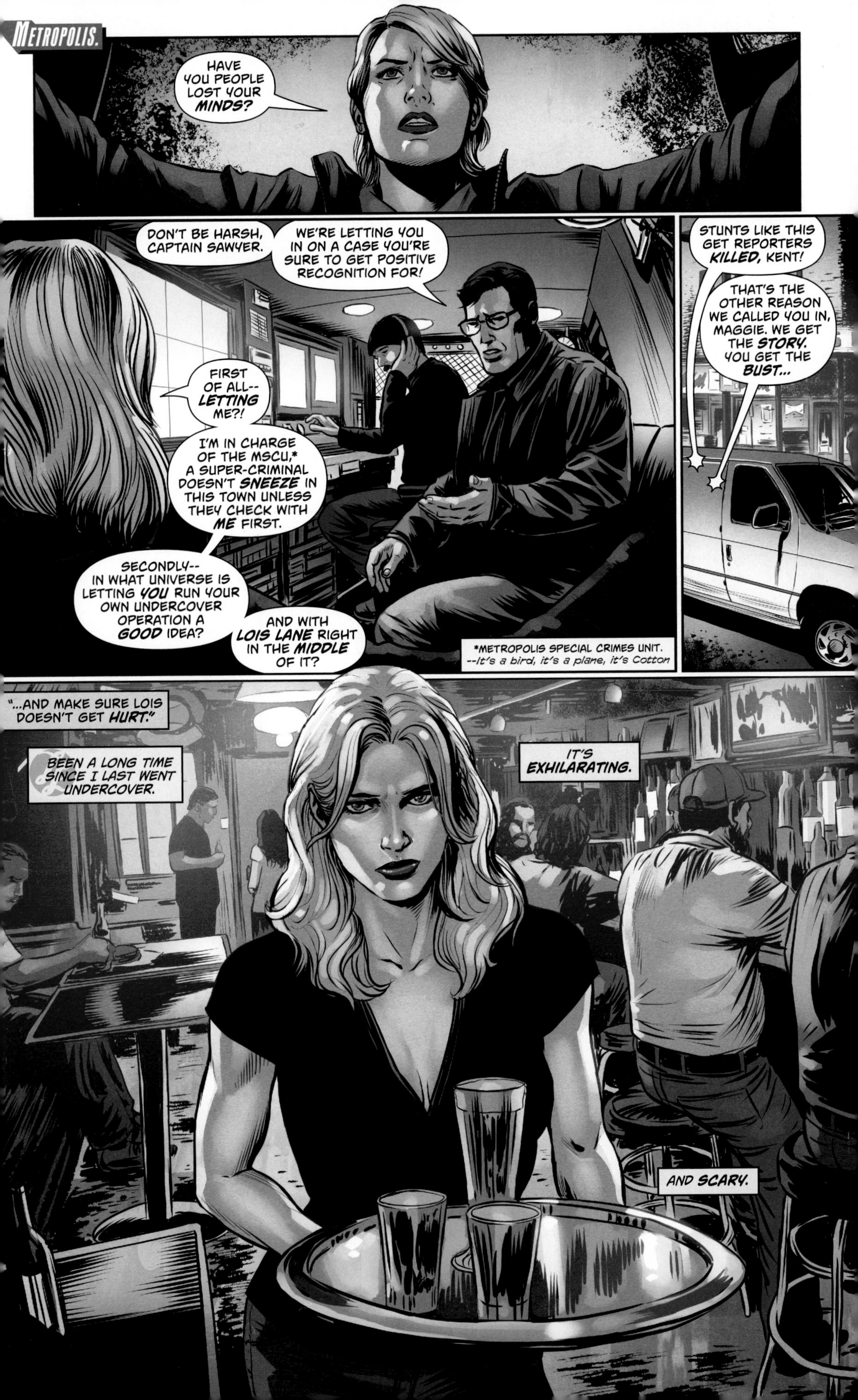
METROPOLIS.
HAVE YOU PEOPLE LOST YOUR MINDS?
DON'T BE HARSH, CAPTAIN SAWYER.
WE'RE LETTING YOU IN ON A CASE YOU'RE SURE TO GET POSITIVE RECOGNITION FOR!
FIRST OF ALL-- LETTING ME?!
I'M IN CHARGE OF THE MSCU,* A SUPER-CRIMINAL DOESN'T SNEEZE IN THIS TOWN UNLESS THEY CHECK WITH ME FIRST.
SECONDLY-- IN WHAT UNIVERSE IS LETTING YOU RUN YOUR OWN UNDERCOVER OPERATION A GOOD IDEA?
AND WITH LOIS LANE RIGHT IN THE MIDDLE OF IT?
*METROPOLIS SPECIAL CRIMES UNIT. --It's a bird, it's a plane, it's Cotton
STUNTS LIKE THIS GET REPORTERS KILLED, KENT!
THAT'S THE OTHER REASON WE CALLED YOU IN, MAGGIE. WE GET THE STORY. YOU GET THE BUST...
"...AND MAKE SURE LOIS DOESN'T GET HURT."
BEEN A LONG TIME SINCE I LAST WENT UNDERCOVER.
IT'S EXHILARATING.
AND SCARY.

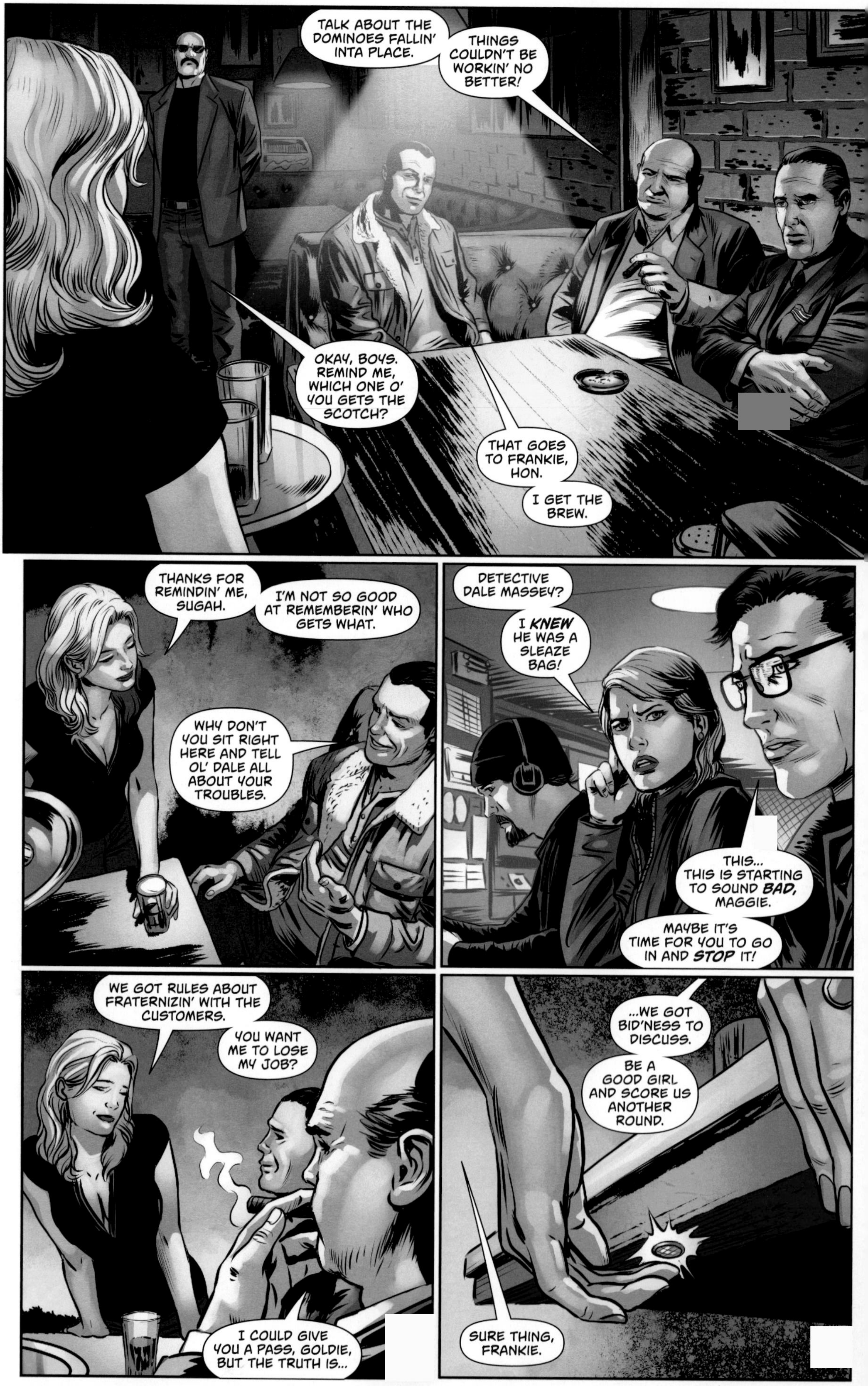

TALK ABOUT THE DOMINOES FALLIN' INTA PLACE.
THINGS COULDN'T BE WORKIN' NO BETTER!
OKAY, BOYS. REMIND ME, WHICH ONE O' YOU GETS THE SCOTCH?
THAT GOES TO FRANKIE, HON.
I GET THE BREW.
THANKS FOR REMINDIN' ME, SUGAH.
I'M NOT SO GOOD AT REMEMBERIN' WHO GETS WHAT.
WHY DON'T YOU SIT RIGHT HERE AND TELL OL' DALE ALL ABOUT YOUR TROUBLES.
DETECTIVE DALE MASSEY?
I KNEW HE WAS A SLEAZE BAG!
THIS... THIS IS STARTING TO SOUND BAD, MAGGIE.
MAYBE IT'S TIME FOR YOU TO GO IN AND STOP IT!
WE GOT RULES ABOUT FRATERNIZIN' WITH THE CUSTOMERS.
YOU WANT ME TO LOSE MY JOB?
I COULD GIVE YOU A PASS, GOLDIE, BUT THE TRUTH IS...
...WE GOT BID'NESS TO DISCUSS.
BE A GOOD GIRL AND SCORE US ANOTHER ROUND.
SURE THING, FRANKIE.

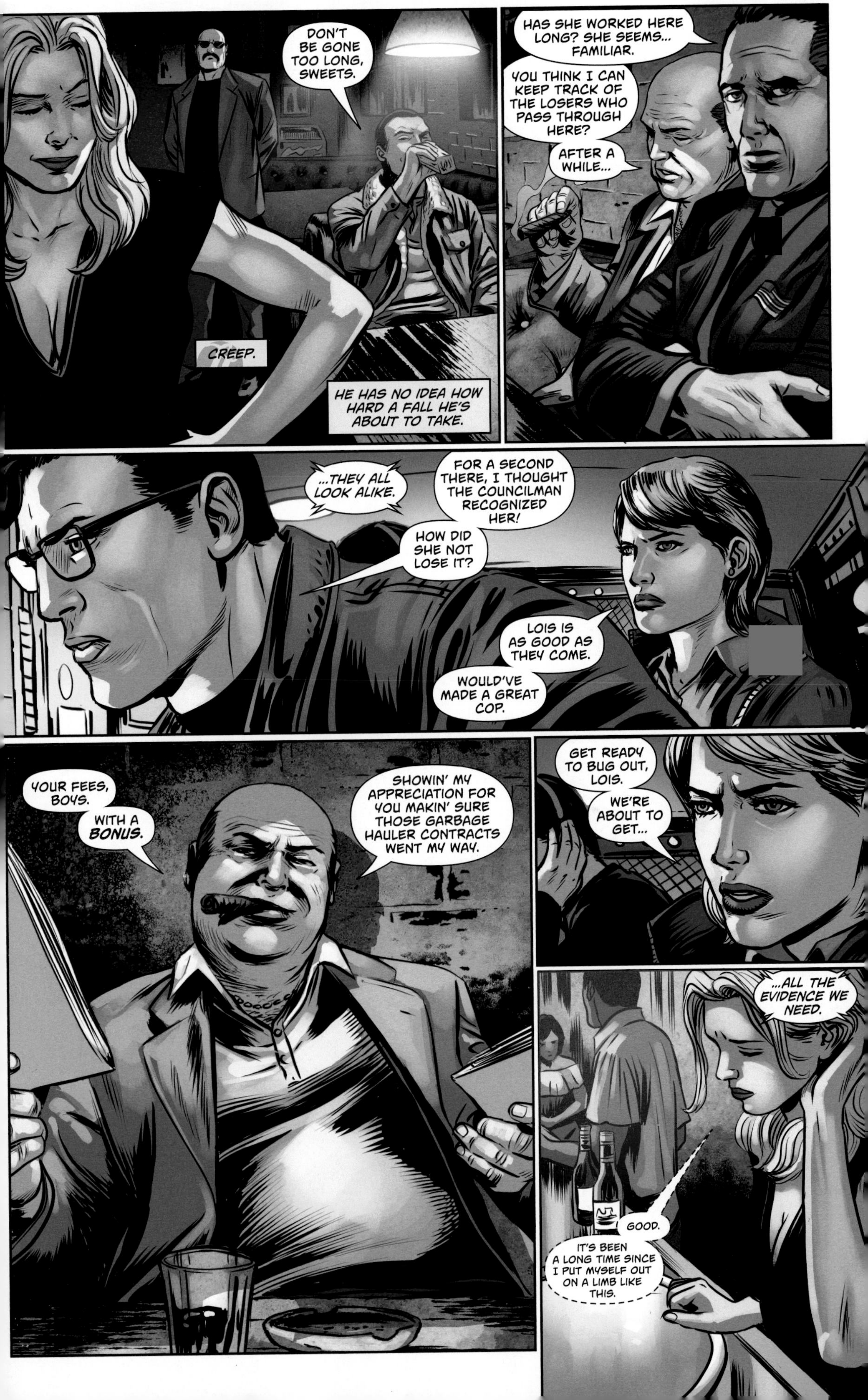
DON'T BE GONE TOO LONG, SWEETS.
CREEP.
HE HAS NO IDEA HOW HARD A FALL HE'S ABOUT TO TAKE.
HAS SHE WORKED HERE LONG? SHE SEEMS... FAMILIAR.
YOU THINK I CAN KEEP TRACK OF THE LOSERS WHO PASS THROUGH HERE?
AFTER A WHILE...
...THEY ALL LOOK ALIKE.
FOR A SECOND THERE, I THOUGHT THE COUNCILMAN RECOGNIZED HER!
HOW DID SHE NOT LOSE IT?
LOIS IS AS GOOD AS THEY COME.
WOULD'VE MADE A GREAT COP.
YOUR FEES, BOYS.
WITH A *BONUS*.
SHOWIN' MY APPRECIATION FOR YOU MAKIN' SURE THOSE GARBAGE HAULER CONTRACTS WENT MY WAY.
GET READY TO BUG OUT, LOIS.
WE'RE ABOUT TO GET...
...ALL THE EVIDENCE WE NEED.
GOOD.
IT'S BEEN A LONG TIME SINCE I PUT MYSELF OUT ON A LIMB LIKE THIS.

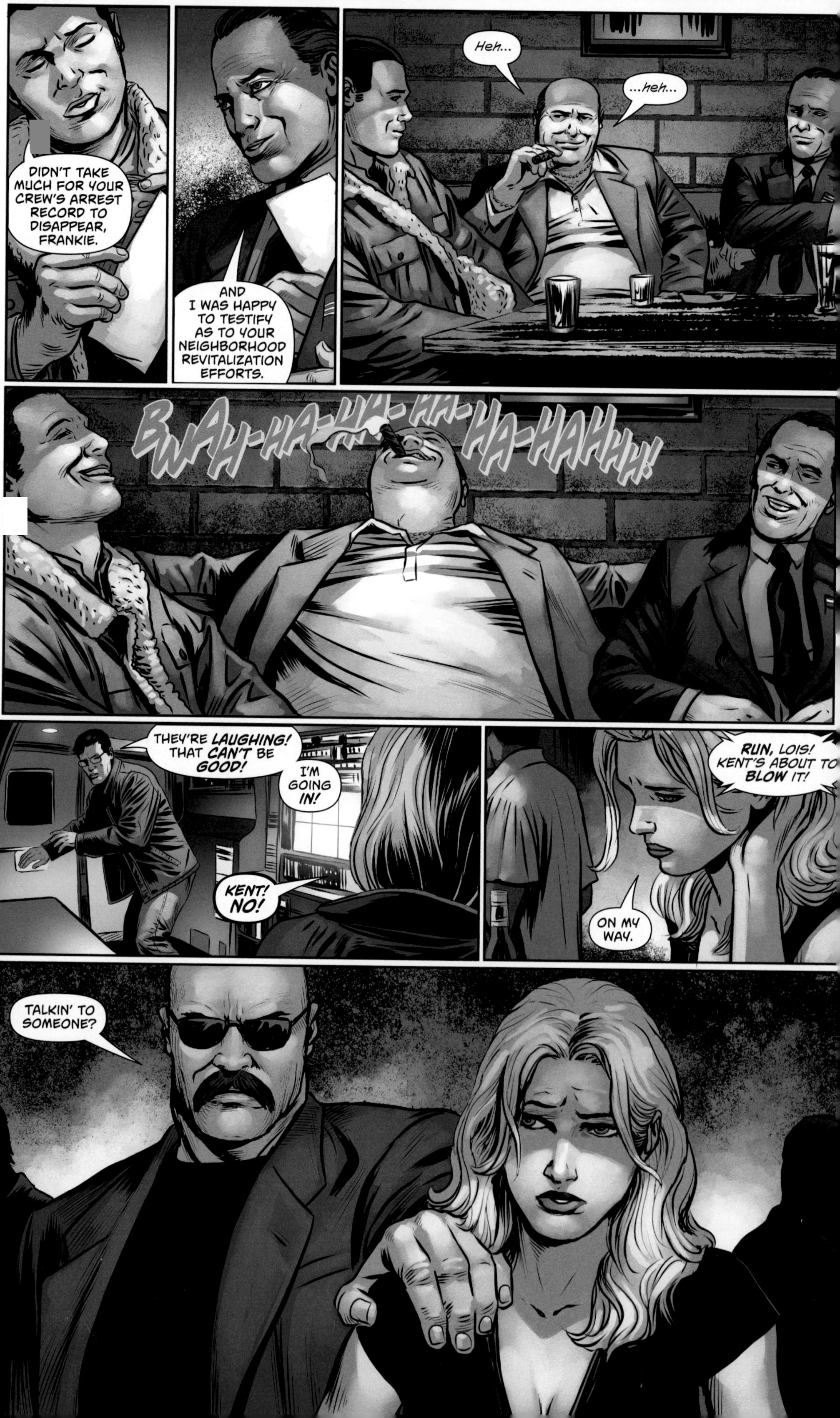
DIDN'T TAKE MUCH FOR YOUR CREW'S ARREST RECORD TO DISAPPEAR, FRANKIE.
AND I WAS HAPPY TO TESTIFY AS TO YOUR NEIGHBORHOOD REVITALIZATION EFFORTS.
Heh...
...heh...
BWAH-HA-HA-HA-HA-HAHHH!
THEY'RE LAUGHING! THAT CAN'T BE GOOD!
I'M GOING IN!
KENT! NO!
RUN, LOIS! KENT'S ABOUT TO BLOW IT!
ON MY WAY.
TALKIN' TO SOMEONE?

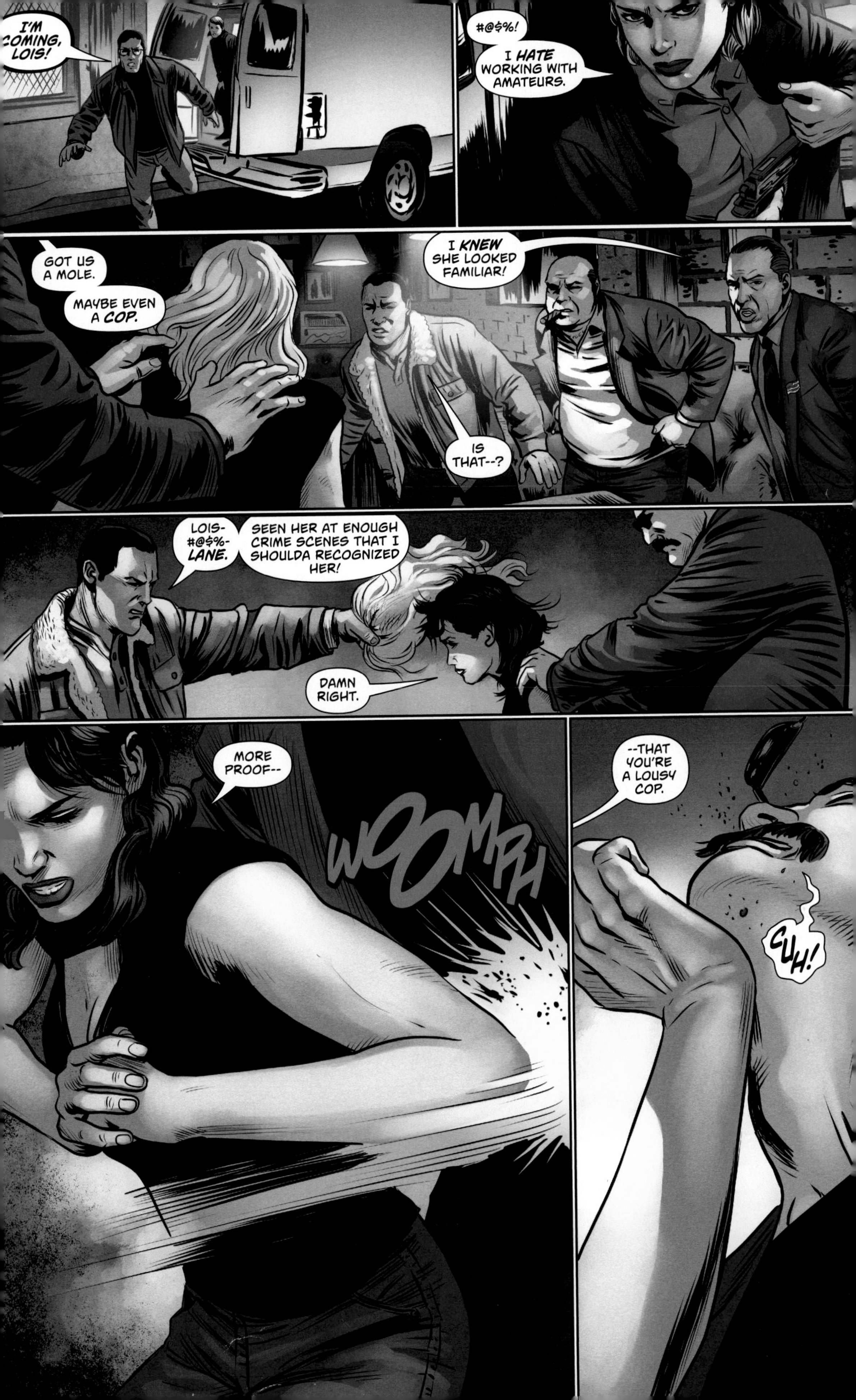
I'M COMING, LOIS!
#@$%!
I HATE WORKING WITH AMATEURS.
GOT US A MOLE.
MAYBE EVEN A COP.
IS THAT--?
I KNEW SHE LOOKED FAMILIAR!
LOIS-#@$%-LANE.
SEEN HER AT ENOUGH CRIME SCENES THAT I SHOULDA RECOGNIZED HER!
DAMN RIGHT.
MORE PROOF--
WOOMPH
--THAT YOU'RE A LOUSY COP.
CUH!

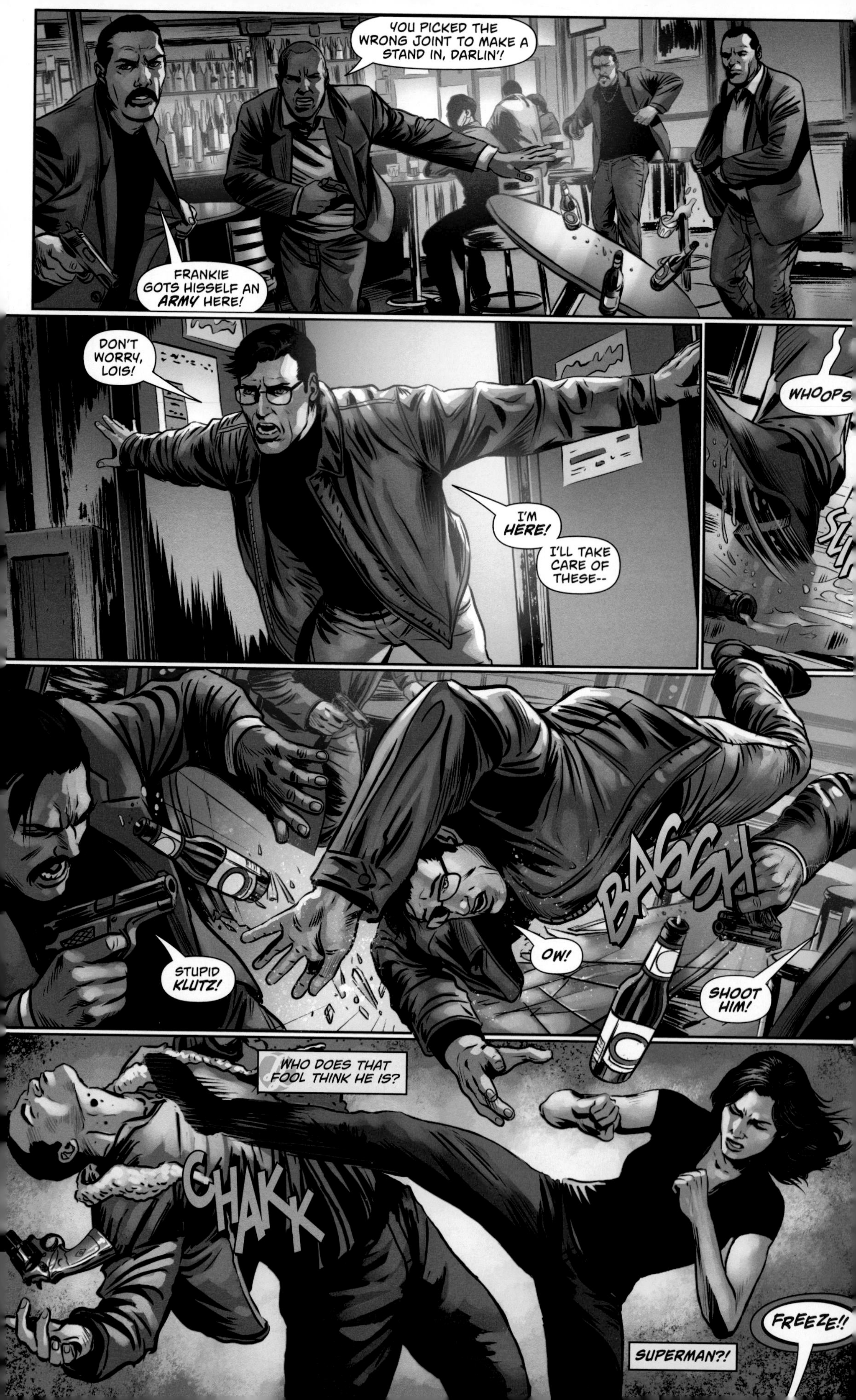
YOU PICKED THE WRONG JOINT TO MAKE A STAND IN, DARLIN'!
FRANKIE GOTS HISSELF AN *ARMY* HERE!
DON'T WORRY, LOIS!
I'M *HERE!*
I'LL TAKE CARE OF THESE--
WHOOPS
BASSH
OW!
STUPID *KLUTZ!*
SHOOT HIM!
WHO DOES THAT FOOL THINK HE IS?
CHAKK
SUPERMAN?!
FREEZE!!

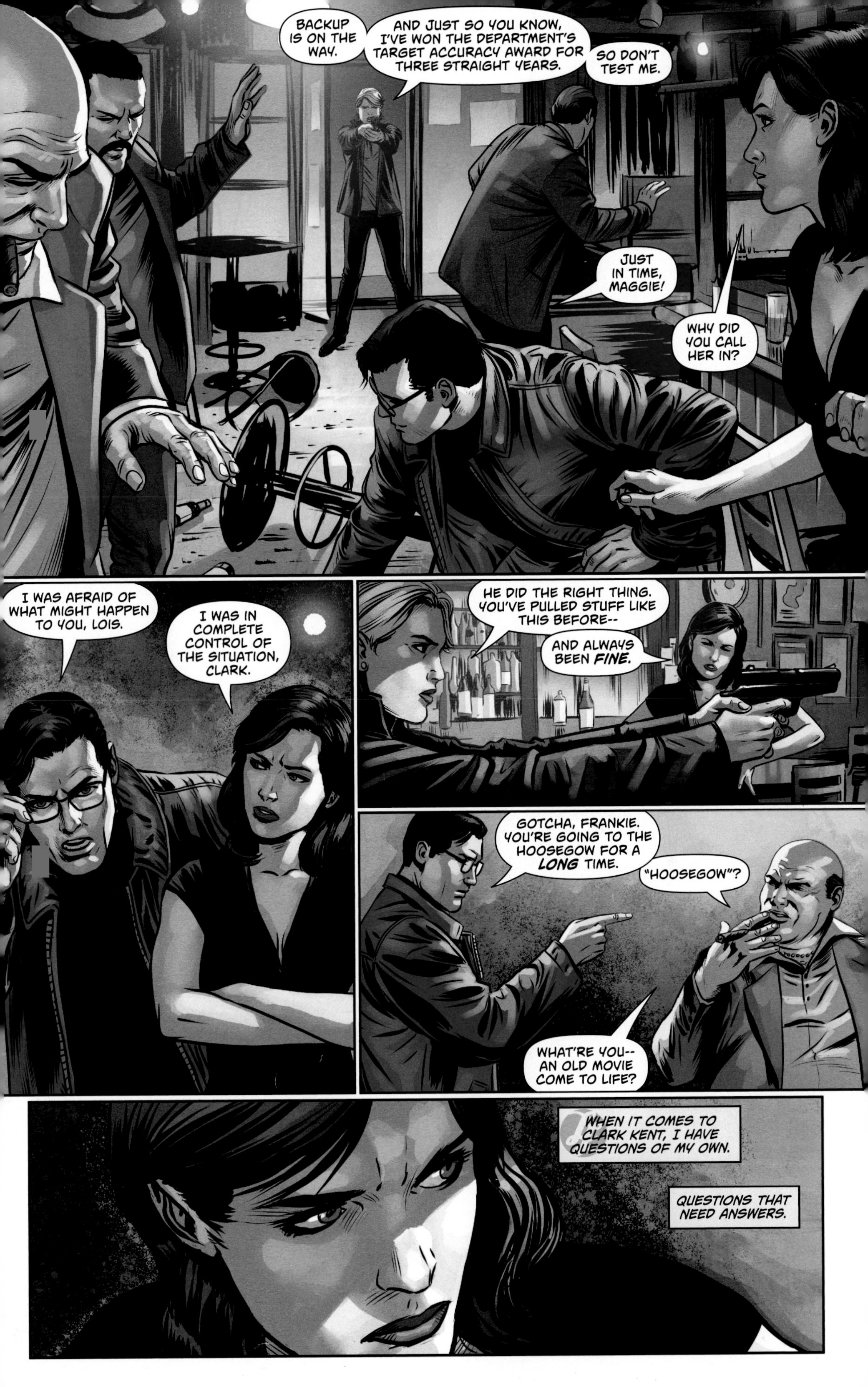
BACKUP IS ON THE WAY.
AND JUST SO YOU KNOW, I'VE WON THE DEPARTMENT'S TARGET ACCURACY AWARD FOR THREE STRAIGHT YEARS.
SO DON'T TEST ME.
JUST IN TIME, MAGGIE!
WHY DID YOU CALL HER IN?
I WAS AFRAID OF WHAT MIGHT HAPPEN TO YOU, LOIS.
I WAS IN COMPLETE CONTROL OF THE SITUATION, CLARK.
HE DID THE RIGHT THING. YOU'VE PULLED STUFF LIKE THIS BEFORE--
AND ALWAYS BEEN FINE.
GOTCHA, FRANKIE. YOU'RE GOING TO THE HOOSEGOW FOR A LONG TIME.
"HOOSEGOW"?
WHAT'RE YOU-- AN OLD MOVIE COME TO LIFE?
WHEN IT COMES TO CLARK KENT, I HAVE QUESTIONS OF MY OWN.
QUESTIONS THAT NEED ANSWERS.

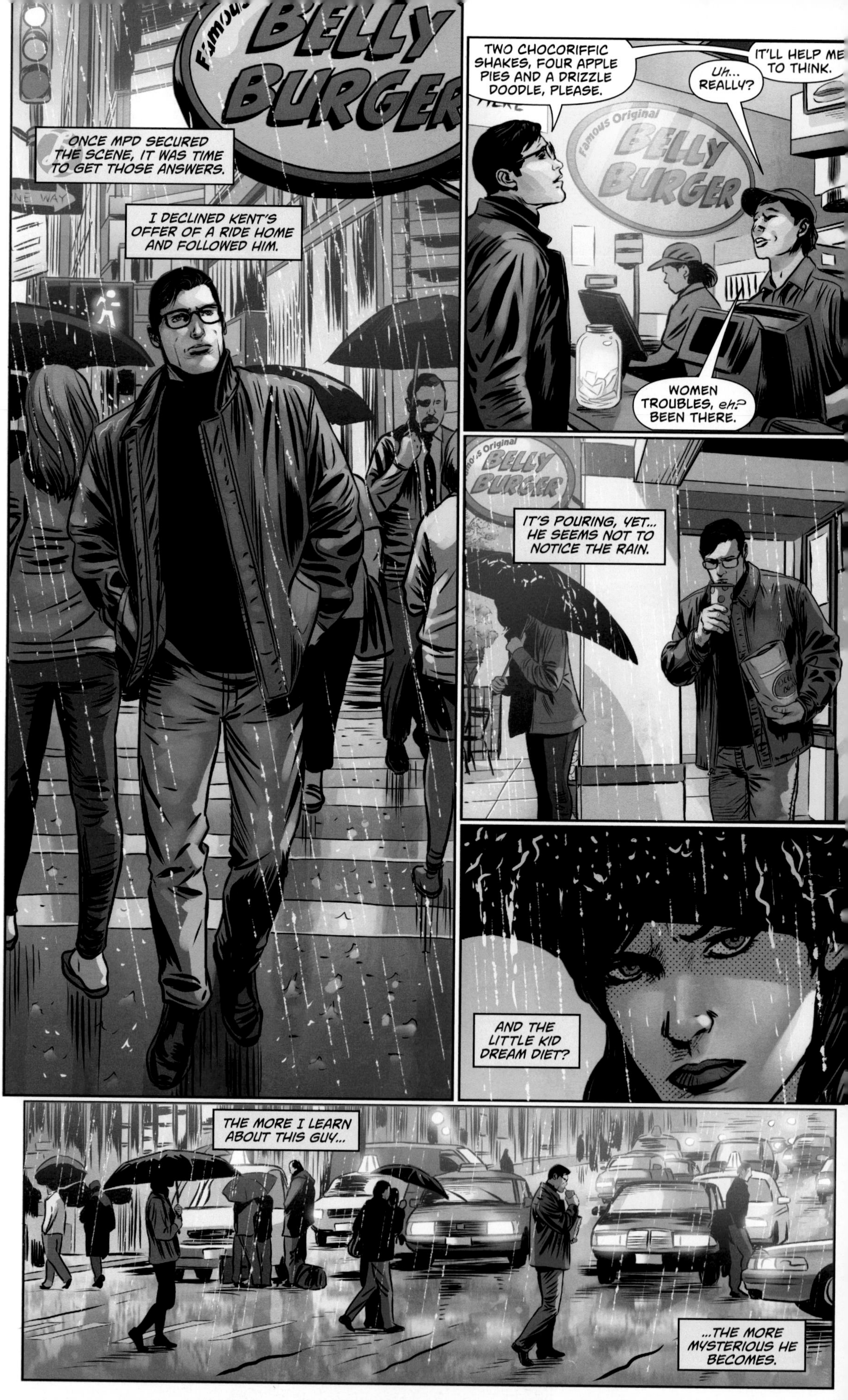
BELLY BURGER
ONCE MPD SECURED THE SCENE, IT WAS TIME TO GET THOSE ANSWERS.
I DECLINED KENT'S OFFER OF A RIDE HOME AND FOLLOWED HIM.
TWO CHOCORIFFIC SHAKES, FOUR APPLE PIES AND A DRIZZLE DOODLE, PLEASE.
Uh... REALLY?
IT'LL HELP ME TO THINK.
Famous Original BELLY BURGER
WOMEN TROUBLES, eh? BEEN THERE.
BELLY BURGER
IT'S POURING, YET... HE SEEMS NOT TO NOTICE THE RAIN.
AND THE LITTLE KID DREAM DIET?
THE MORE I LEARN ABOUT THIS GUY...
...THE MORE MYSTERIOUS HE BECOMES.

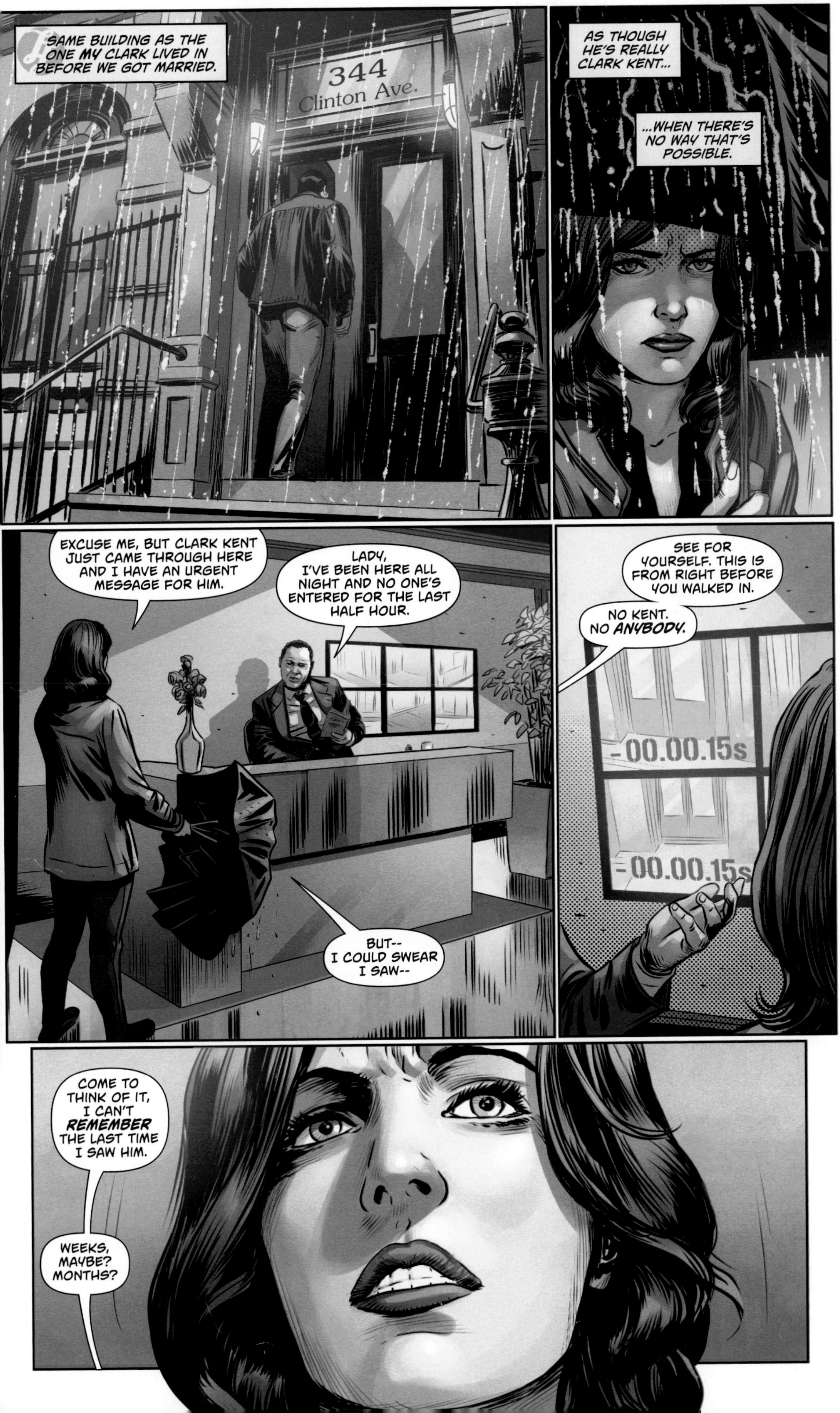
SAME BUILDING AS THE ONE MY CLARK LIVED IN BEFORE WE GOT MARRIED.
344 Clinton Ave.
AS THOUGH HE'S REALLY CLARK KENT...
...WHEN THERE'S NO WAY THAT'S POSSIBLE.
EXCUSE ME, BUT CLARK KENT JUST CAME THROUGH HERE AND I HAVE AN URGENT MESSAGE FOR HIM.
LADY, I'VE BEEN HERE ALL NIGHT AND NO ONE'S ENTERED FOR THE LAST HALF HOUR.
BUT-- I COULD SWEAR I SAW--
SEE FOR YOURSELF. THIS IS FROM RIGHT BEFORE YOU WALKED IN.
NO KENT. NO ANYBODY.
-00.00.15s
-00.00.15s
COME TO THINK OF IT, I CAN'T REMEMBER THE LAST TIME I SAW HIM.
WEEKS, MAYBE? MONTHS?

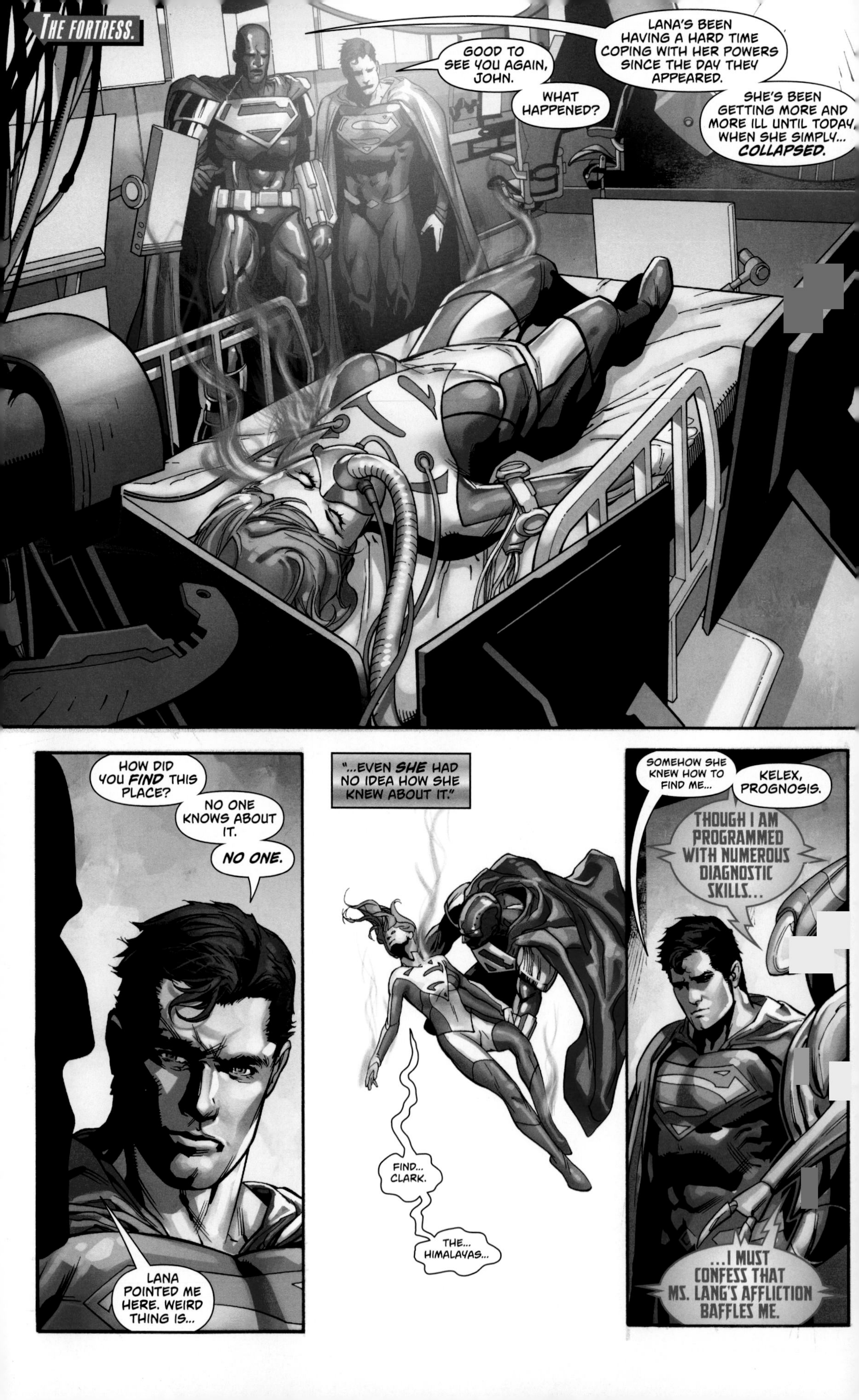
THE FORTRESS.
GOOD TO SEE YOU AGAIN, JOHN.
WHAT HAPPENED?
LANA'S BEEN HAVING A HARD TIME COPING WITH HER POWERS SINCE THE DAY THEY APPEARED.
SHE'S BEEN GETTING MORE AND MORE ILL UNTIL TODAY, WHEN SHE SIMPLY... COLLAPSED.
HOW DID YOU FIND THIS PLACE?
NO ONE KNOWS ABOUT IT.
NO ONE.
LANA POINTED ME HERE. WEIRD THING IS...
"...EVEN SHE HAD NO IDEA HOW SHE KNEW ABOUT IT."
FIND... CLARK.
THE... HIMALAYAS...
SOMEHOW SHE KNEW HOW TO FIND ME...
KELEX, PROGNOSIS.
THOUGH I AM PROGRAMMED WITH NUMEROUS DIAGNOSTIC SKILLS...
...I MUST CONFESS THAT MS. LANG'S AFFLICTION BAFFLES ME.

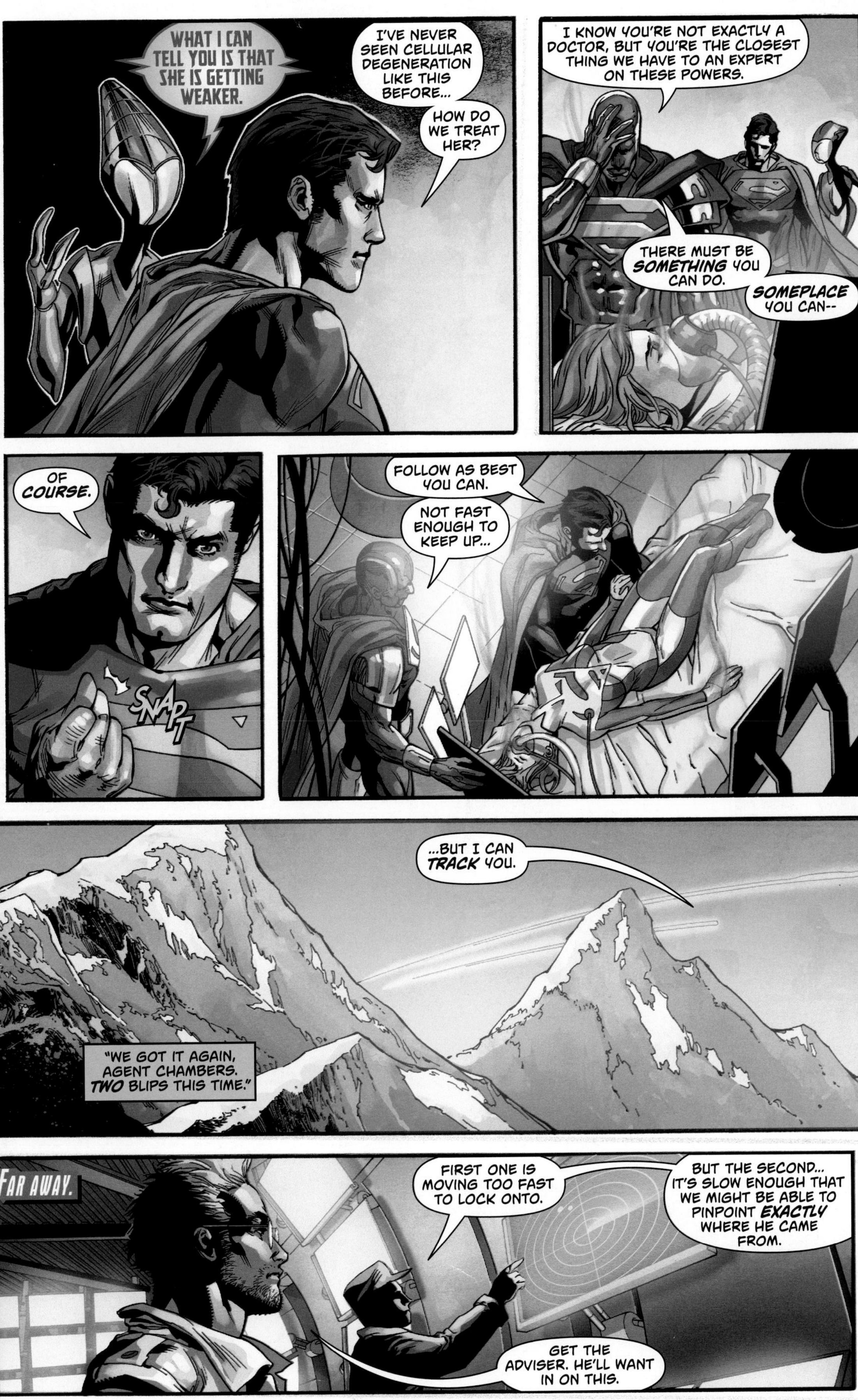
WHAT I CAN TELL YOU IS THAT SHE IS GETTING WEAKER.
I'VE NEVER SEEN CELLULAR DEGENERATION LIKE THIS BEFORE...
HOW DO WE TREAT HER?
I KNOW YOU'RE NOT EXACTLY A DOCTOR, BUT YOU'RE THE CLOSEST THING WE HAVE TO AN EXPERT ON THESE POWERS.
THERE MUST BE SOMETHING YOU CAN DO.
SOMEPLACE YOU CAN--
OF COURSE.
SNAPT
FOLLOW AS BEST YOU CAN.
NOT FAST ENOUGH TO KEEP UP...
...BUT I CAN TRACK YOU.
"WE GOT IT AGAIN, AGENT CHAMBERS. TWO BLIPS THIS TIME."
FAR AWAY.
FIRST ONE IS MOVING TOO FAST TO LOCK ONTO.
BUT THE SECOND... IT'S SLOW ENOUGH THAT WE MIGHT BE ABLE TO PINPOINT EXACTLY WHERE HE CAME FROM.
GET THE ADVISER. HE'LL WANT IN ON THIS.

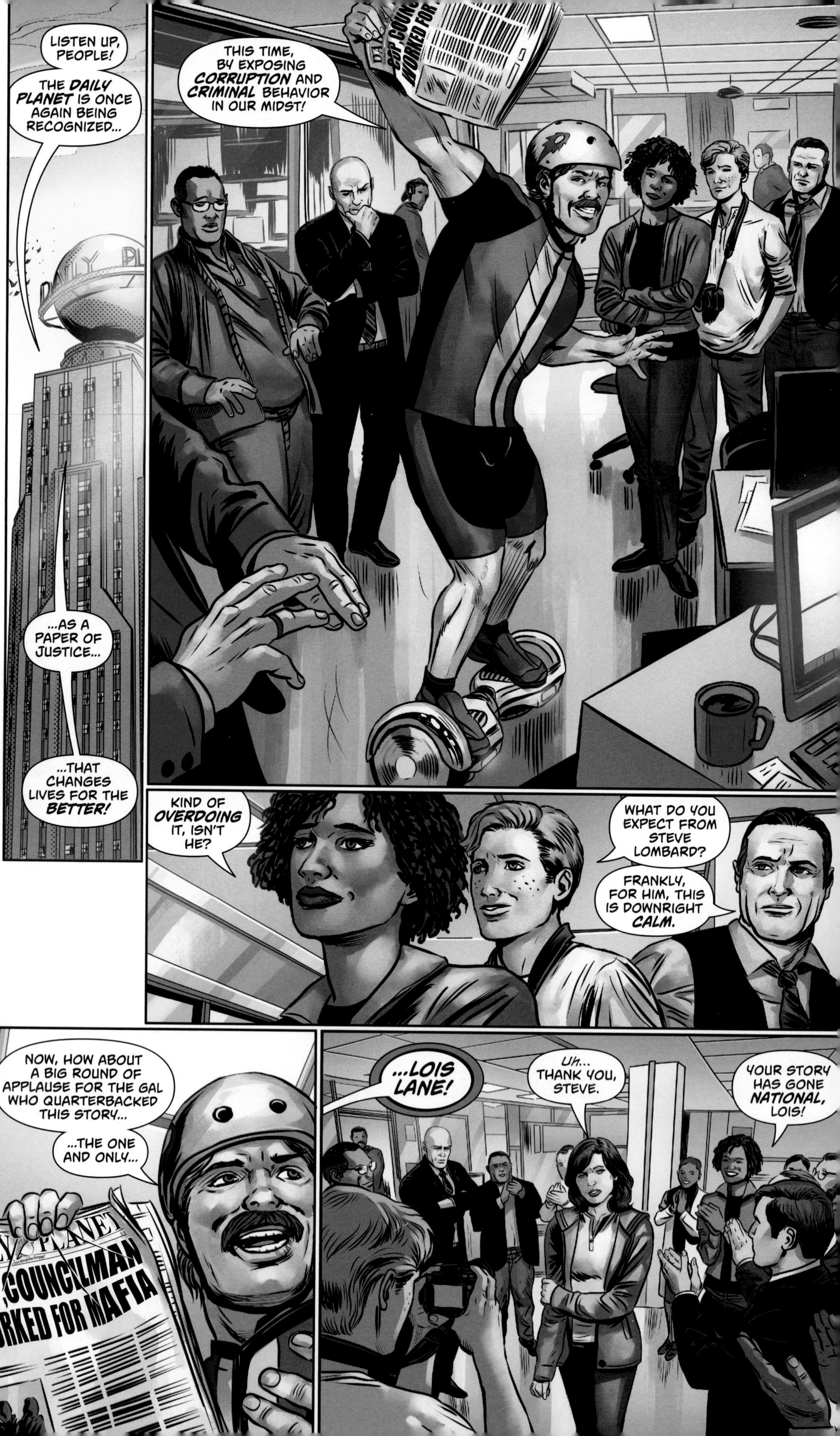
LISTEN UP, PEOPLE!
THE DAILY PLANET IS ONCE AGAIN BEING RECOGNIZED...
THIS TIME, BY EXPOSING CORRUPTION AND CRIMINAL BEHAVIOR IN OUR MIDST!
...AS A PAPER OF JUSTICE...
...THAT CHANGES LIVES FOR THE BETTER!
KIND OF OVERDOING IT, ISN'T HE?
WHAT DO YOU EXPECT FROM STEVE LOMBARD?
FRANKLY, FOR HIM, THIS IS DOWNRIGHT CALM.
NOW, HOW ABOUT A BIG ROUND OF APPLAUSE FOR THE GAL WHO QUARTERBACKED THIS STORY...
...THE ONE AND ONLY...
AILY PLANET
OP COUNCILMAN WORKED FOR MAFIA
...LOIS LANE!
Uh... THANK YOU, STEVE.
YOUR STORY HAS GONE NATIONAL, LOIS!

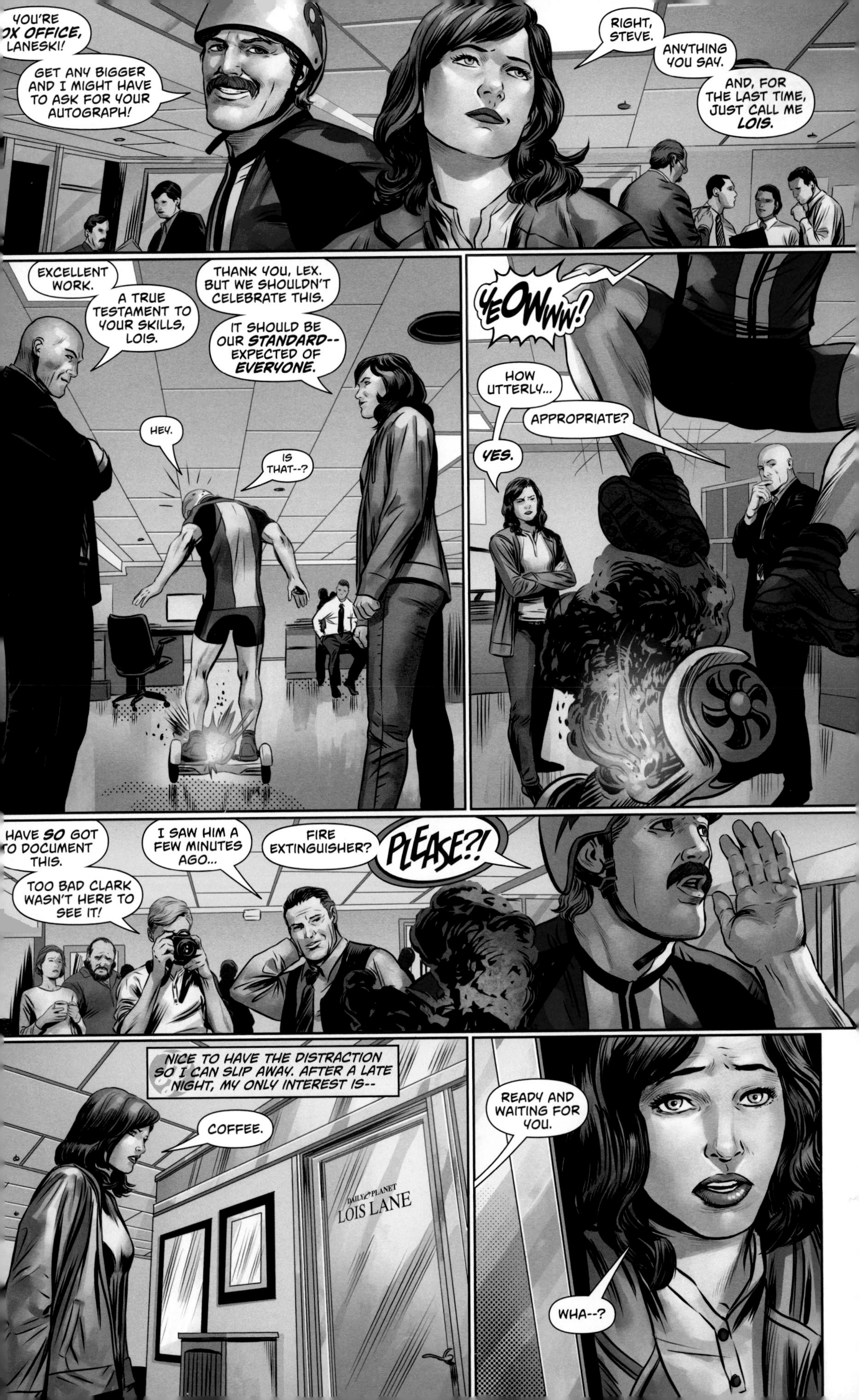
YOU'RE
OX OFFICE, LANESKI!
GET ANY BIGGER AND I MIGHT HAVE TO ASK FOR YOUR AUTOGRAPH!
RIGHT, STEVE.
ANYTHING YOU SAY.
AND, FOR THE LAST TIME, JUST CALL ME LOIS.
EXCELLENT WORK.
A TRUE TESTAMENT TO YOUR SKILLS, LOIS.
THANK YOU, LEX. BUT WE SHOULDN'T CELEBRATE THIS.
IT SHOULD BE OUR STANDARD-- EXPECTED OF EVERYONE.
HEY.
IS THAT--?
YEOWWW!
HOW UTTERLY...
APPROPRIATE?
YES.
HAVE SO GOT
O DOCUMENT THIS.
TOO BAD CLARK WASN'T HERE TO SEE IT!
I SAW HIM A FEW MINUTES AGO...
FIRE EXTINGUISHER?
PLEASE?!
NICE TO HAVE THE DISTRACTION SO I CAN SLIP AWAY. AFTER A LATE NIGHT, MY ONLY INTEREST IS--
COFFEE.
DAILY PLANET
LOIS LANE
READY AND WAITING FOR YOU.
WHA--?

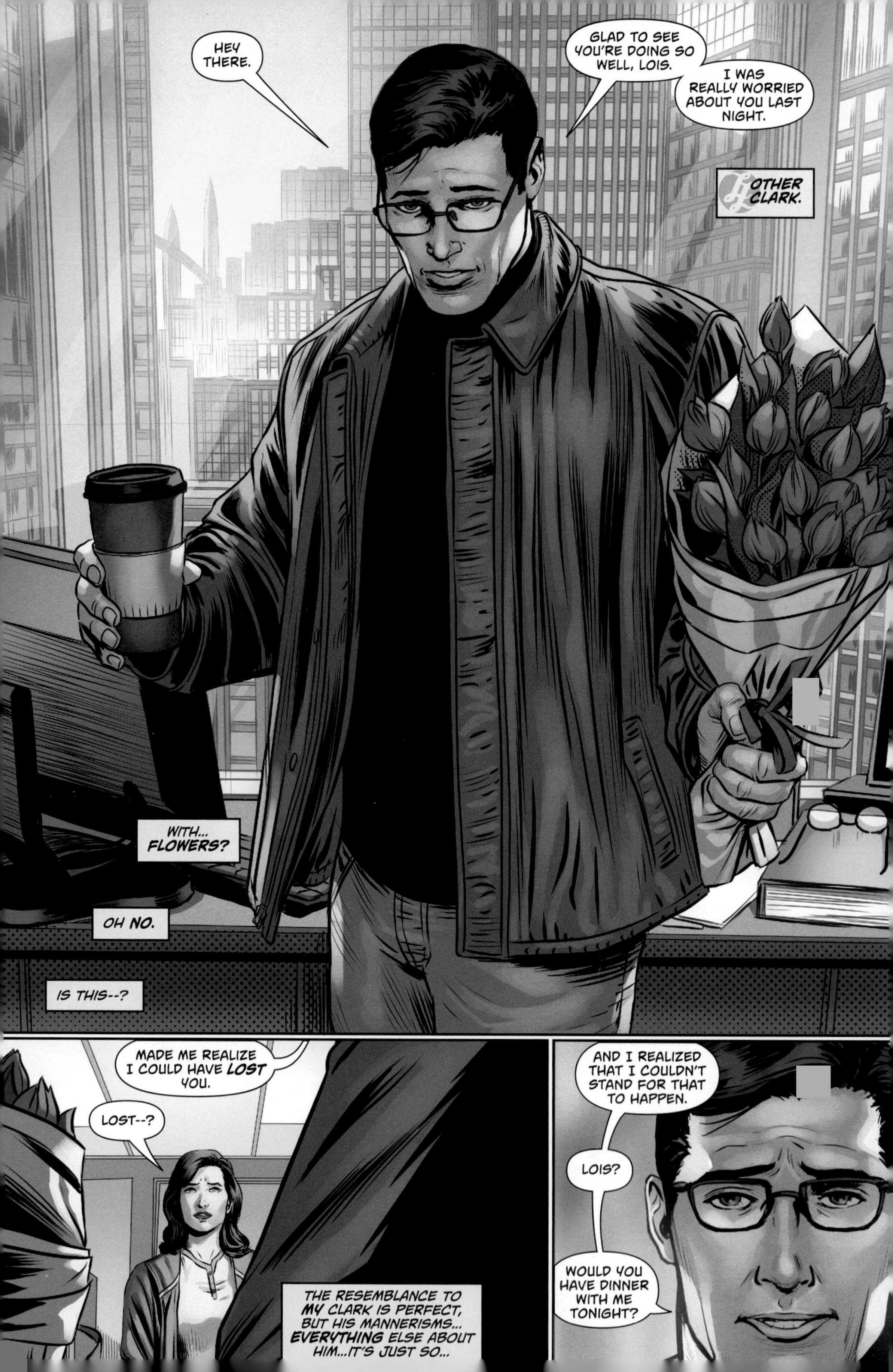
HEY THERE.
GLAD TO SEE YOU'RE DOING SO WELL, LOIS.
I WAS REALLY WORRIED ABOUT YOU LAST NIGHT.
OTHER CLARK.
WITH... FLOWERS?
OH NO.
IS THIS--?
MADE ME REALIZE I COULD HAVE LOST YOU.
LOST--?
THE RESEMBLANCE TO MY CLARK IS PERFECT, BUT HIS MANNERISMS... EVERYTHING ELSE ABOUT HIM...IT'S JUST SO...
AND I REALIZED THAT I COULDN'T STAND FOR THAT TO HAPPEN.
LOIS?
WOULD YOU HAVE DINNER WITH ME TONIGHT?

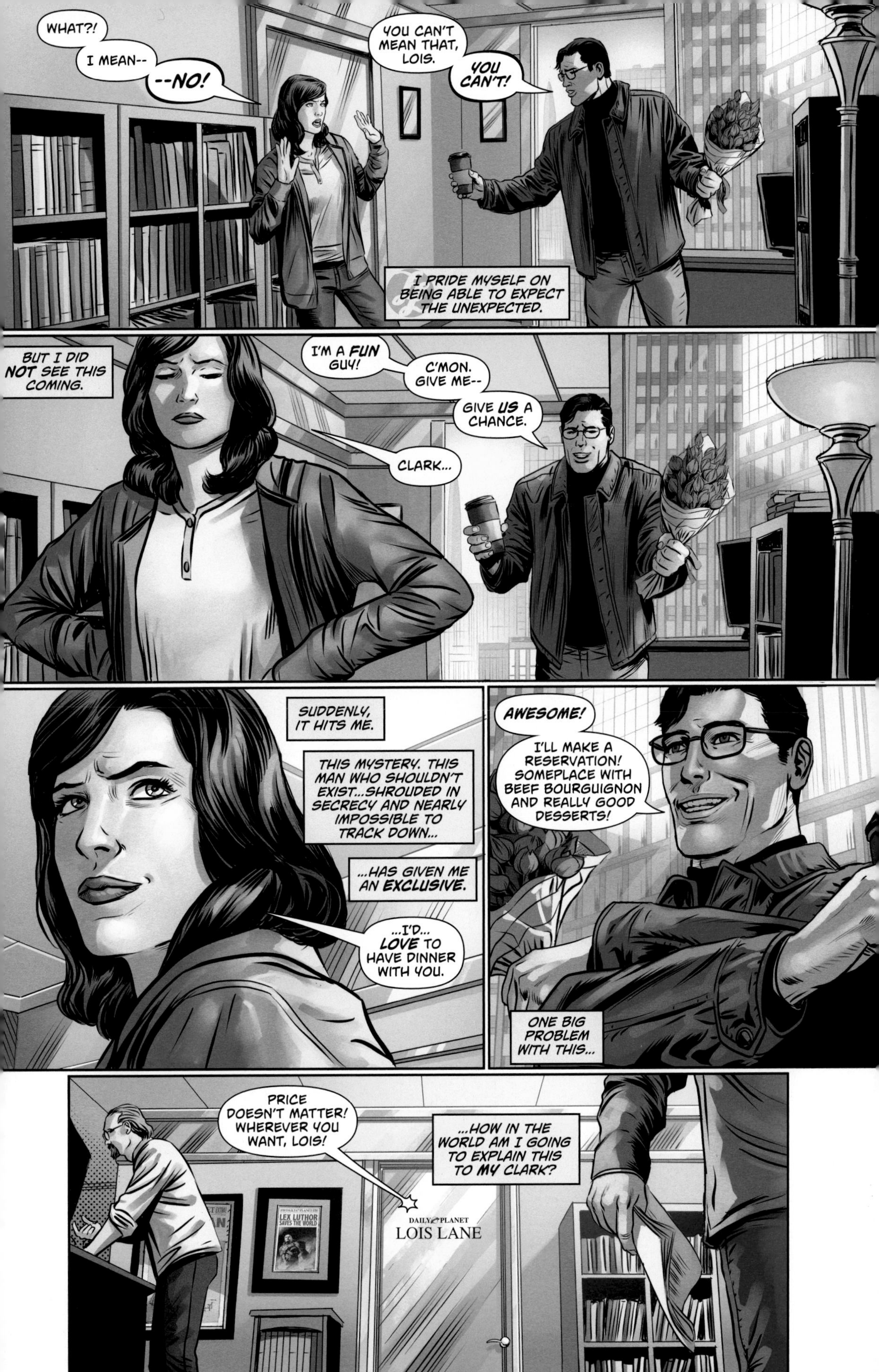
WHAT?!
I MEAN--
--NO!
YOU CAN'T MEAN THAT, LOIS.
YOU CAN'T!
I PRIDE MYSELF ON BEING ABLE TO EXPECT THE UNEXPECTED.
BUT I DID NOT SEE THIS COMING.
I'M A FUN GUY!
C'MON. GIVE ME--
GIVE US A CHANCE.
CLARK...
SUDDENLY, IT HITS ME.
THIS MYSTERY. THIS MAN WHO SHOULDN'T EXIST...SHROUDED IN SECRECY AND NEARLY IMPOSSIBLE TO TRACK DOWN...
...HAS GIVEN ME AN EXCLUSIVE.
...I'D... LOVE TO HAVE DINNER WITH YOU.
AWESOME!
I'LL MAKE A RESERVATION! SOMEPLACE WITH BEEF BOURGUIGNON AND REALLY GOOD DESSERTS!
ONE BIG PROBLEM WITH THIS...
PRICE DOESN'T MATTER! WHEREVER YOU WANT, LOIS!
...HOW IN THE WORLD AM I GOING TO EXPLAIN THIS TO MY CLARK?
LEX LUTHOR SAVES THE WORLD
DAILY PLANET
LOIS LANE

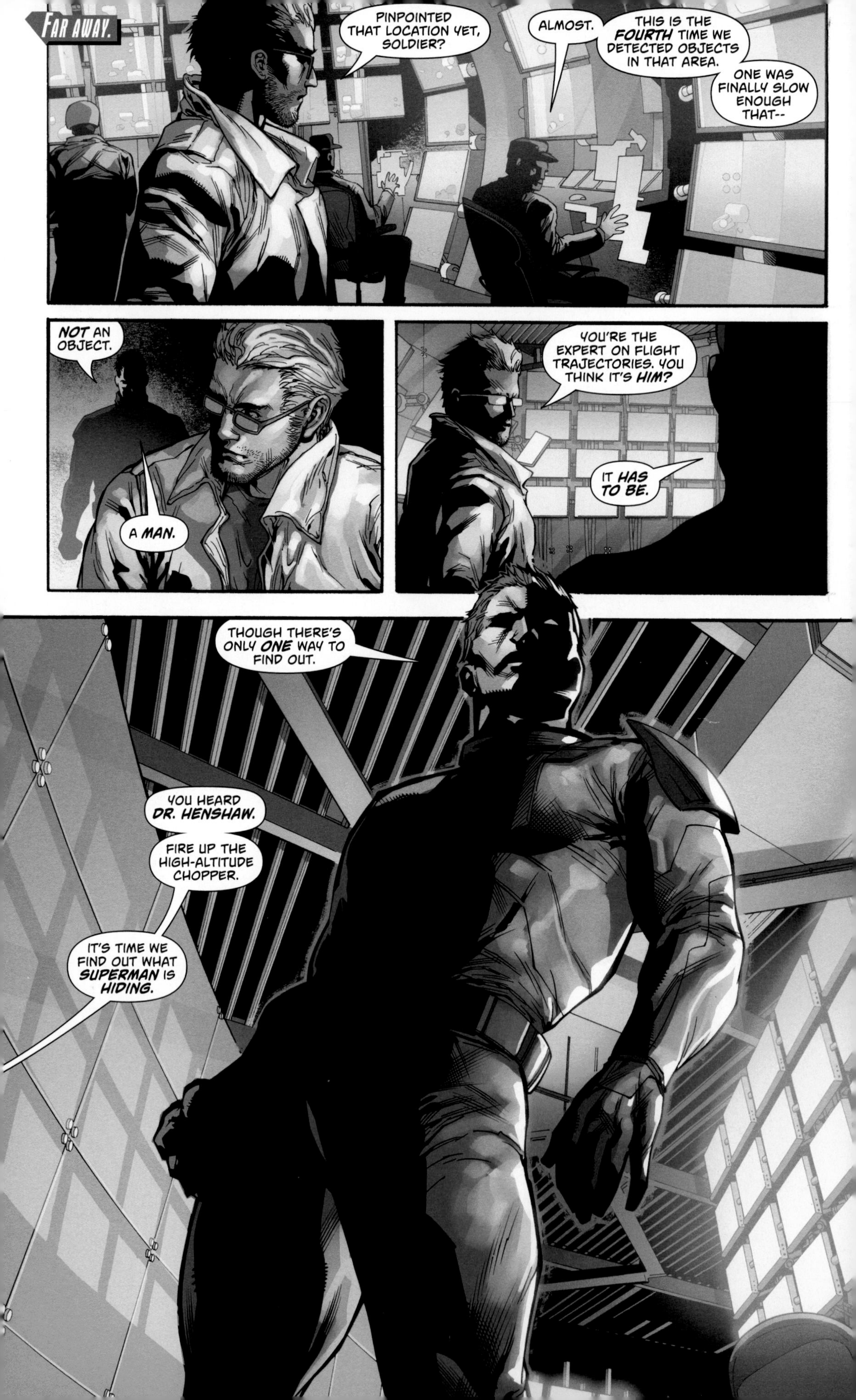
FAR AWAY.
PINPOINTED THAT LOCATION YET, SOLDIER?
ALMOST.
THIS IS THE FOURTH TIME WE DETECTED OBJECTS IN THAT AREA.
ONE WAS FINALLY SLOW ENOUGH THAT--
NOT AN OBJECT.
A MAN.
YOU'RE THE EXPERT ON FLIGHT TRAJECTORIES. YOU THINK IT'S HIM?
IT HAS TO BE.
THOUGH THERE'S ONLY ONE WAY TO FIND OUT.
YOU HEARD DR. HENSHAW.
FIRE UP THE HIGH-ALTITUDE CHOPPER.
IT'S TIME WE FIND OUT WHAT SUPERMAN IS HIDING.

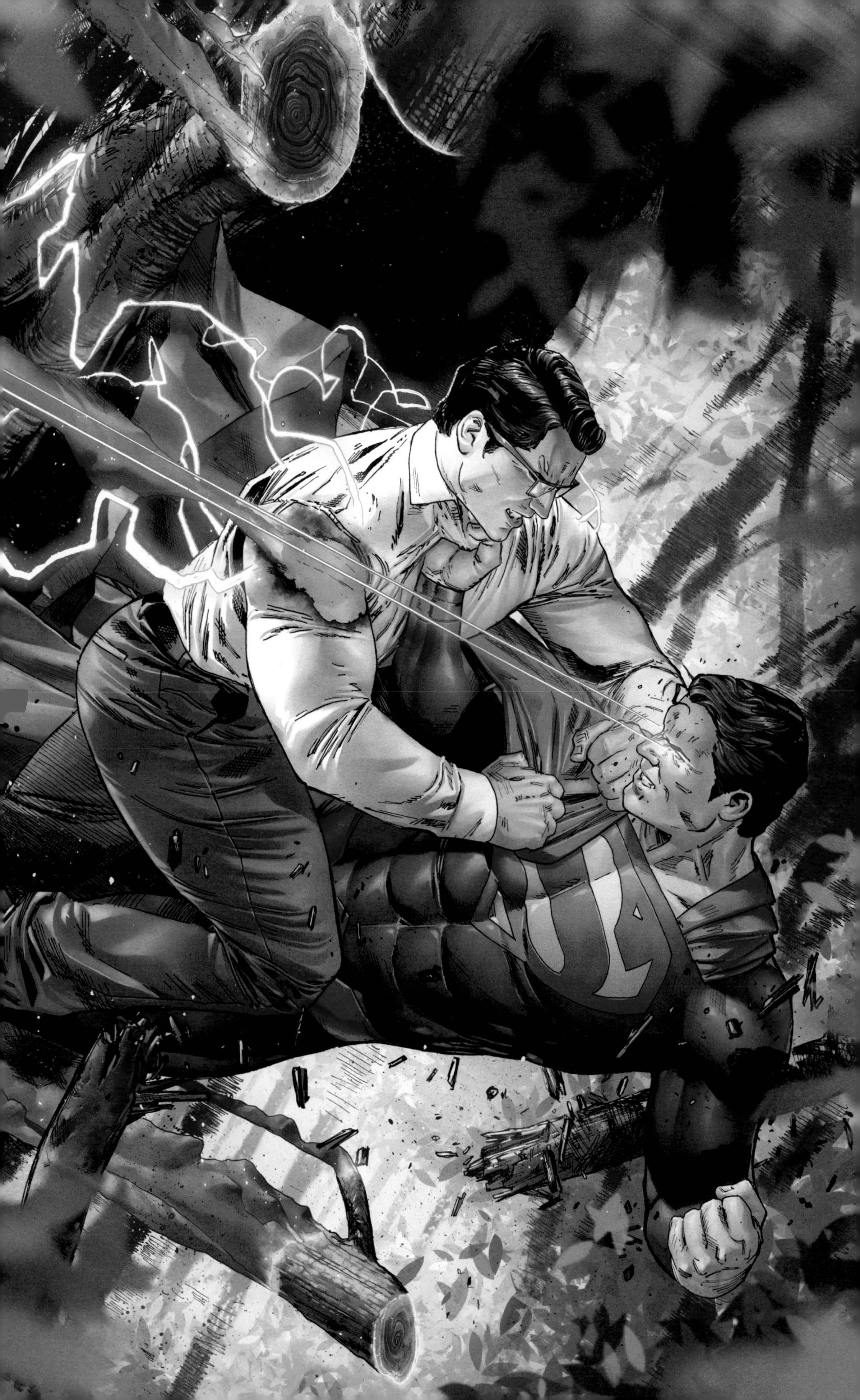

MILD MANNERED part two

DAN JURGENS writer * PATCH ZIRCHER & STEPHEN SEGOVIA pencillers
PATCH ZIRCHER & ART THIBERT inkers * ULISES ARREOLA colorist
CLAY MANN & TOMEU MOREY cover art

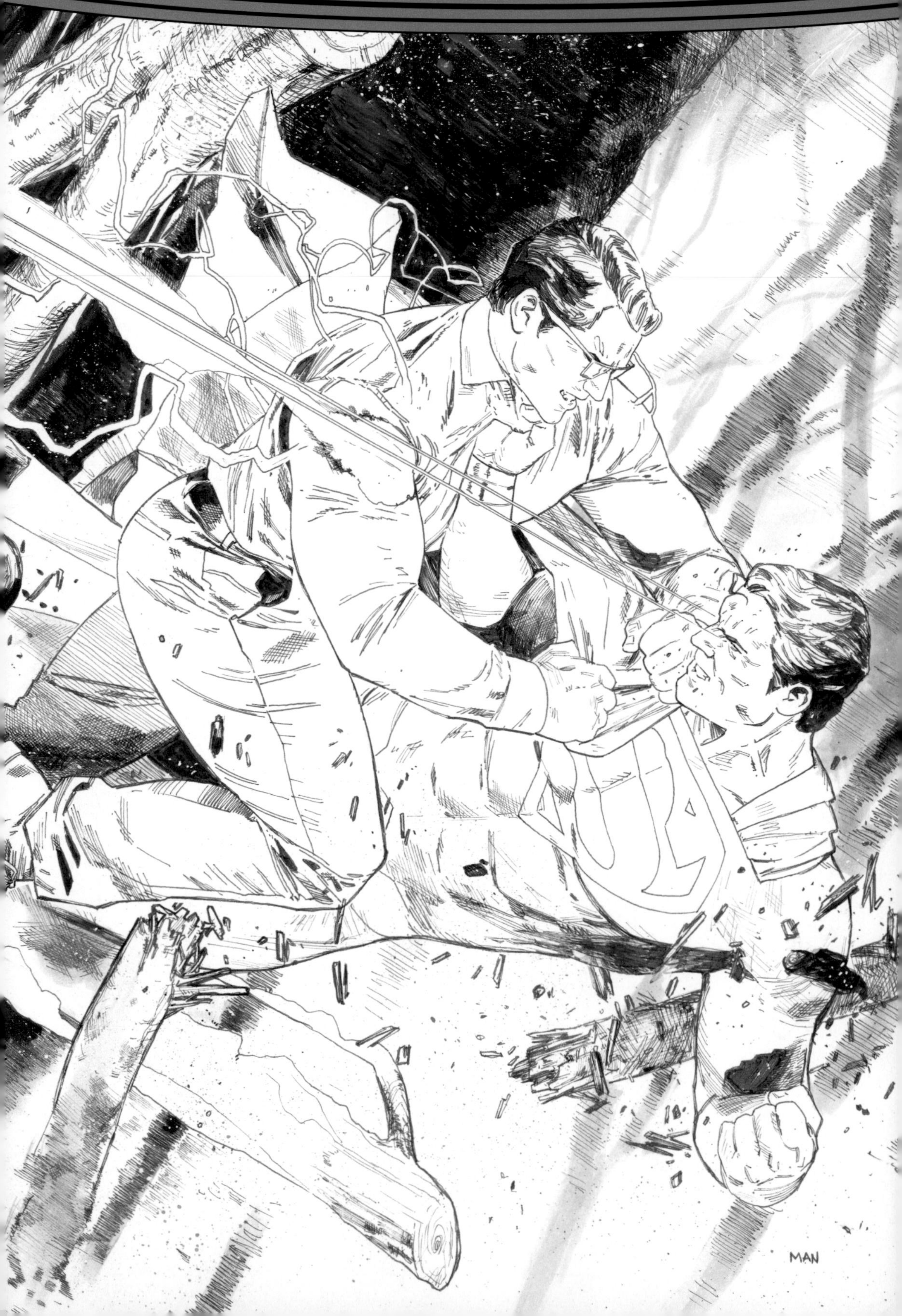
MAN

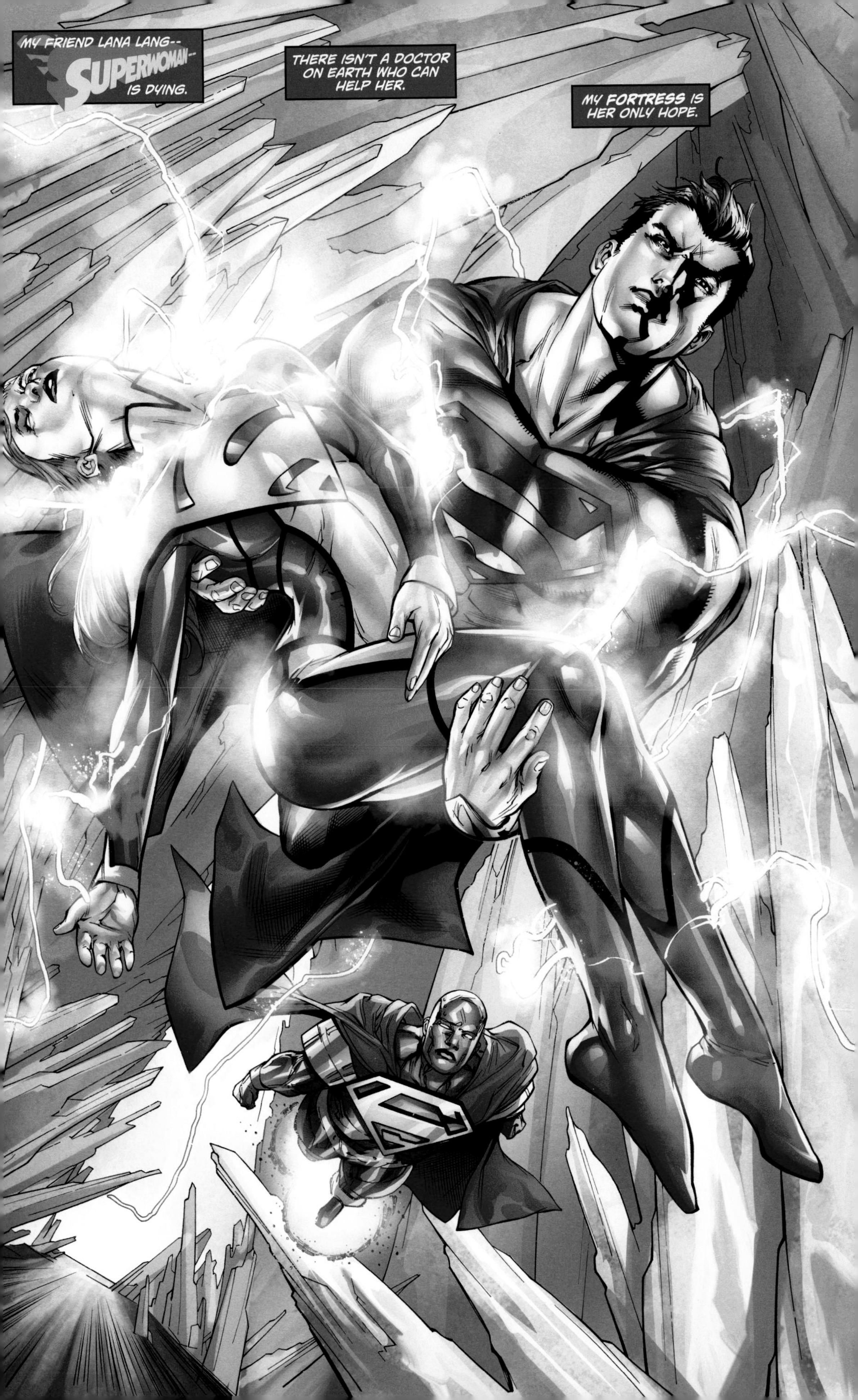
MY FRIEND LANA LANG--
SUPERWOMAN--
IS DYING.
THERE ISN'T A DOCTOR ON EARTH WHO CAN HELP HER.
MY FORTRESS IS HER ONLY HOPE.

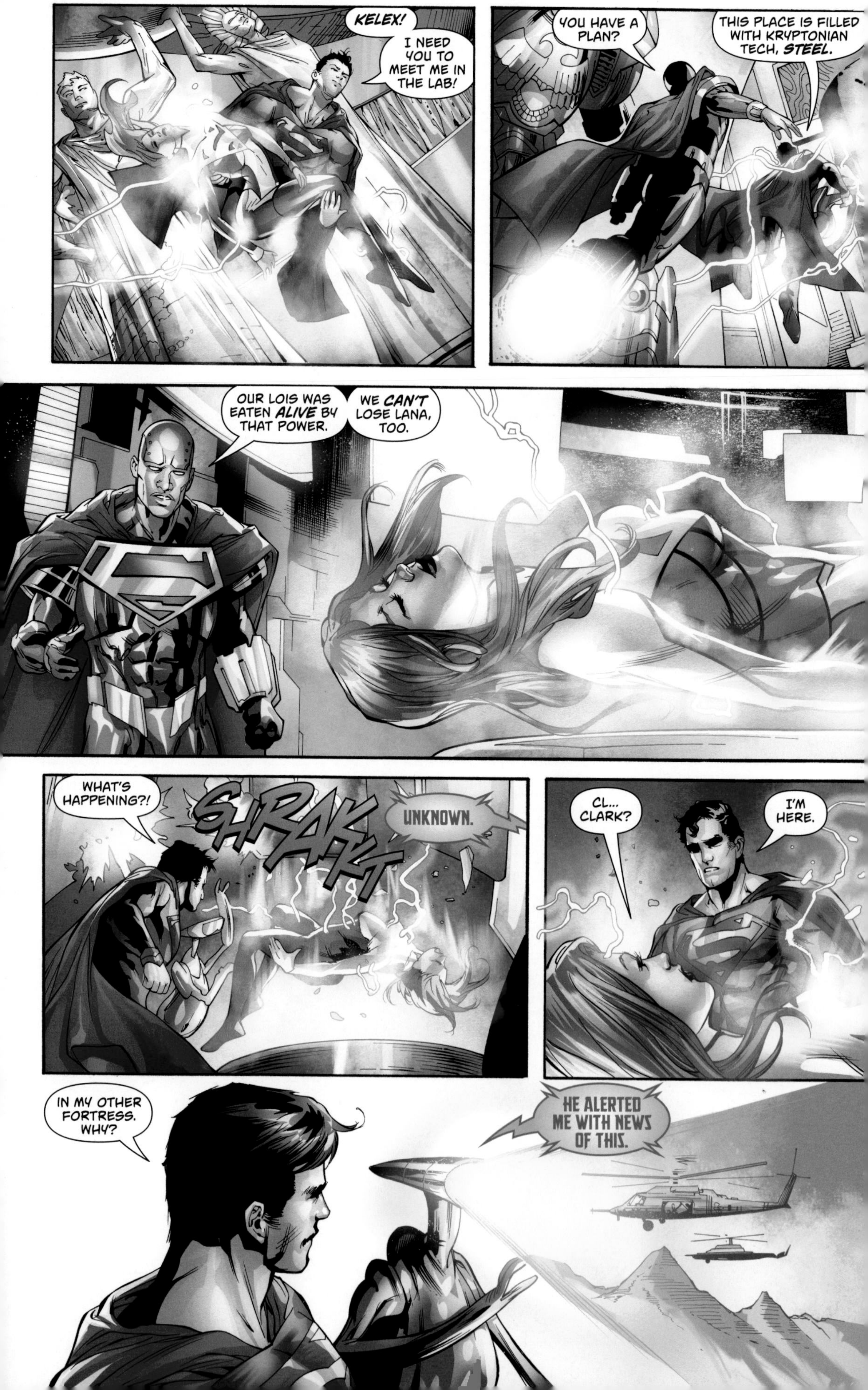
KELEX!
I NEED YOU TO MEET ME IN THE LAB!
YOU HAVE A PLAN?
THIS PLACE IS FILLED WITH KRYPTONIAN TECH, STEEL.
OUR LOIS WAS EATEN ALIVE BY THAT POWER.
WE CAN'T LOSE LANA, TOO.
WHAT'S HAPPENING?!
SHRAKT
UNKNOWN.
CL... CLARK?
I'M HERE.
IN MY OTHER FORTRESS. WHY?
HE ALERTED ME WITH NEWS OF THIS.

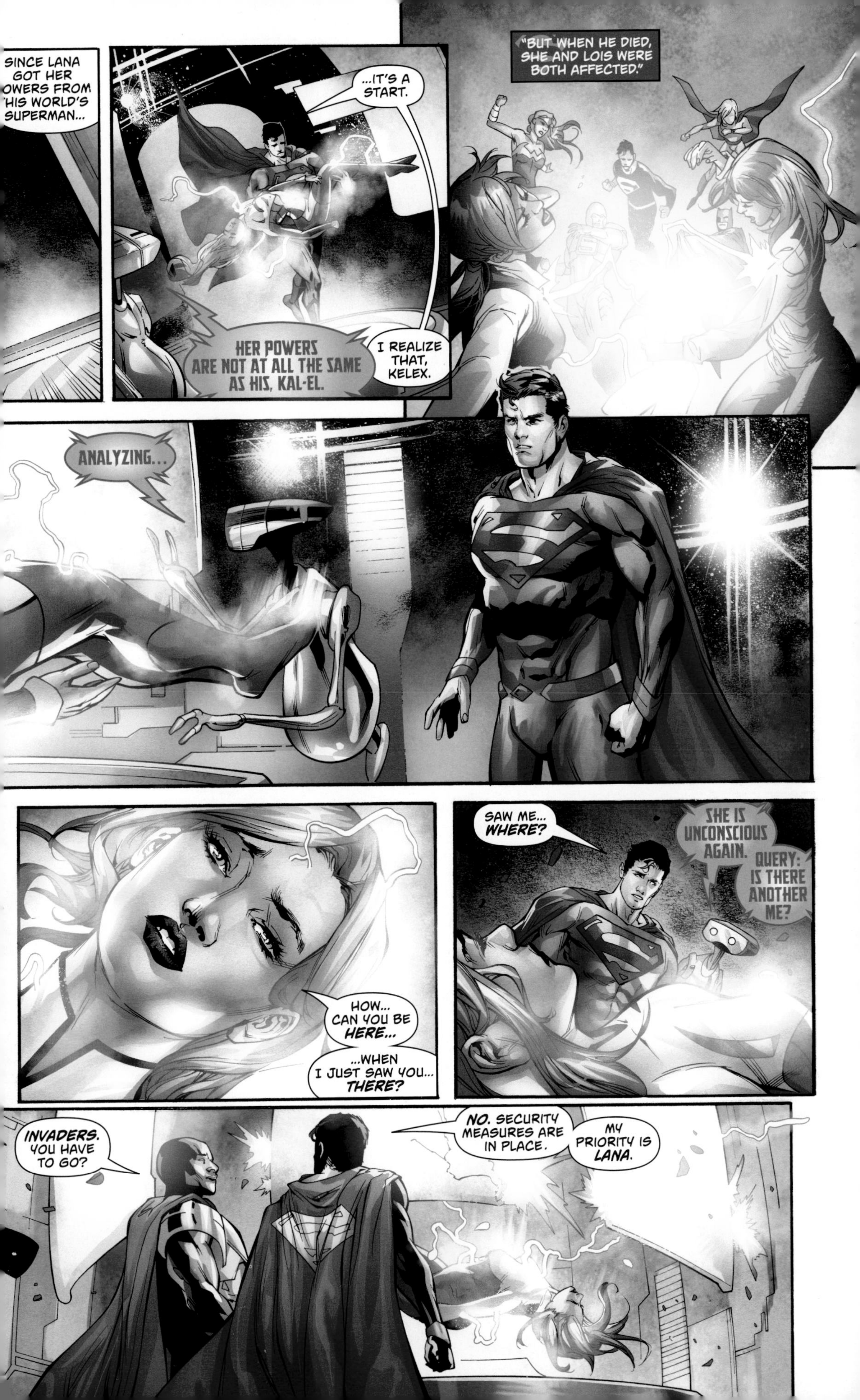
SINCE LANA GOT HER POWERS FROM THIS WORLD'S SUPERMAN...
...IT'S A START.
HER POWERS ARE NOT AT ALL THE SAME AS HIS, KAL-EL.
I REALIZE THAT, KELEX.
"BUT WHEN HE DIED, SHE AND LOIS WERE BOTH AFFECTED."
ANALYZING...
HOW... CAN YOU BE HERE...
...WHEN I JUST SAW YOU... THERE?
SAW ME... WHERE?
SHE IS UNCONSCIOUS AGAIN.
QUERY: IS THERE ANOTHER ME?
INVADERS. YOU HAVE TO GO?
NO. SECURITY MEASURES ARE IN PLACE.
MY PRIORITY IS LANA.

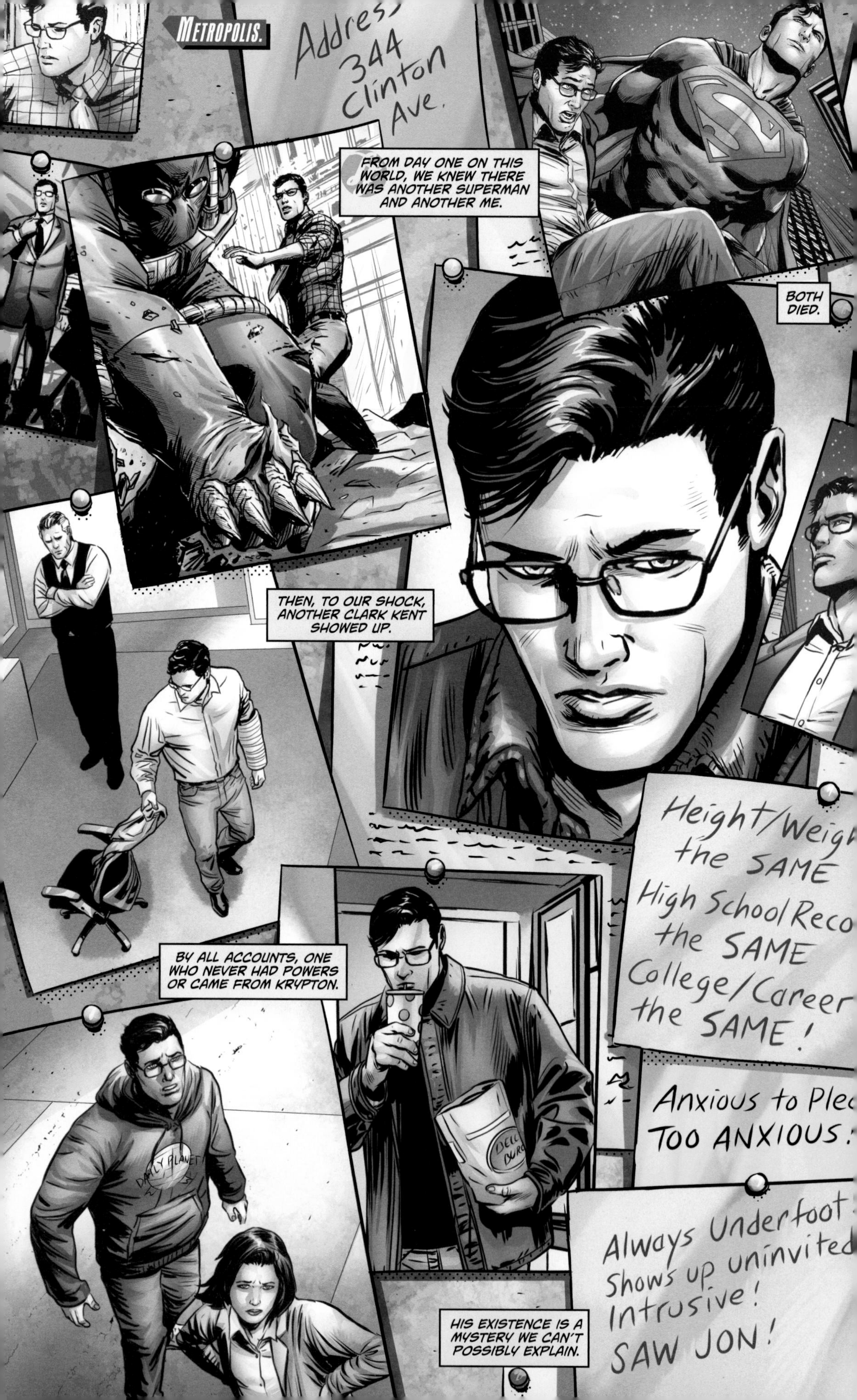
METROPOLIS.
Address 344 Clinton Ave.
FROM DAY ONE ON THIS WORLD, WE KNEW THERE WAS ANOTHER SUPERMAN AND ANOTHER ME.
BOTH DIED.
THEN, TO OUR SHOCK, ANOTHER CLARK KENT SHOWED UP.
Height/Weig the SAME
High School Reco the SAME
College/Career the SAME!
BY ALL ACCOUNTS, ONE WHO NEVER HAD POWERS OR CAME FROM KRYPTON.
Anxious to Plea TOO ANXIOUS!
DAILY PLANET
Always Underfoot! Shows up uninvited Intrusive! SAW JON!
HIS EXISTENCE IS A MYSTERY WE CAN'T POSSIBLY EXPLAIN.

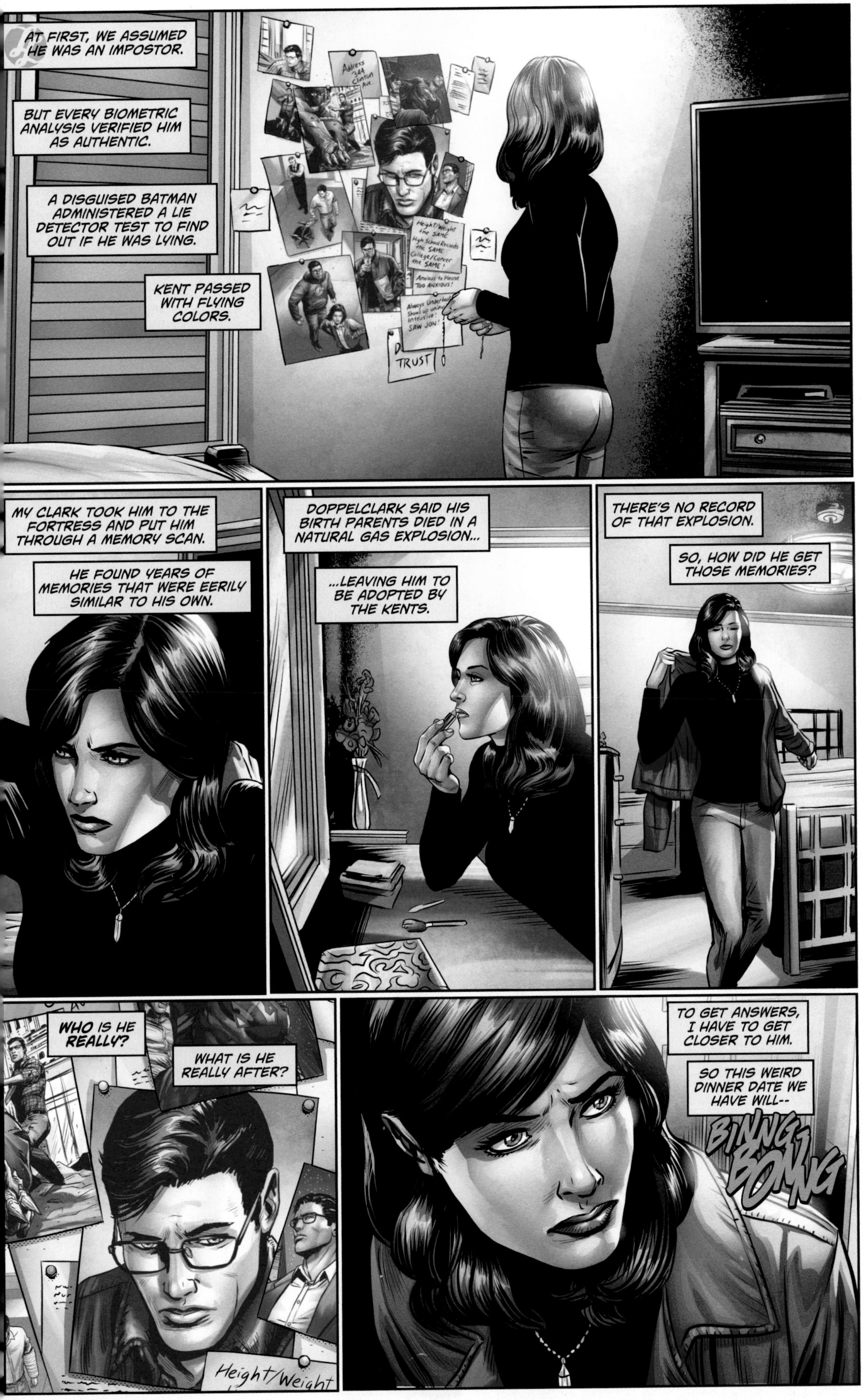
AT FIRST, WE ASSUMED HE WAS AN IMPOSTOR.
BUT EVERY BIOMETRIC ANALYSIS VERIFIED HIM AS AUTHENTIC.
A DISGUISED BATMAN ADMINISTERED A LIE DETECTOR TEST TO FIND OUT IF HE WAS LYING.
KENT PASSED WITH FLYING COLORS.
TRUST
MY CLARK TOOK HIM TO THE FORTRESS AND PUT HIM THROUGH A MEMORY SCAN.
HE FOUND YEARS OF MEMORIES THAT WERE EERILY SIMILAR TO HIS OWN.
DOPPELCLARK SAID HIS BIRTH PARENTS DIED IN A NATURAL GAS EXPLOSION...
...LEAVING HIM TO BE ADOPTED BY THE KENTS.
THERE'S NO RECORD OF THAT EXPLOSION.
SO, HOW DID HE GET THOSE MEMORIES?
WHO IS HE REALLY?
WHAT IS HE REALLY AFTER?
Height/Weight
TO GET ANSWERS, I HAVE TO GET CLOSER TO HIM.
SO THIS WEIRD DINNER DATE WE HAVE WILL--
BINNG BONNG

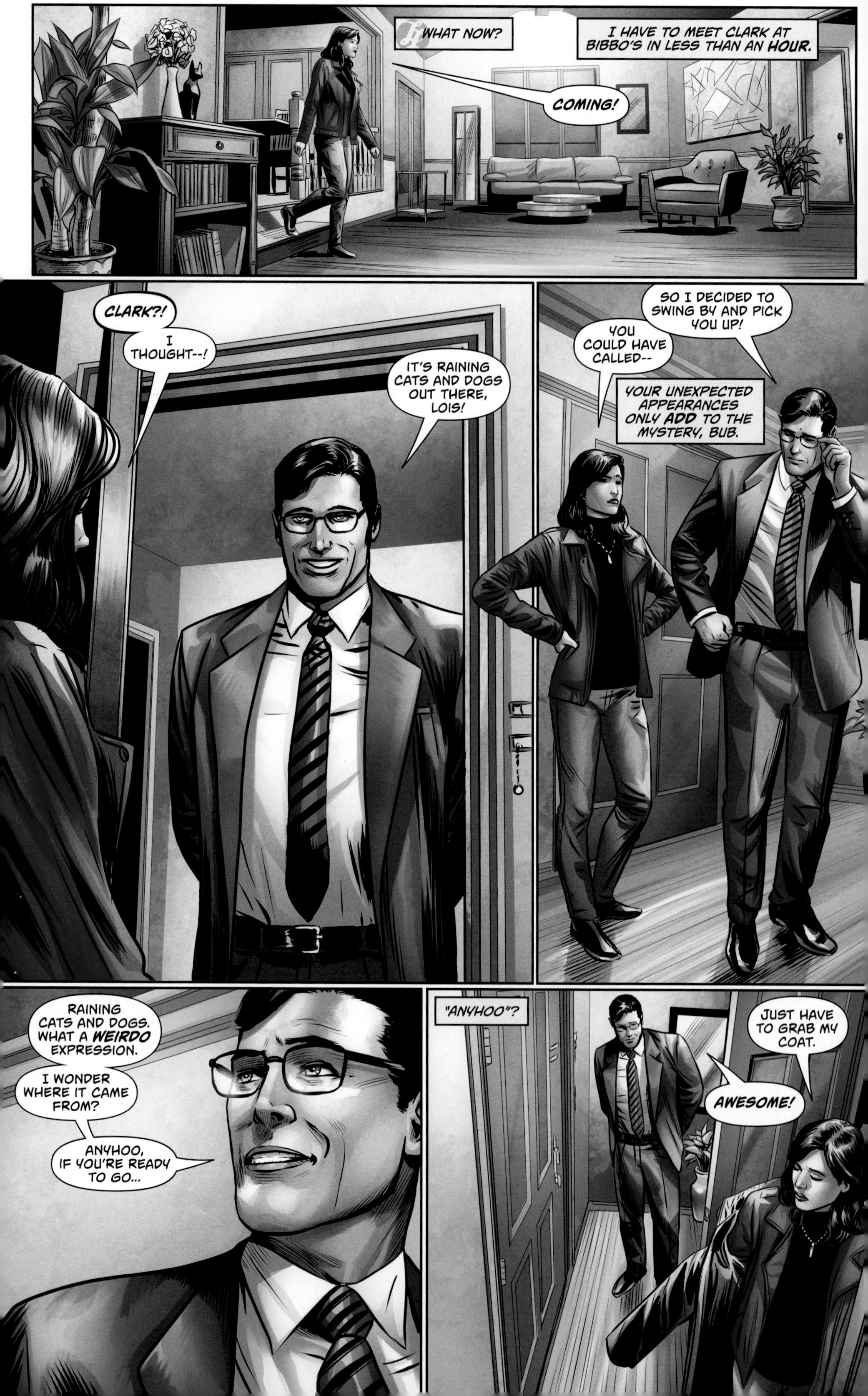
WHAT NOW?
I HAVE TO MEET CLARK AT BIBBO'S IN LESS THAN AN HOUR.
COMING!
CLARK?!
I THOUGHT--!
IT'S RAINING CATS AND DOGS OUT THERE, LOIS!
SO I DECIDED TO SWING BY AND PICK YOU UP!
YOU COULD HAVE CALLED--
YOUR UNEXPECTED APPEARANCES ONLY ADD TO THE MYSTERY, BUB.
RAINING CATS AND DOGS. WHAT A WEIRDO EXPRESSION.
I WONDER WHERE IT CAME FROM?
ANYHOO, IF YOU'RE READY TO GO...
"ANYHOO"?
JUST HAVE TO GRAB MY COAT.
AWESOME!

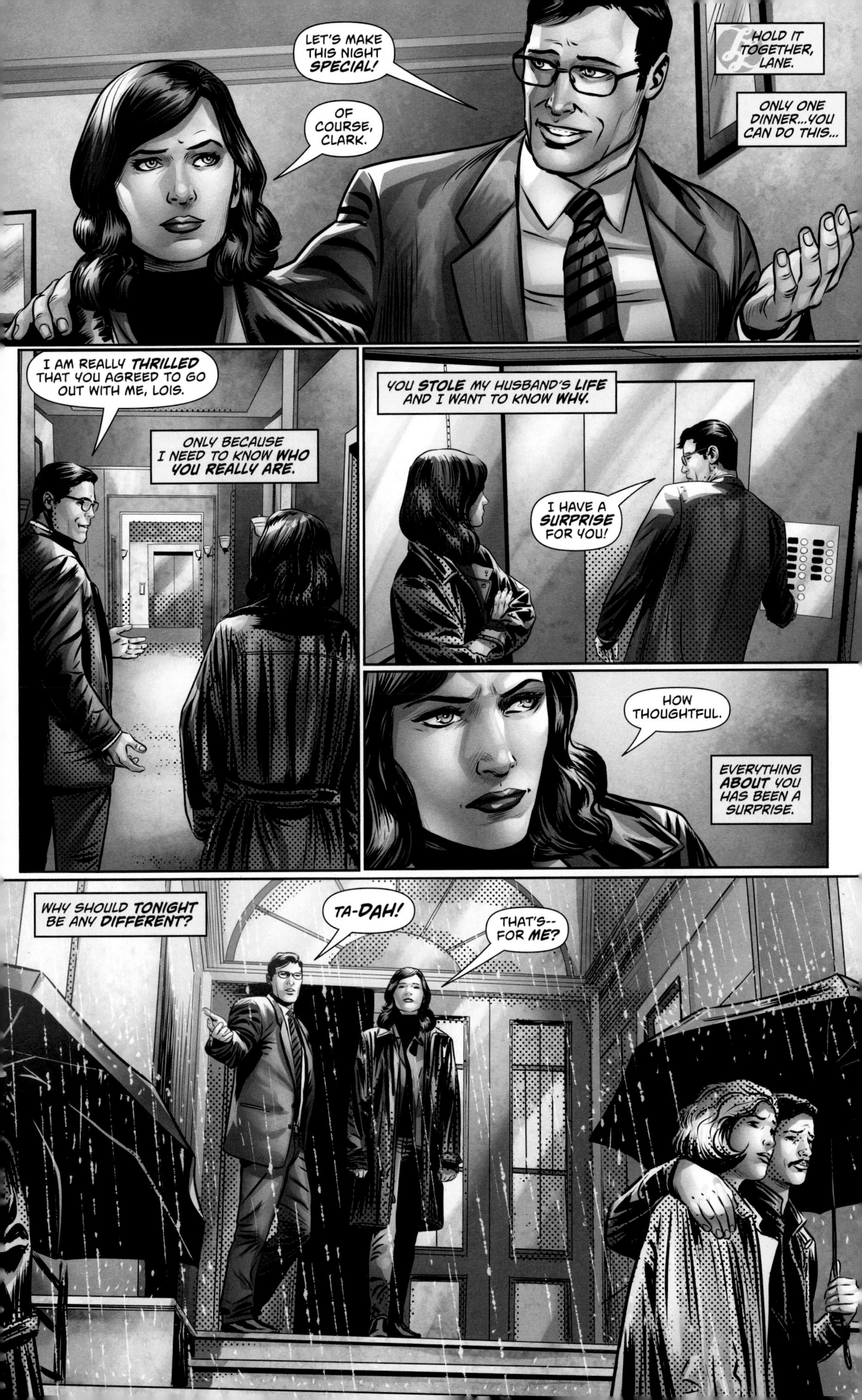
LET'S MAKE THIS NIGHT SPECIAL!
OF COURSE, CLARK.
HOLD IT TOGETHER, LANE.
ONLY ONE DINNER...YOU CAN DO THIS...
I AM REALLY THRILLED THAT YOU AGREED TO GO OUT WITH ME, LOIS.
ONLY BECAUSE I NEED TO KNOW WHO YOU REALLY ARE.
YOU STOLE MY HUSBAND'S LIFE AND I WANT TO KNOW WHY.
I HAVE A SURPRISE FOR YOU!
HOW THOUGHTFUL.
EVERYTHING ABOUT YOU HAS BEEN A SURPRISE.
WHY SHOULD TONIGHT BE ANY DIFFERENT?
TA-DAH!
THAT'S-- FOR ME?

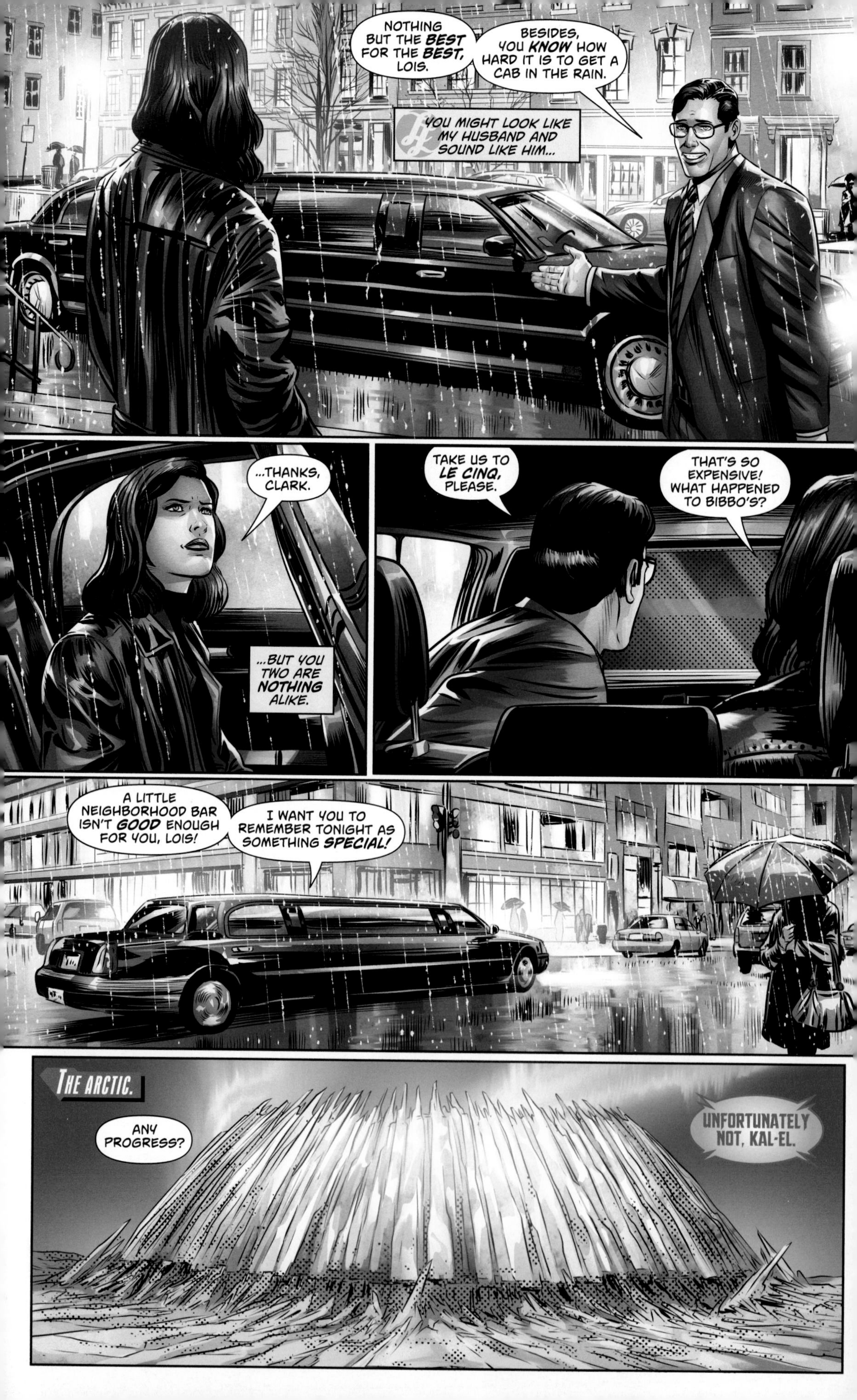
NOTHING BUT THE BEST FOR THE BEST, LOIS.
BESIDES, YOU KNOW HOW HARD IT IS TO GET A CAB IN THE RAIN.
YOU MIGHT LOOK LIKE MY HUSBAND AND SOUND LIKE HIM...
...THANKS, CLARK.
...BUT YOU TWO ARE NOTHING ALIKE.
TAKE US TO LE CINQ, PLEASE.
THAT'S SO EXPENSIVE! WHAT HAPPENED TO BIBBO'S?
A LITTLE NEIGHBORHOOD BAR ISN'T GOOD ENOUGH FOR YOU, LOIS!
I WANT YOU TO REMEMBER TONIGHT AS SOMETHING SPECIAL!
THE ARCTIC.
ANY PROGRESS?
UNFORTUNATELY NOT, KAL-EL.

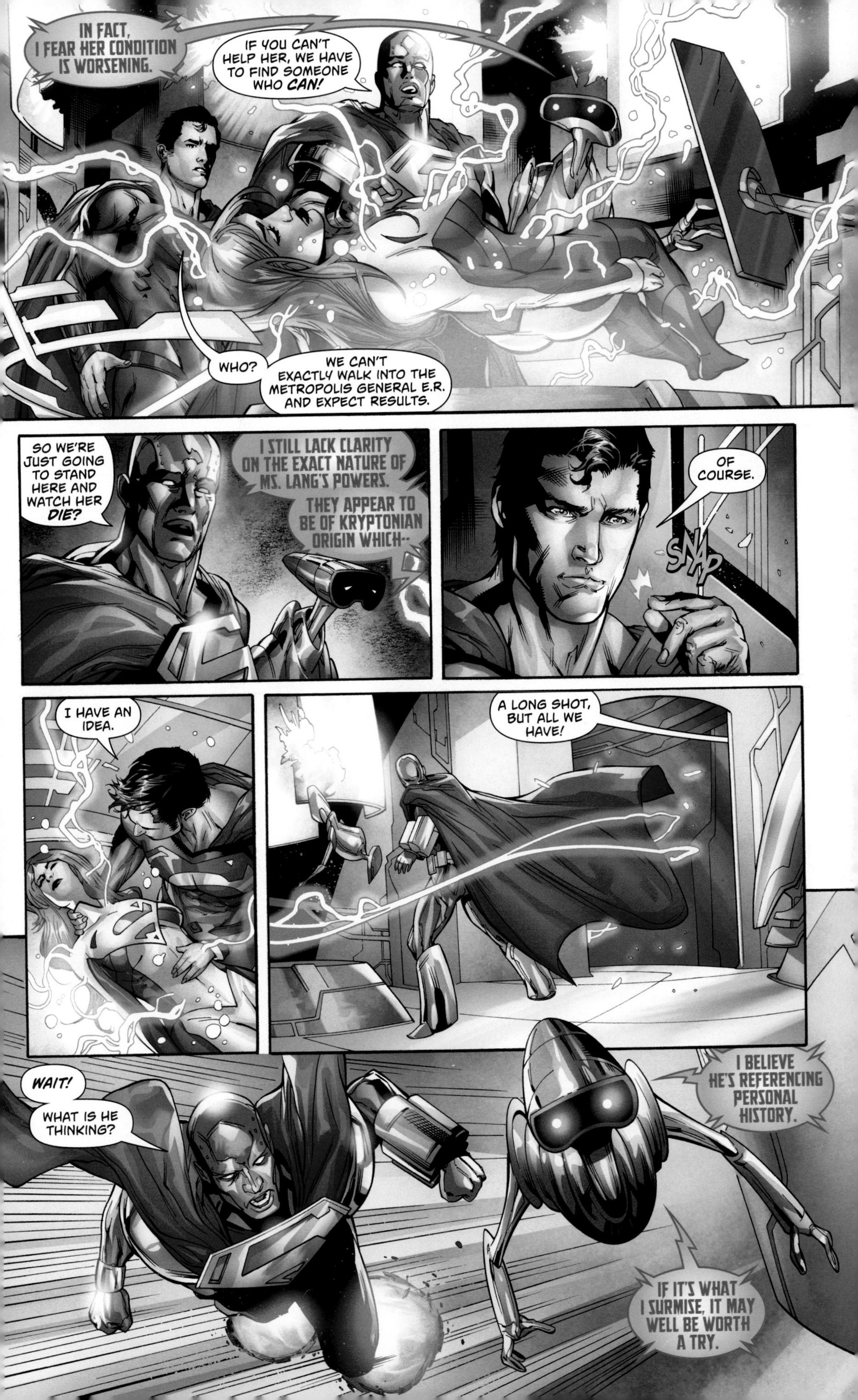
IN FACT, I FEAR HER CONDITION IS WORSENING.
IF YOU CAN'T HELP HER, WE HAVE TO FIND SOMEONE WHO CAN!
WHO?
WE CAN'T EXACTLY WALK INTO THE METROPOLIS GENERAL E.R. AND EXPECT RESULTS.
SO WE'RE JUST GOING TO STAND HERE AND WATCH HER DIE?
I STILL LACK CLARITY ON THE EXACT NATURE OF MS. LANG'S POWERS.
THEY APPEAR TO BE OF KRYPTONIAN ORIGIN WHICH--
OF COURSE.
SNAP
I HAVE AN IDEA.
A LONG SHOT, BUT ALL WE HAVE!
WAIT!
WHAT IS HE THINKING?
I BELIEVE HE'S REFERENCING PERSONAL HISTORY.
IF IT'S WHAT I SURMISE, IT MAY WELL BE WORTH A TRY.

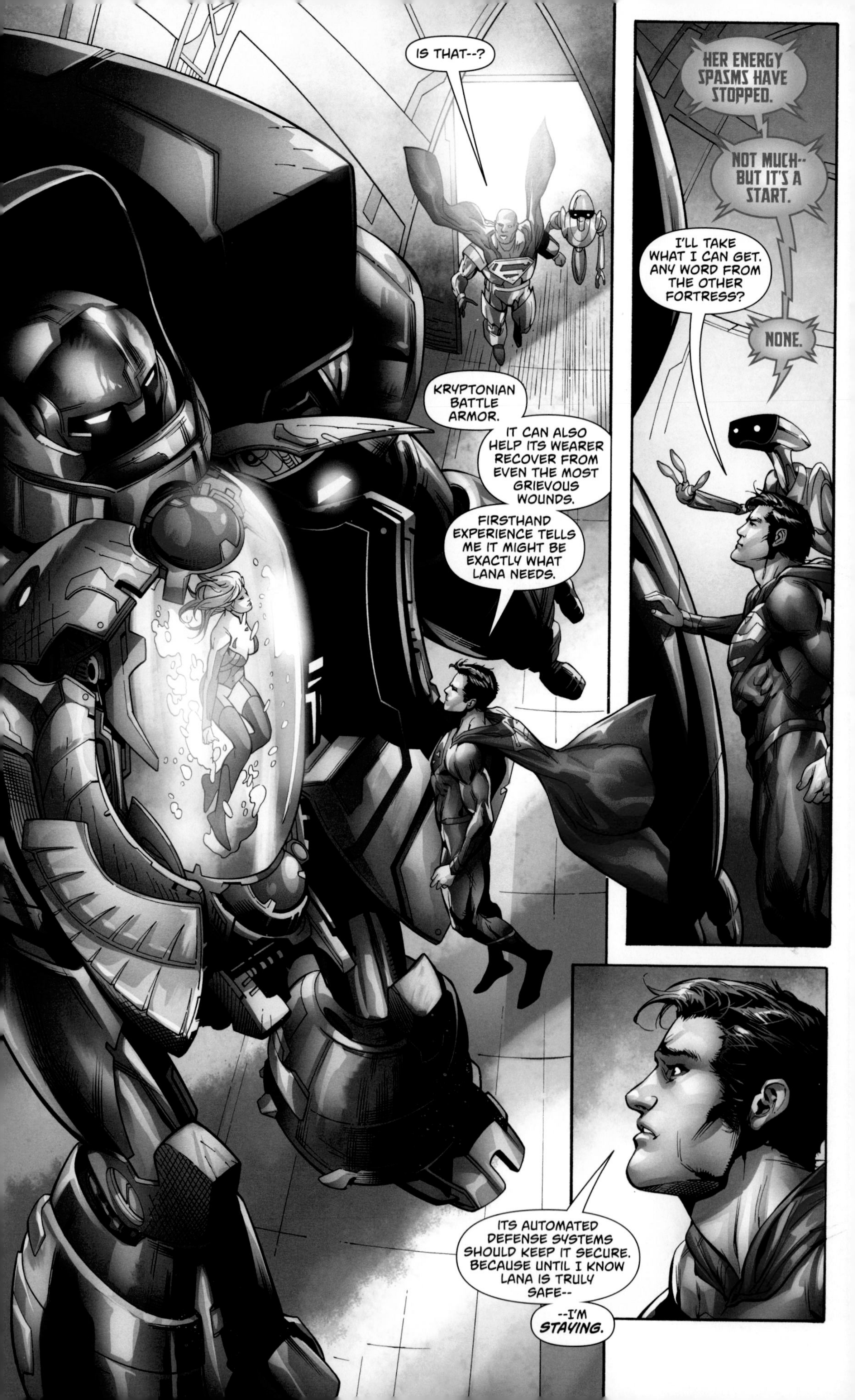
IS THAT--?
KRYPTONIAN BATTLE ARMOR.
IT CAN ALSO HELP ITS WEARER RECOVER FROM EVEN THE MOST GRIEVOUS WOUNDS.
FIRSTHAND EXPERIENCE TELLS ME IT MIGHT BE EXACTLY WHAT LANA NEEDS.
HER ENERGY SPASMS HAVE STOPPED.
NOT MUCH-- BUT IT'S A START.
I'LL TAKE WHAT I CAN GET. ANY WORD FROM THE OTHER FORTRESS?
NONE.
ITS AUTOMATED DEFENSE SYSTEMS SHOULD KEEP IT SECURE. BECAUSE UNTIL I KNOW LANA IS TRULY SAFE--
--I'M STAYING.

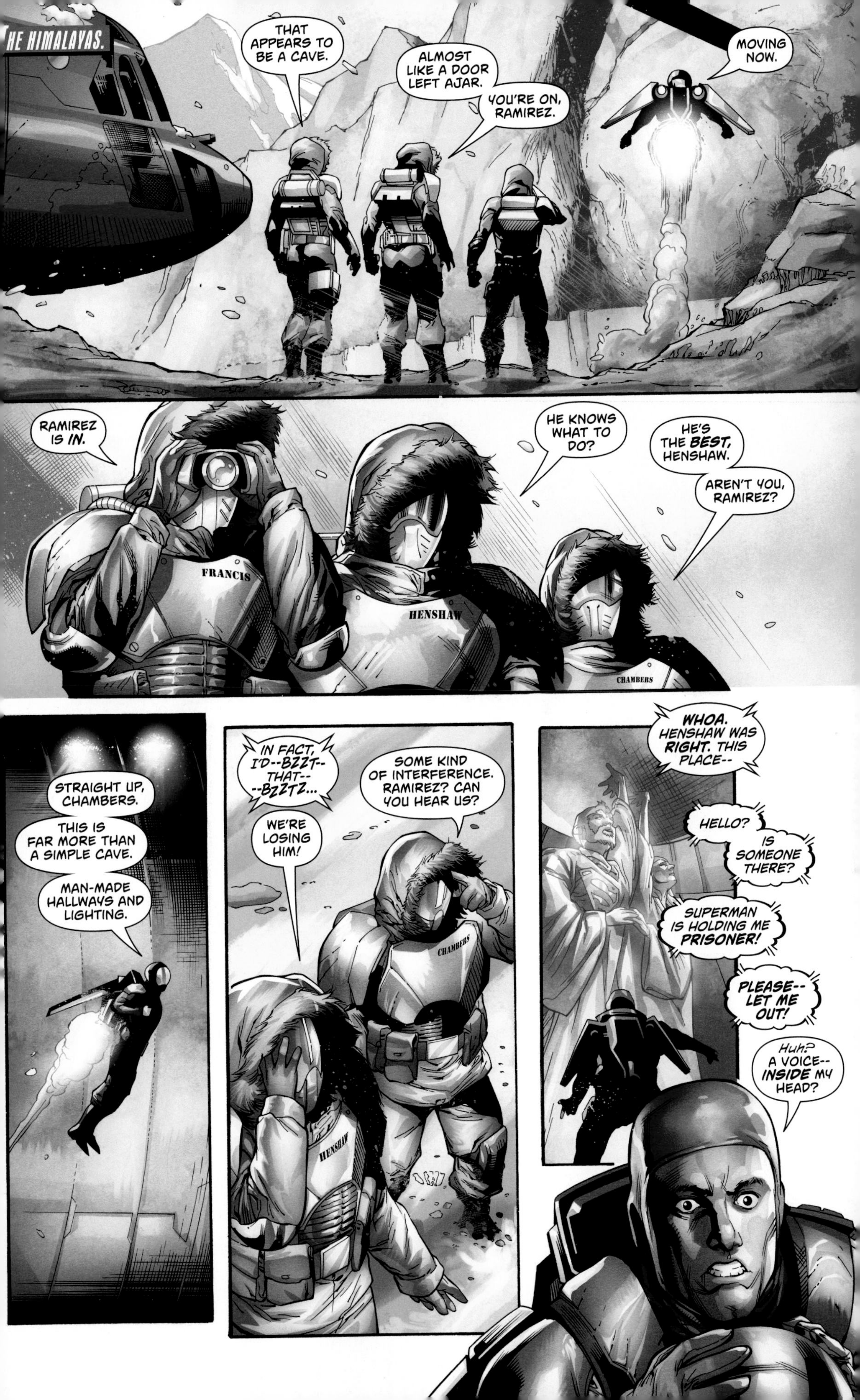
HE HIMALAYAS.
THAT APPEARS TO BE A CAVE.
ALMOST LIKE A DOOR LEFT AJAR.
YOU'RE ON, RAMIREZ.
MOVING NOW.
RAMIREZ IS IN.
HE KNOWS WHAT TO DO?
HE'S THE BEST, HENSHAW.
AREN'T YOU, RAMIREZ?
FRANCIS
HENSHAW
CHAMBERS
STRAIGHT UP, CHAMBERS.
THIS IS FAR MORE THAN A SIMPLE CAVE.
MAN-MADE HALLWAYS AND LIGHTING.
IN FACT, I'D--BZZT--THAT----BZZTZ...
WE'RE LOSING HIM!
SOME KIND OF INTERFERENCE. RAMIREZ? CAN YOU HEAR US?
CHAMBERS
HENSHAW
WHOA. HENSHAW WAS RIGHT. THIS PLACE--
HELLO?
IS SOMEONE THERE?
SUPERMAN IS HOLDING ME PRISONER!
PLEASE--LET ME OUT!
Huh? A VOICE--INSIDE MY HEAD?

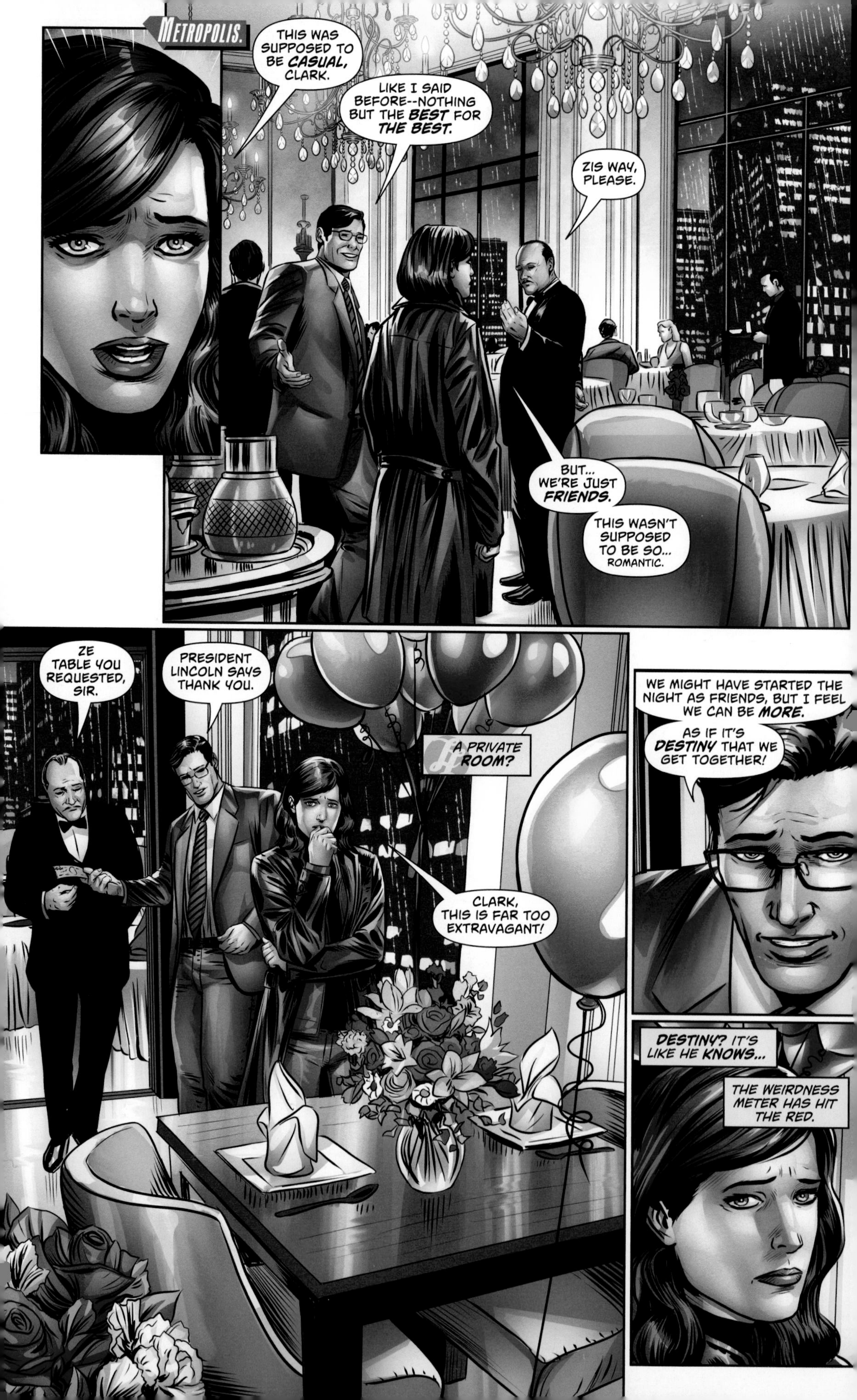
METROPOLIS.
THIS WAS SUPPOSED TO BE CASUAL, CLARK.
LIKE I SAID BEFORE--NOTHING BUT THE BEST FOR THE BEST.
ZIS WAY, PLEASE.
BUT... WE'RE JUST FRIENDS.
THIS WASN'T SUPPOSED TO BE SO... ROMANTIC.
ZE TABLE YOU REQUESTED, SIR.
PRESIDENT LINCOLN SAYS THANK YOU.
A PRIVATE ROOM?
CLARK, THIS IS FAR TOO EXTRAVAGANT!
WE MIGHT HAVE STARTED THE NIGHT AS FRIENDS, BUT I FEEL WE CAN BE MORE.
AS IF IT'S DESTINY THAT WE GET TOGETHER!
DESTINY? IT'S LIKE HE KNOWS...
THE WEIRDNESS METER HAS HIT THE RED.

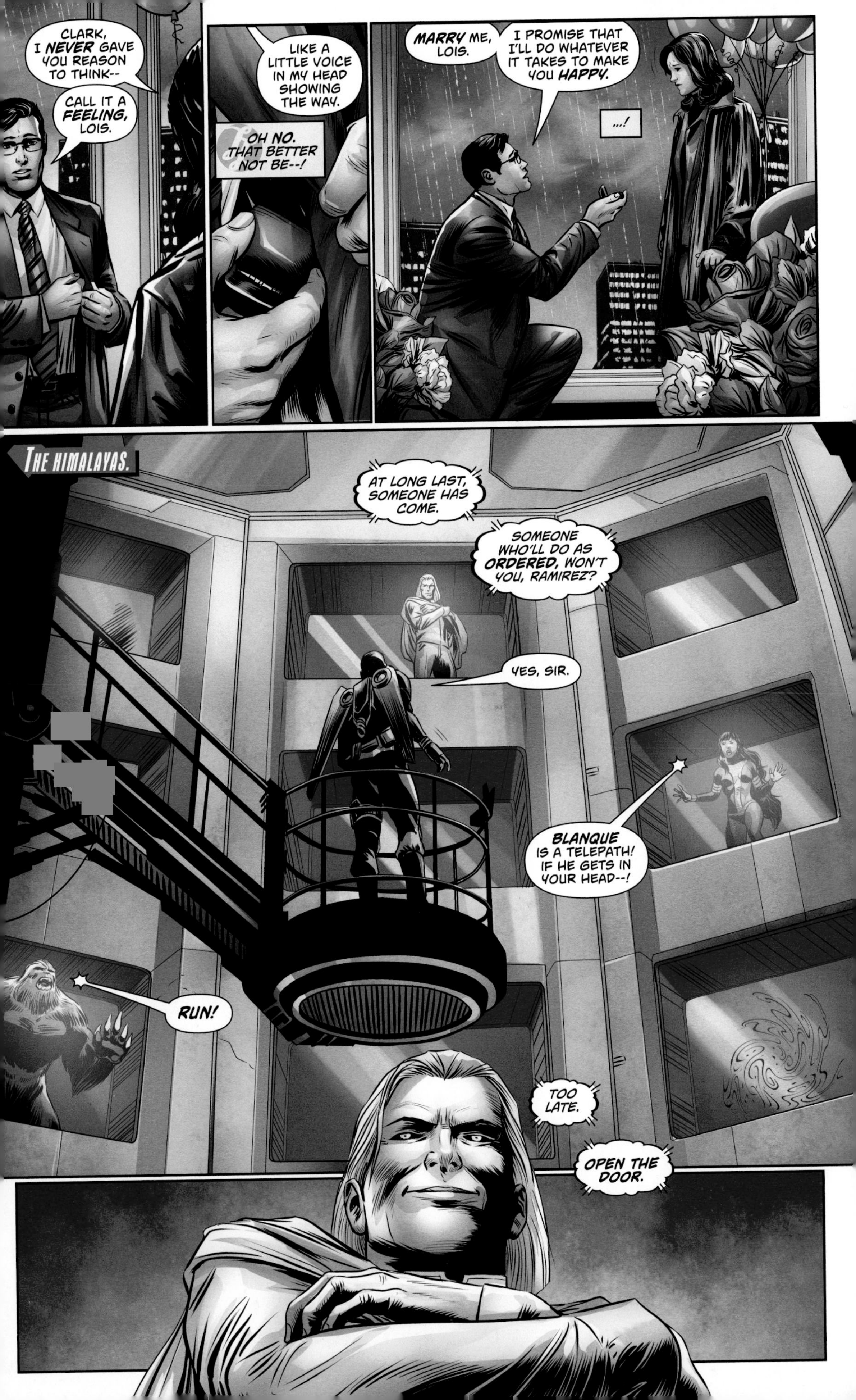
CLARK, I NEVER GAVE YOU REASON TO THINK--
CALL IT A FEELING, LOIS.
LIKE A LITTLE VOICE IN MY HEAD SHOWING THE WAY.
OH NO. THAT BETTER NOT BE--!
MARRY ME, LOIS.
I PROMISE THAT I'LL DO WHATEVER IT TAKES TO MAKE YOU HAPPY.
...!
THE HIMALAYAS.
AT LONG LAST, SOMEONE HAS COME.
SOMEONE WHO'LL DO AS ORDERED, WON'T YOU, RAMIREZ?
YES, SIR.
BLANQUE IS A TELEPATH! IF HE GETS IN YOUR HEAD--!
RUN!
TOO LATE.
OPEN THE DOOR.

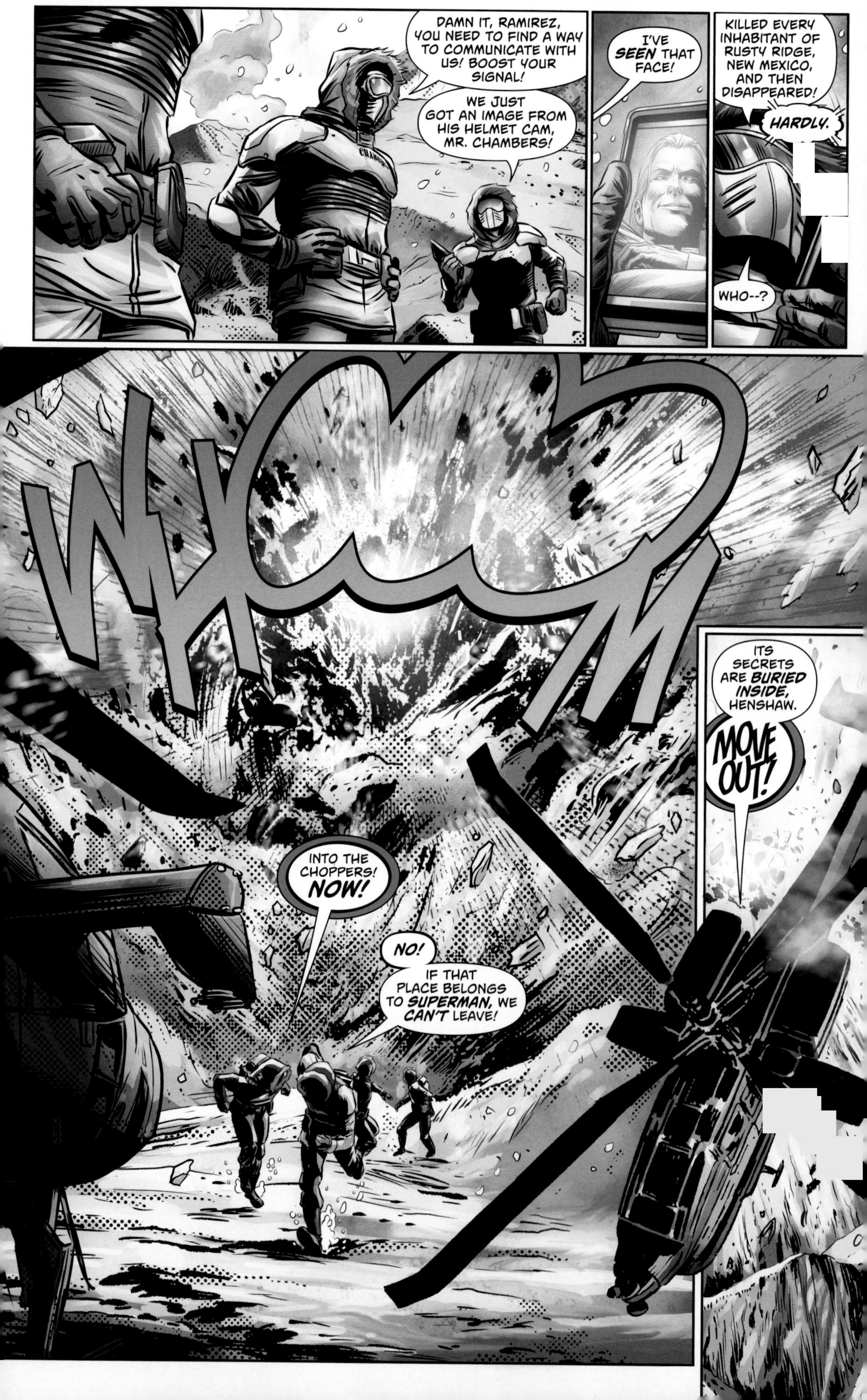
DAMN IT, RAMIREZ, YOU NEED TO FIND A WAY TO COMMUNICATE WITH US! BOOST YOUR SIGNAL!
WE JUST GOT AN IMAGE FROM HIS HELMET CAM, MR. CHAMBERS!
I'VE SEEN THAT FACE!
KILLED EVERY INHABITANT OF RUSTY RIDGE, NEW MEXICO, AND THEN DISAPPEARED!
HARDLY.
WHO--?
WHOOM
ITS SECRETS ARE BURIED INSIDE, HENSHAW.
MOVE OUT!
INTO THE CHOPPERS! NOW!
NO!
IF THAT PLACE BELONGS TO SUPERMAN, WE CAN'T LEAVE!

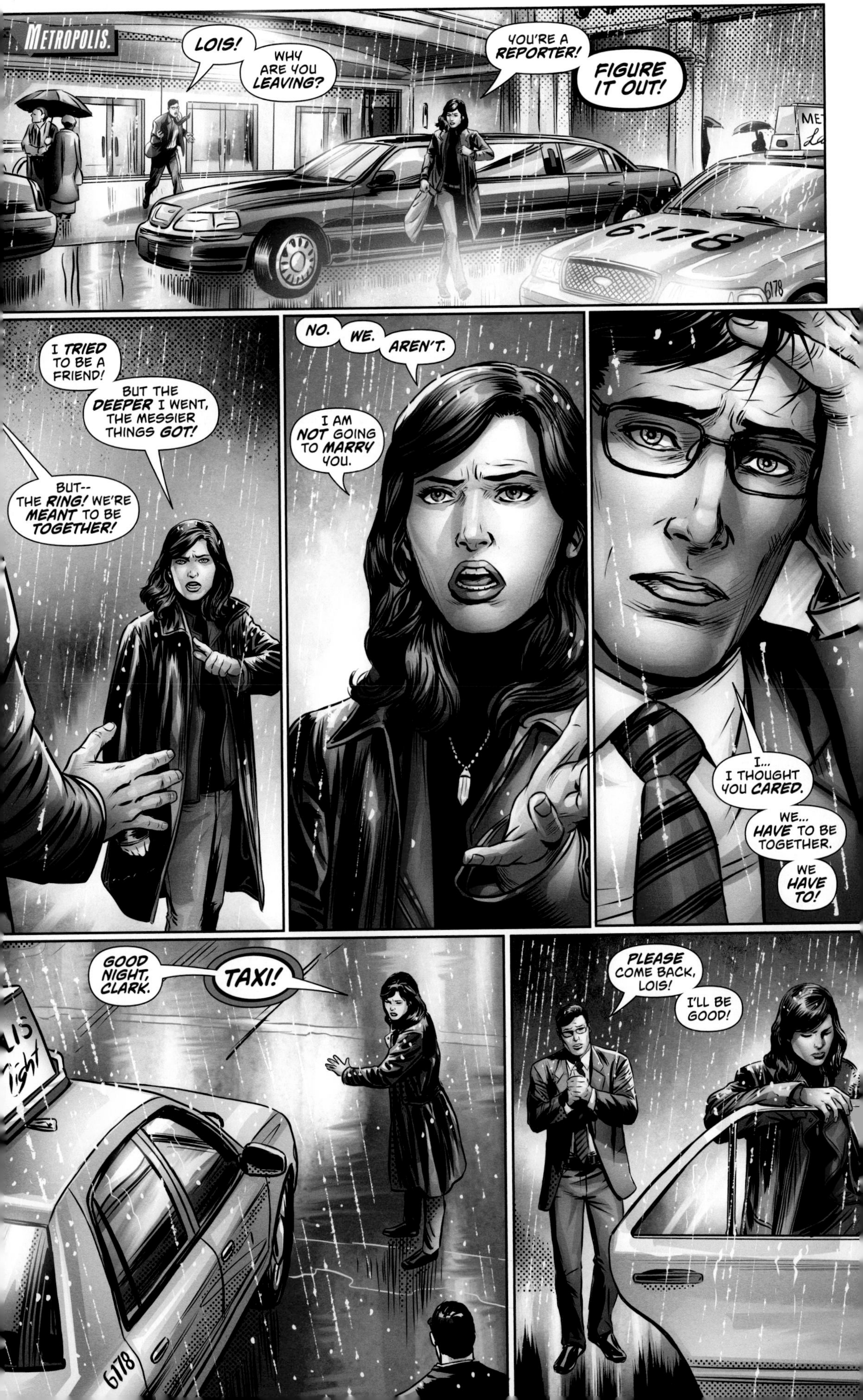
METROPOLIS.
LOIS!
WHY ARE YOU LEAVING?
YOU'RE A REPORTER!
FIGURE IT OUT!
6178
I TRIED TO BE A FRIEND!
BUT THE DEEPER I WENT, THE MESSIER THINGS GOT!
BUT-- THE RING! WE'RE MEANT TO BE TOGETHER!
NO.
WE.
AREN'T.
I AM NOT GOING TO MARRY YOU.
I... I THOUGHT YOU CARED.
WE... HAVE TO BE TOGETHER.
WE HAVE TO!
GOOD NIGHT, CLARK.
TAXI!
PLEASE COME BACK, LOIS!
I'LL BE GOOD!
6178

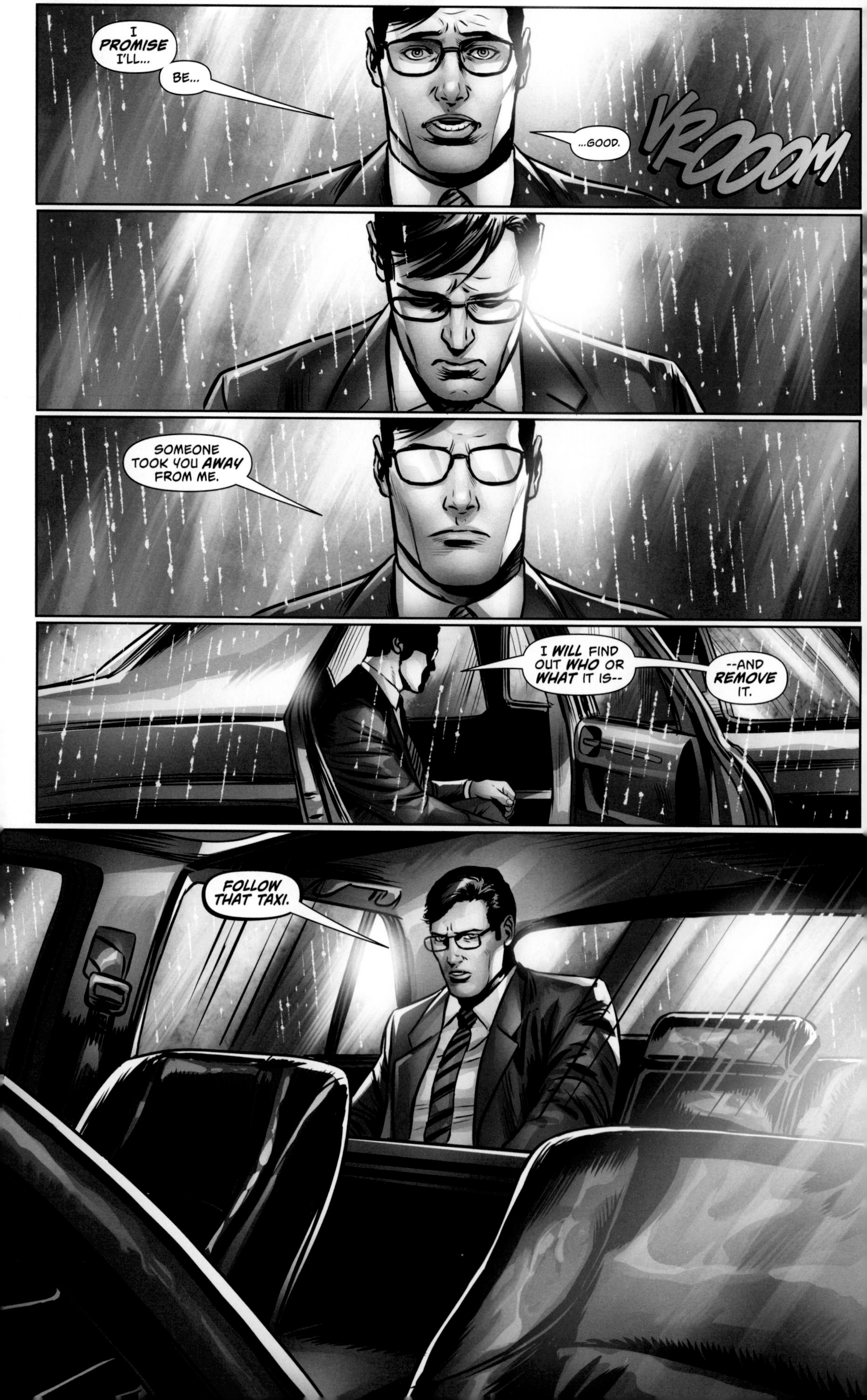
I PROMISE I'LL...
BE...
...GOOD.
VROOOM
SOMEONE TOOK YOU AWAY FROM ME.
I WILL FIND OUT WHO OR WHAT IT IS--
--AND REMOVE IT.
FOLLOW THAT TAXI.

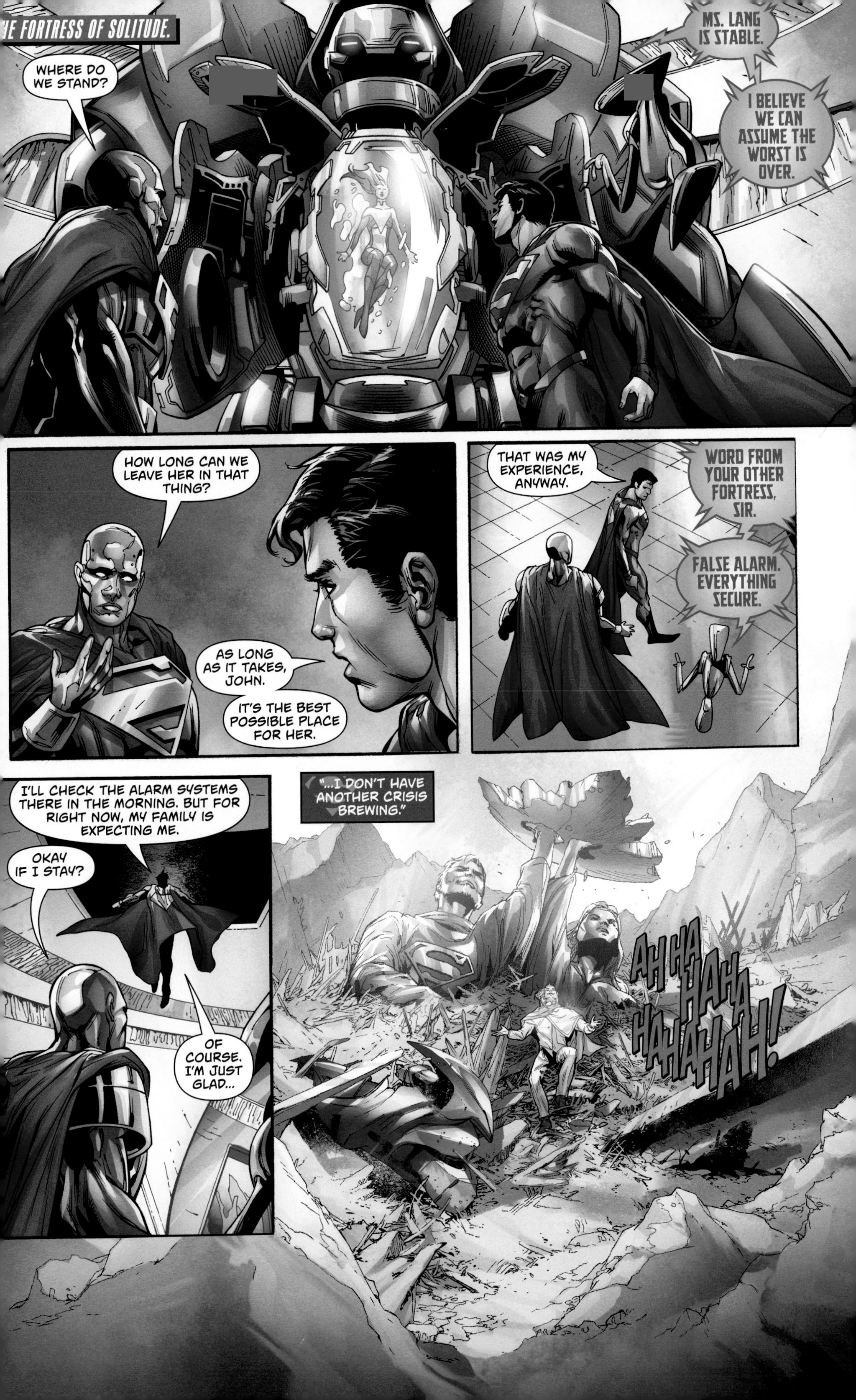

E FORTRESS OF SOLITUDE.
WHERE DO WE STAND?
MS. LANG IS STABLE.
I BELIEVE WE CAN ASSUME THE WORST IS OVER.
HOW LONG CAN WE LEAVE HER IN THAT THING?
AS LONG AS IT TAKES, JOHN.
IT'S THE BEST POSSIBLE PLACE FOR HER.
THAT WAS MY EXPERIENCE, ANYWAY.
WORD FROM YOUR OTHER FORTRESS, SIR.
FALSE ALARM. EVERYTHING SECURE.
I'LL CHECK THE ALARM SYSTEMS THERE IN THE MORNING. BUT FOR RIGHT NOW, MY FAMILY IS EXPECTING ME.
OKAY IF I STAY?
OF COURSE. I'M JUST GLAD...
"...I DON'T HAVE ANOTHER CRISIS BREWING."
AH HA HAHA HAHAHAH!

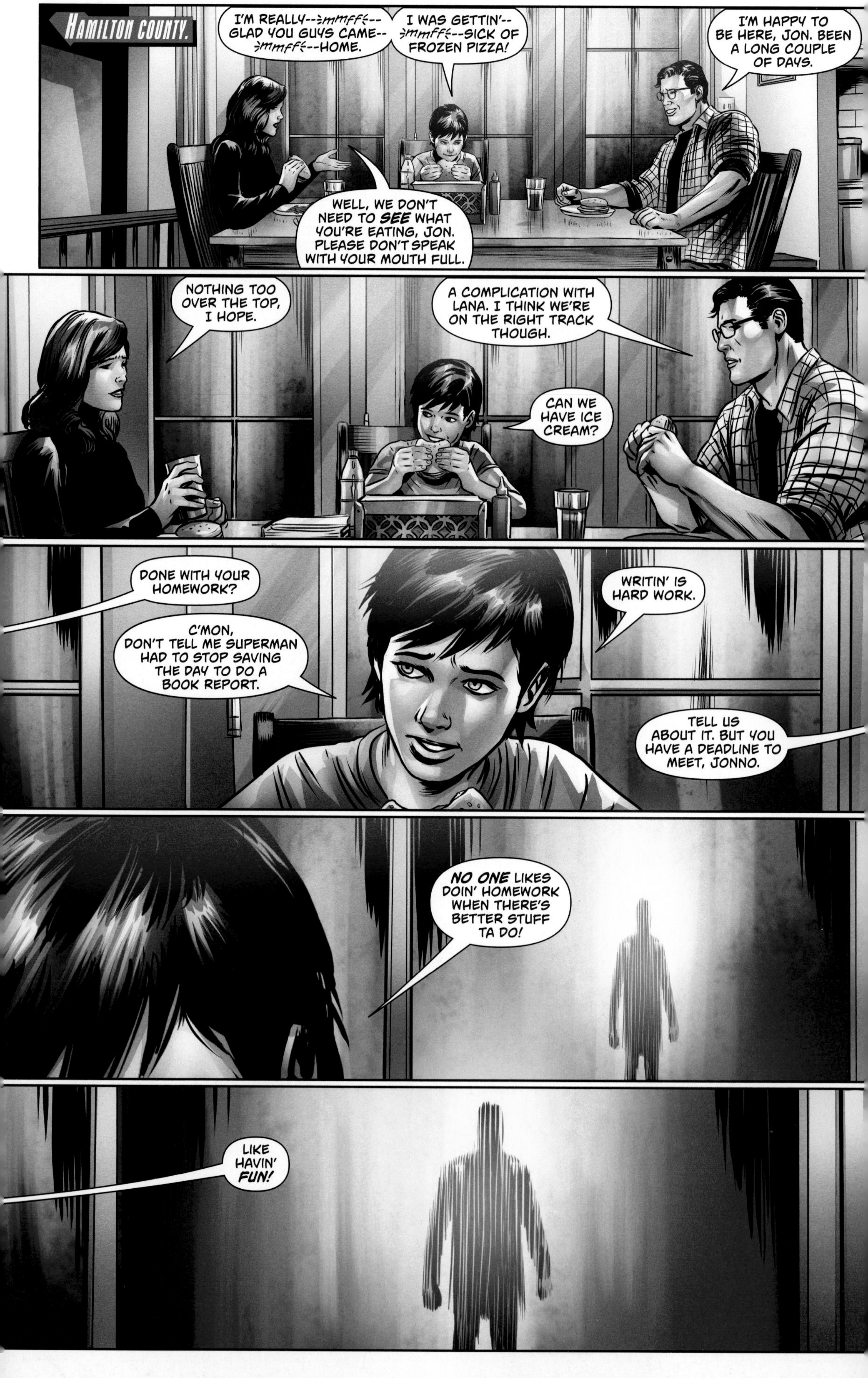
HAMILTON COUNTY.
I'M REALLY--mmff--GLAD YOU GUYS CAME--mmff--HOME.
I WAS GETTIN'--mmff--SICK OF FROZEN PIZZA!
I'M HAPPY TO BE HERE, JON. BEEN A LONG COUPLE OF DAYS.
WELL, WE DON'T NEED TO SEE WHAT YOU'RE EATING, JON. PLEASE DON'T SPEAK WITH YOUR MOUTH FULL.
NOTHING TOO OVER THE TOP, I HOPE.
A COMPLICATION WITH LANA. I THINK WE'RE ON THE RIGHT TRACK THOUGH.
CAN WE HAVE ICE CREAM?
DONE WITH YOUR HOMEWORK?
C'MON, DON'T TELL ME SUPERMAN HAD TO STOP SAVING THE DAY TO DO A BOOK REPORT.
WRITIN' IS HARD WORK.
TELL US ABOUT IT. BUT YOU HAVE A DEADLINE TO MEET, JONNO.
NO ONE LIKES DOIN' HOMEWORK WHEN THERE'S BETTER STUFF TA DO!
LIKE HAVIN' FUN!

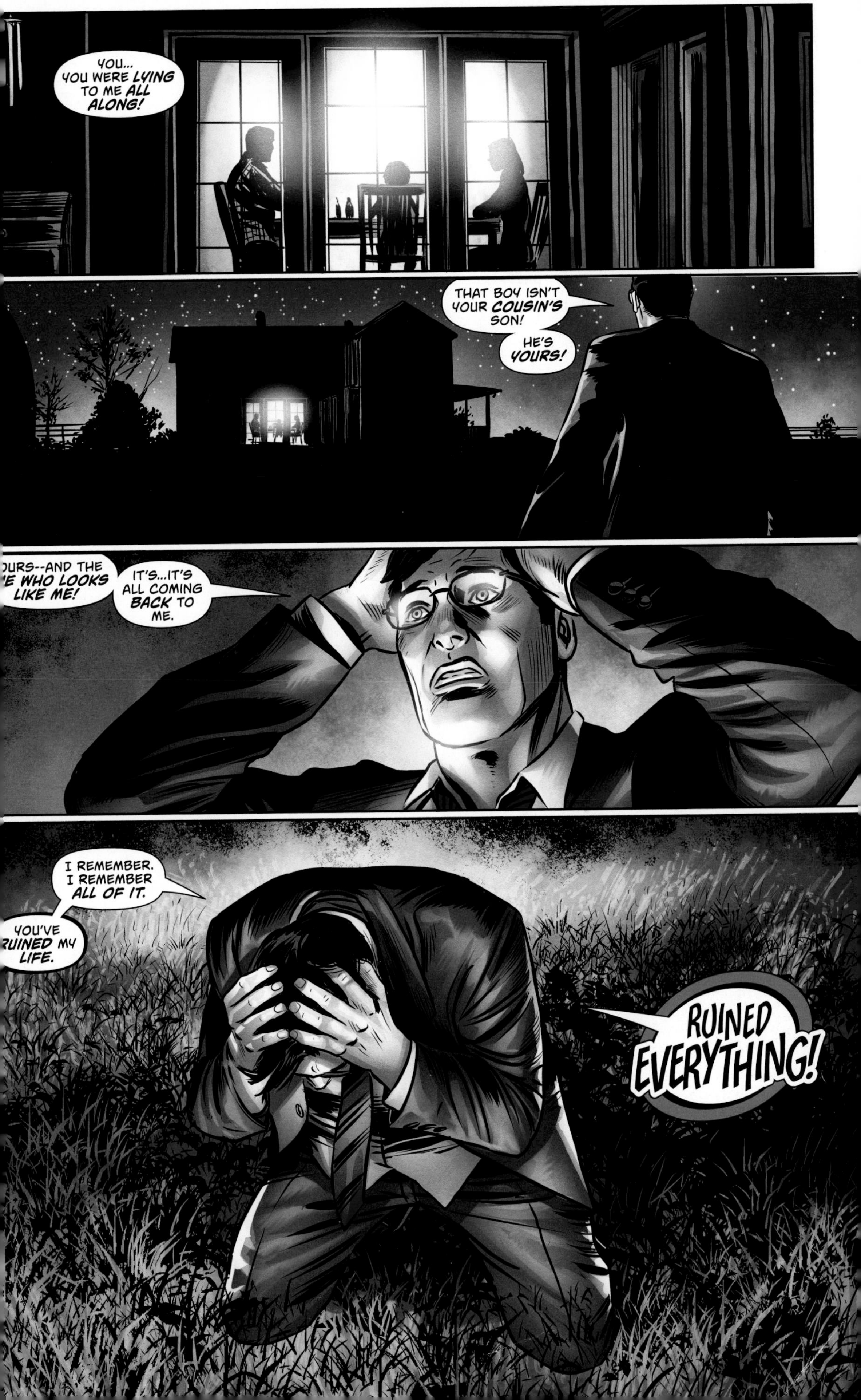
YOU... YOU WERE LYING TO ME ALL ALONG!
THAT BOY ISN'T YOUR COUSIN'S SON!
HE'S YOURS!
OURS--AND THE E WHO LOOKS LIKE ME!
IT'S...IT'S ALL COMING BACK TO ME.
I REMEMBER. I REMEMBER ALL OF IT.
YOU'VE RUINED MY LIFE.
RUINED EVERYTHING!

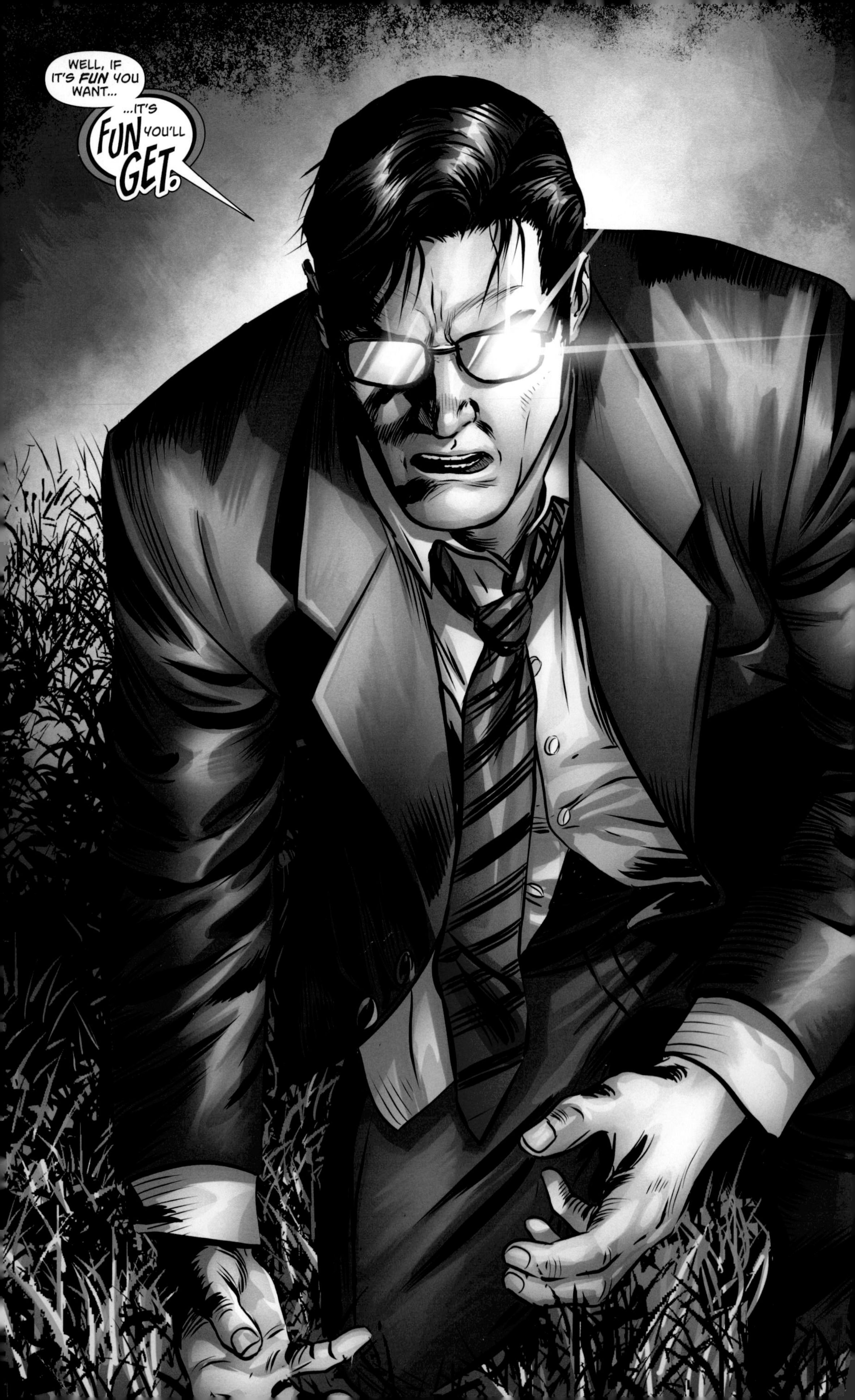
WELL, IF IT'S FUN YOU WANT...
...IT'S FUN YOU'LL GET.

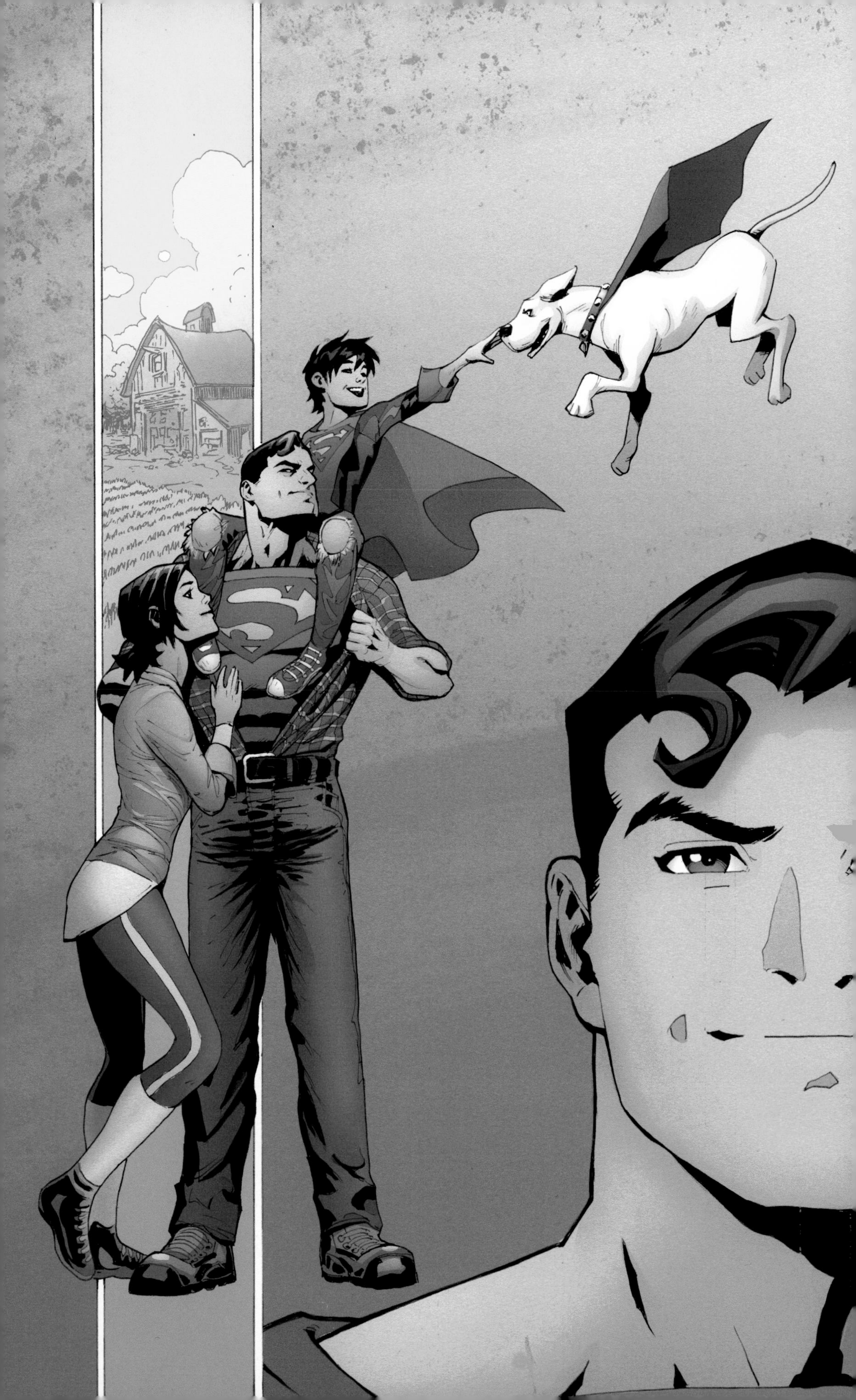

SUPERMAN: REBORN part one

PETER J. TOMASI & PATRICK GLEASON writers * PATRICK GLEASON penciller

MICK GRAY inker * JOHN KALISZ colorist

PATRICK GLEASON & JOHN KALISZ cover art

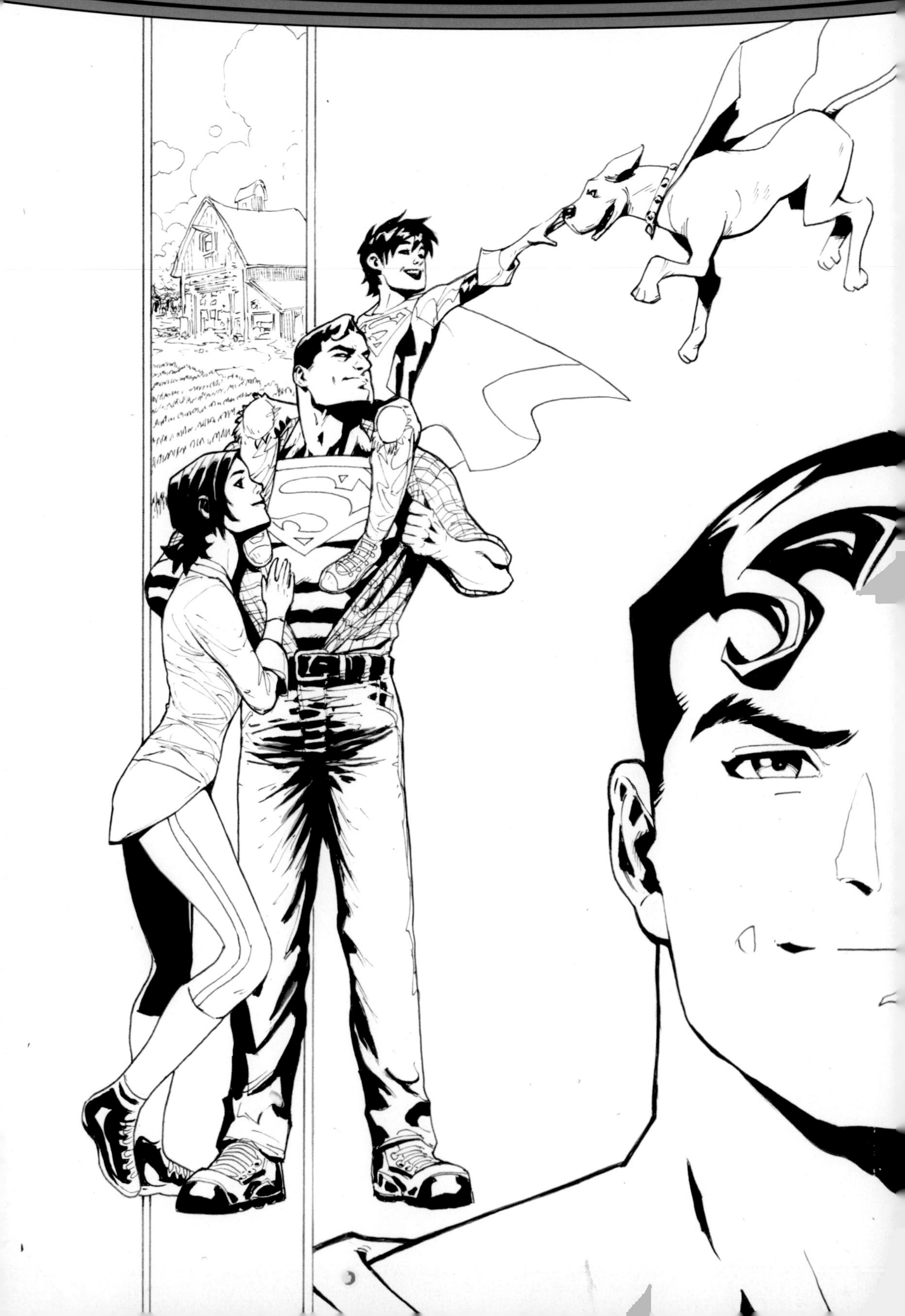

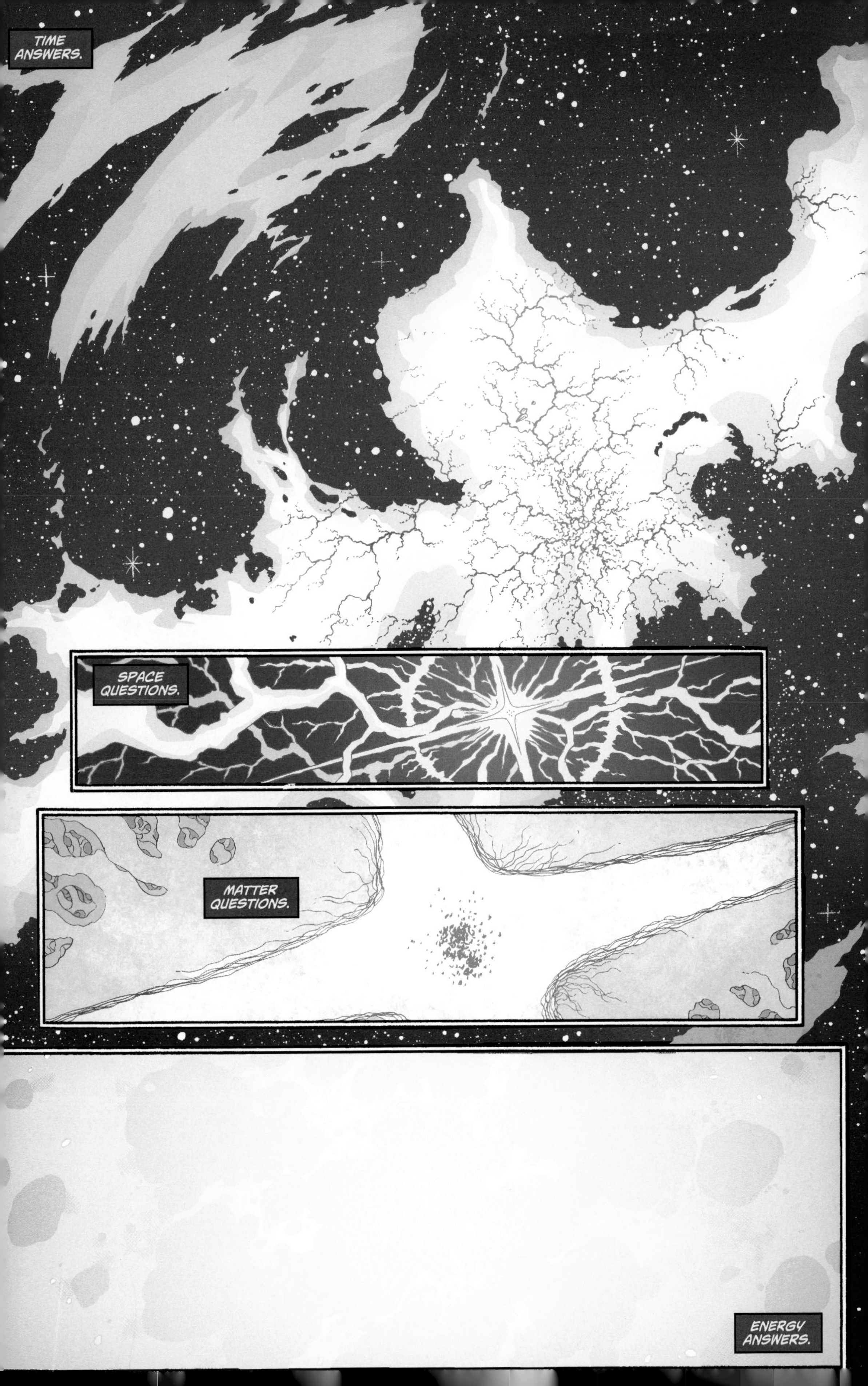
TIME ANSWERS.
SPACE QUESTIONS.
MATTER QUESTIONS.
ENERGY ANSWERS.

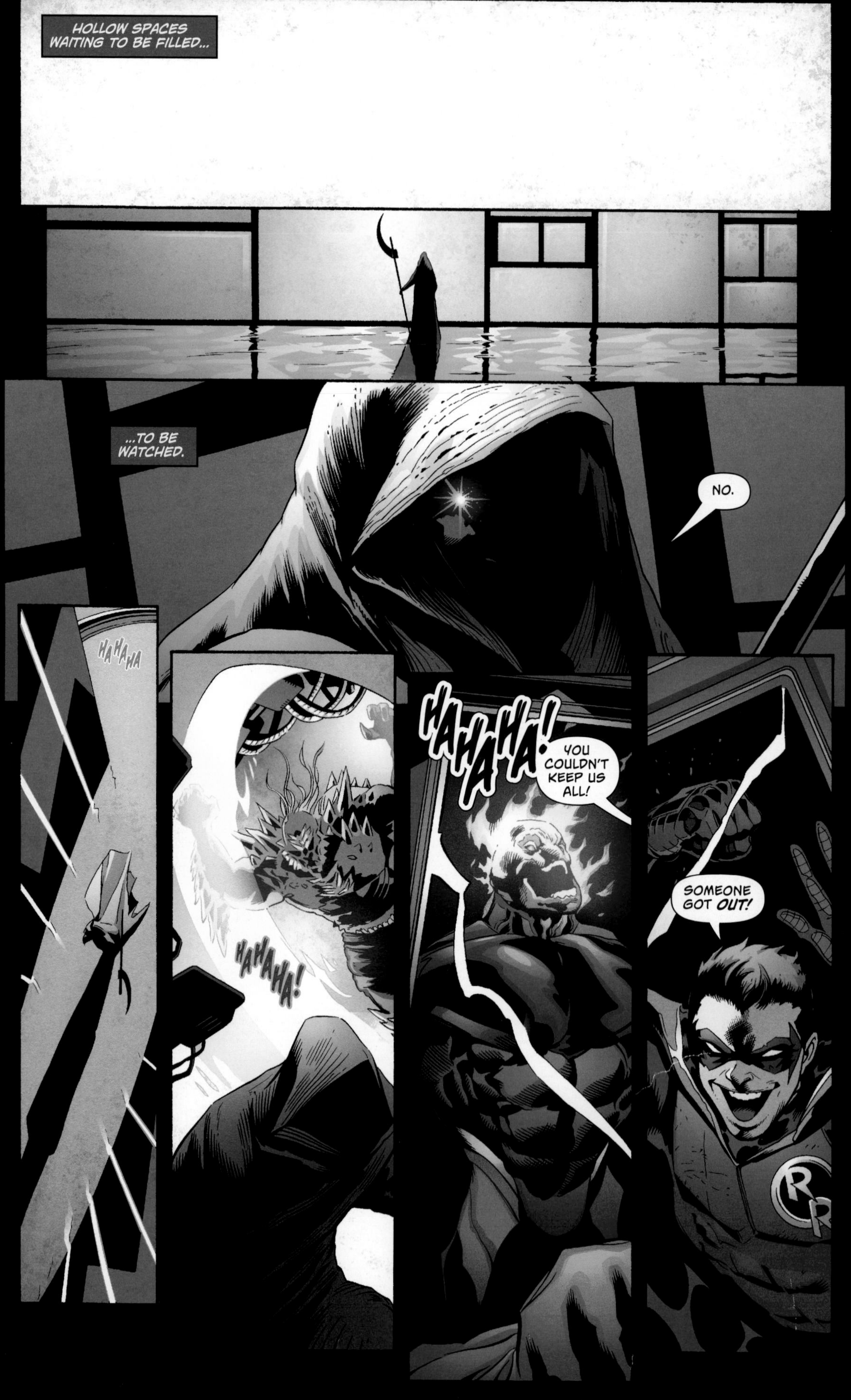
HOLLOW SPACES WAITING TO BE FILLED...
...TO BE WATCHED.
NO.
HAHAHA
HAHAHA!
HAHAHA!
YOU COULDN'T KEEP US ALL!
SOMEONE GOT OUT!

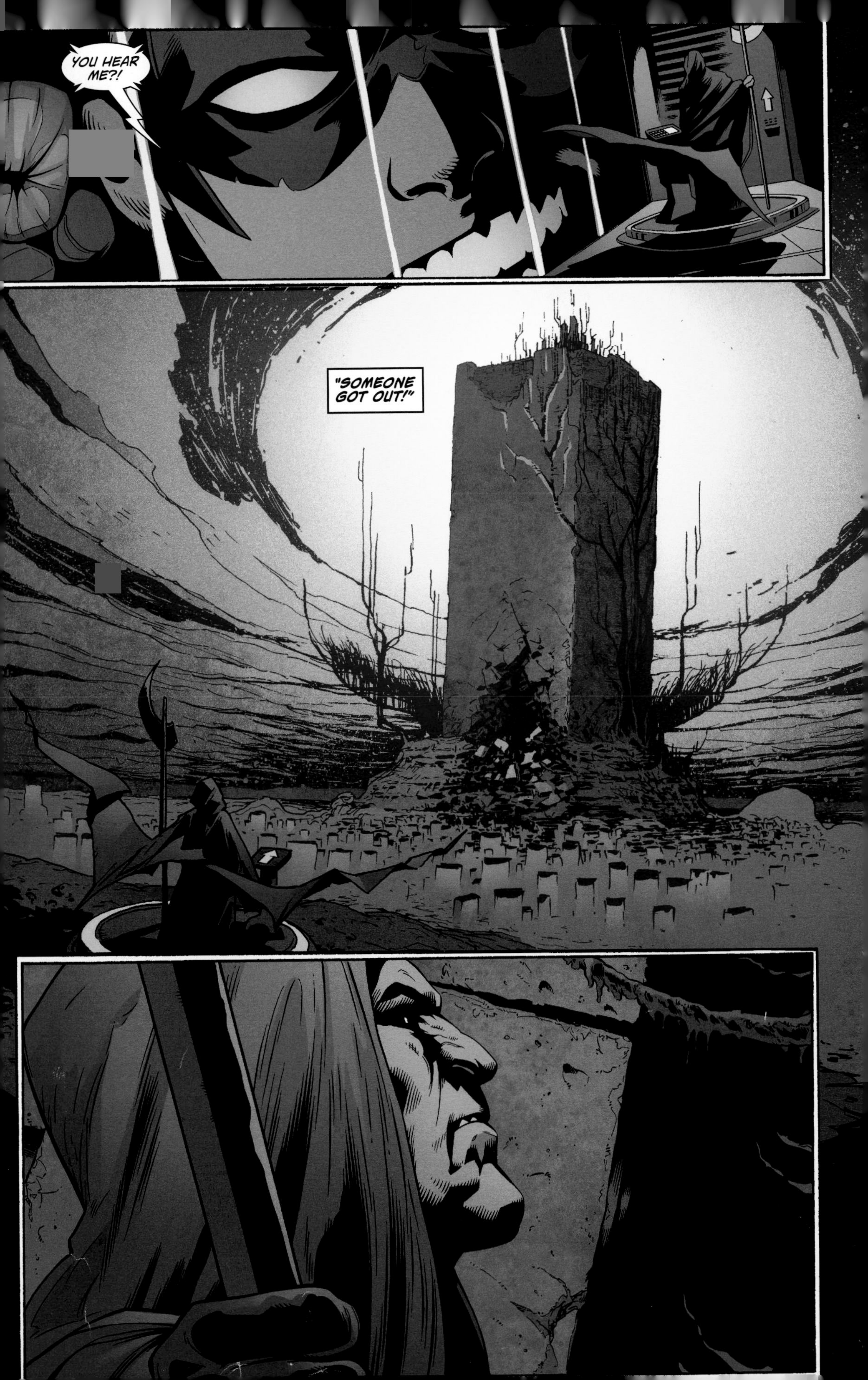
YOU HEAR ME?!
"SOMEONE GOT OUT!"

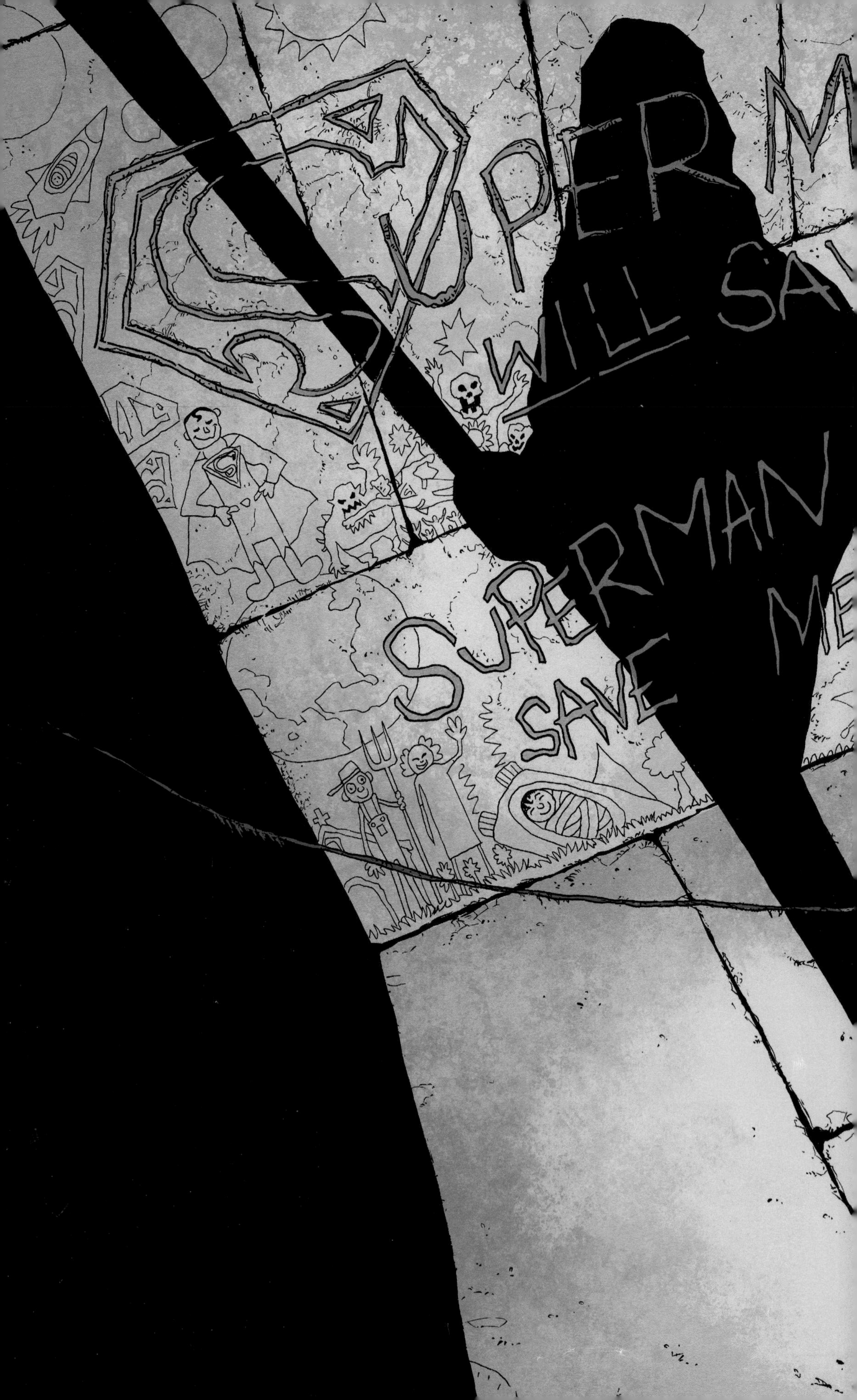
SUPER M
WILL SA
SUPERMAN
SAVE
ME

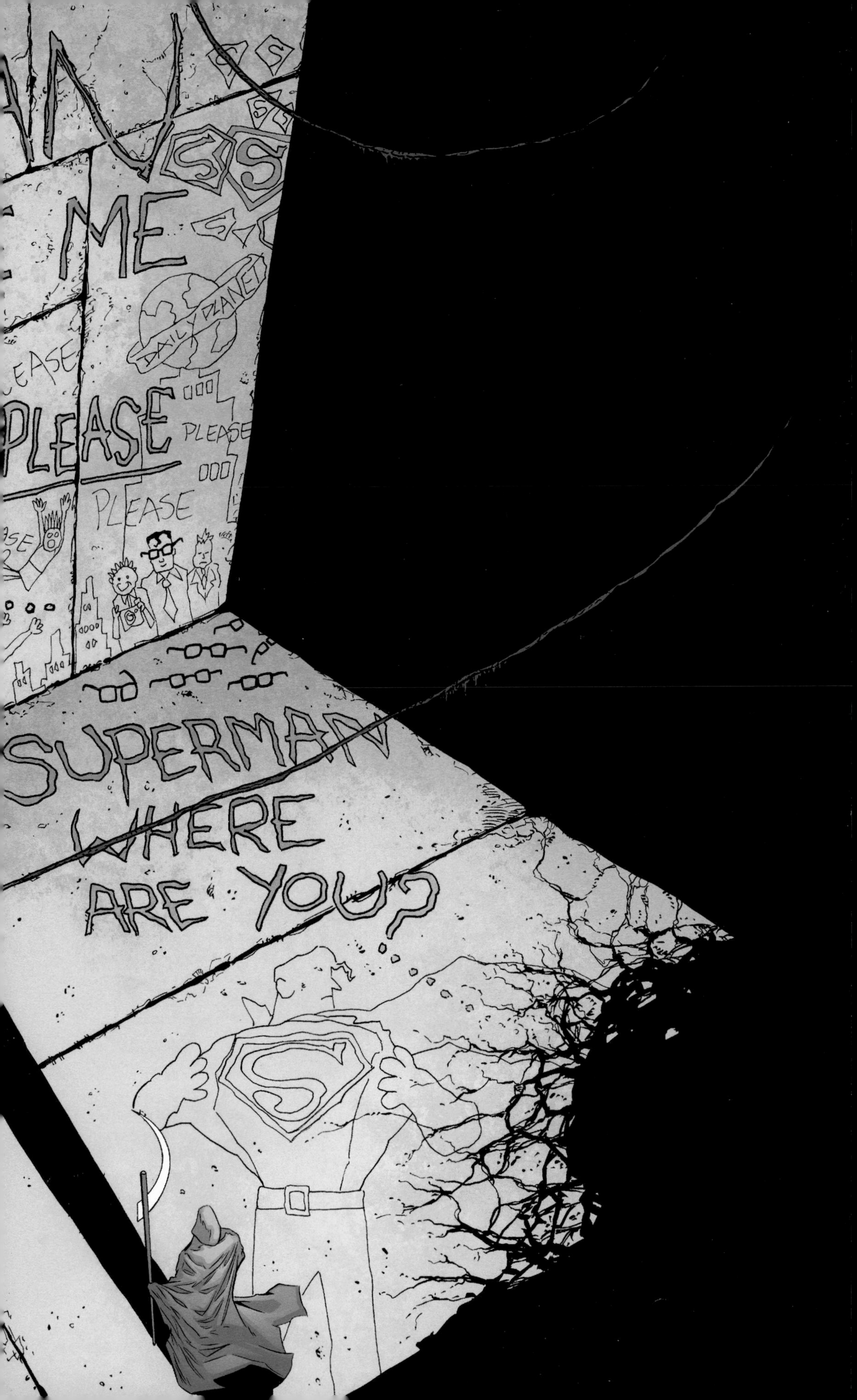

ME
DAILY PLANET
PLEASE
PLEASE
SUPERMAN
WHERE
ARE YOU?

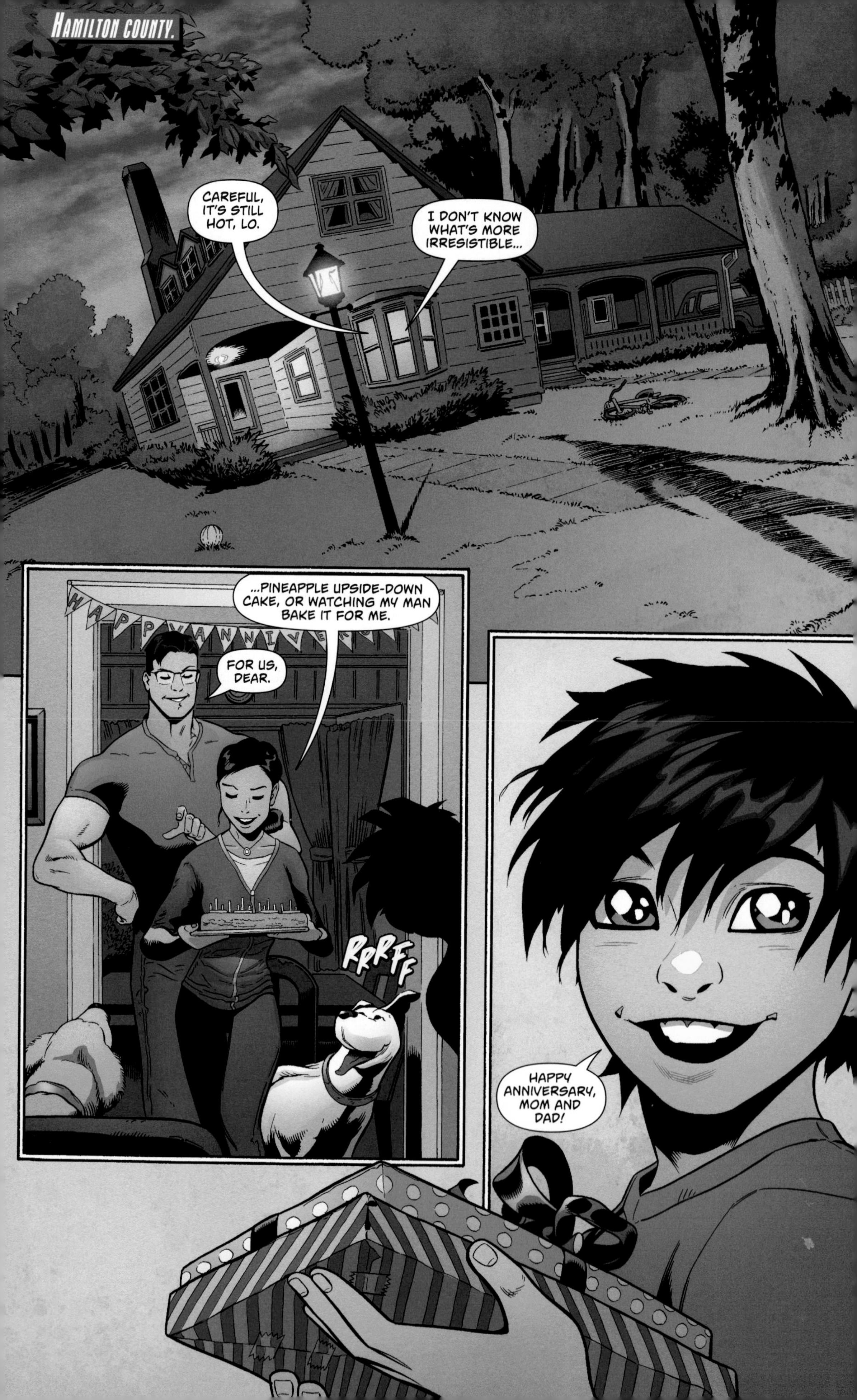
HAMILTON COUNTY.
CAREFUL, IT'S STILL HOT, LO.
I DON'T KNOW WHAT'S MORE IRRESISTIBLE...
...PINEAPPLE UPSIDE-DOWN CAKE, OR WATCHING MY MAN BAKE IT FOR ME.
FOR US, DEAR.
RRRFF
HAPPY ANNIVERSARY, MOM AND DAD!

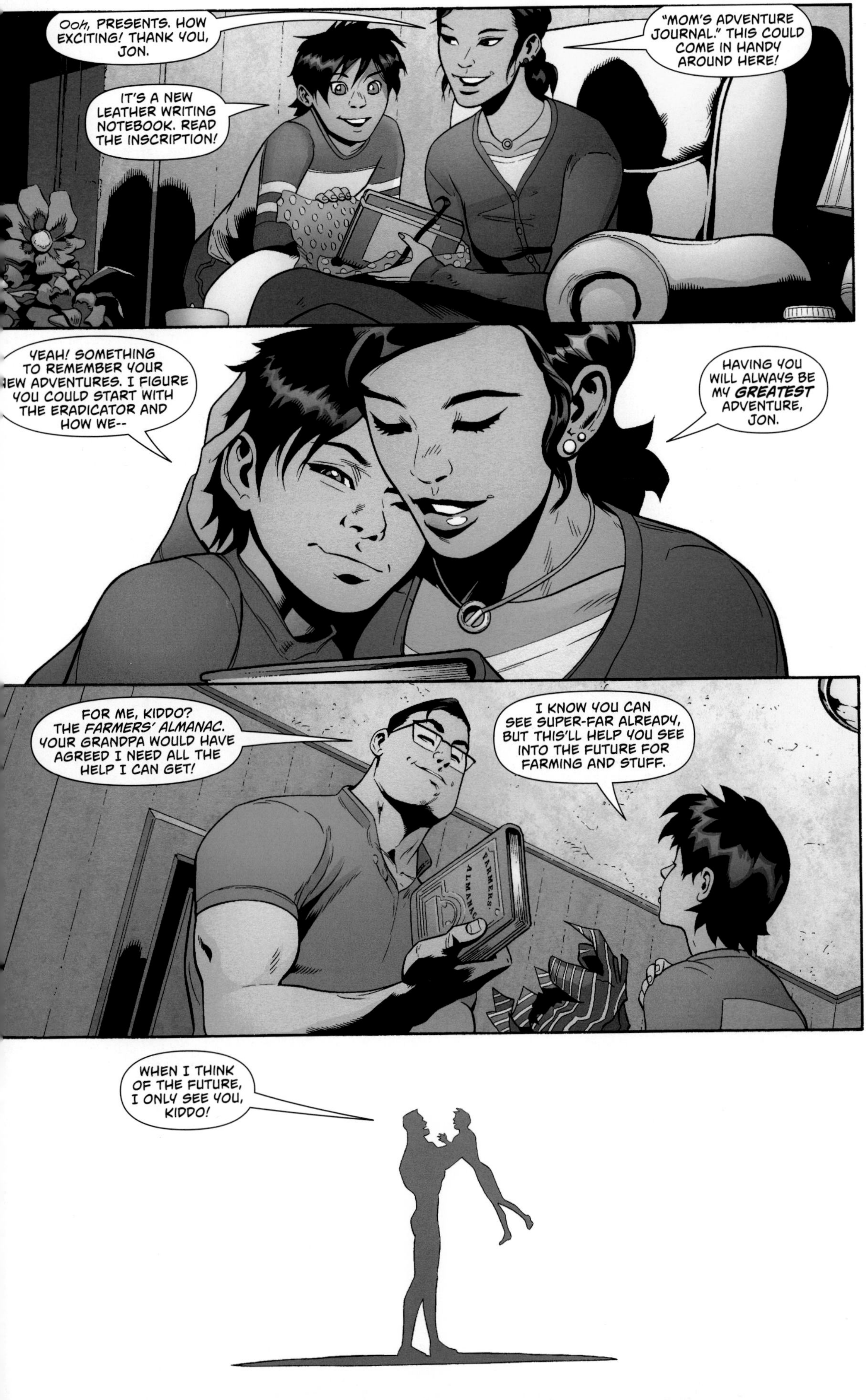

OOH, PRESENTS. HOW EXCITING! THANK YOU, JON.
IT'S A NEW LEATHER WRITING NOTEBOOK. READ THE INSCRIPTION!
"MOM'S ADVENTURE JOURNAL." THIS COULD COME IN HANDY AROUND HERE!
YEAH! SOMETHING TO REMEMBER YOUR NEW ADVENTURES. I FIGURE YOU COULD START WITH THE ERADICATOR AND HOW WE--
HAVING YOU WILL ALWAYS BE MY GREATEST ADVENTURE, JON.
FOR ME, KIDDO? THE FARMERS' ALMANAC. YOUR GRANDPA WOULD HAVE AGREED I NEED ALL THE HELP I CAN GET!
I KNOW YOU CAN SEE SUPER-FAR ALREADY, BUT THIS'LL HELP YOU SEE INTO THE FUTURE FOR FARMING AND STUFF.
FARMERS' ALMANAC
WHEN I THINK OF THE FUTURE, I ONLY SEE YOU, KIDDO!

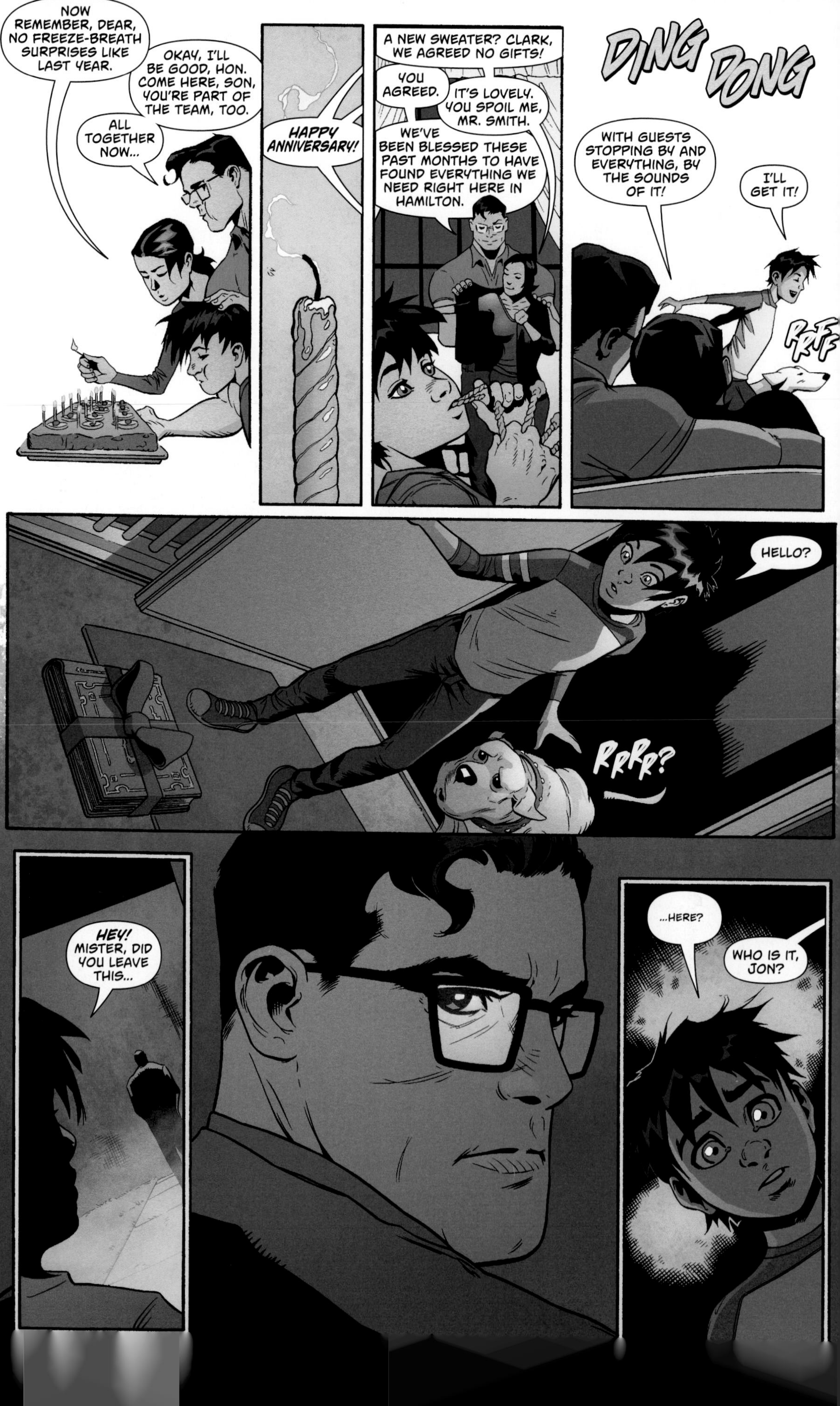
NOW REMEMBER, DEAR, NO FREEZE-BREATH SURPRISES LIKE LAST YEAR.
OKAY, I'LL BE GOOD, HON. COME HERE, SON, YOU'RE PART OF THE TEAM, TOO.
ALL TOGETHER NOW...
HAPPY ANNIVERSARY!
A NEW SWEATER? CLARK, WE AGREED NO GIFTS!
YOU AGREED.
IT'S LOVELY. YOU SPOIL ME, MR. SMITH.
WE'VE BEEN BLESSED THESE PAST MONTHS TO HAVE FOUND EVERYTHING WE NEED RIGHT HERE IN HAMILTON.
DING DONG
WITH GUESTS STOPPING BY AND EVERYTHING, BY THE SOUNDS OF IT!
I'LL GET IT!
RRFF
HELLO?
RRRR?
HEY! MISTER, DID YOU LEAVE THIS...
...HERE?
WHO IS IT, JON?

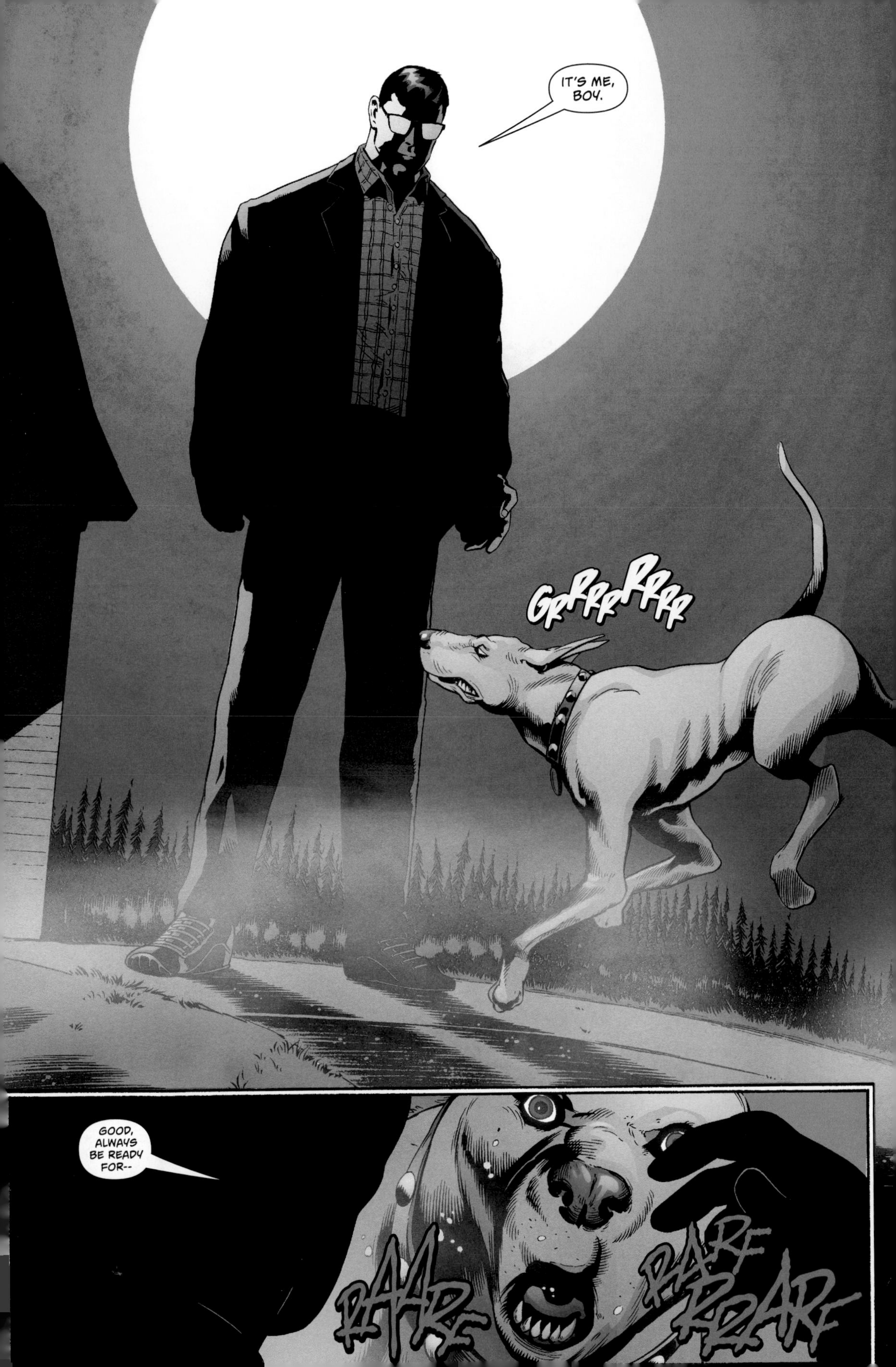
IT'S ME, BOY.
GOOD, ALWAYS BE READY FOR--

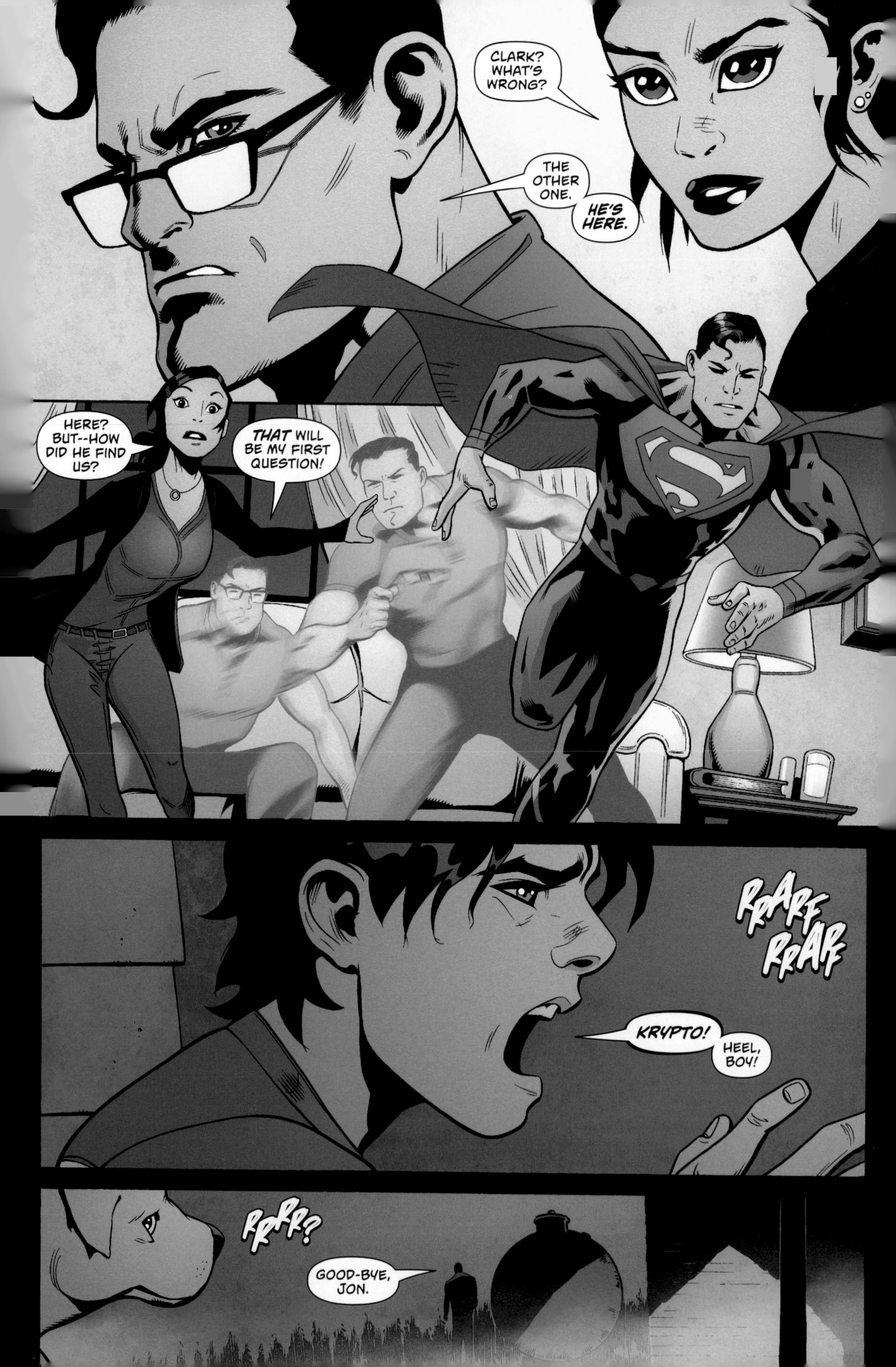
CLARK? WHAT'S WRONG?
THE OTHER ONE.
HE'S HERE.
HERE? BUT--HOW DID HE FIND US?
THAT WILL BE MY FIRST QUESTION!
RRARF RRAR
KRYPTO!
HEEL, BOY!
RRRR?
GOOD-BYE, JON.

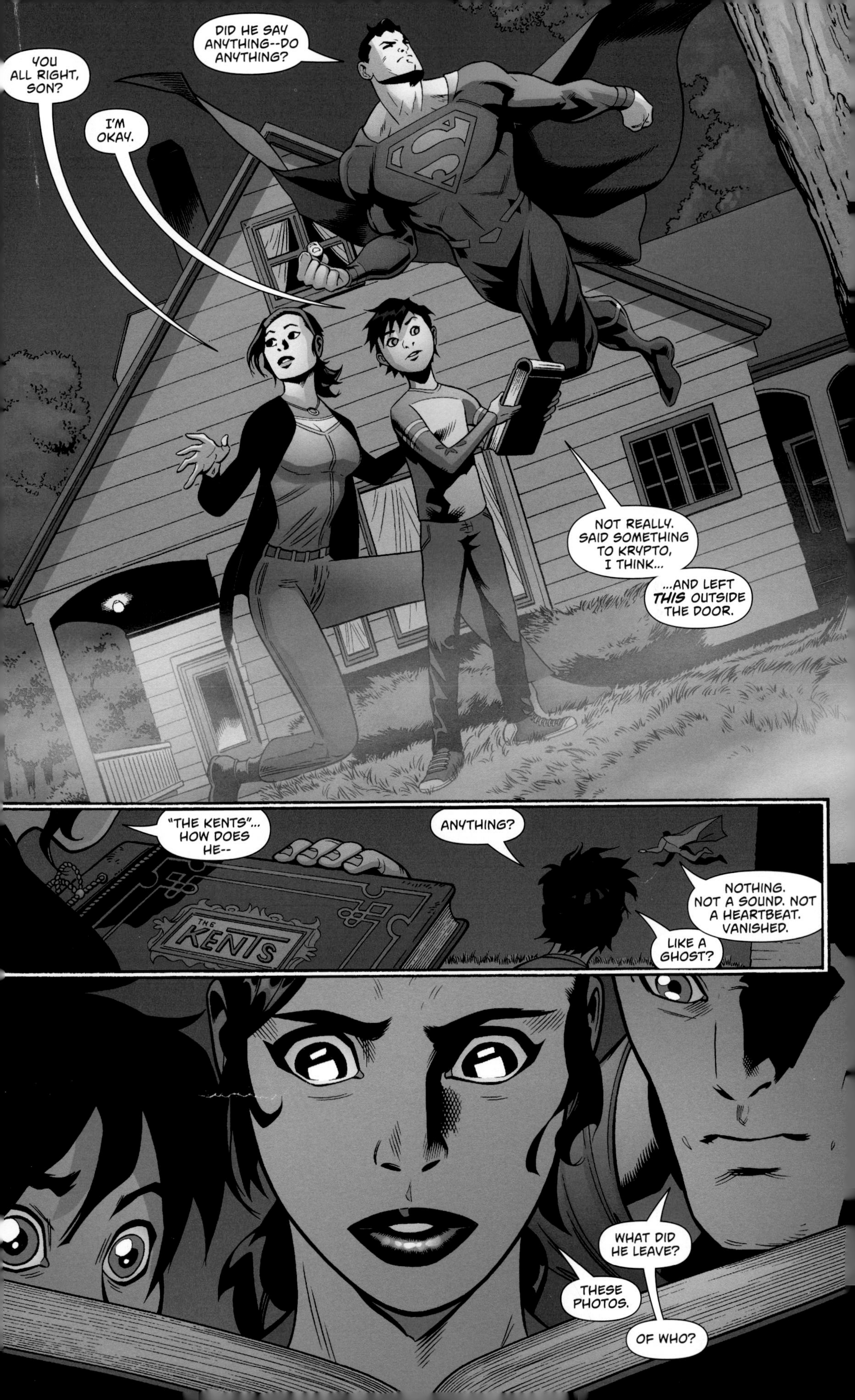
YOU ALL RIGHT, SON?
DID HE SAY ANYTHING--DO ANYTHING?
I'M OKAY.
NOT REALLY. SAID SOMETHING TO KRYPTO, I THINK...
...AND LEFT THIS OUTSIDE THE DOOR.
"THE KENTS"... HOW DOES HE--
THE KENTS
ANYTHING?
NOTHING. NOT A SOUND. NOT A HEARTBEAT. VANISHED.
LIKE A GHOST?
WHAT DID HE LEAVE?
THESE PHOTOS.
OF WHO?

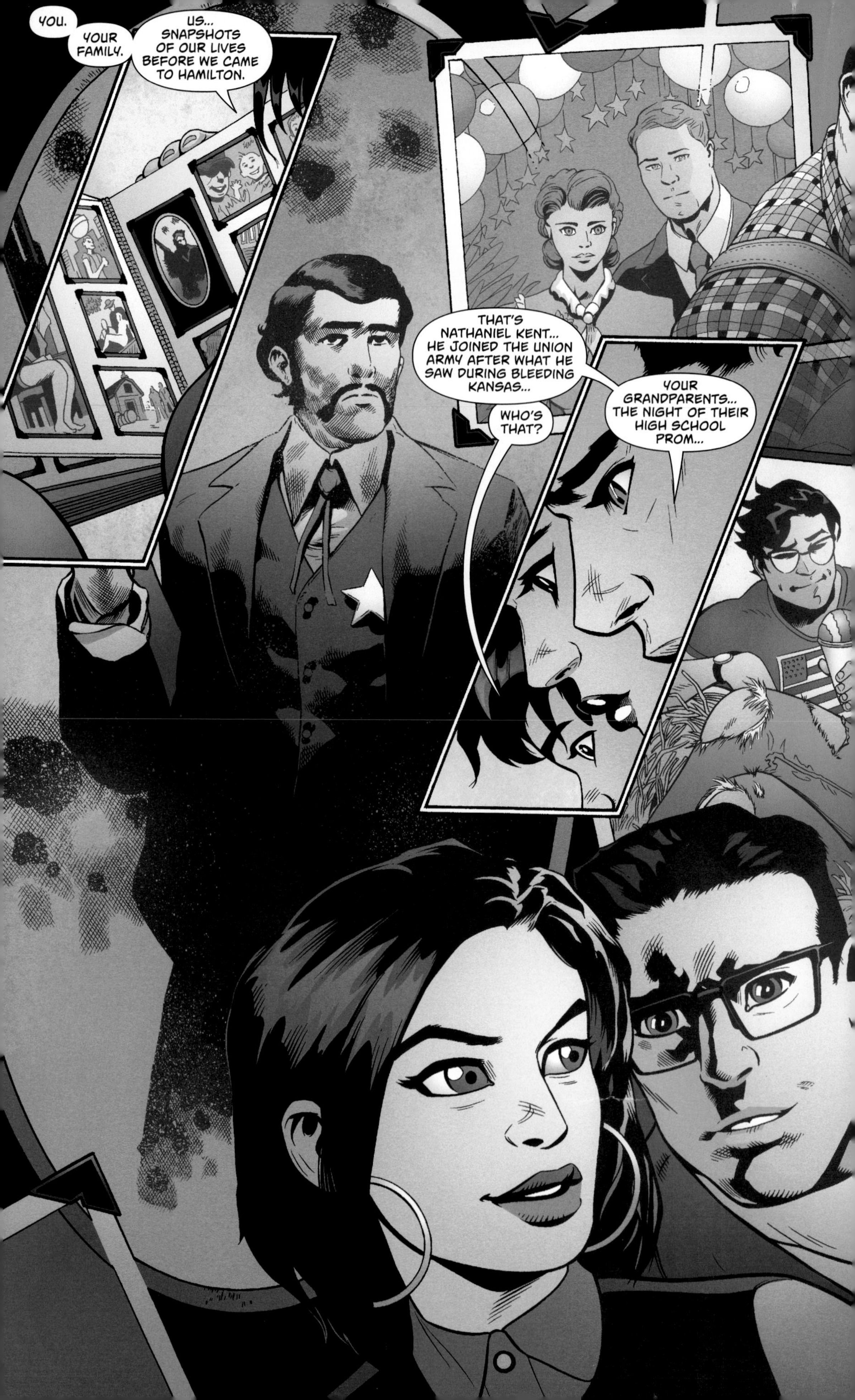
YOU.
YOUR FAMILY.
US... SNAPSHOTS OF OUR LIVES BEFORE WE CAME TO HAMILTON.
THAT'S NATHANIEL KENT... HE JOINED THE UNION ARMY AFTER WHAT HE SAW DURING BLEEDING KANSAS...
WHO'S THAT?
YOUR GRANDPARENTS... THE NIGHT OF THEIR HIGH SCHOOL PROM...

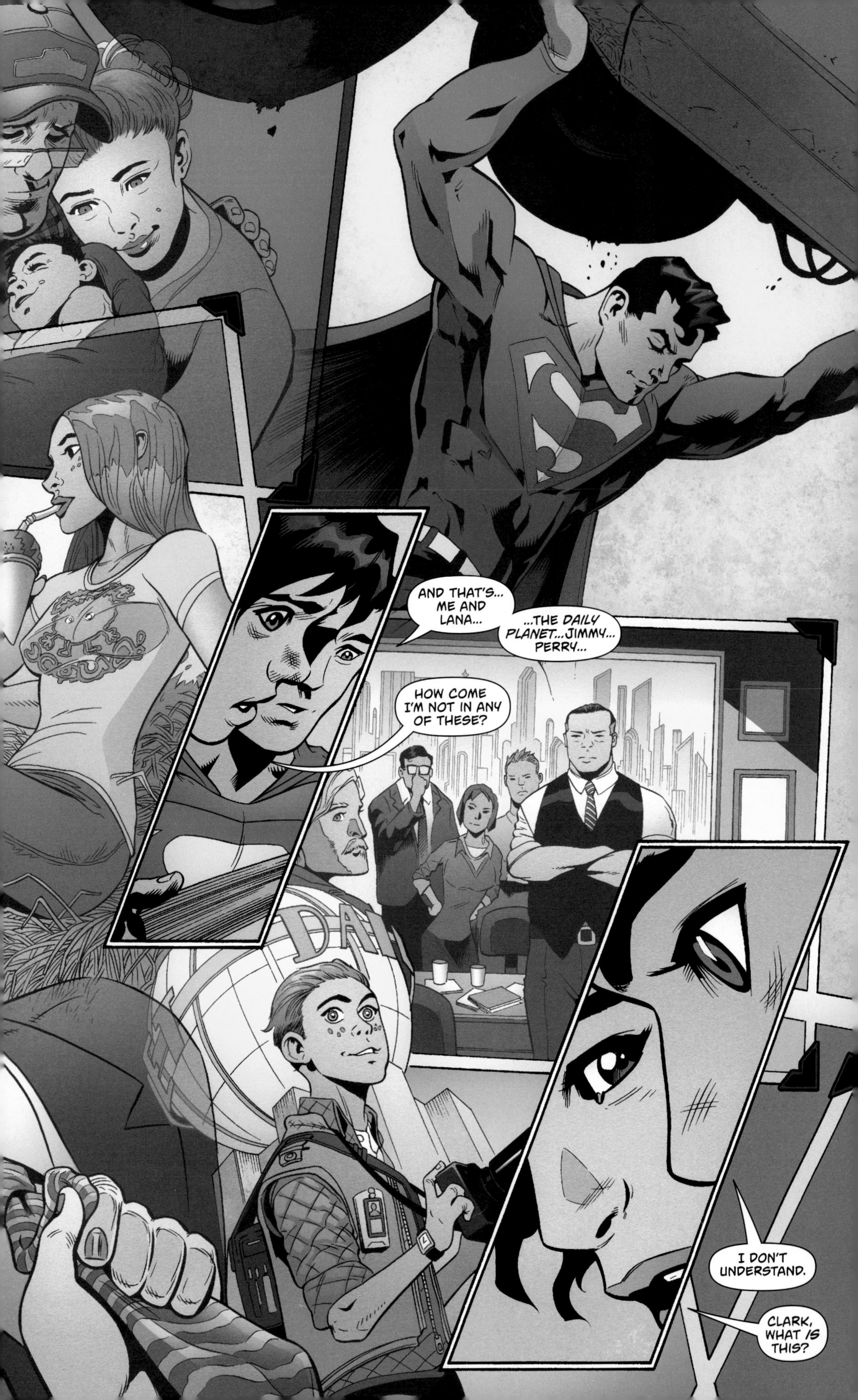

AND THAT'S... ME AND LANA...
...THE *DAILY PLANET*...JIMMY... PERRY...
HOW COME I'M NOT IN ANY OF THESE?
I DON'T UNDERSTAND.
CLARK, WHAT *IS* THIS?

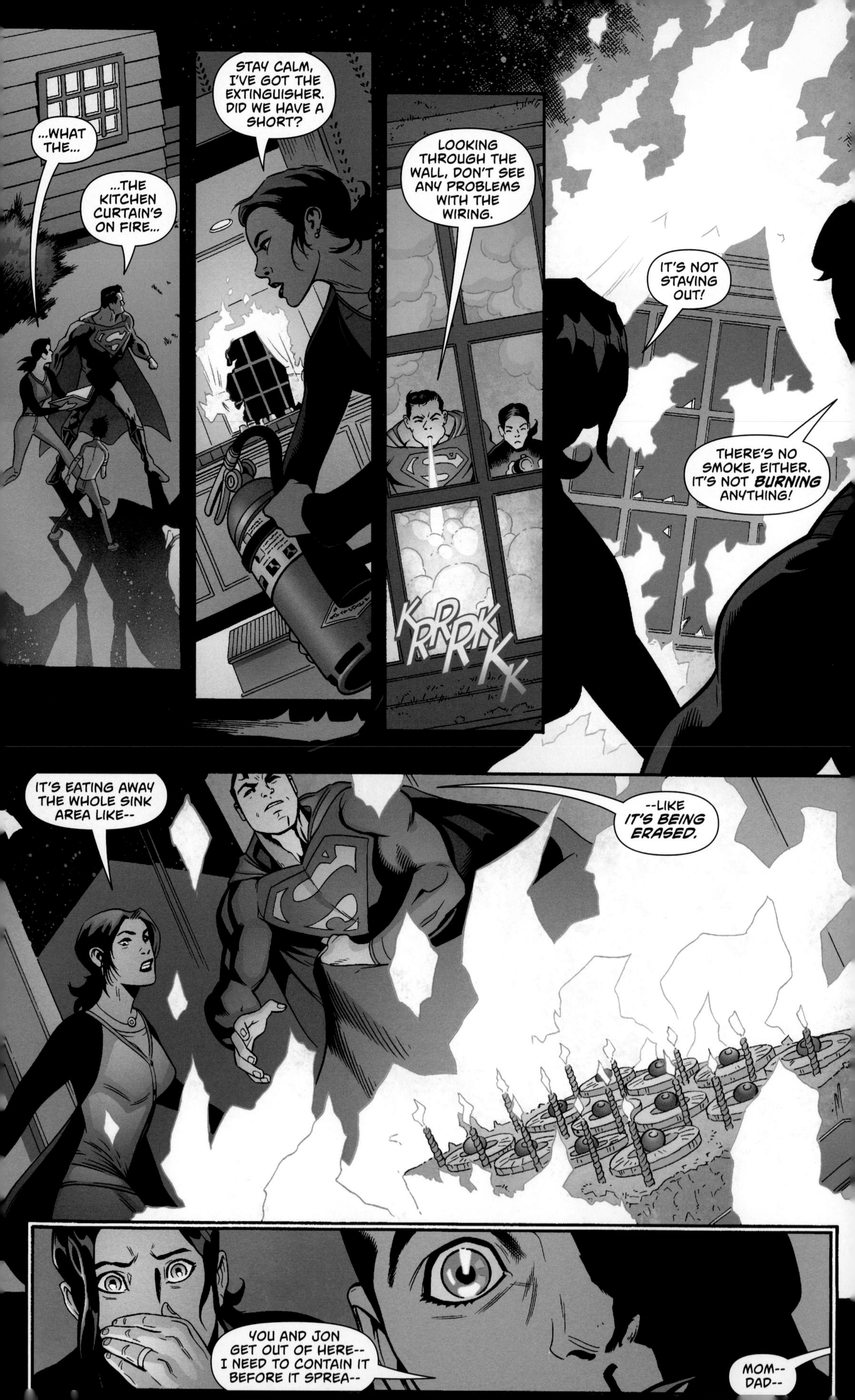
...WHAT THE...
...THE KITCHEN CURTAIN'S ON FIRE...
STAY CALM, I'VE GOT THE EXTINGUISHER. DID WE HAVE A SHORT?
LOOKING THROUGH THE WALL, DON'T SEE ANY PROBLEMS WITH THE WIRING.
KRRRDKKK
IT'S NOT STAYING OUT!
THERE'S NO SMOKE, EITHER. IT'S NOT BURNING ANYTHING!
IT'S EATING AWAY THE WHOLE SINK AREA LIKE--
--LIKE IT'S BEING ERASED.
YOU AND JON GET OUT OF HERE-- I NEED TO CONTAIN IT BEFORE IT SPREA--
MOM-- DAD--

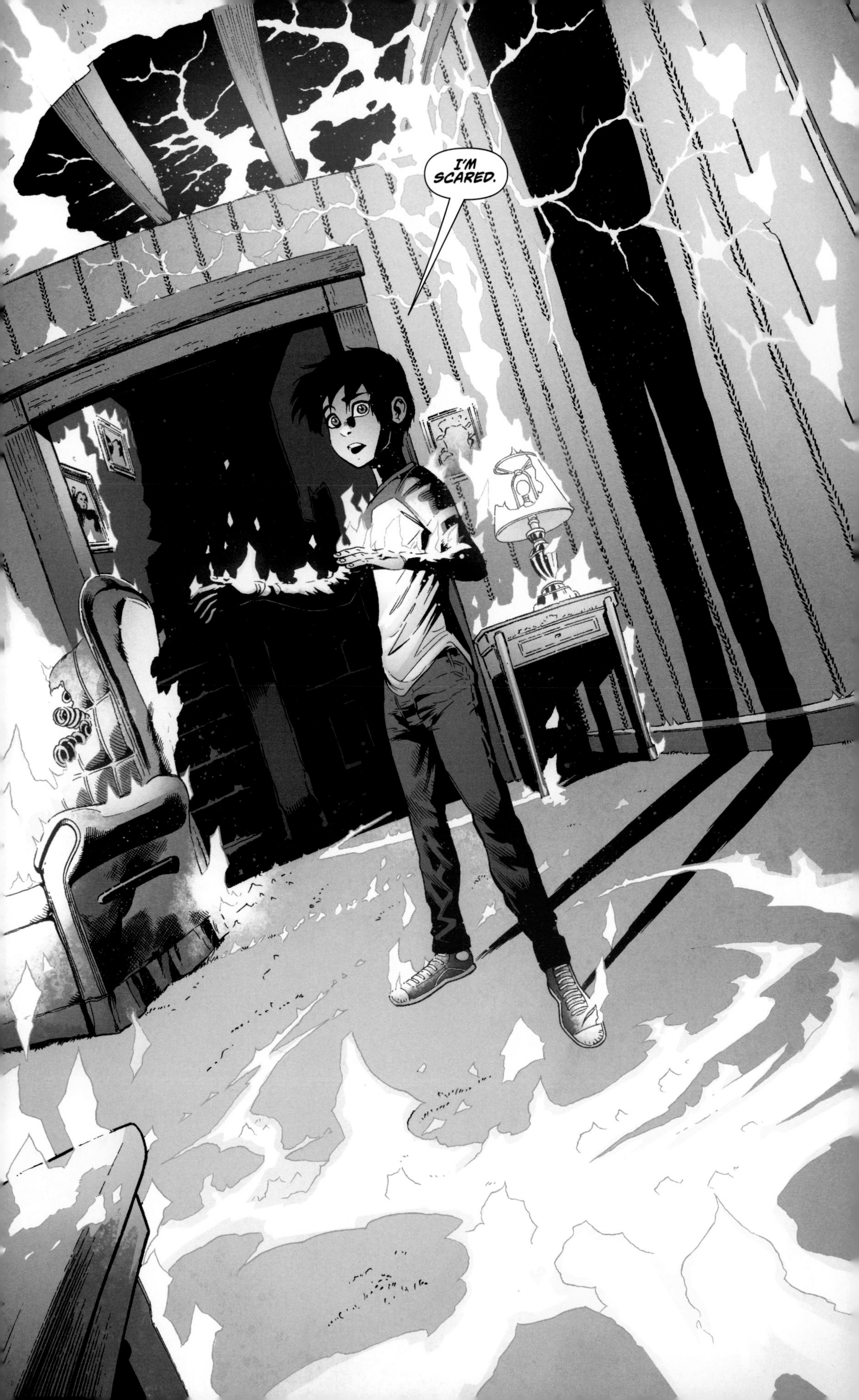
I'M SCARED.

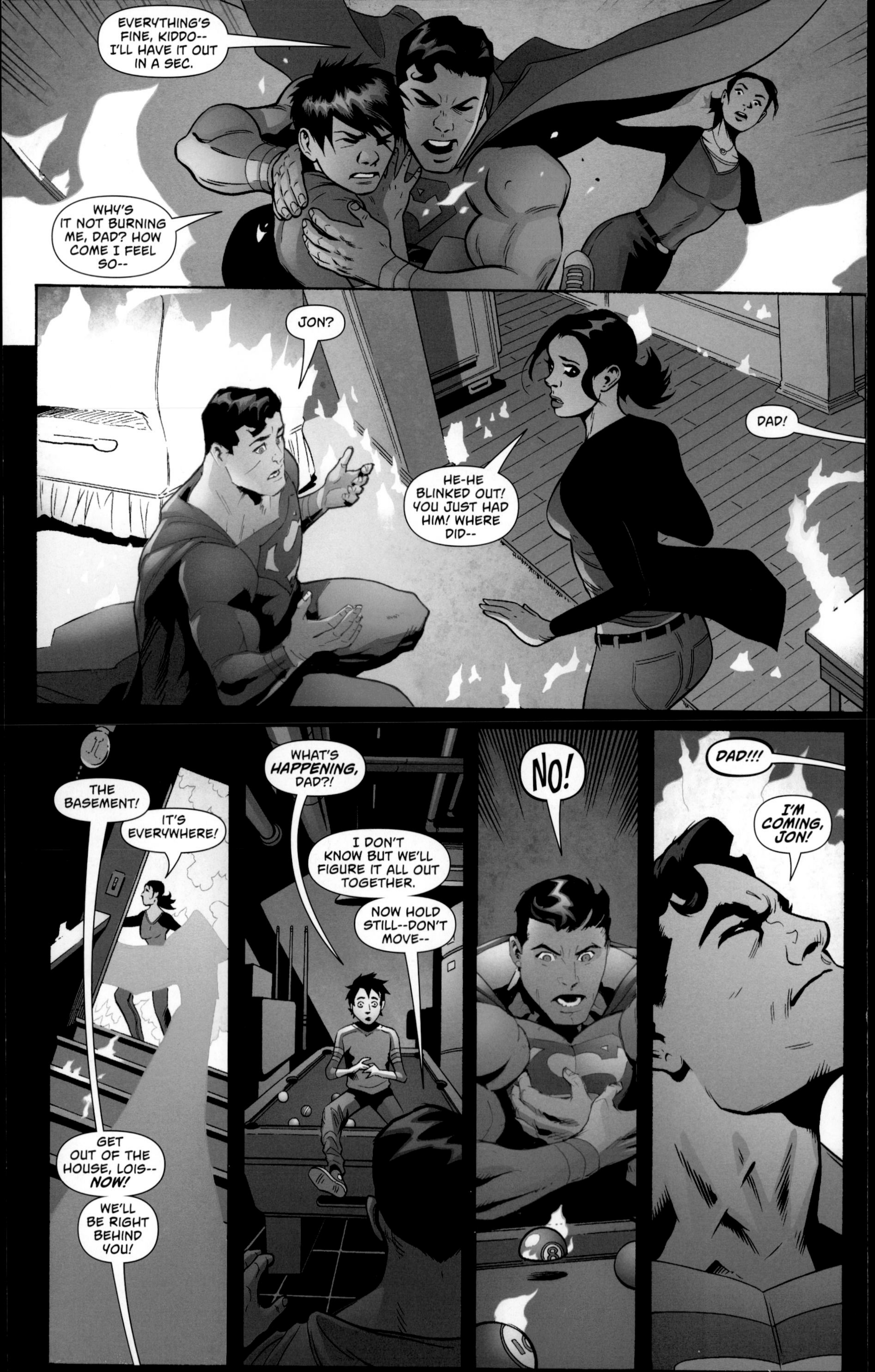
EVERYTHING'S FINE, KIDDO-- I'LL HAVE IT OUT IN A SEC.
WHY'S IT NOT BURNING ME, DAD? HOW COME I FEEL SO--
JON?
HE-HE BLINKED OUT! YOU JUST HAD HIM! WHERE DID--
DAD!
THE BASEMENT!
IT'S EVERYWHERE!
GET OUT OF THE HOUSE, LOIS-- NOW!
WE'LL BE RIGHT BEHIND YOU!
WHAT'S HAPPENING, DAD?!
I DON'T KNOW BUT WE'LL FIGURE IT ALL OUT TOGETHER.
NOW HOLD STILL--DON'T MOVE--
NO!
DAD!!!
I'M COMING, JON!

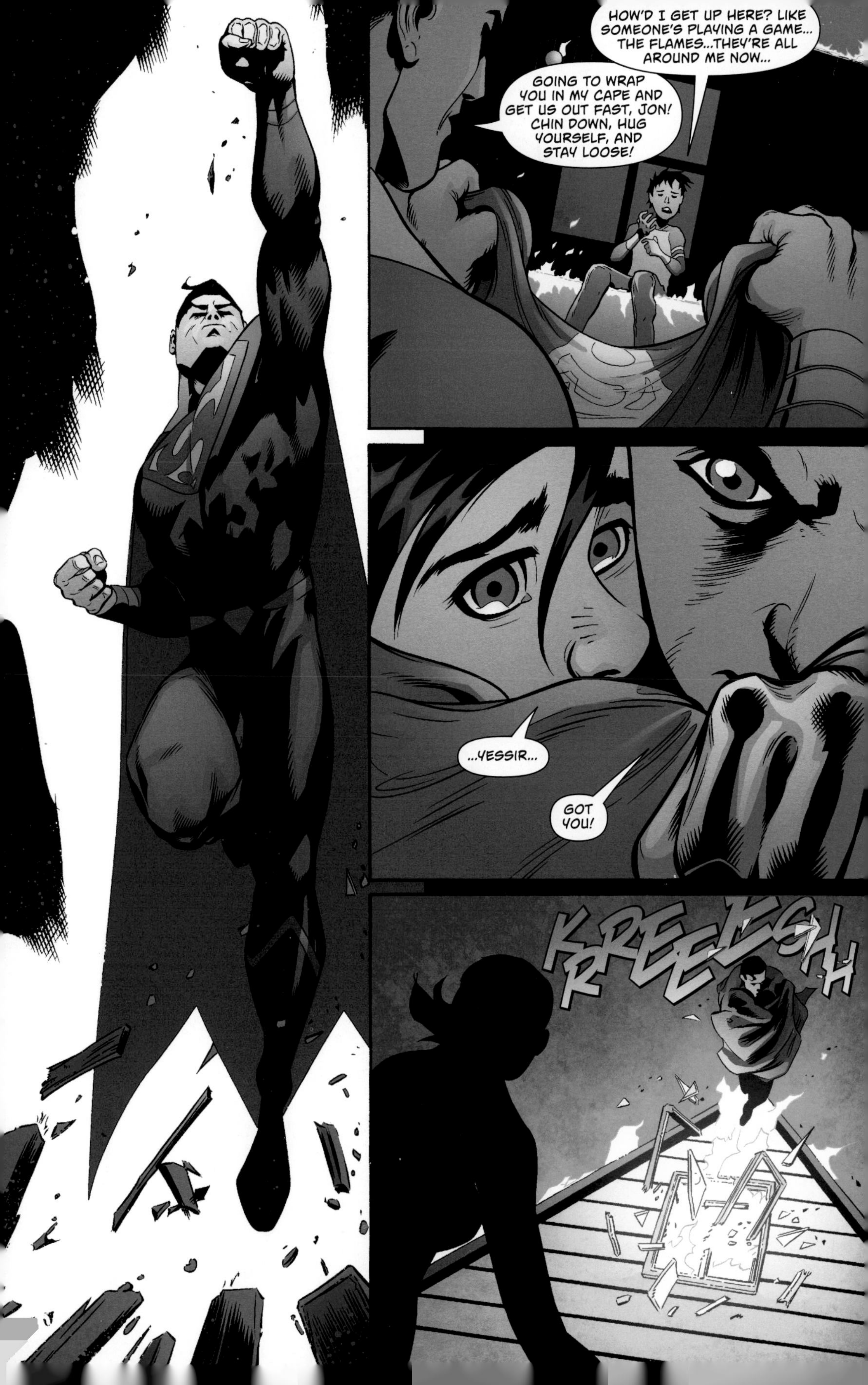
HOW'D I GET UP HERE? LIKE SOMEONE'S PLAYING A GAME... THE FLAMES...THEY'RE ALL AROUND ME NOW...
GOING TO WRAP YOU IN MY CAPE AND GET US OUT FAST, JON! CHIN DOWN, HUG YOURSELF, AND STAY LOOSE!
...YESSIR...
GOT YOU!
KRREEESSHH

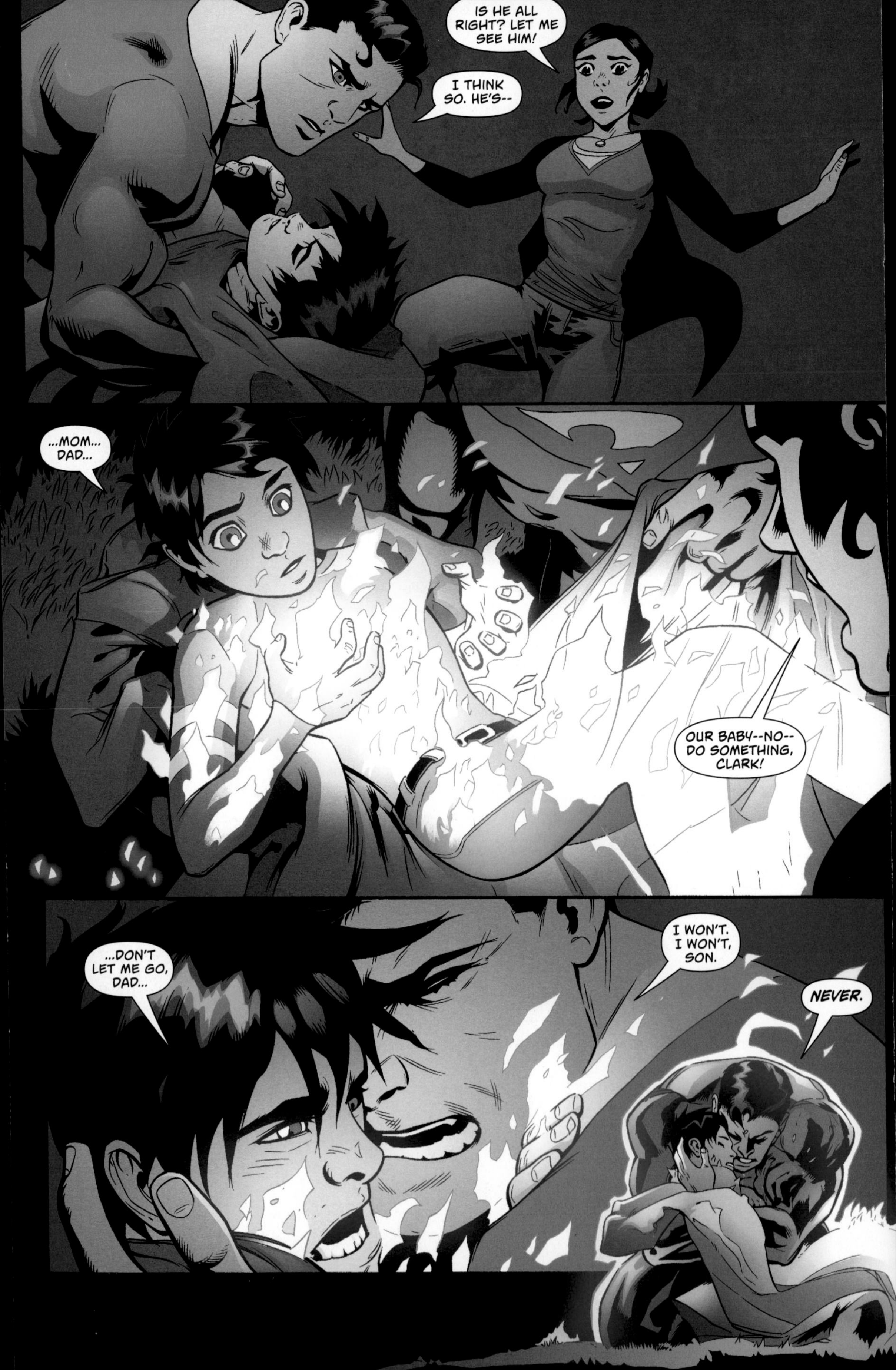

IS HE ALL RIGHT? LET ME SEE HIM!
I THINK SO. HE'S--
...MOM... DAD...
OUR BABY--NO-- DO SOMETHING, CLARK!
...DON'T LET ME GO, DAD...
I WON'T. I WON'T, SON.
NEVER.

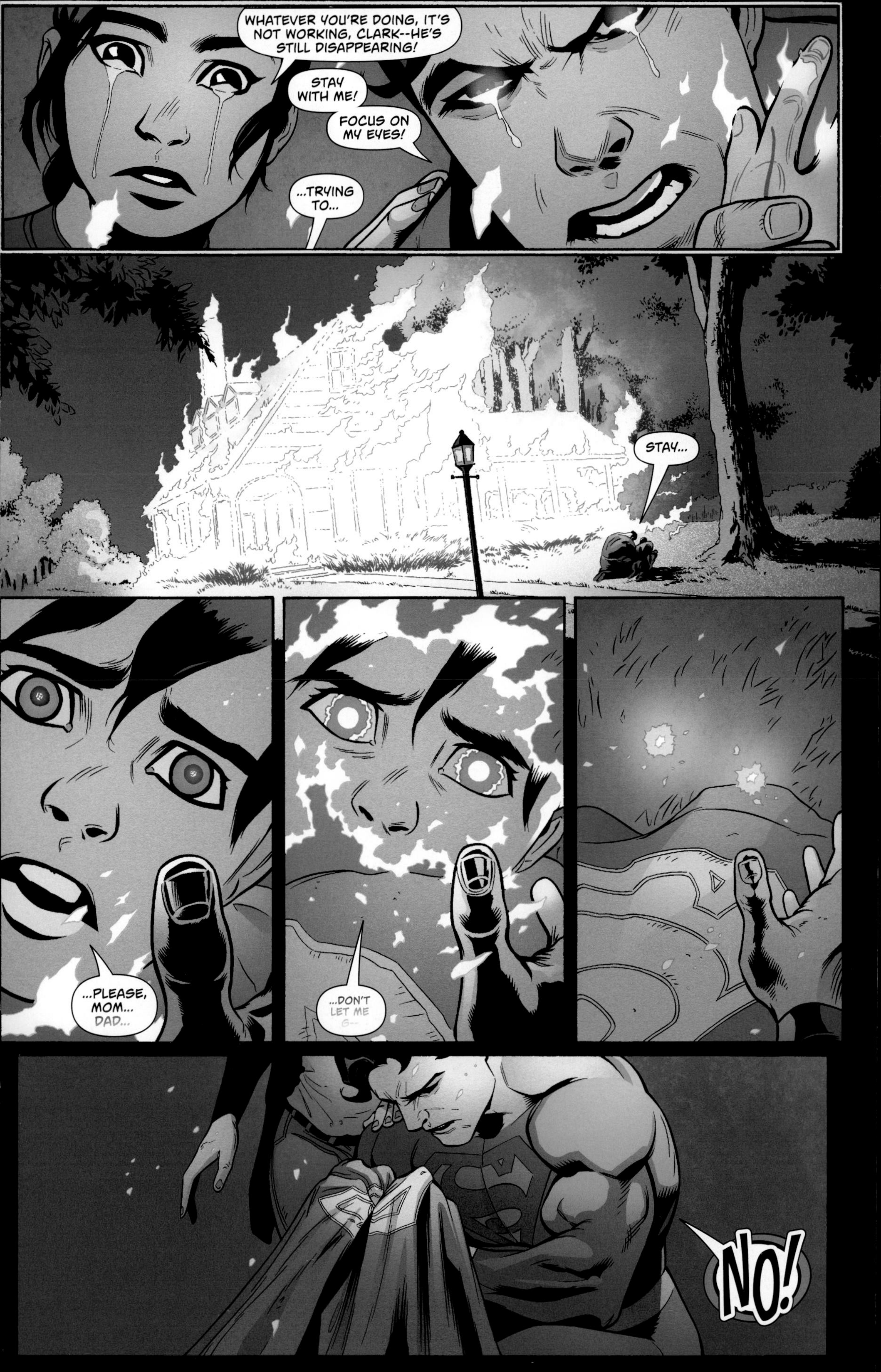
WHATEVER YOU'RE DOING, IT'S NOT WORKING, CLARK--HE'S STILL DISAPPEARING!
STAY WITH ME!
FOCUS ON MY EYES!
...TRYING TO...
STAY...
...PLEASE, MOM... DAD...
...DON'T LET ME G--
NO!

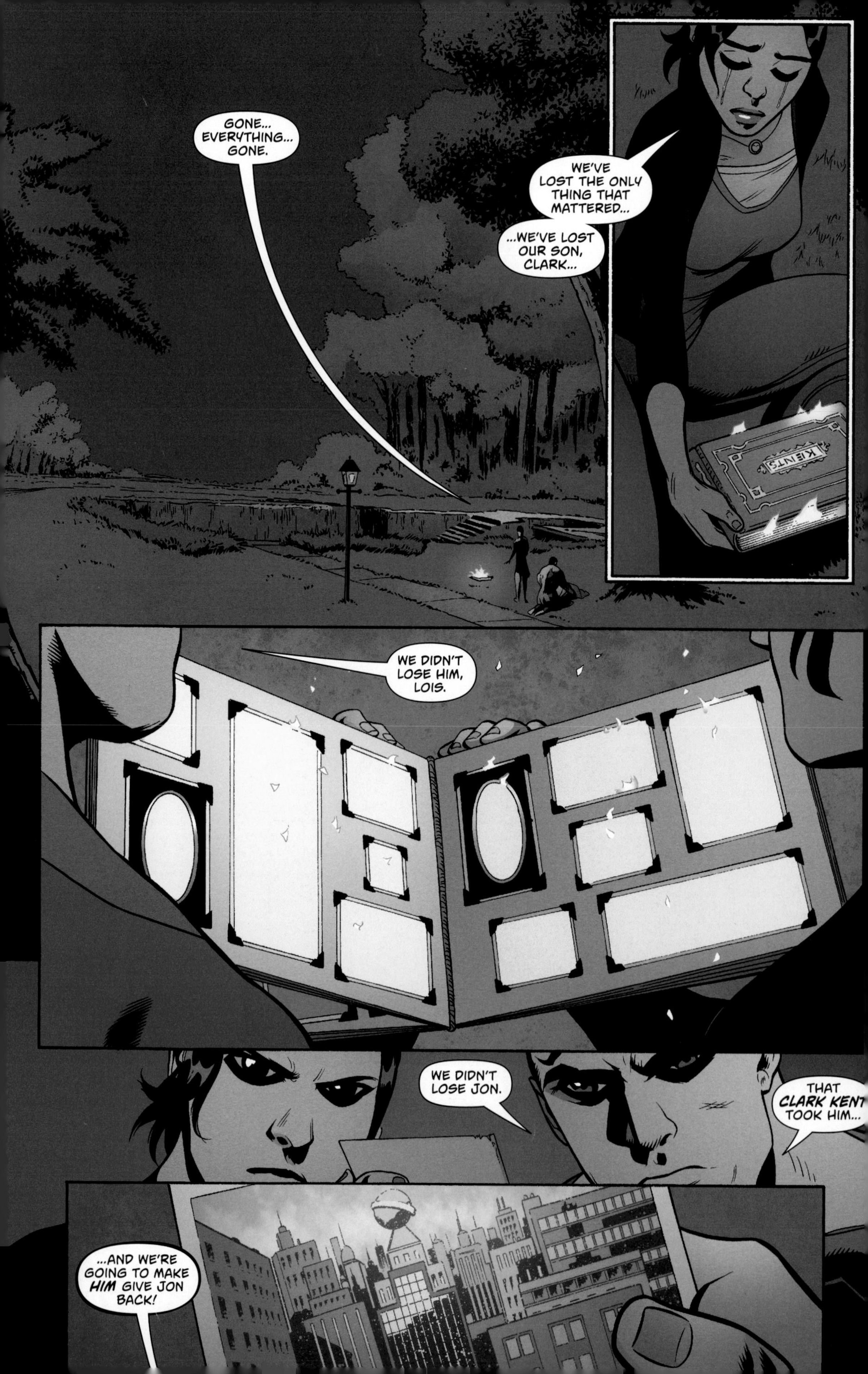

GONE... EVERYTHING... GONE.
WE'VE LOST THE ONLY THING THAT MATTERED...
...WE'VE LOST OUR SON, CLARK...
KENTS
WE DIDN'T LOSE HIM, LOIS.
WE DIDN'T LOSE JON.
THAT CLARK KENT TOOK HIM...
...AND WE'RE GOING TO MAKE HIM GIVE JON BACK!

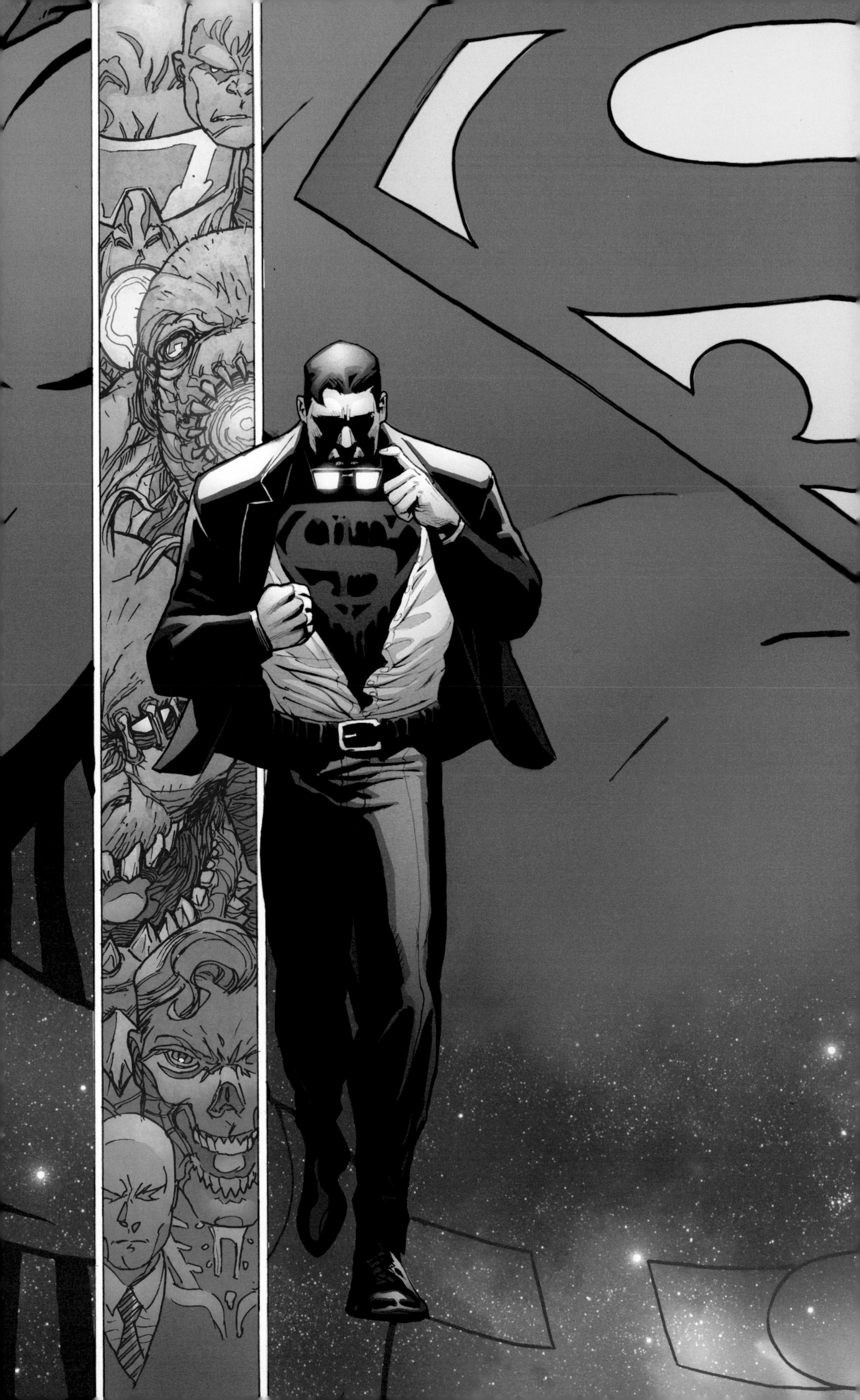

SUPERMAN: REBORN part two

DAN JURGENS writer * DOUG MAHNKE penciller
JAIME MENDOZA inker * WIL QUINTANA colorist
PATRICK GLEASON & JOHN KALISZ cover art

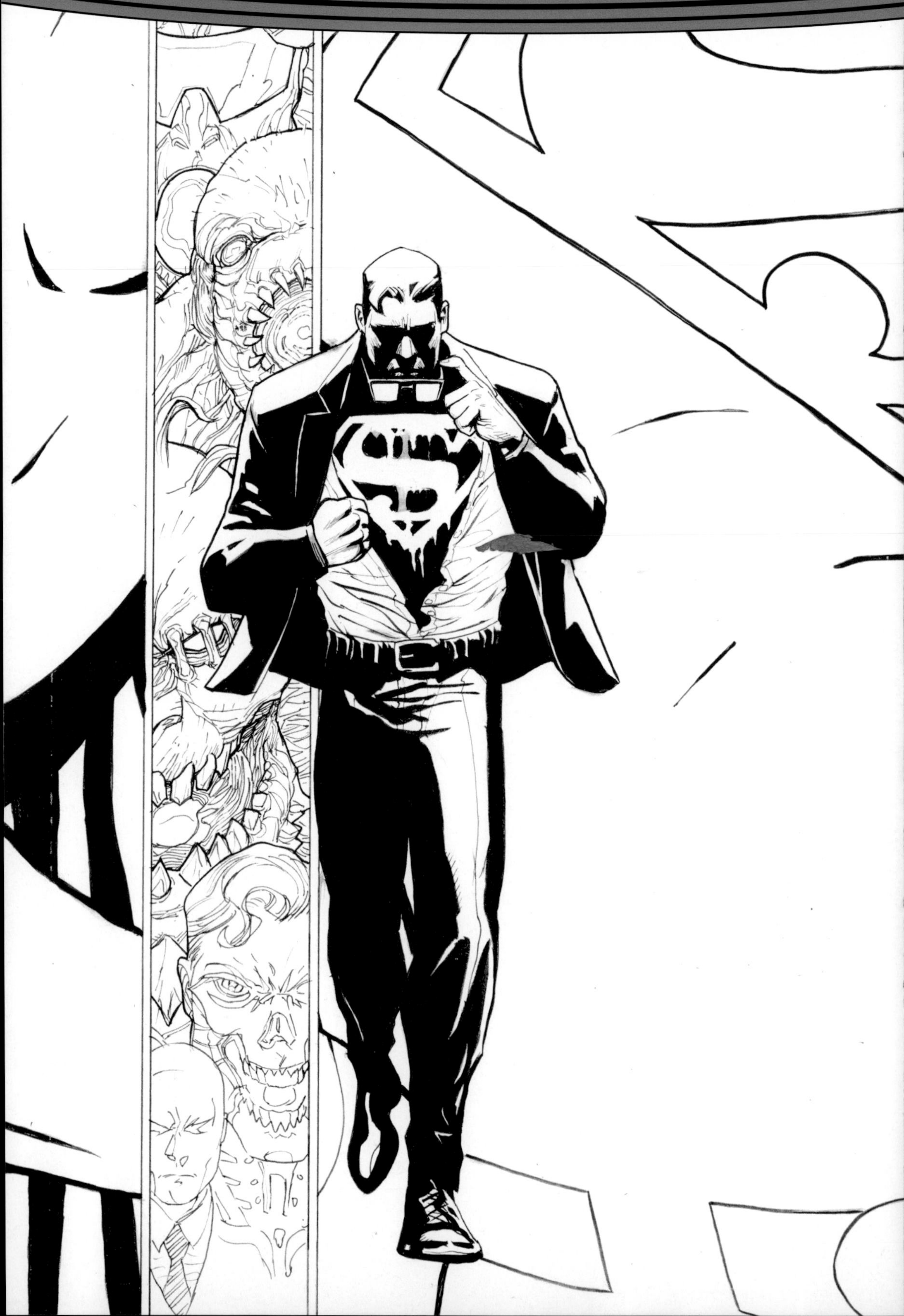

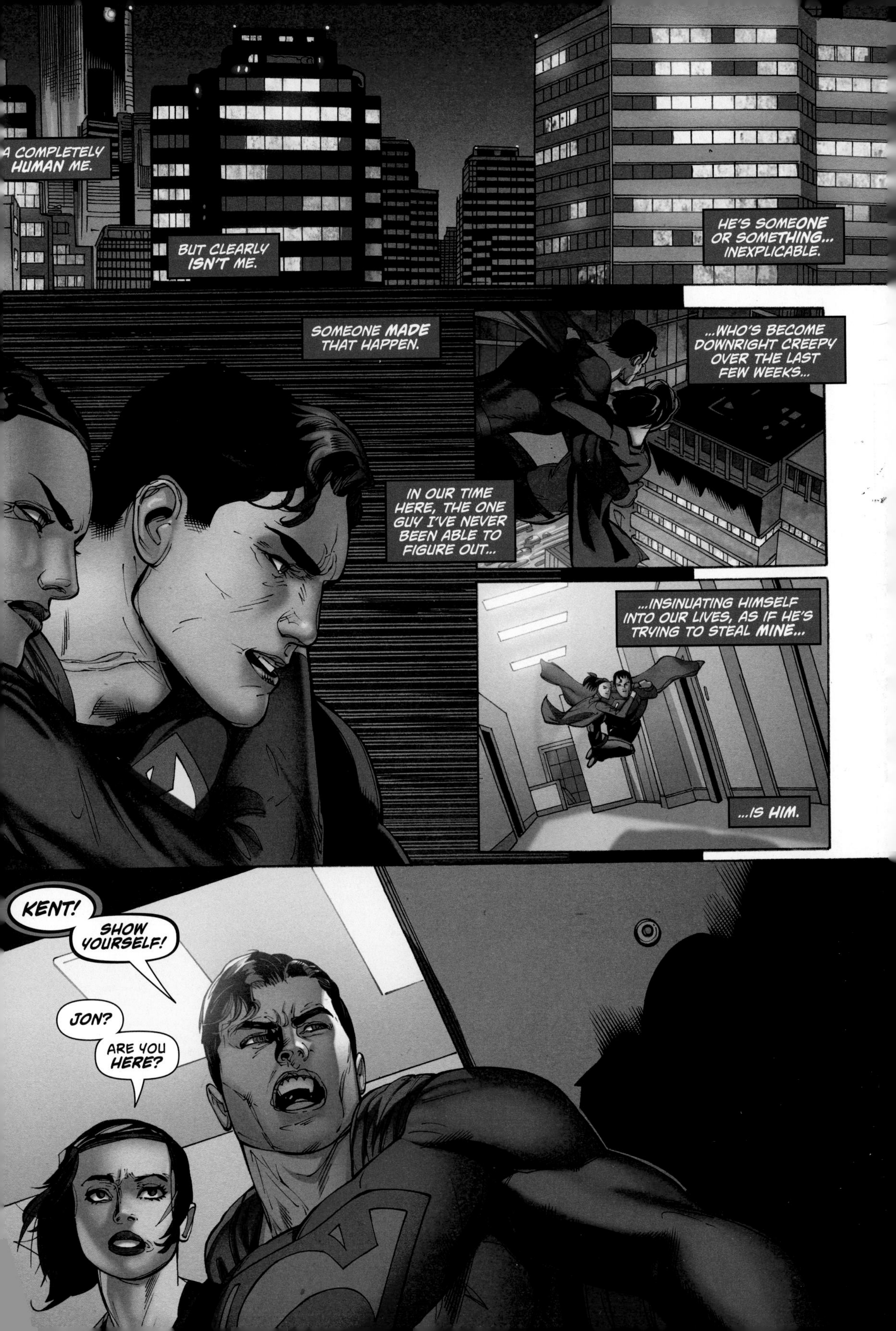
A COMPLETELY HUMAN ME.
BUT CLEARLY ISN'T ME.
HE'S SOMEONE OR SOMETHING... INEXPLICABLE.
SOMEONE MADE THAT HAPPEN.
IN OUR TIME HERE, THE ONE GUY I'VE NEVER BEEN ABLE TO FIGURE OUT...
...WHO'S BECOME DOWNRIGHT CREEPY OVER THE LAST FEW WEEKS...
...INSINUATING HIMSELF INTO OUR LIVES, AS IF HE'S TRYING TO STEAL MINE...
...IS HIM.
KENT!
SHOW YOURSELF!
JON?
ARE YOU HERE?

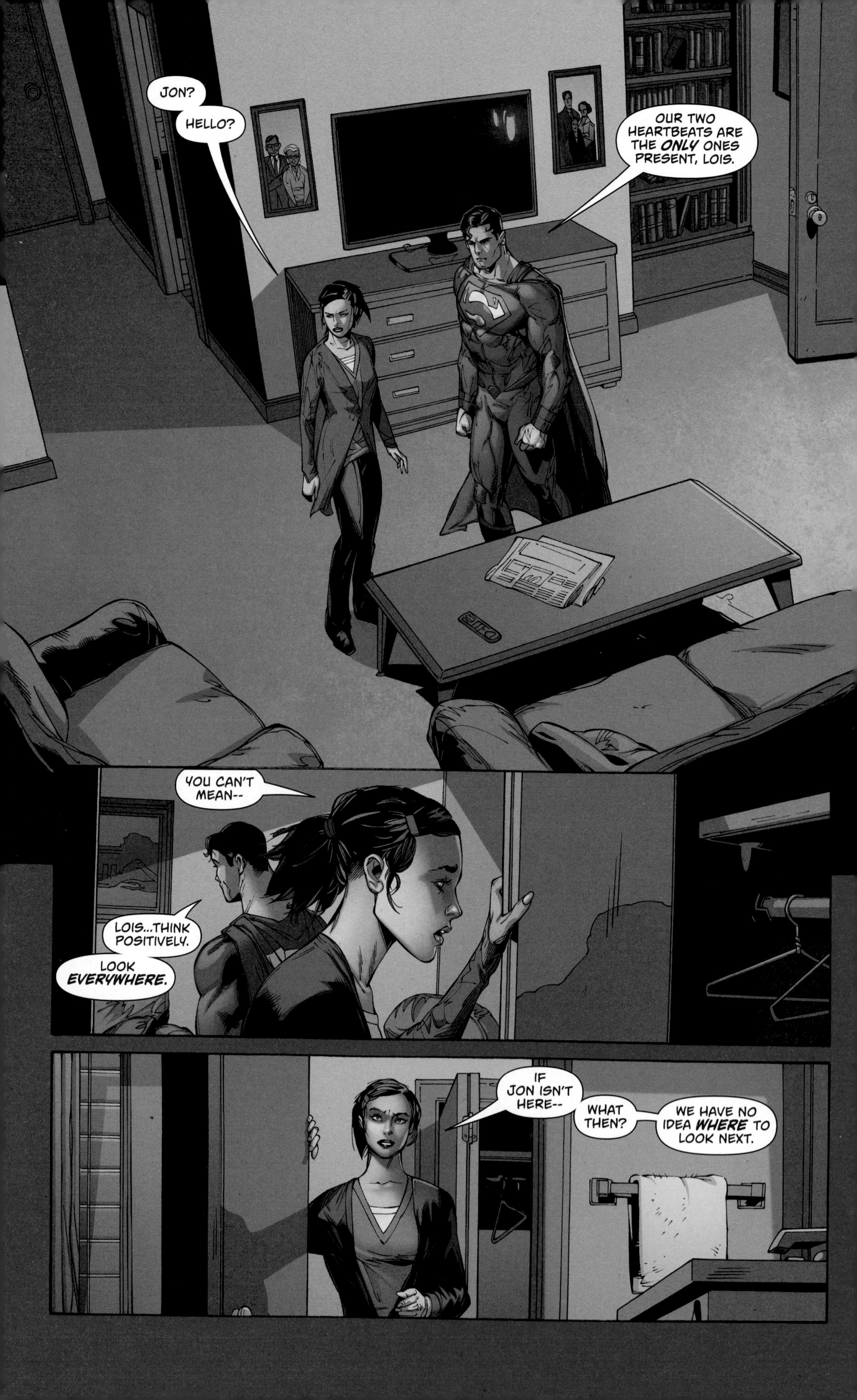
JON?
HELLO?
OUR TWO HEARTBEATS ARE THE ONLY ONES PRESENT, LOIS.
YOU CAN'T MEAN--
LOIS...THINK POSITIVELY.
LOOK EVERYWHERE.
IF JON ISN'T HERE--
WHAT THEN?
WE HAVE NO IDEA WHERE TO LOOK NEXT.

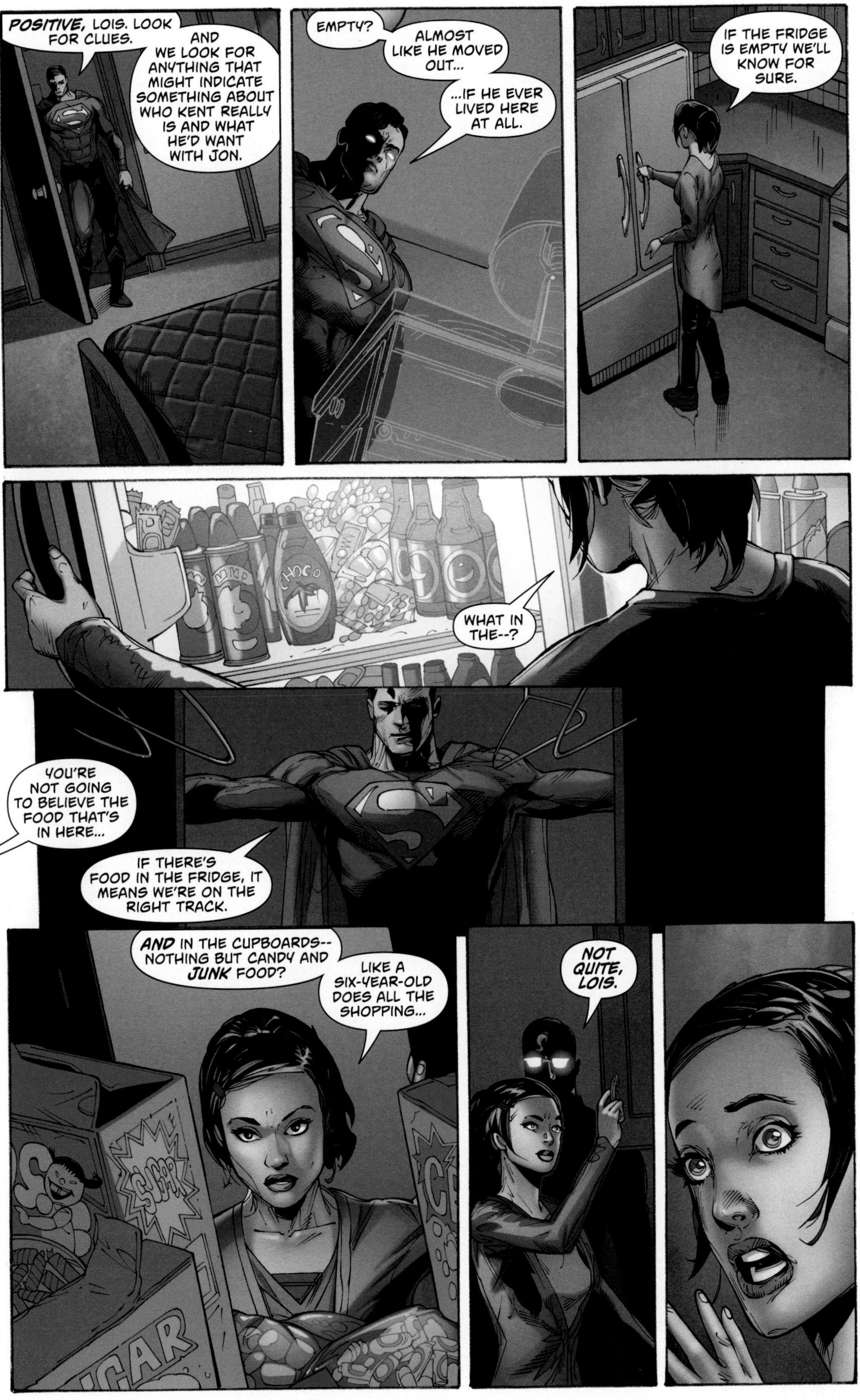
POSITIVE, LOIS. LOOK FOR CLUES.
AND WE LOOK FOR ANYTHING THAT MIGHT INDICATE SOMETHING ABOUT WHO KENT REALLY IS AND WHAT HE'D WANT WITH JON.
EMPTY?
ALMOST LIKE HE MOVED OUT...
...IF HE EVER LIVED HERE AT ALL.
IF THE FRIDGE IS EMPTY WE'LL KNOW FOR SURE.
CHOCO
WHAT IN THE--?
YOU'RE NOT GOING TO BELIEVE THE FOOD THAT'S IN HERE...
IF THERE'S FOOD IN THE FRIDGE, IT MEANS WE'RE ON THE RIGHT TRACK.
AND IN THE CUPBOARDS-- NOTHING BUT CANDY AND JUNK FOOD?
LIKE A SIX-YEAR-OLD DOES ALL THE SHOPPING...
SUGAR
NOT QUITE, LOIS.

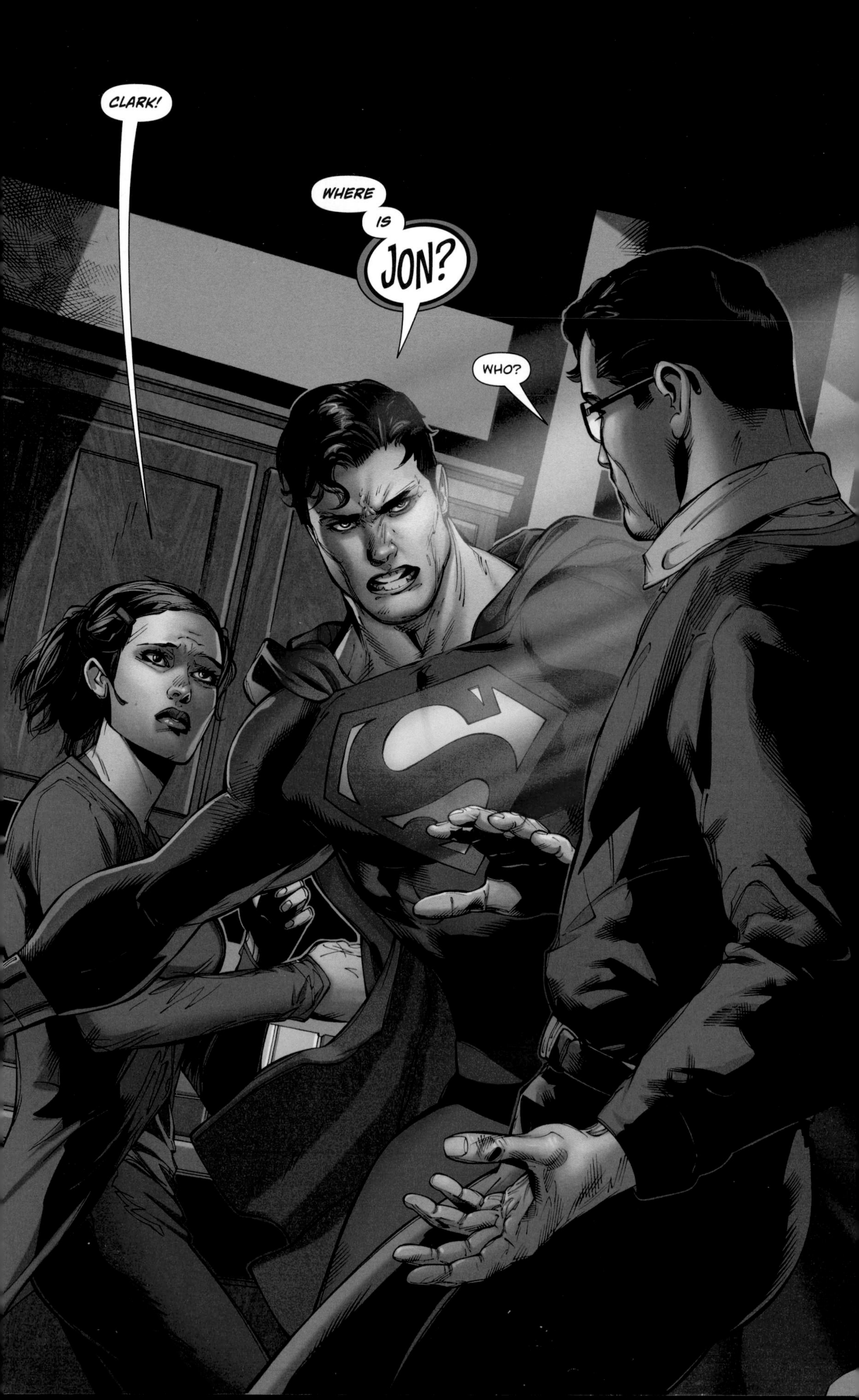
CLARK!
WHERE IS JON?
WHO?

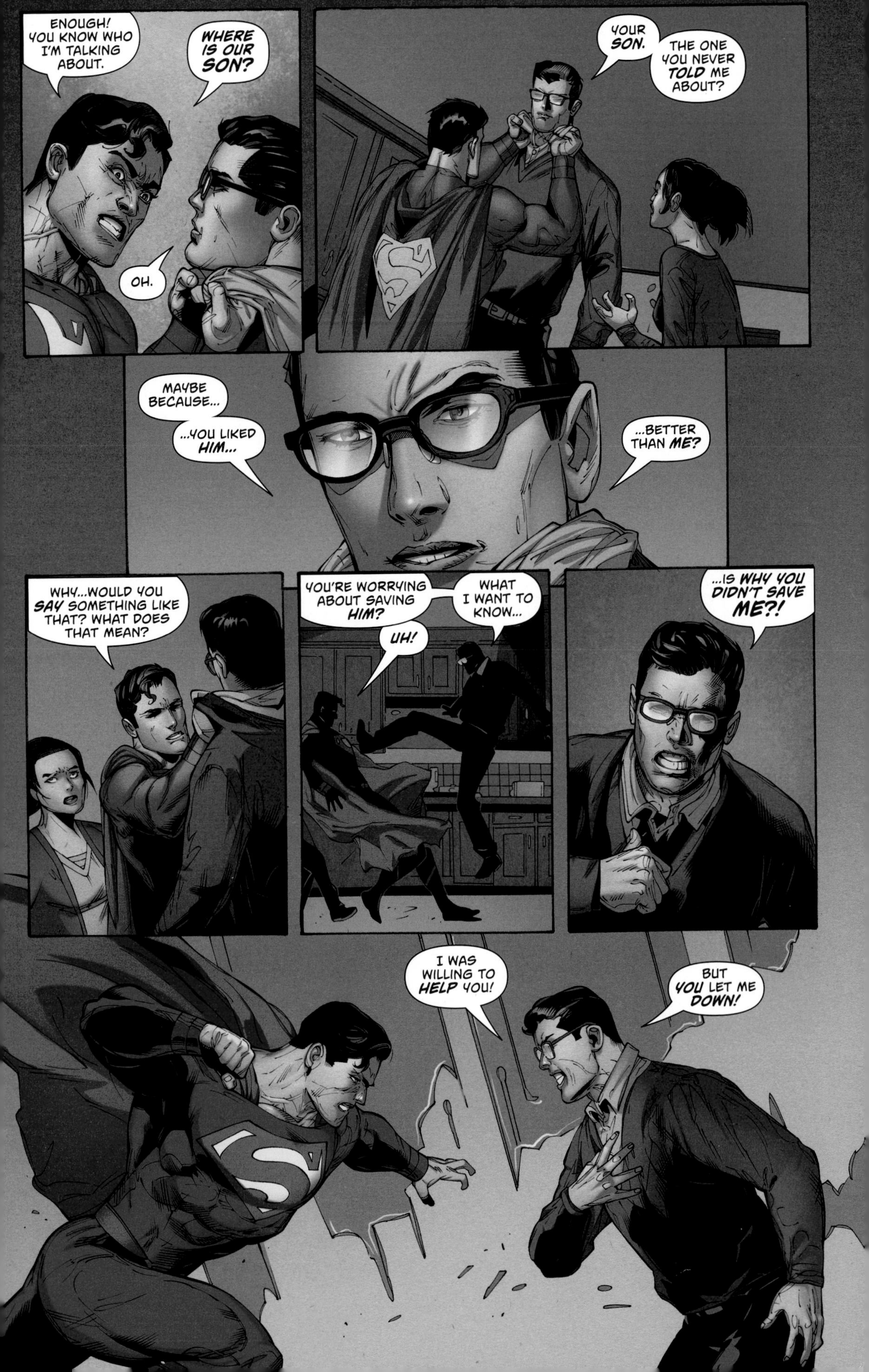
ENOUGH! YOU KNOW WHO I'M TALKING ABOUT.
WHERE IS OUR SON?
OH.
YOUR SON.
THE ONE YOU NEVER TOLD ME ABOUT?
MAYBE BECAUSE...
...YOU LIKED HIM...
...BETTER THAN ME?
WHY...WOULD YOU SAY SOMETHING LIKE THAT? WHAT DOES THAT MEAN?
YOU'RE WORRYING ABOUT SAVING HIM?
WHAT I WANT TO KNOW...
UH!
...IS WHY YOU DIDN'T SAVE ME?!
I WAS WILLING TO HELP YOU!
BUT YOU LET ME DOWN!

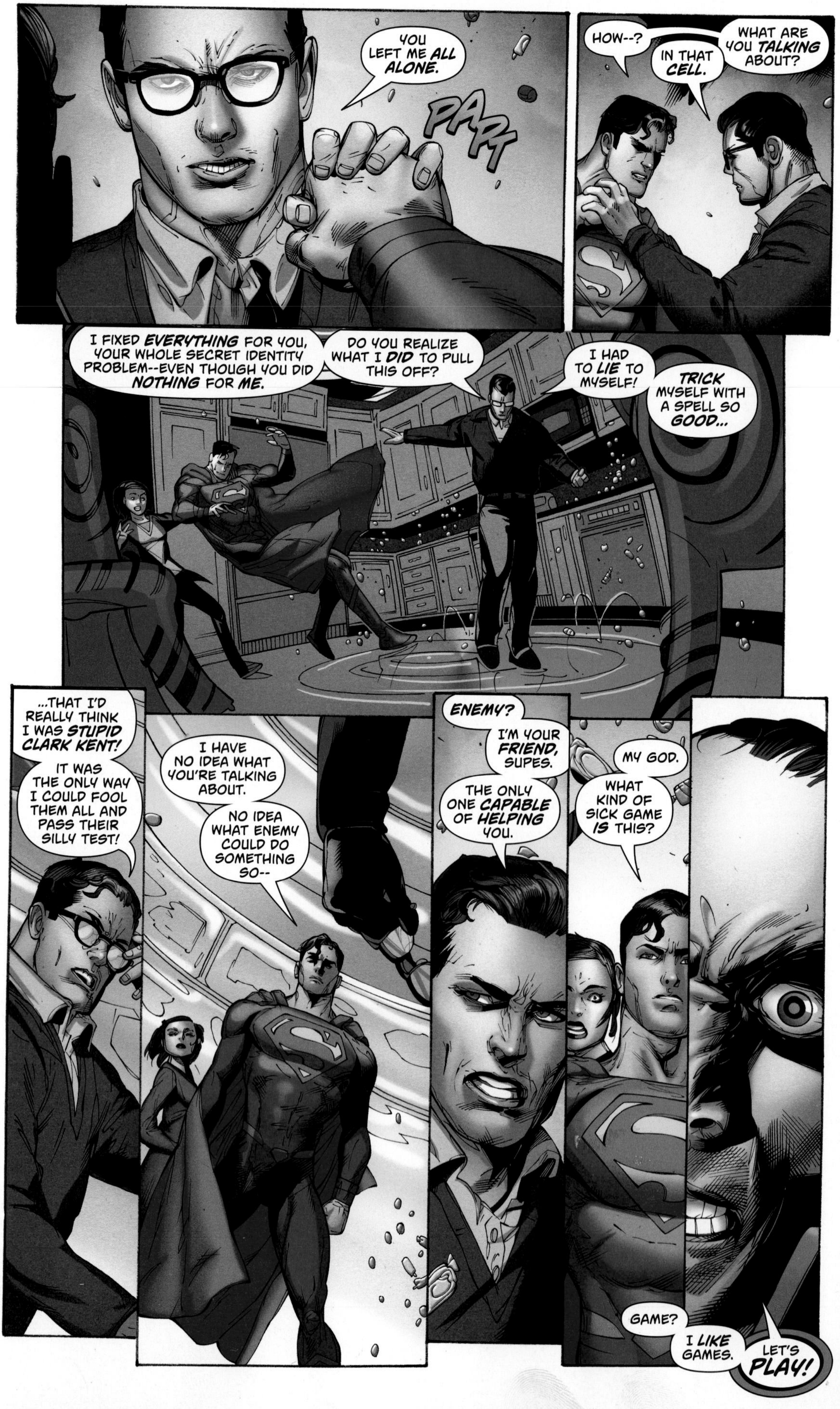
YOU LEFT ME ALL ALONE.
PAPH
HOW--?
WHAT ARE YOU TALKING ABOUT?
IN THAT CELL.
I FIXED EVERYTHING FOR YOU, YOUR WHOLE SECRET IDENTITY PROBLEM--EVEN THOUGH YOU DID NOTHING FOR ME.
DO YOU REALIZE WHAT I DID TO PULL THIS OFF?
I HAD TO LIE TO MYSELF!
TRICK MYSELF WITH A SPELL SO GOOD...
...THAT I'D REALLY THINK I WAS STUPID CLARK KENT!
IT WAS THE ONLY WAY I COULD FOOL THEM ALL AND PASS THEIR SILLY TEST!
I HAVE NO IDEA WHAT YOU'RE TALKING ABOUT.
NO IDEA WHAT ENEMY COULD DO SOMETHING SO--
ENEMY?
I'M YOUR FRIEND, SUPES.
THE ONLY ONE CAPABLE OF HELPING YOU.
MY GOD.
WHAT KIND OF SICK GAME IS THIS?
GAME?
I LIKE GAMES.
LET'S PLAY!

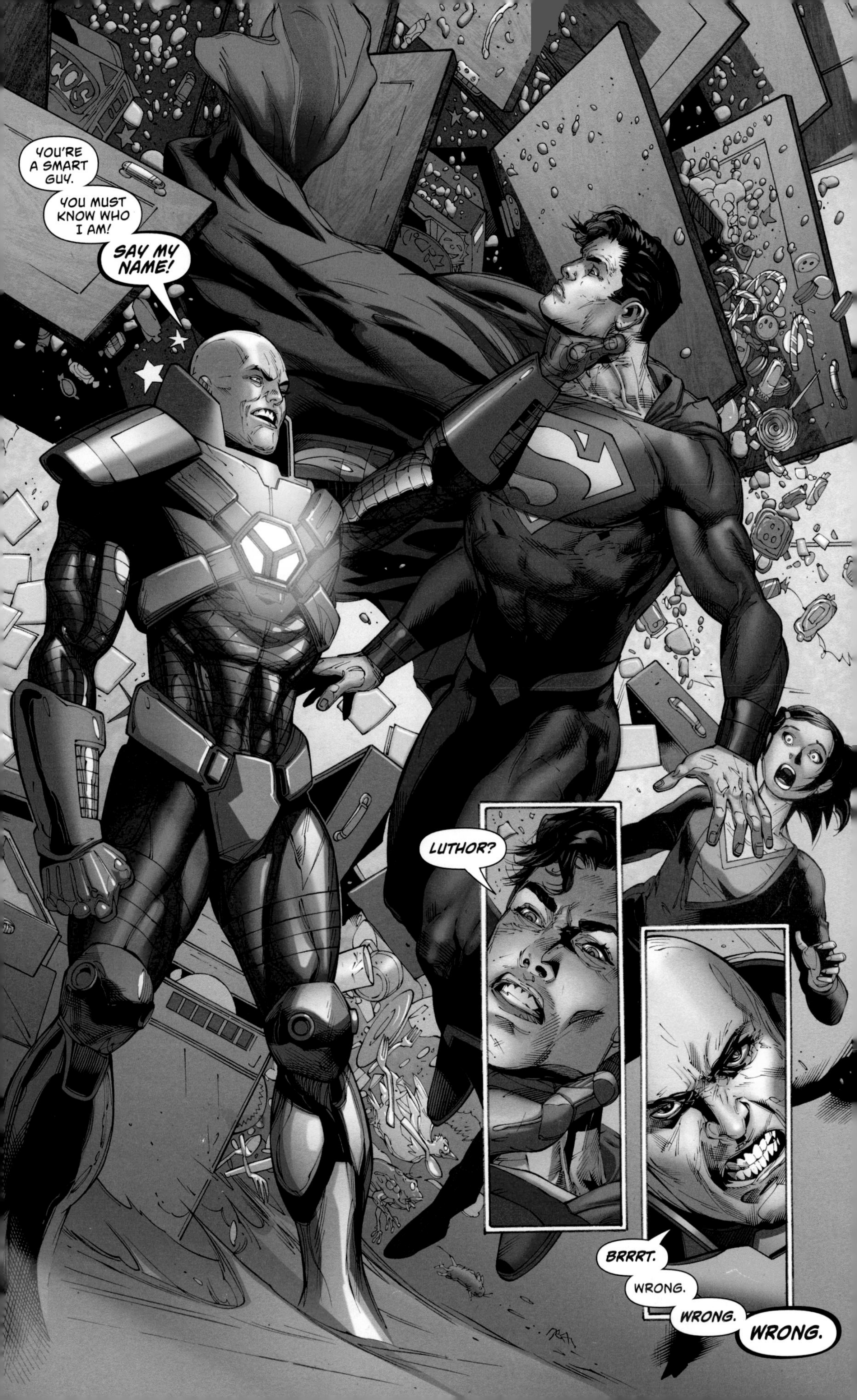
YOU'RE A SMART GUY.
YOU MUST KNOW WHO I AM!
SAY MY NAME!
LUTHOR?
BRRRT.
WRONG.
WRONG.
WRONG.

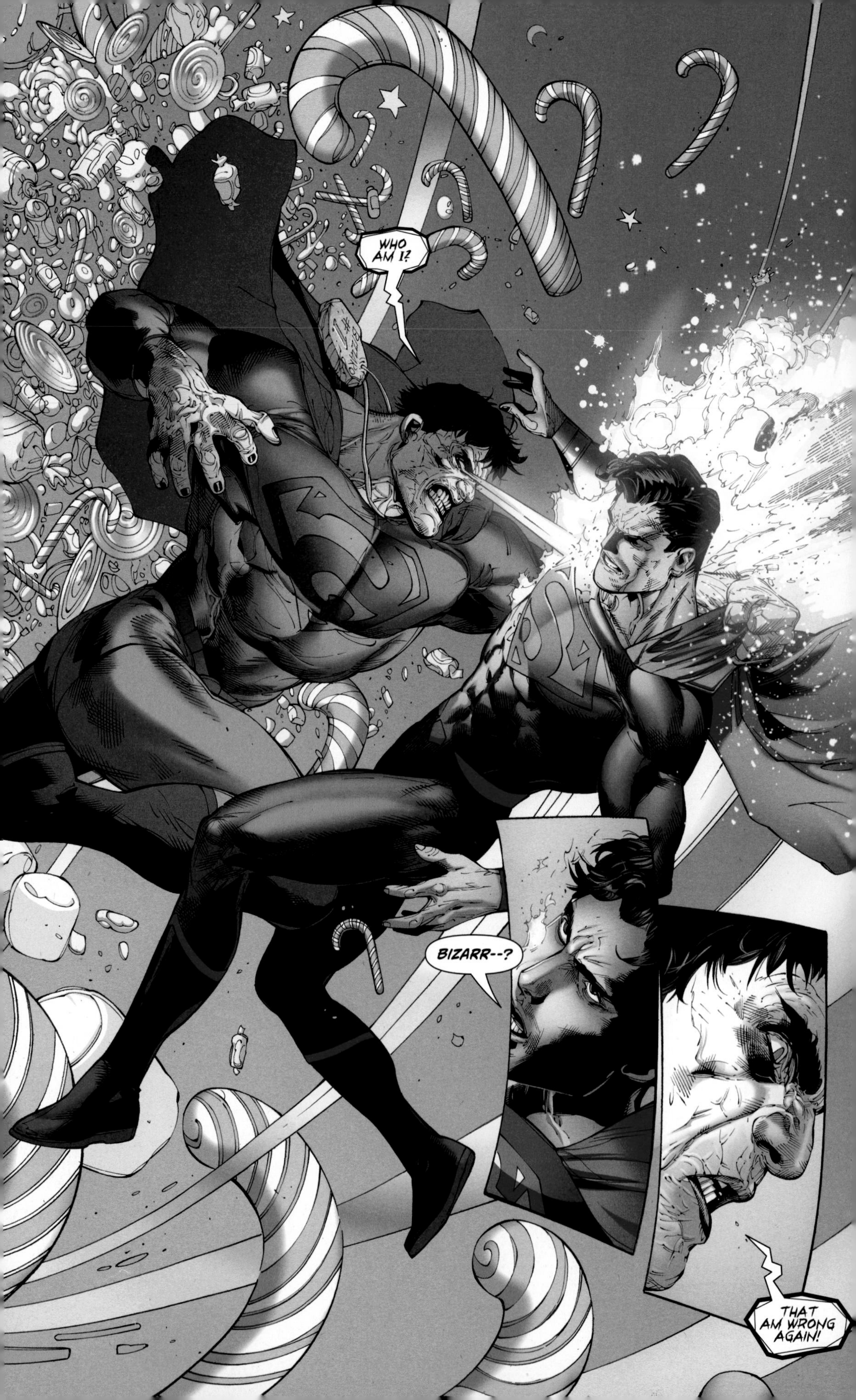
WHO AM I?
BIZARR--?
THAT AM WRONG AGAIN!

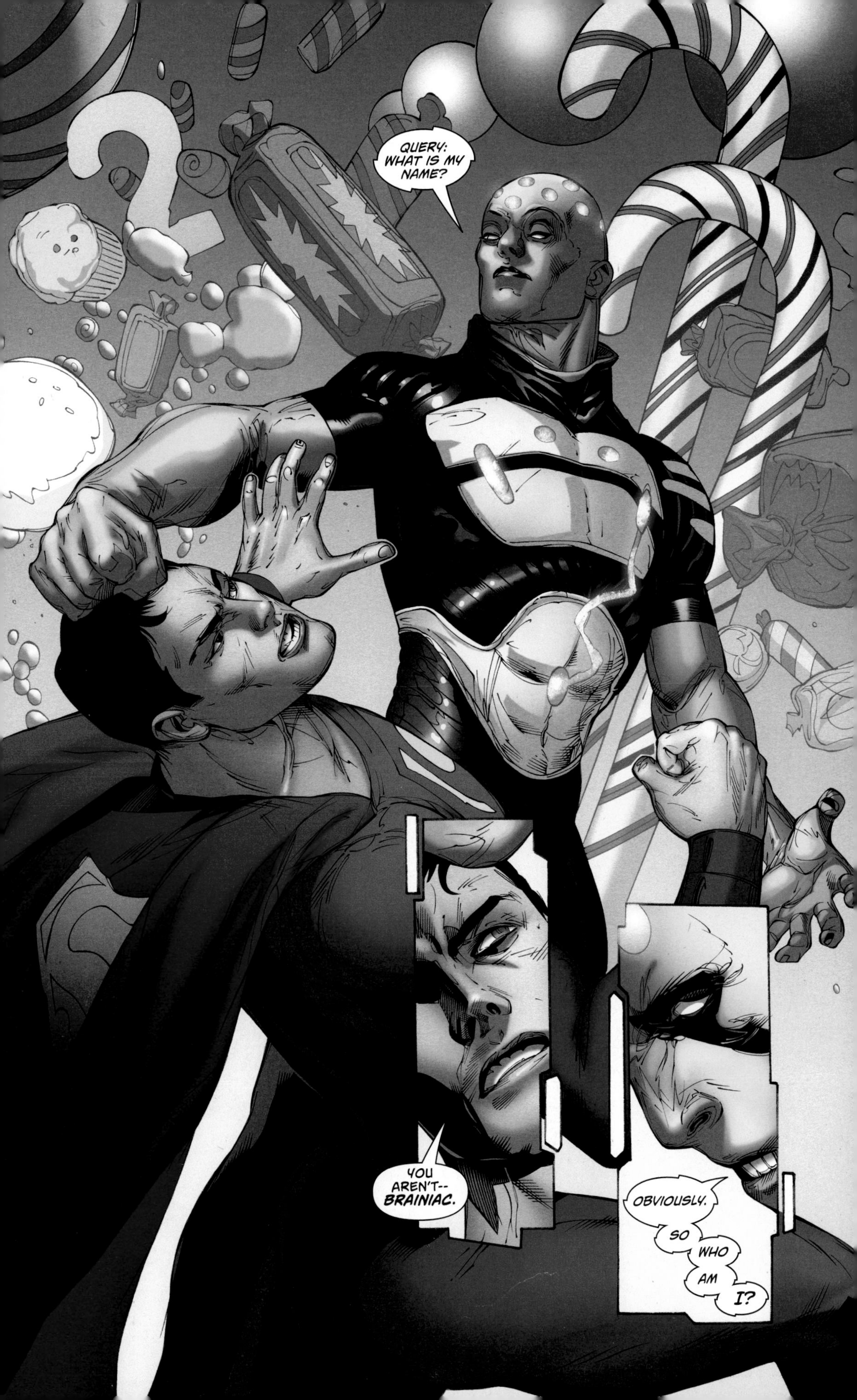
QUERY: WHAT IS MY NAME?
YOU AREN'T-- BRAINIAC.
OBVIOUSLY.
SO
WHO
AM
I?

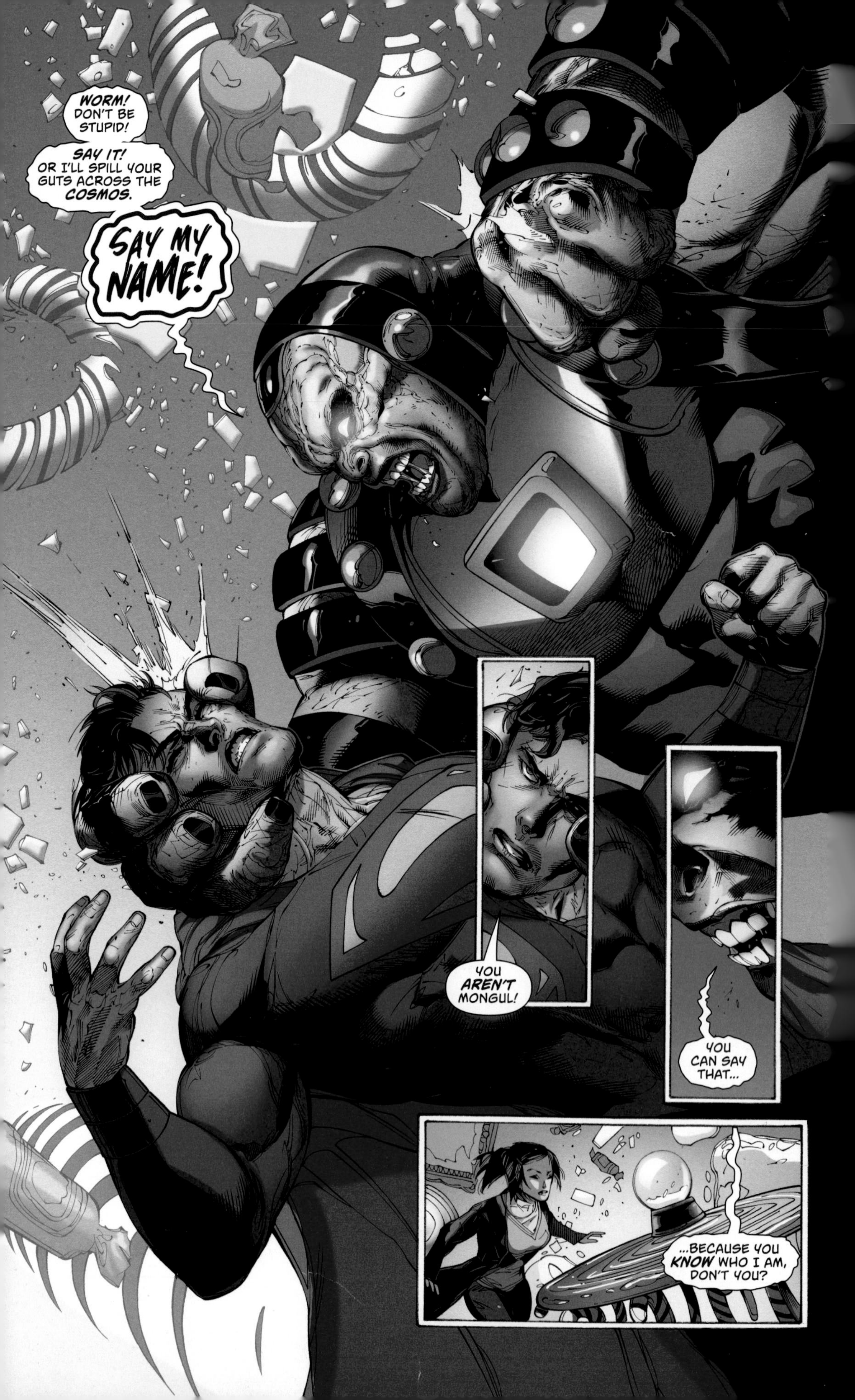
WORM! DON'T BE STUPID!
SAY IT! OR I'LL SPILL YOUR GUTS ACROSS THE COSMOS.
SAY MY NAME!
YOU AREN'T MONGUL!
YOU CAN SAY THAT...
...BECAUSE YOU KNOW WHO I AM, DON'T YOU?

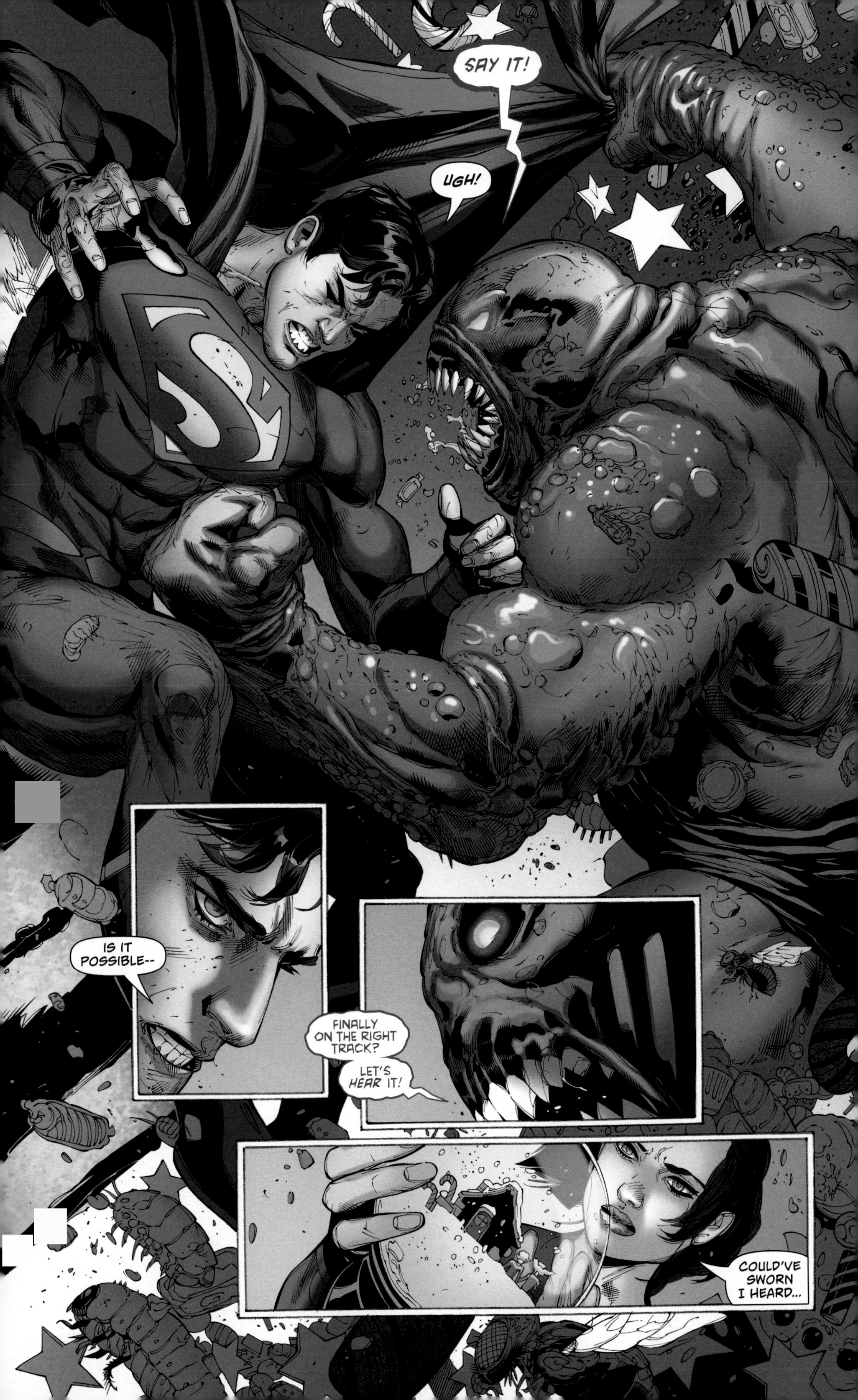
SAY IT!
UGH!
IS IT POSSIBLE--
FINALLY ON THE RIGHT TRACK?
LET'S HEAR IT!
COULD'VE SWORN I HEARD...

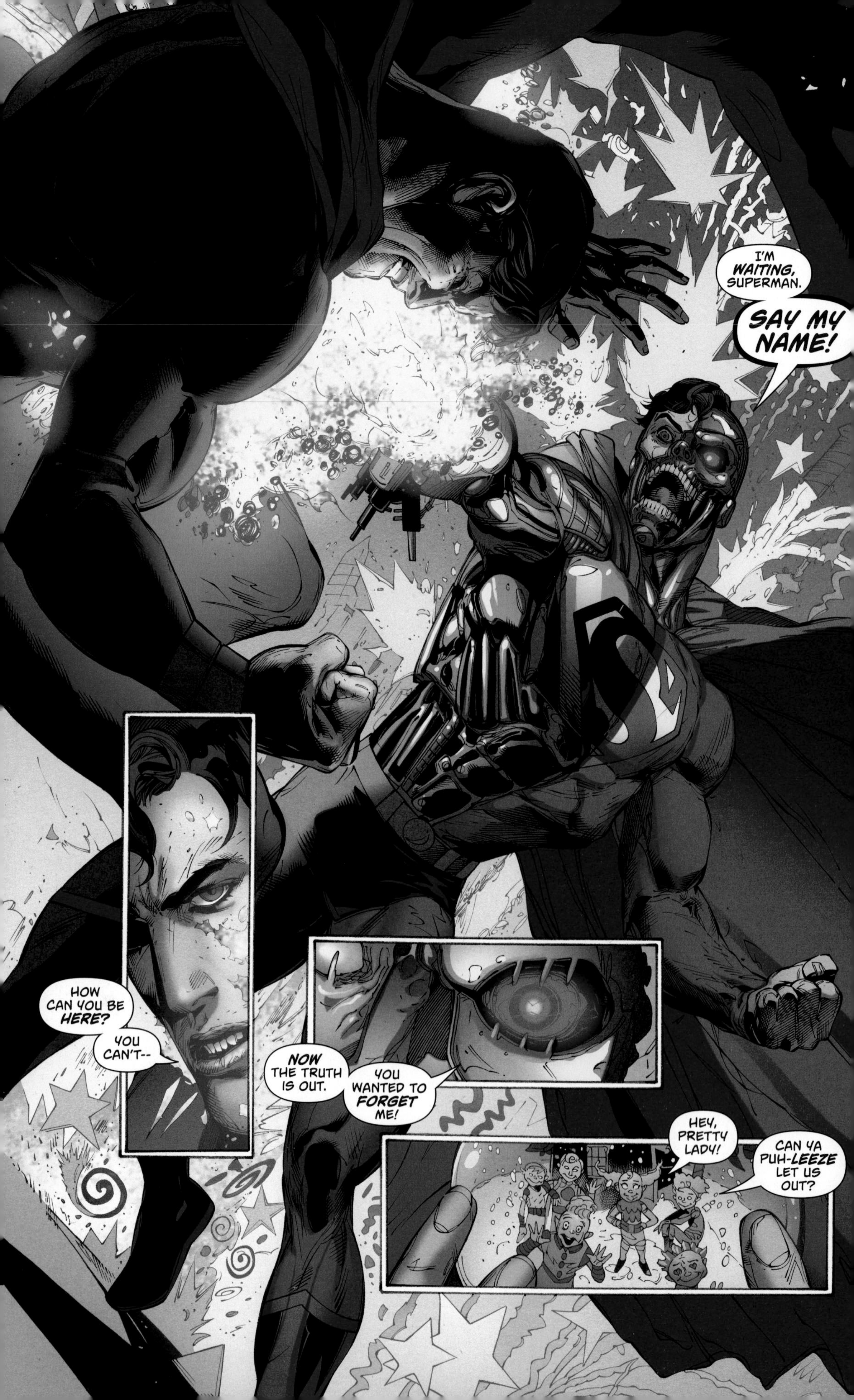
I'M *WAITING,* SUPERMAN.
SAY MY NAME!
HOW CAN YOU BE *HERE?*
YOU CAN'T--
NOW THE TRUTH IS OUT.
YOU WANTED TO *FORGET* ME!
HEY, PRETTY LADY!
CAN YA PUH-*LEEZE* LET US OUT?

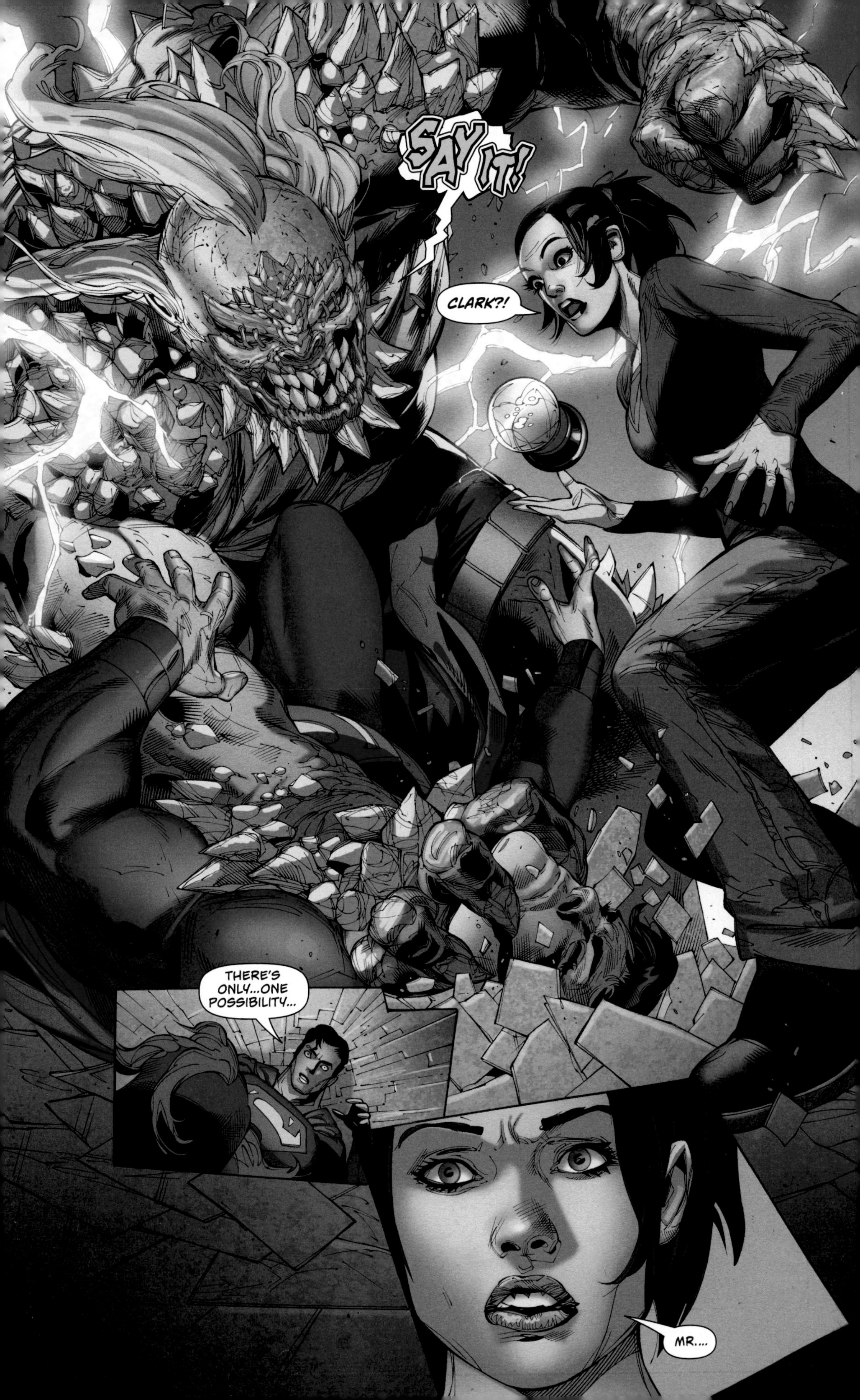
SAY IT!
CLARK?!
THERE'S ONLY...ONE POSSIBILITY...
MR....

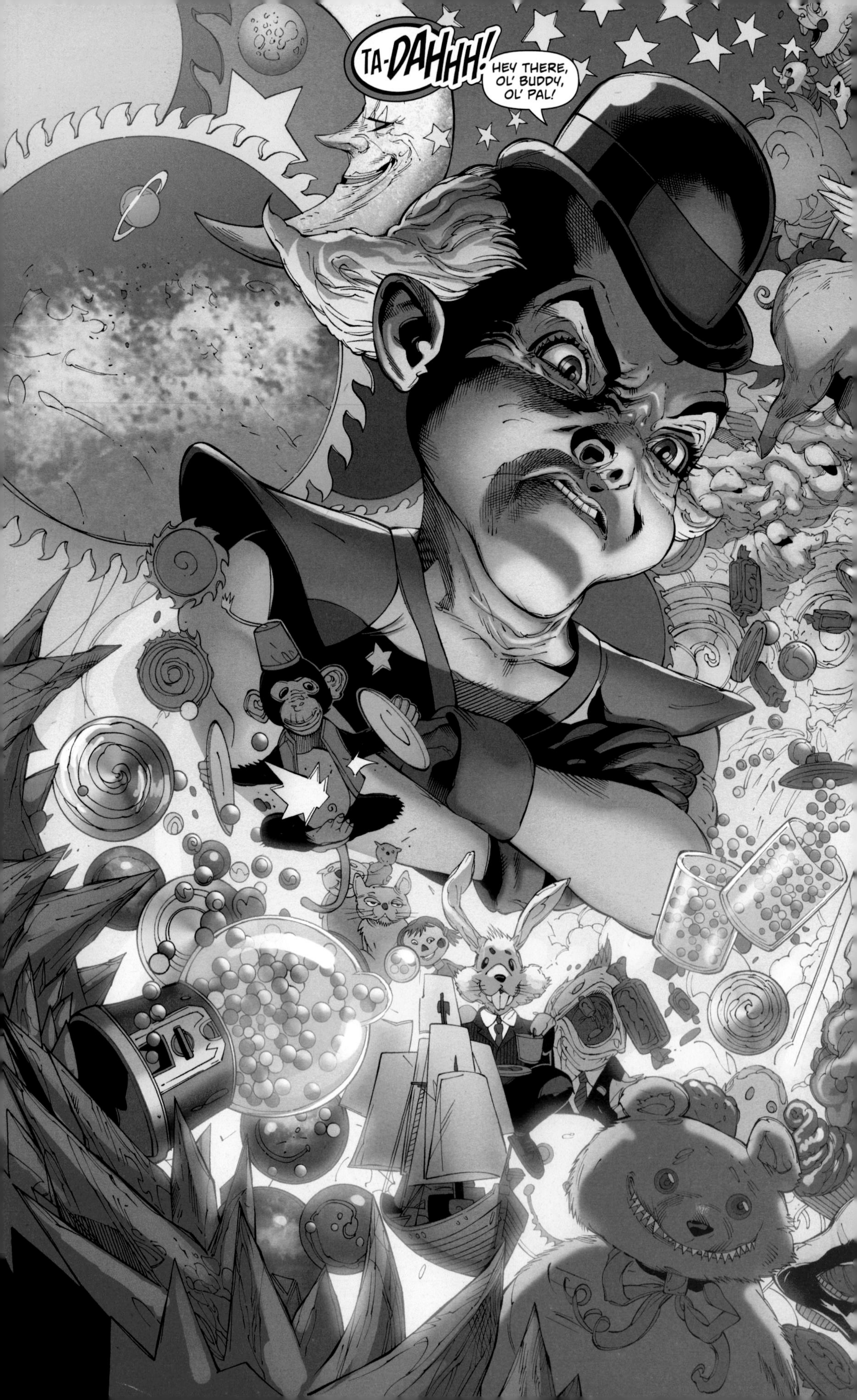
TA-DAHHH!
HEY THERE, OL' BUDDY, OL' PAL!

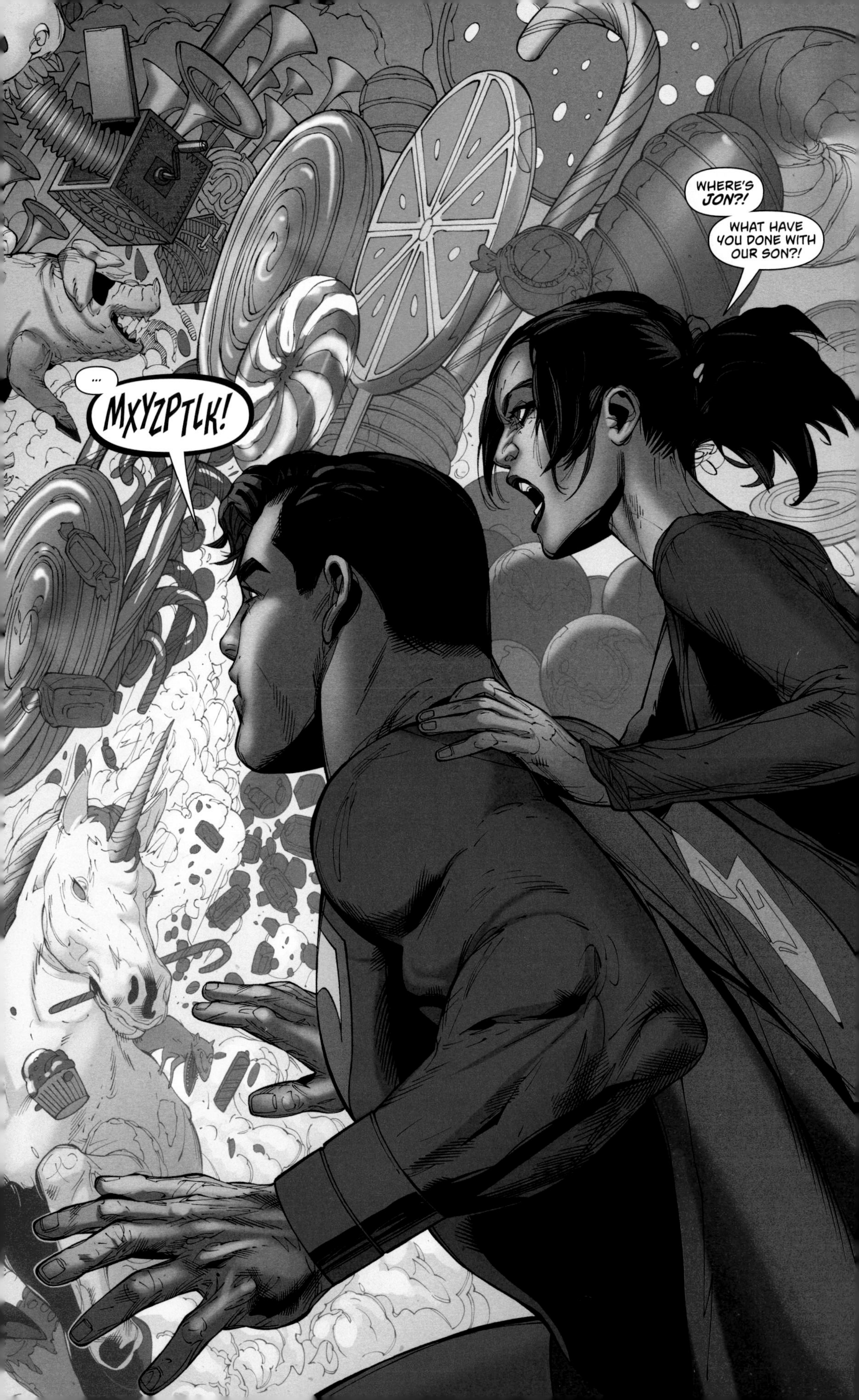

WHERE'S JON?!
WHAT HAVE YOU DONE WITH OUR SON?!
...
MXYZPTLK!

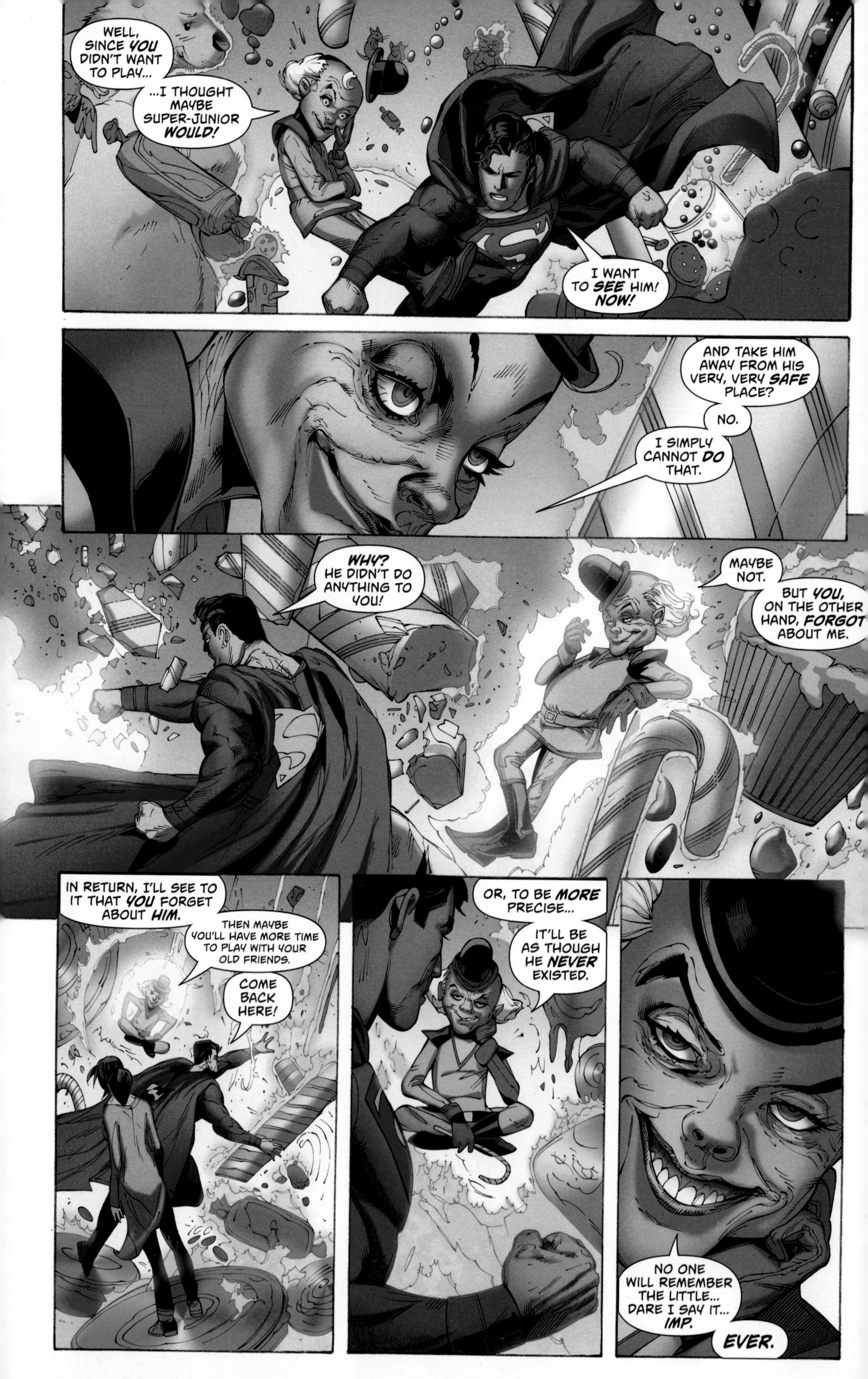

WELL, SINCE YOU DIDN'T WANT TO PLAY...
...I THOUGHT MAYBE SUPER-JUNIOR WOULD!
I WANT TO SEE HIM! NOW!
AND TAKE HIM AWAY FROM HIS VERY, VERY SAFE PLACE?
NO.
I SIMPLY CANNOT DO THAT.
WHY? HE DIDN'T DO ANYTHING TO YOU!
MAYBE NOT.
BUT YOU, ON THE OTHER HAND, FORGOT ABOUT ME.
IN RETURN, I'LL SEE TO IT THAT YOU FORGET ABOUT HIM.
THEN MAYBE YOU'LL HAVE MORE TIME TO PLAY WITH YOUR OLD FRIENDS.
COME BACK HERE!
OR, TO BE MORE PRECISE...
IT'LL BE AS THOUGH HE NEVER EXISTED.
NO ONE WILL REMEMBER THE LITTLE... DARE I SAY IT... IMP.
EVER.

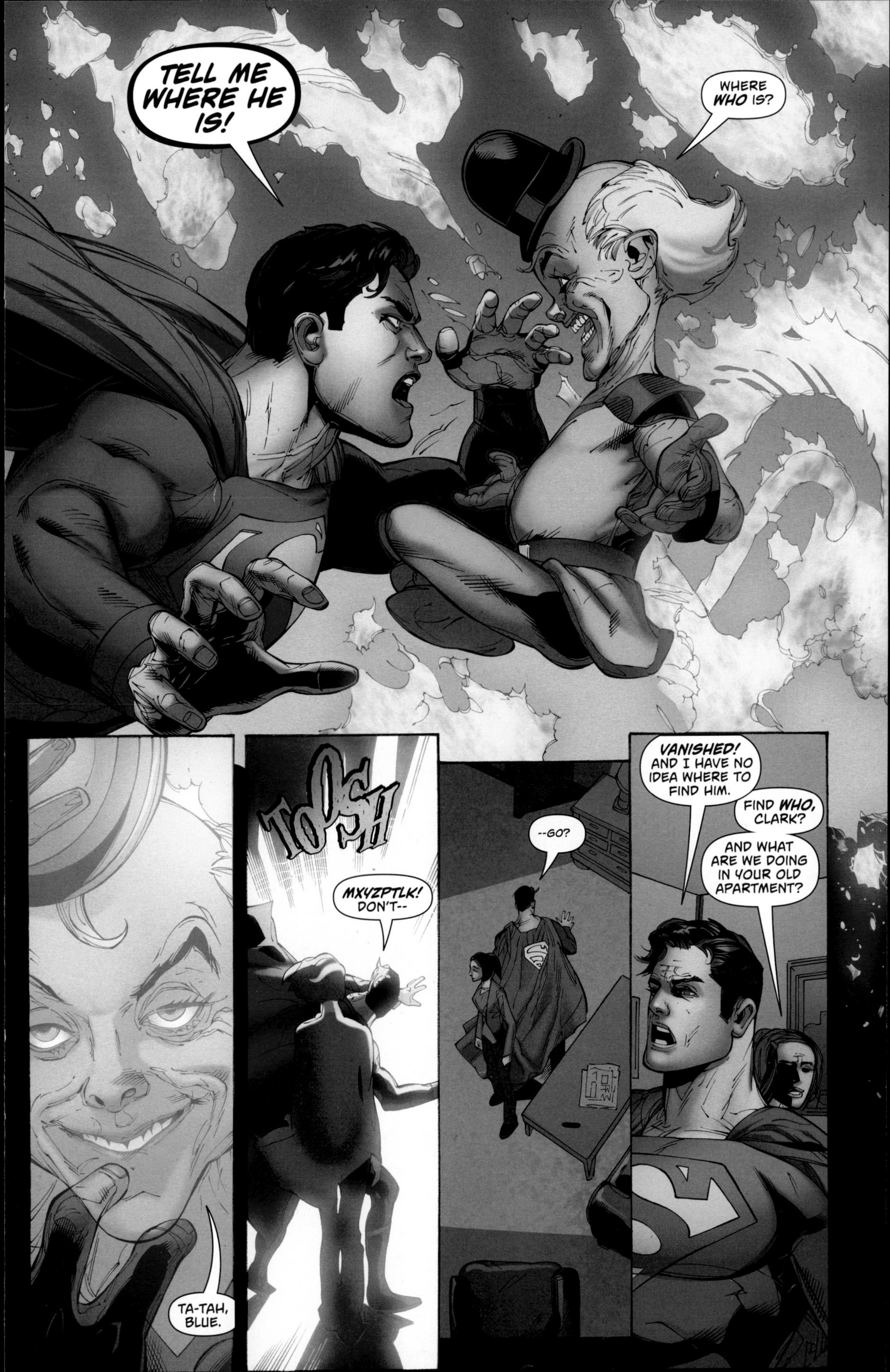
TELL ME WHERE HE IS!
WHERE *WHO* IS?
TA-TAH, BLUE.
TOOSH
MXYZPTLK! DON'T--
--GO?
VANISHED! AND I HAVE NO IDEA WHERE TO FIND HIM.
FIND *WHO,* CLARK?
AND WHAT ARE WE DOING IN YOUR OLD APARTMENT?

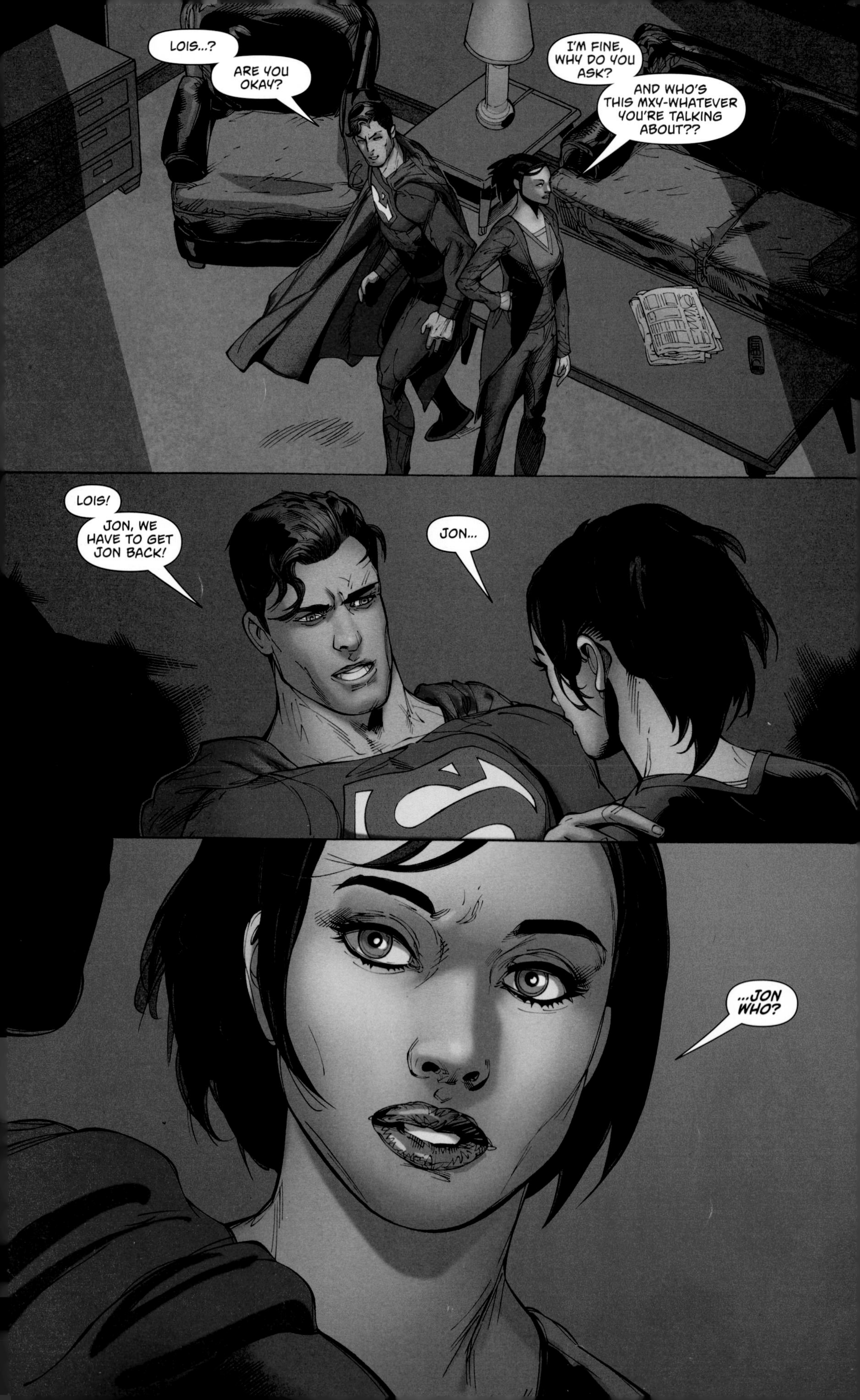
LOIS...?
ARE YOU OKAY?
I'M FINE, WHY DO YOU ASK?
AND WHO'S THIS MXY-WHATEVER YOU'RE TALKING ABOUT??
LOIS!
JON, WE HAVE TO GET JON BACK!
JON...
...JON WHO?

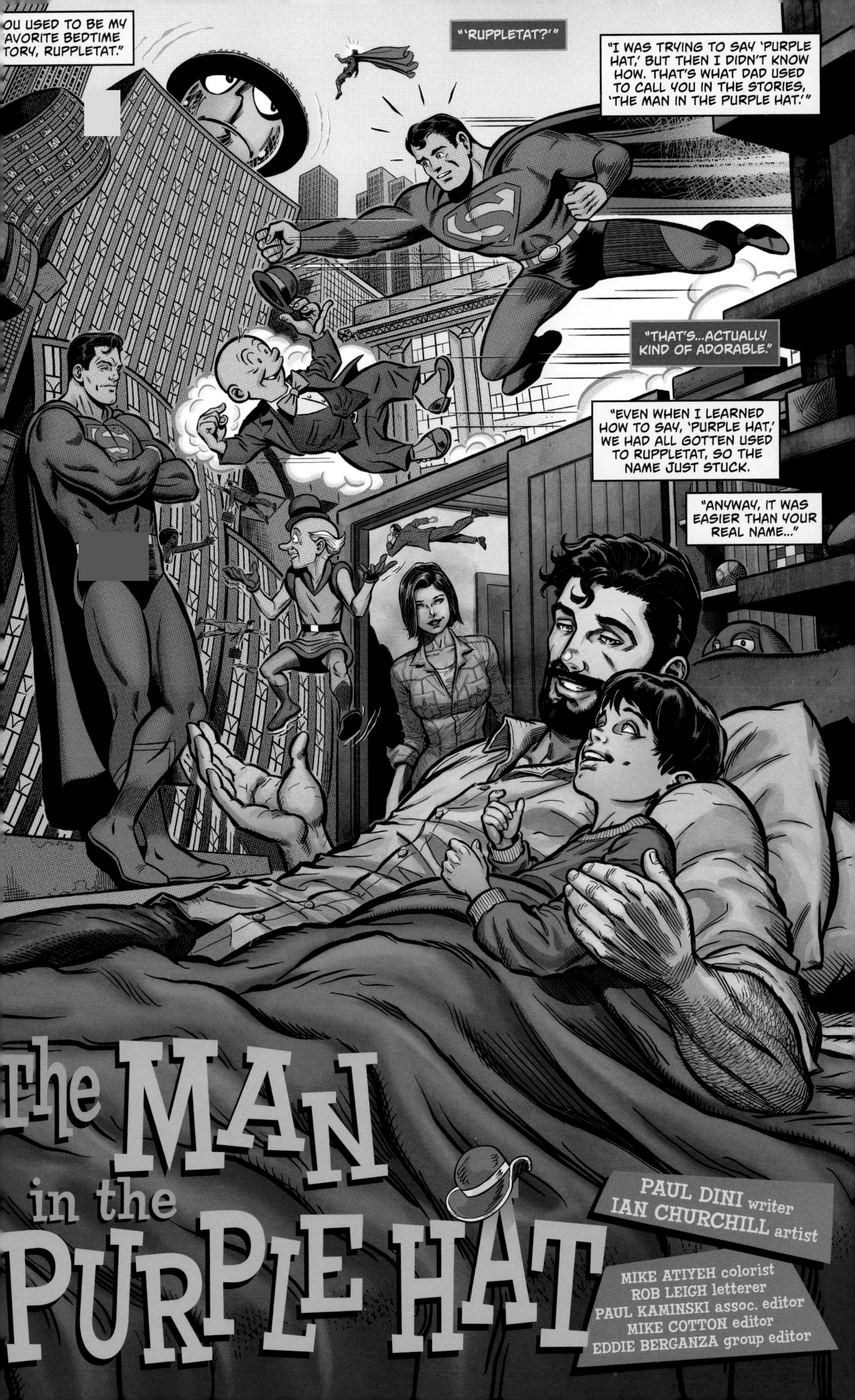
OU USED TO BE MY AVORITE BEDTIME TORY, RUPPLETAT."
"'RUPPLETAT?'"
"I WAS TRYING TO SAY 'PURPLE HAT,' BUT THEN I DIDN'T KNOW HOW. THAT'S WHAT DAD USED TO CALL YOU IN THE STORIES, 'THE MAN IN THE PURPLE HAT.'"
"THAT'S...ACTUALLY KIND OF ADORABLE."
"EVEN WHEN I LEARNED HOW TO SAY, 'PURPLE HAT,' WE HAD ALL GOTTEN USED TO RUPPLETAT, SO THE NAME JUST STUCK.
"ANYWAY, IT WAS EASIER THAN YOUR REAL NAME..."
The MAN in the PURPLE HAT
PAUL DINI writer
IAN CHURCHILL artist
MIKE ATIYEH colorist
ROB LEIGH letterer
PAUL KAMINSKI assoc. editor
MIKE COTTON editor
EDDIE BERGANZA group editor

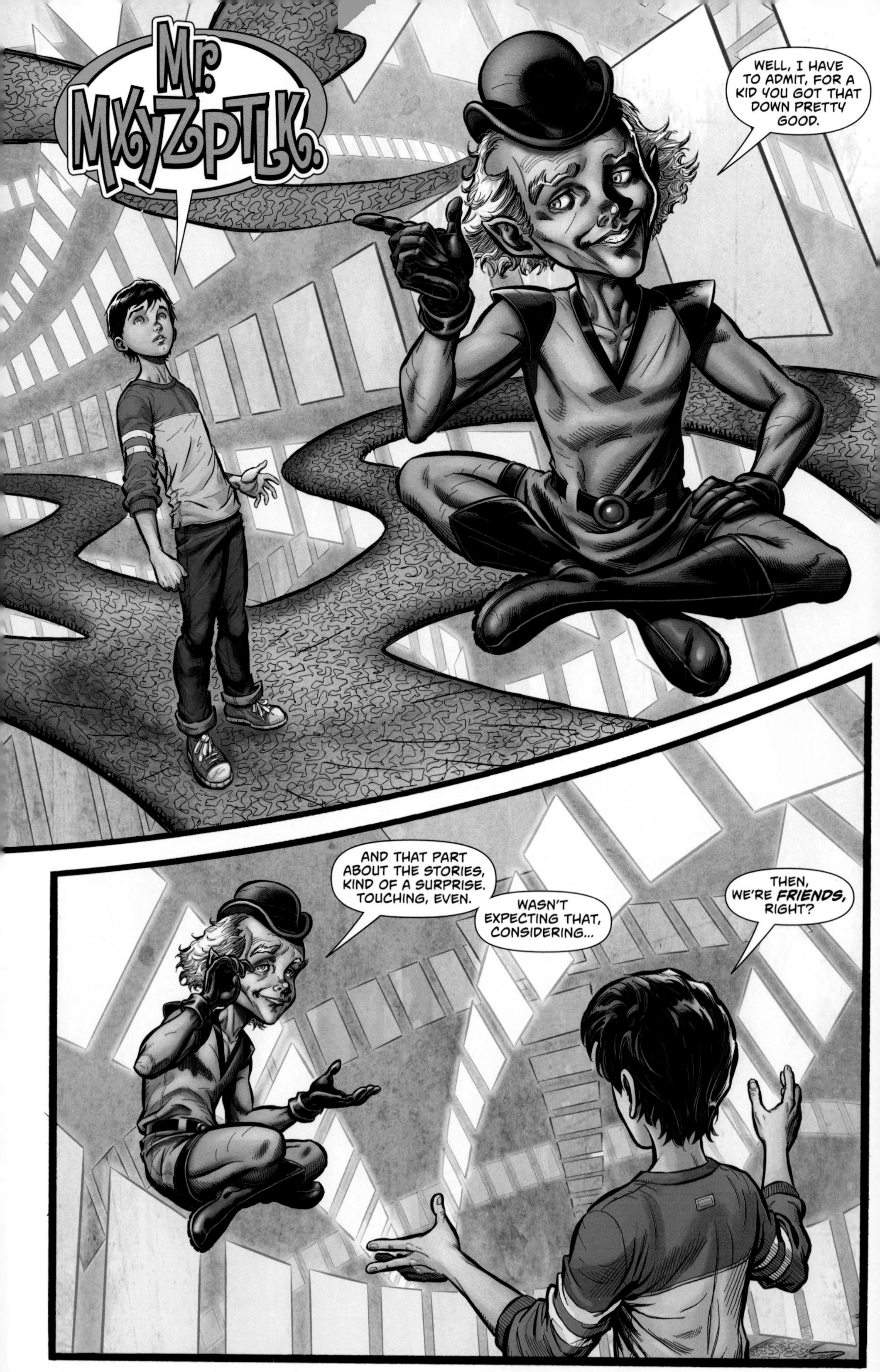

Mr. MXYZPTLK.
WELL, I HAVE TO ADMIT, FOR A KID YOU GOT THAT DOWN PRETTY GOOD.
AND THAT PART ABOUT THE STORIES, KIND OF A SURPRISE. TOUCHING, EVEN.
WASN'T EXPECTING THAT, CONSIDERING...
THEN, WE'RE *FRIENDS,* RIGHT?

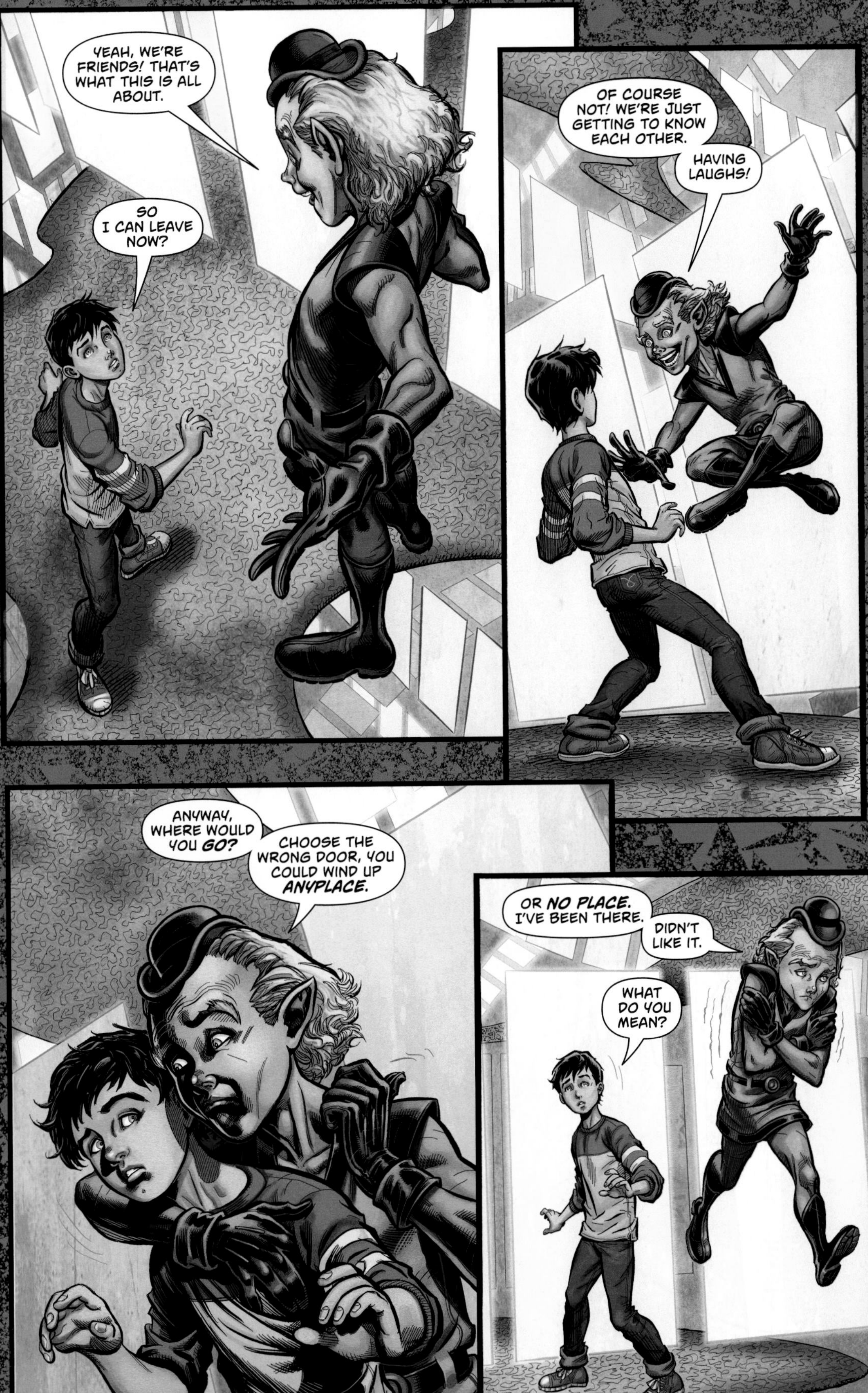
YEAH, WE'RE FRIENDS! THAT'S WHAT THIS IS ALL ABOUT.
SO I CAN LEAVE NOW?
OF COURSE NOT! WE'RE JUST GETTING TO KNOW EACH OTHER.
HAVING LAUGHS!
ANYWAY, WHERE WOULD YOU *GO?*
CHOOSE THE WRONG DOOR, YOU COULD WIND UP *ANYPLACE*.
OR *NO PLACE*. I'VE BEEN THERE.
DIDN'T LIKE IT.
WHAT DO YOU MEAN?

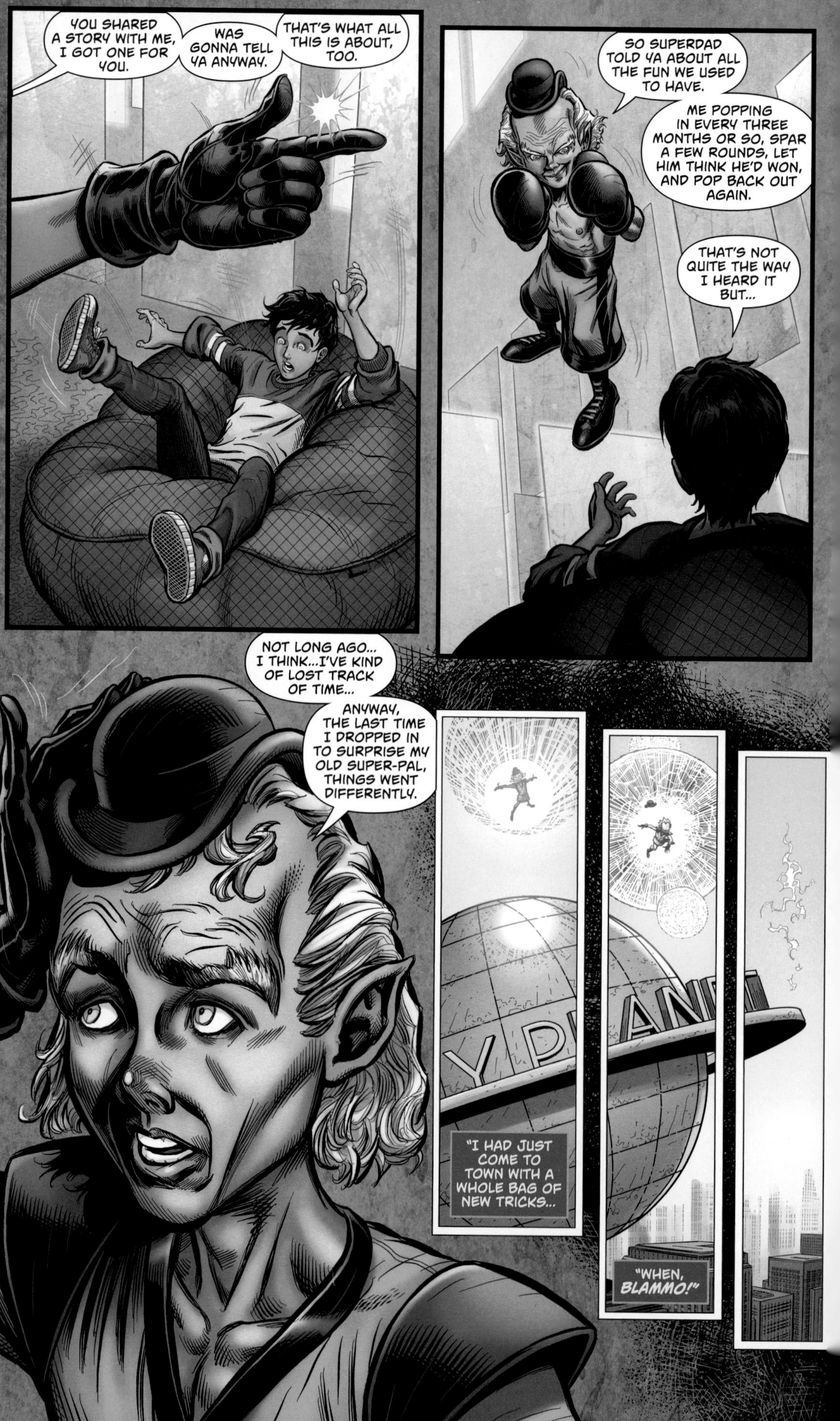

YOU SHARED A STORY WITH ME, I GOT ONE FOR YOU.
WAS GONNA TELL YA ANYWAY.
THAT'S WHAT ALL THIS IS ABOUT, TOO.
SO SUPERDAD TOLD YA ABOUT ALL THE FUN WE USED TO HAVE.
ME POPPING IN EVERY THREE MONTHS OR SO, SPAR A FEW ROUNDS, LET HIM THINK HE'D WON, AND POP BACK OUT AGAIN.
THAT'S NOT QUITE THE WAY I HEARD IT BUT...
NOT LONG AGO... I THINK...I'VE KIND OF LOST TRACK OF TIME...
ANYWAY, THE LAST TIME I DROPPED IN TO SURPRISE MY OLD SUPER-PAL, THINGS WENT DIFFERENTLY.
"I HAD JUST COME TO TOWN WITH A WHOLE BAG OF NEW TRICKS...
"WHEN, *BLAMMO!*"

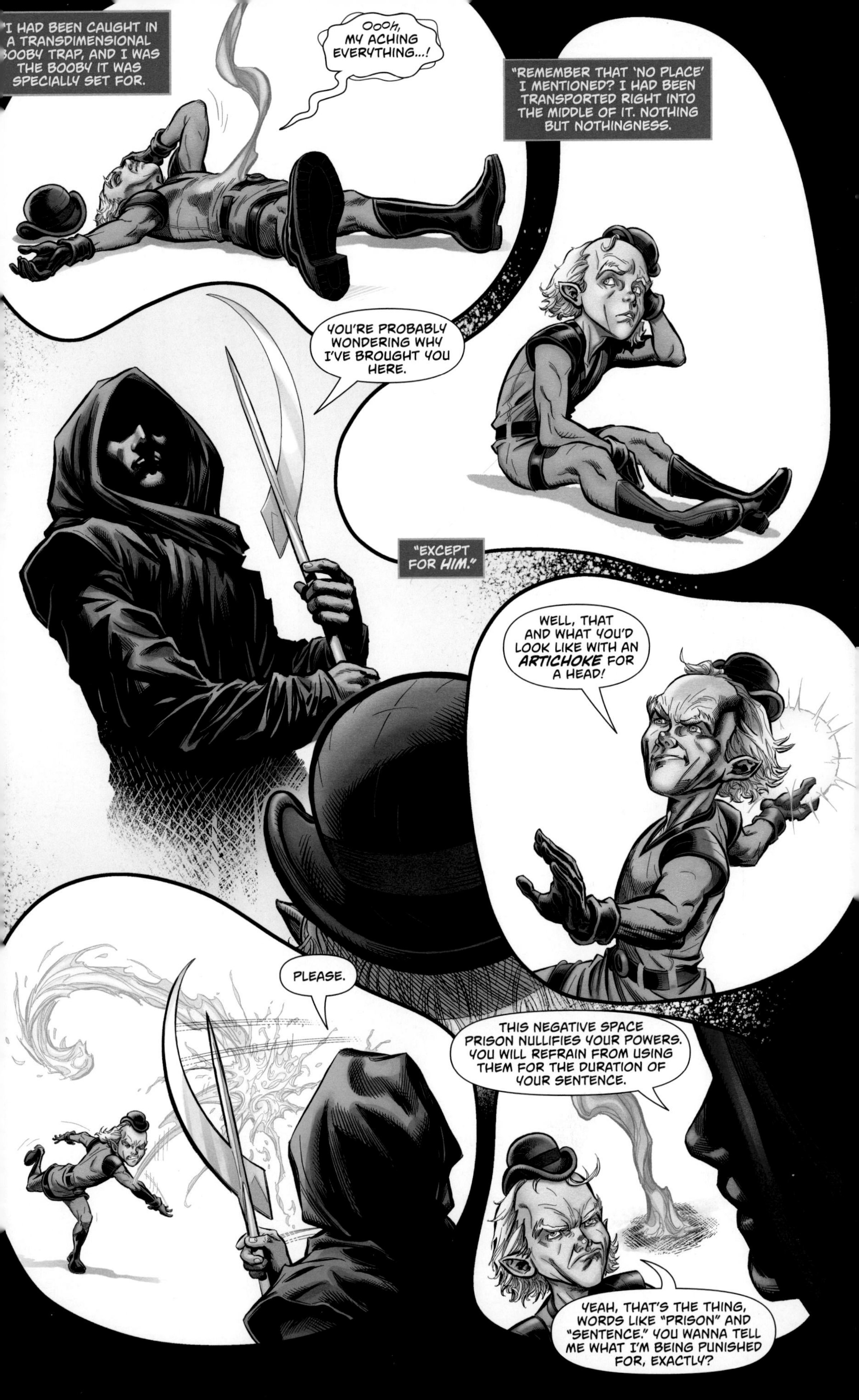
"I HAD BEEN CAUGHT IN A TRANSDIMENSIONAL BOOBY TRAP, AND I WAS THE BOOBY IT WAS SPECIALLY SET FOR.
OOOH, MY ACHING EVERYTHING...!
"REMEMBER THAT 'NO PLACE' I MENTIONED? I HAD BEEN TRANSPORTED RIGHT INTO THE MIDDLE OF IT. NOTHING BUT NOTHINGNESS.
"EXCEPT FOR HIM."
YOU'RE PROBABLY WONDERING WHY I'VE BROUGHT YOU HERE.
WELL, THAT AND WHAT YOU'D LOOK LIKE WITH AN ARTICHOKE FOR A HEAD!
PLEASE.
THIS NEGATIVE SPACE PRISON NULLIFIES YOUR POWERS. YOU WILL REFRAIN FROM USING THEM FOR THE DURATION OF YOUR SENTENCE.
YEAH, THAT'S THE THING, WORDS LIKE "PRISON" AND "SENTENCE." YOU WANNA TELL ME WHAT I'M BEING PUNISHED FOR, EXACTLY?

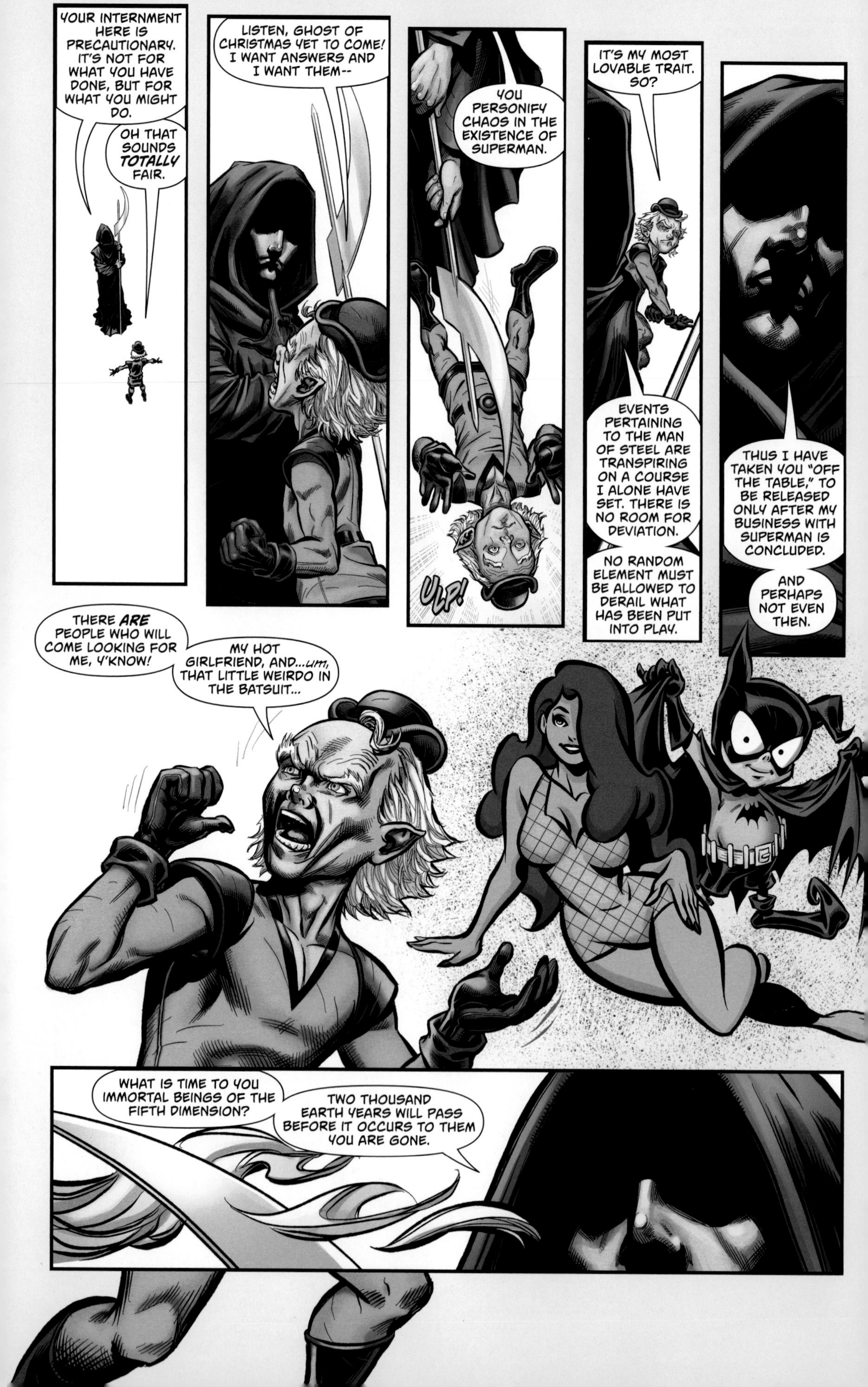
YOUR INTERNMENT HERE IS PRECAUTIONARY. IT'S NOT FOR WHAT YOU HAVE DONE, BUT FOR WHAT YOU MIGHT DO.
OH THAT SOUNDS TOTALLY FAIR.
LISTEN, GHOST OF CHRISTMAS YET TO COME! I WANT ANSWERS AND I WANT THEM--
YOU PERSONIFY CHAOS IN THE EXISTENCE OF SUPERMAN.
ULP!
IT'S MY MOST LOVABLE TRAIT. SO?
EVENTS PERTAINING TO THE MAN OF STEEL ARE TRANSPIRING ON A COURSE I ALONE HAVE SET. THERE IS NO ROOM FOR DEVIATION.
NO RANDOM ELEMENT MUST BE ALLOWED TO DERAIL WHAT HAS BEEN PUT INTO PLAY.
THUS I HAVE TAKEN YOU "OFF THE TABLE," TO BE RELEASED ONLY AFTER MY BUSINESS WITH SUPERMAN IS CONCLUDED.
AND PERHAPS NOT EVEN THEN.
THERE ARE PEOPLE WHO WILL COME LOOKING FOR ME, Y'KNOW!
MY HOT GIRLFRIEND, AND...UM, THAT LITTLE WEIRDO IN THE BATSUIT...
WHAT IS TIME TO YOU IMMORTAL BEINGS OF THE FIFTH DIMENSION?
TWO THOUSAND EARTH YEARS WILL PASS BEFORE IT OCCURS TO THEM YOU ARE GONE.

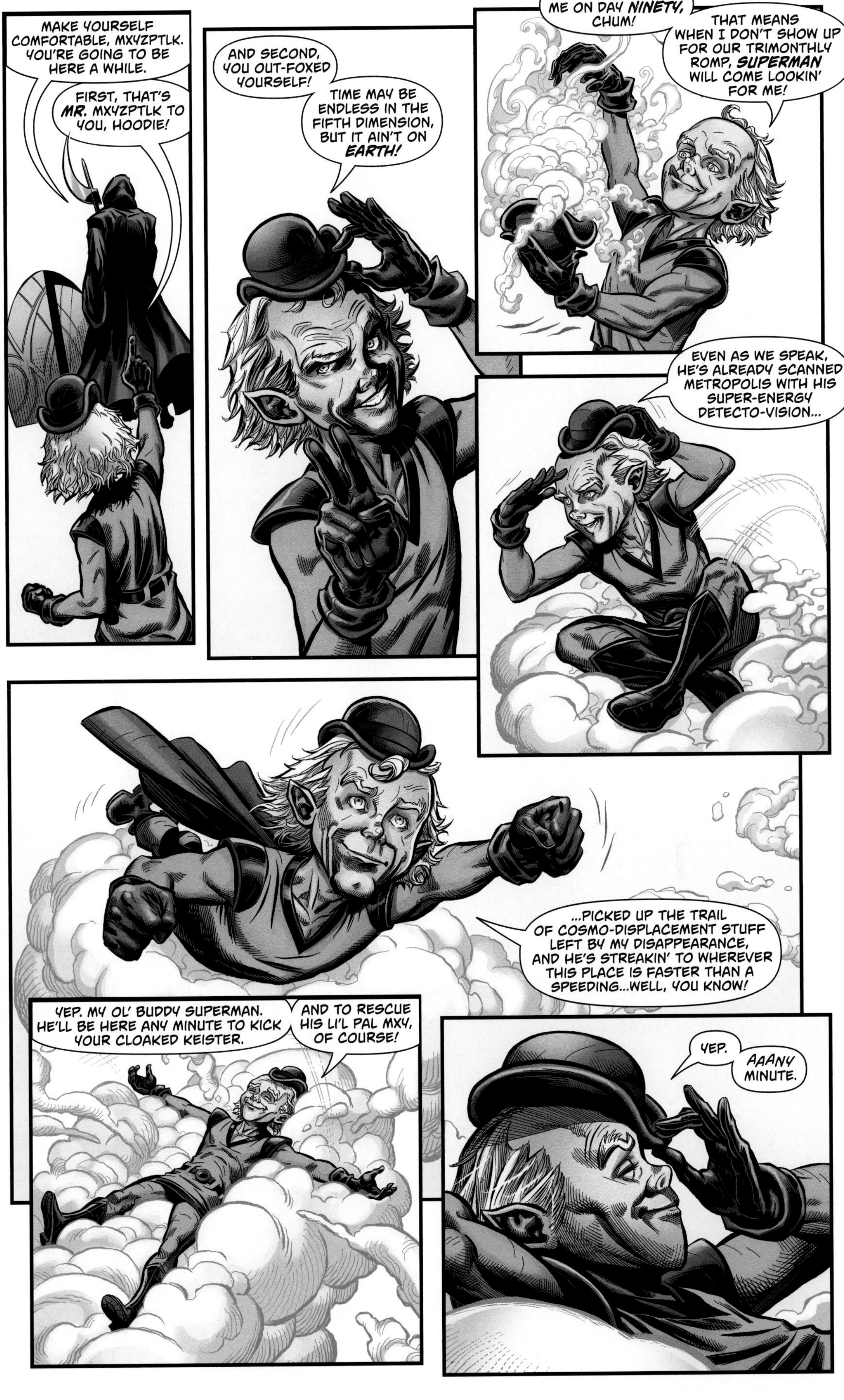
MAKE YOURSELF COMFORTABLE, MXYZPTLK. YOU'RE GOING TO BE HERE A WHILE.
FIRST, THAT'S *MR.* MXYZPTLK TO YOU, HOODIE!
AND SECOND, YOU OUT-FOXED YOURSELF!
TIME MAY BE ENDLESS IN THE FIFTH DIMENSION, BUT IT AIN'T ON *EARTH!*
YOU SNATCHED ME ON DAY *NINETY,* CHUM!
THAT MEANS WHEN I DON'T SHOW UP FOR OUR TRIMONTHLY ROMP, *SUPERMAN* WILL COME LOOKIN' FOR ME!
EVEN AS WE SPEAK, HE'S ALREADY SCANNED METROPOLIS WITH HIS SUPER-ENERGY DETECTO-VISION...
...PICKED UP THE TRAIL OF COSMO-DISPLACEMENT STUFF LEFT BY MY DISAPPEARANCE, AND HE'S STREAKIN' TO WHEREVER THIS PLACE IS FASTER THAN A SPEEDING...WELL, YOU KNOW!
YEP. MY OL' BUDDY SUPERMAN. HE'LL BE HERE ANY MINUTE TO KICK YOUR CLOAKED KEISTER.
AND TO RESCUE HIS LI'L PAL MXY, OF COURSE!
YEP.
AAANY MINUTE.

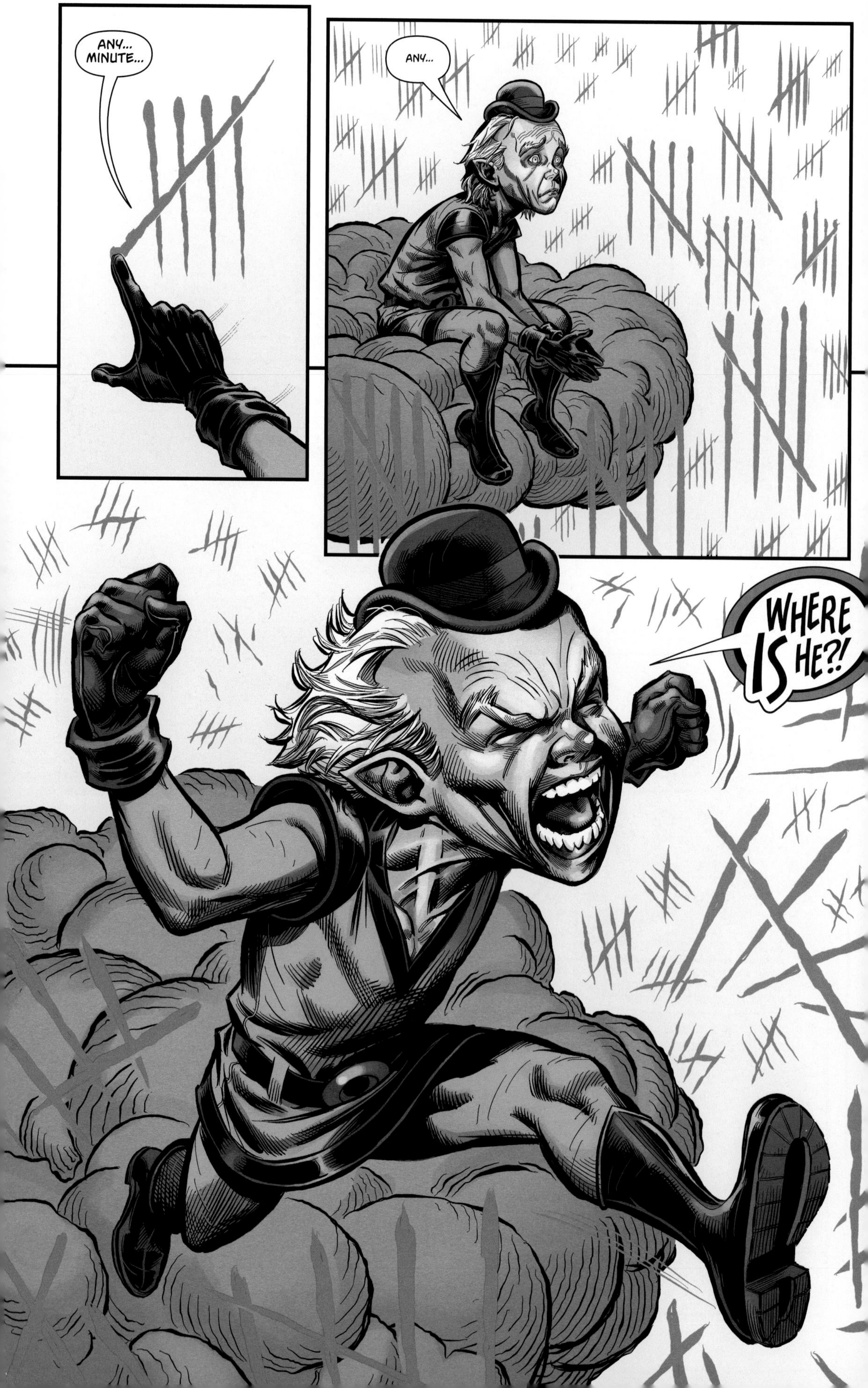
ANY... MINUTE...
ANY...
WHERE IS HE?!

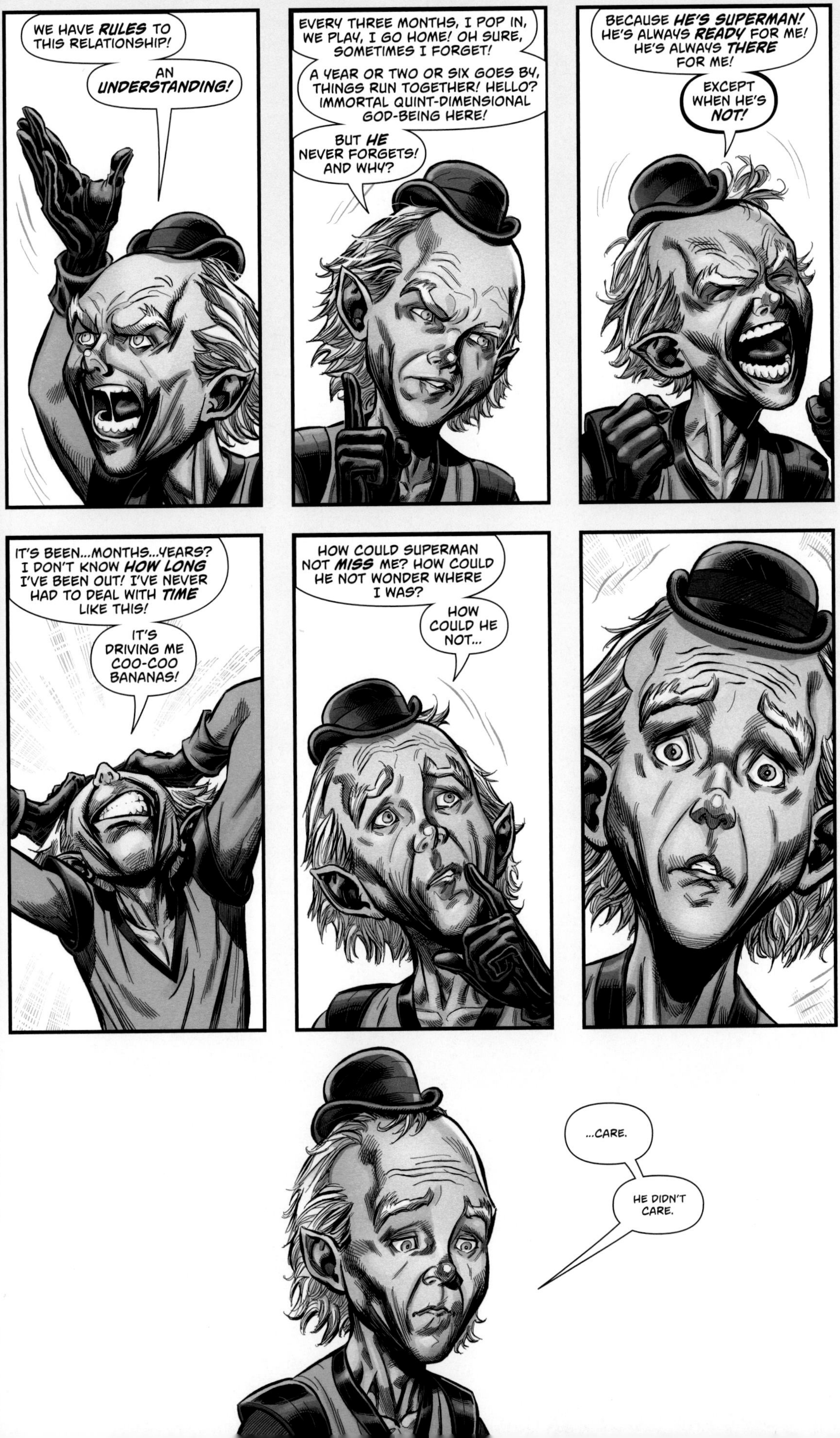
WE HAVE RULES TO THIS RELATIONSHIP!
AN UNDERSTANDING!
EVERY THREE MONTHS, I POP IN, WE PLAY, I GO HOME! OH SURE, SOMETIMES I FORGET!
A YEAR OR TWO OR SIX GOES BY, THINGS RUN TOGETHER! HELLO? IMMORTAL QUINT-DIMENSIONAL GOD-BEING HERE!
BUT HE NEVER FORGETS! AND WHY?
BECAUSE HE'S SUPERMAN! HE'S ALWAYS READY FOR ME! HE'S ALWAYS THERE FOR ME!
EXCEPT WHEN HE'S NOT!
IT'S BEEN...MONTHS...YEARS? I DON'T KNOW HOW LONG I'VE BEEN OUT! I'VE NEVER HAD TO DEAL WITH TIME LIKE THIS!
IT'S DRIVING ME COO-COO BANANAS!
HOW COULD SUPERMAN NOT MISS ME? HOW COULD HE NOT WONDER WHERE I WAS?
HOW COULD HE NOT...
...CARE.
HE DIDN'T CARE.

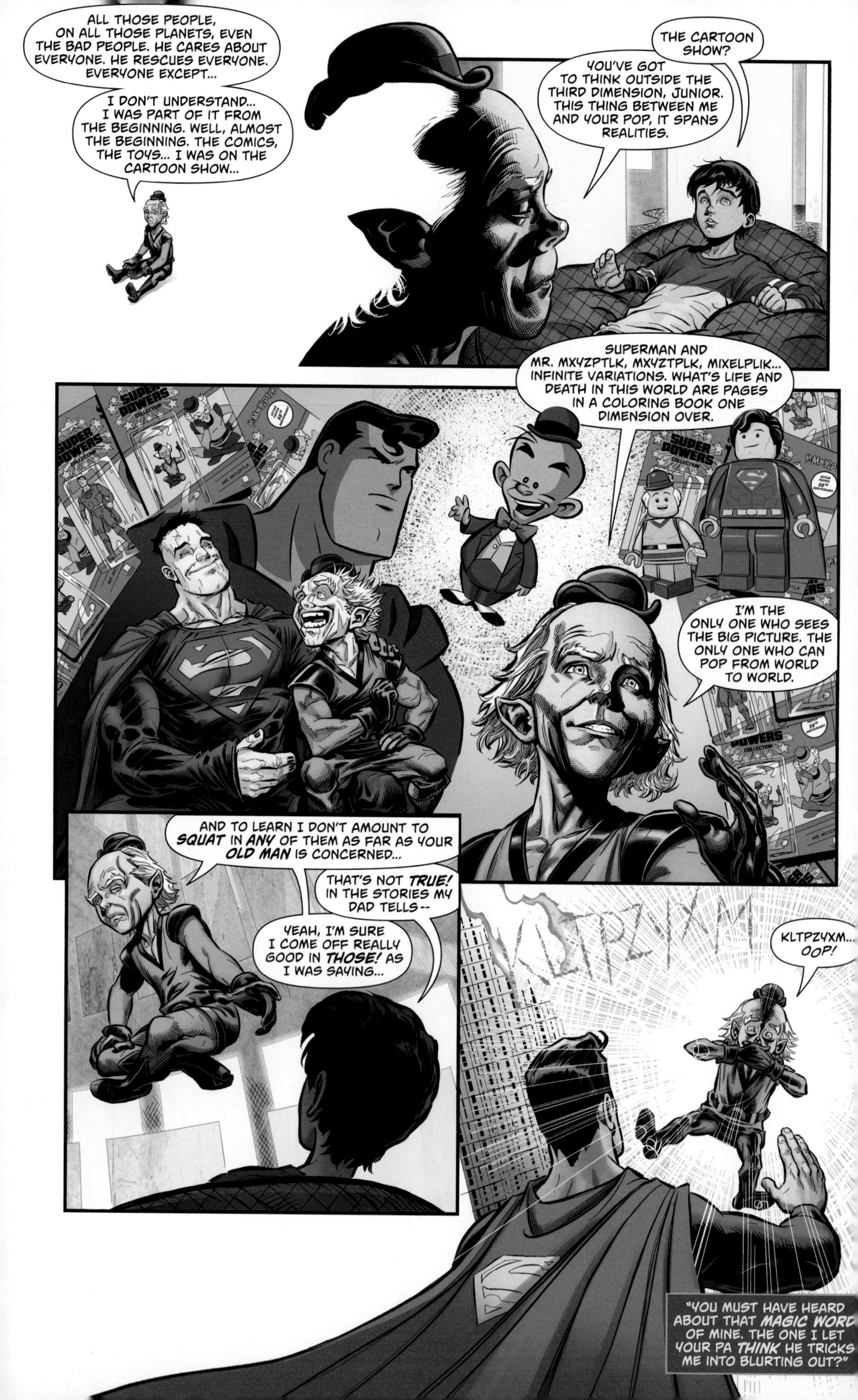
ALL THOSE PEOPLE, ON ALL THOSE PLANETS, EVEN THE BAD PEOPLE. HE CARES ABOUT EVERYONE. HE RESCUES EVERYONE. EVERYONE EXCEPT...
I DON'T UNDERSTAND... I WAS PART OF IT FROM THE BEGINNING. WELL, ALMOST THE BEGINNING. THE COMICS, THE TOYS... I WAS ON THE CARTOON SHOW...
THE CARTOON SHOW?
YOU'VE GOT TO THINK OUTSIDE THE THIRD DIMENSION, JUNIOR. THIS THING BETWEEN ME AND YOUR POP, IT SPANS REALITIES.
SUPERMAN AND MR. MXYZPTLK, MXYZTPLK, MIXELPLIK... INFINITE VARIATIONS. WHAT'S LIFE AND DEATH IN THIS WORLD ARE PAGES IN A COLORING BOOK ONE DIMENSION OVER.
SUPER POWERS COLLECTION
I'M THE ONLY ONE WHO SEES THE BIG PICTURE. THE ONLY ONE WHO CAN POP FROM WORLD TO WORLD.
AND TO LEARN I DON'T AMOUNT TO SQUAT IN ANY OF THEM AS FAR AS YOUR OLD MAN IS CONCERNED...
THAT'S NOT TRUE! IN THE STORIES MY DAD TELLS--
YEAH, I'M SURE I COME OFF REALLY GOOD IN THOSE! AS I WAS SAYING...
KLTPZYXM
KLTPZYXM... OOP!
"YOU MUST HAVE HEARD ABOUT THAT MAGIC WORD OF MINE. THE ONE I LET YOUR PA THINK HE TRICKS ME INTO BLURTING OUT?"

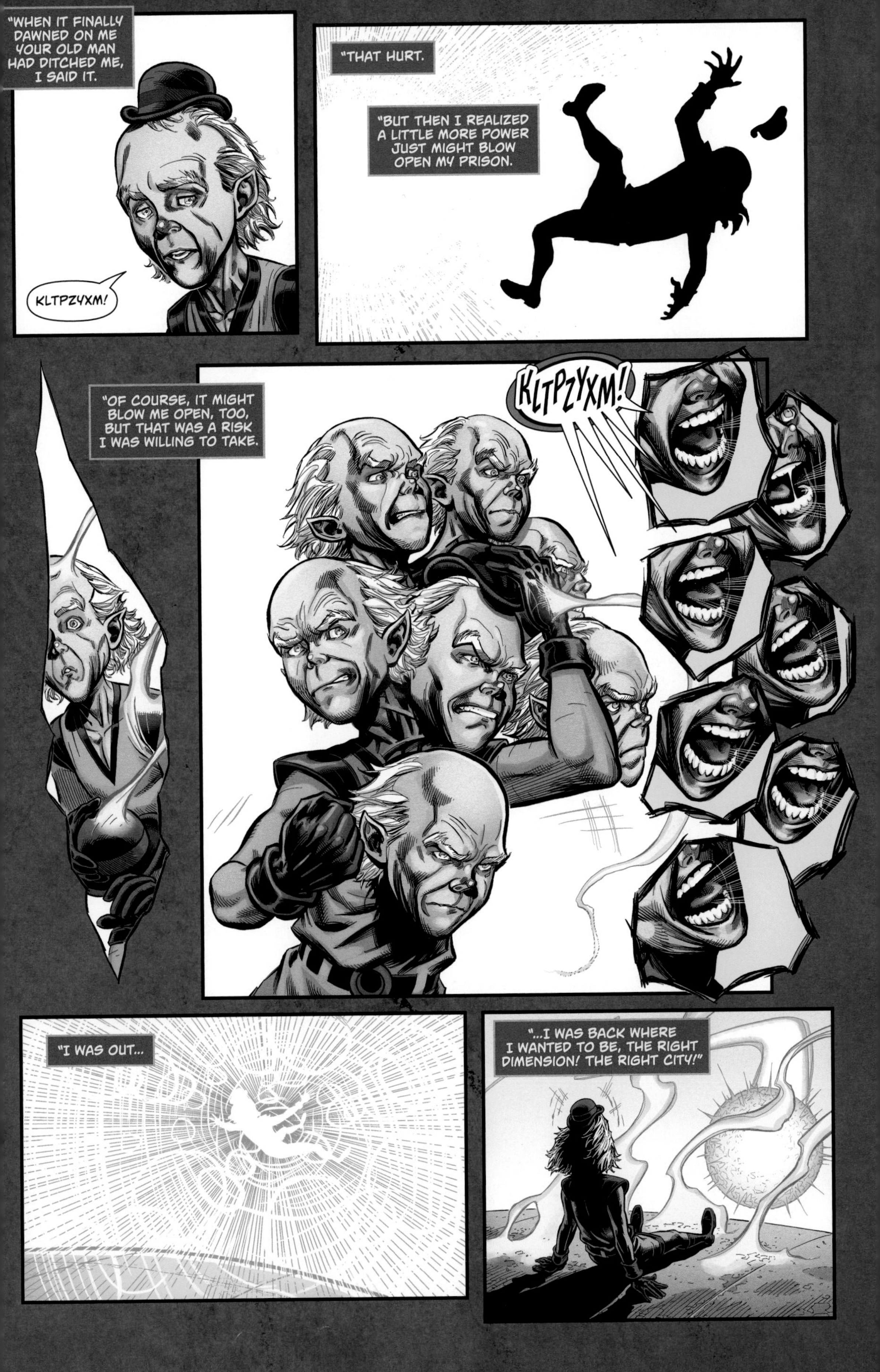
"WHEN IT FINALLY DAWNED ON ME YOUR OLD MAN HAD DITCHED ME, I SAID IT.
KLTPZYXM!
"THAT HURT.
"BUT THEN I REALIZED A LITTLE MORE POWER JUST MIGHT BLOW OPEN MY PRISON.
"OF COURSE, IT MIGHT BLOW ME OPEN, TOO, BUT THAT WAS A RISK I WAS WILLING TO TAKE.
KLTPZYXM!
"I WAS OUT...
"...I WAS BACK WHERE I WANTED TO BE, THE RIGHT DIMENSION! THE RIGHT CITY!"

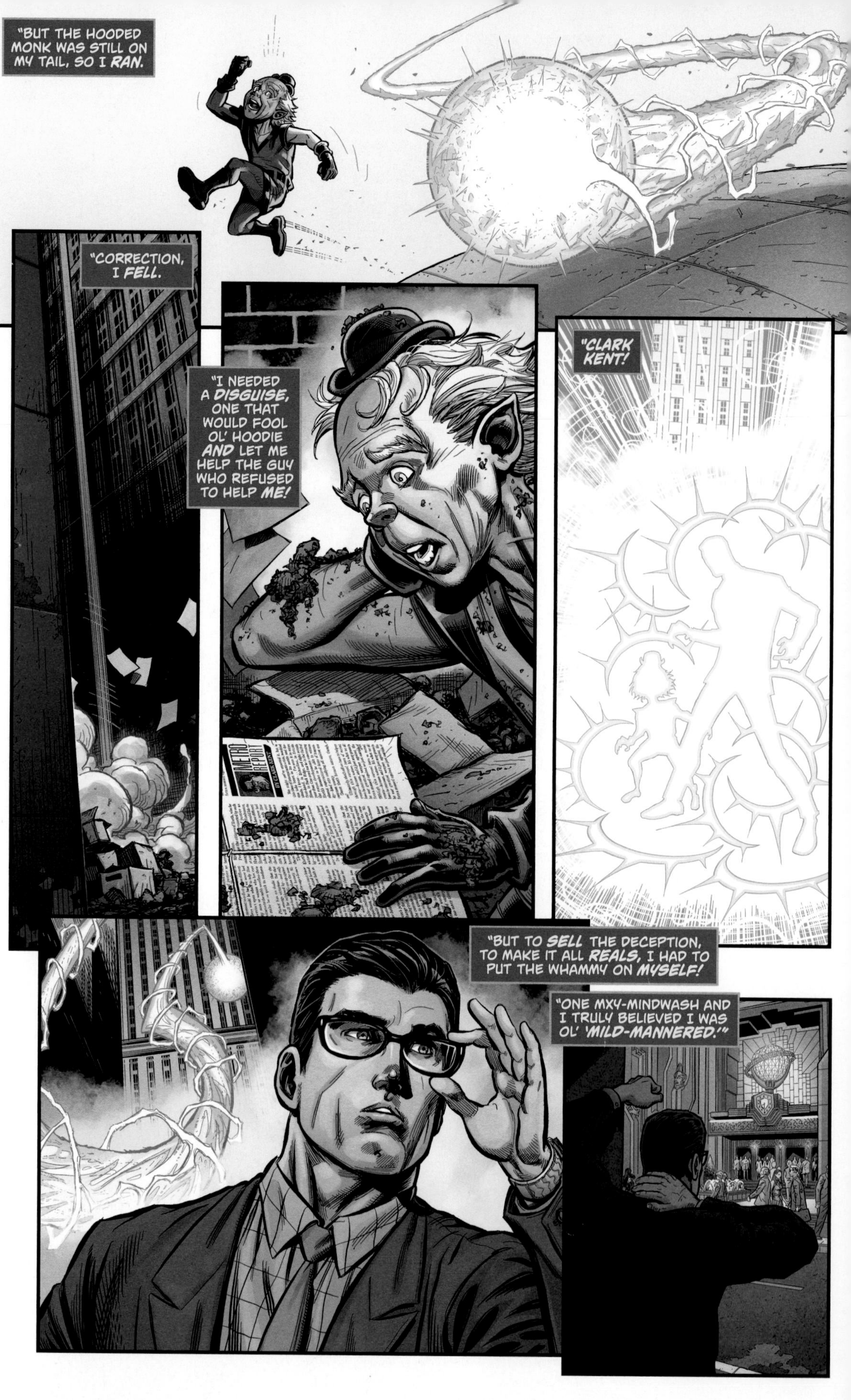
"BUT THE HOODED MONK WAS STILL ON MY TAIL, SO I RAN.
"CORRECTION, I FELL.
"I NEEDED A DISGUISE, ONE THAT WOULD FOOL OL' HOODIE AND LET ME HELP THE GUY WHO REFUSED TO HELP ME!
METRO REPORT
"CLARK KENT!
"BUT TO SELL THE DECEPTION, TO MAKE IT ALL REALS, I HAD TO PUT THE WHAMMY ON MYSELF!
"ONE MXY-MINDWASH AND I TRULY BELIEVED I WAS OL' 'MILD-MANNERED.'"

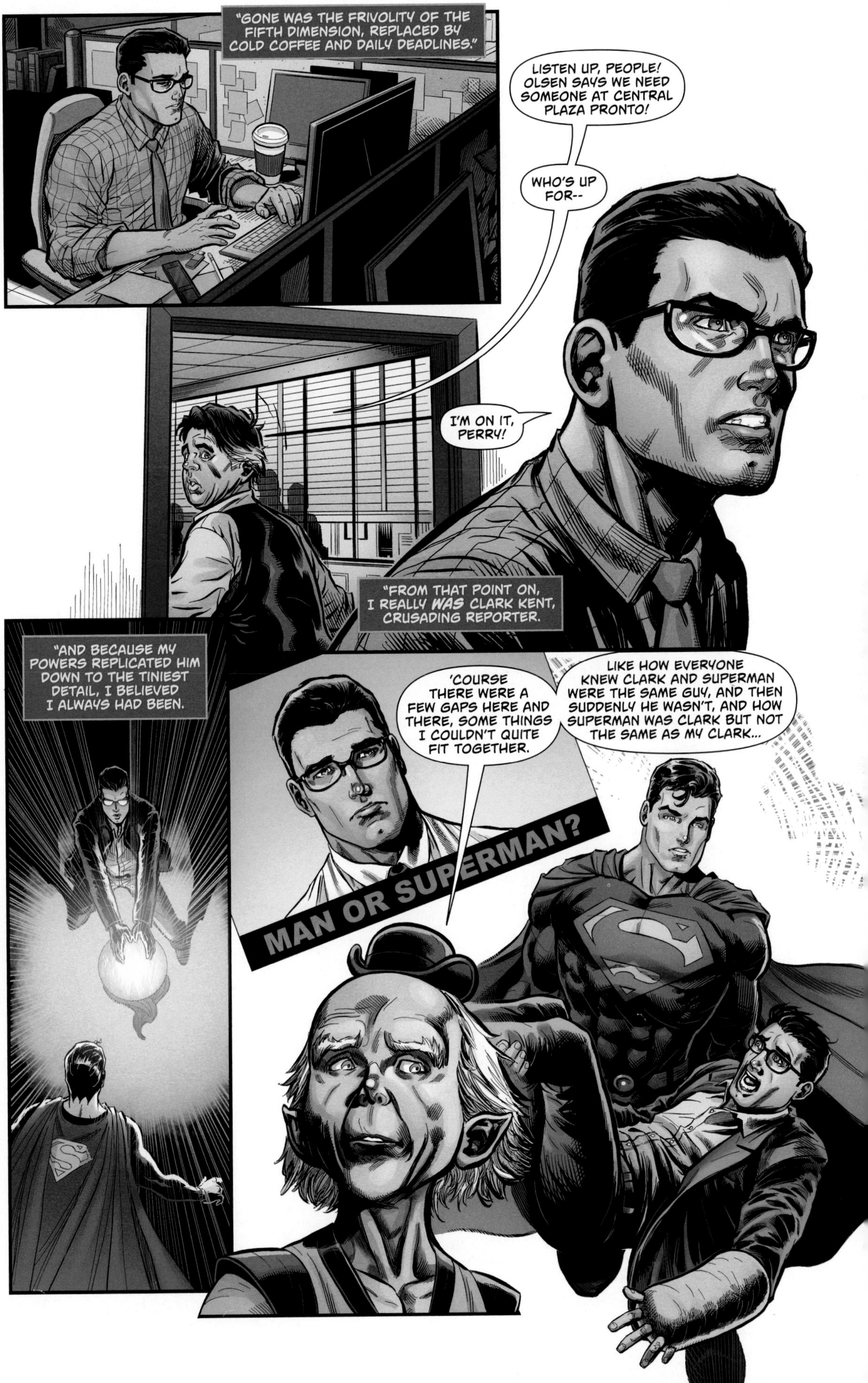
"GONE WAS THE FRIVOLITY OF THE FIFTH DIMENSION, REPLACED BY COLD COFFEE AND DAILY DEADLINES."
LISTEN UP, PEOPLE! OLSEN SAYS WE NEED SOMEONE AT CENTRAL PLAZA PRONTO!
WHO'S UP FOR--
I'M ON IT, PERRY!
"FROM THAT POINT ON, I REALLY WAS CLARK KENT, CRUSADING REPORTER.
"AND BECAUSE MY POWERS REPLICATED HIM DOWN TO THE TINIEST DETAIL, I BELIEVED I ALWAYS HAD BEEN.
'COURSE THERE WERE A FEW GAPS HERE AND THERE, SOME THINGS I COULDN'T QUITE FIT TOGETHER.
LIKE HOW EVERYONE KNEW CLARK AND SUPERMAN WERE THE SAME GUY, AND THEN SUDDENLY HE WASN'T, AND HOW SUPERMAN WAS CLARK BUT NOT THE SAME AS MY CLARK...
MAN OR SUPERMAN?

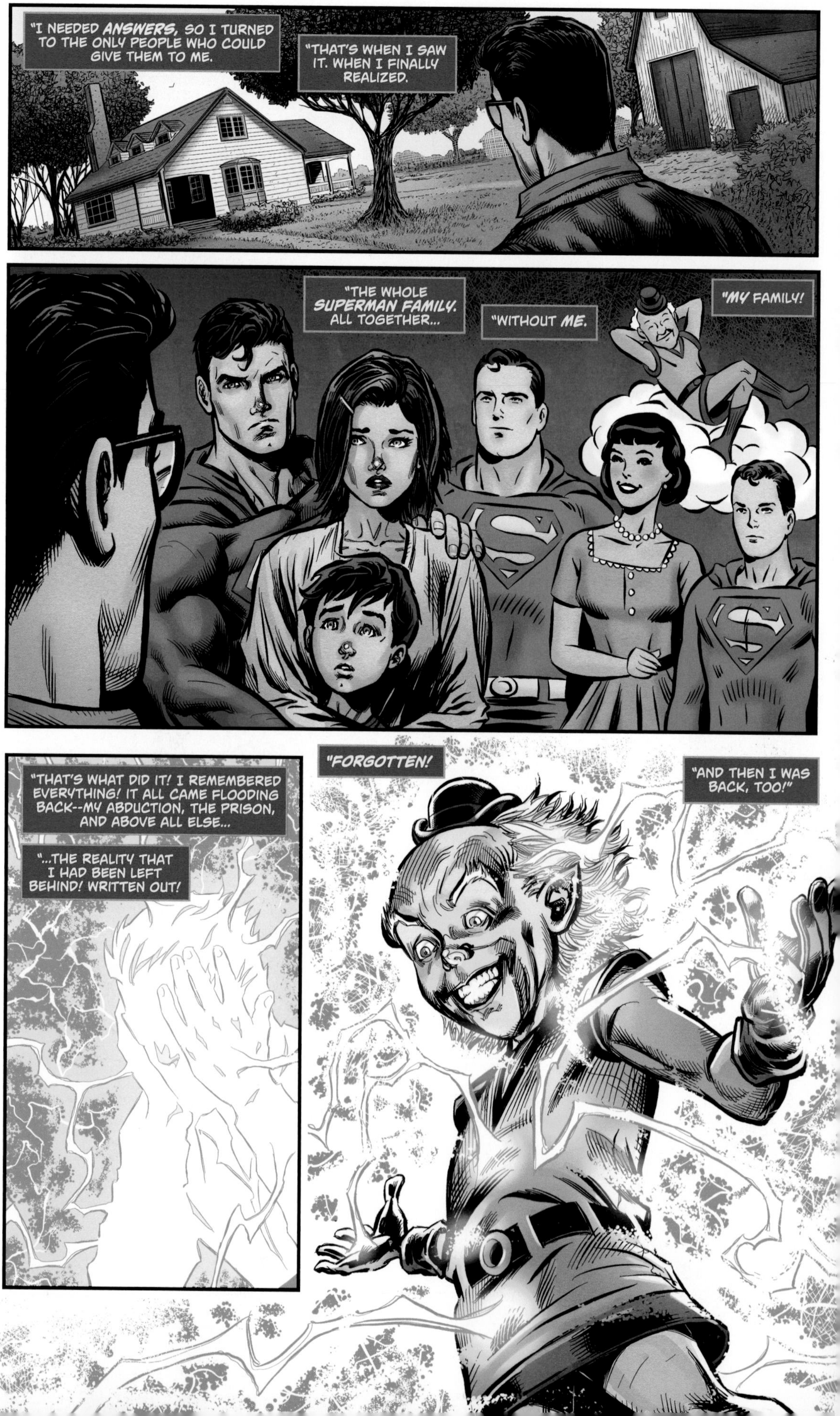
"I NEEDED ANSWERS, SO I TURNED TO THE ONLY PEOPLE WHO COULD GIVE THEM TO ME.
"THAT'S WHEN I SAW IT. WHEN I FINALLY REALIZED.
"THE WHOLE SUPERMAN FAMILY. ALL TOGETHER...
"WITHOUT ME.
"MY FAMILY!
"THAT'S WHAT DID IT! I REMEMBERED EVERYTHING! IT ALL CAME FLOODING BACK--MY ABDUCTION, THE PRISON, AND ABOVE ALL ELSE...
"...THE REALITY THAT I HAD BEEN LEFT BEHIND! WRITTEN OUT!
"FORGOTTEN!
"AND THEN I WAS BACK, TOO!"

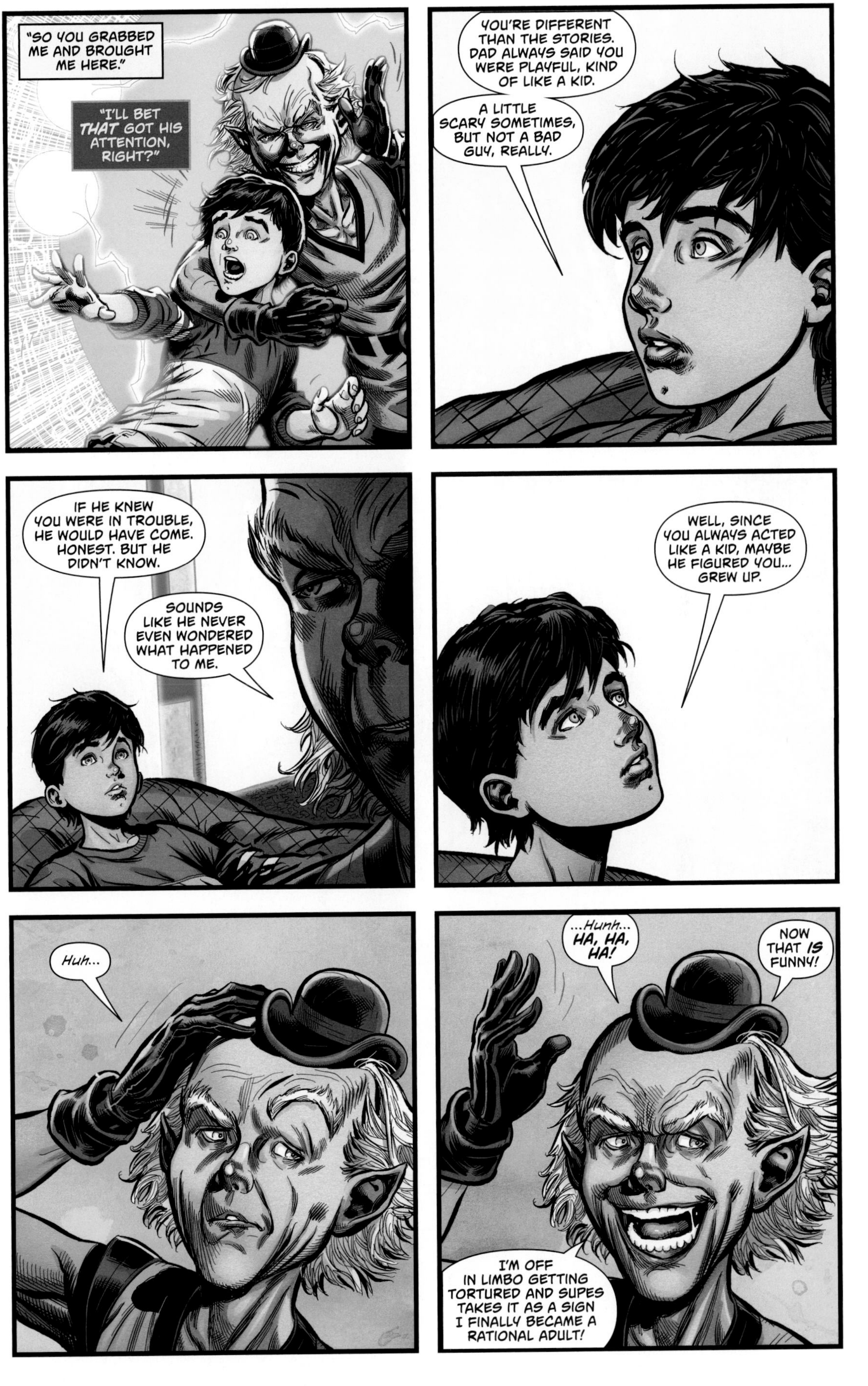
"SO YOU GRABBED ME AND BROUGHT ME HERE."
"I'LL BET *THAT* GOT HIS ATTENTION, RIGHT?"
YOU'RE DIFFERENT THAN THE STORIES. DAD ALWAYS SAID YOU WERE PLAYFUL, KIND OF LIKE A KID.
A LITTLE SCARY SOMETIMES, BUT NOT A BAD GUY, REALLY.
IF HE KNEW YOU WERE IN TROUBLE, HE WOULD HAVE COME. HONEST. BUT HE DIDN'T KNOW.
SOUNDS LIKE HE NEVER EVEN WONDERED WHAT HAPPENED TO ME.
WELL, SINCE YOU ALWAYS ACTED LIKE A KID, MAYBE HE FIGURED YOU... GREW UP.
Huh...
...Hunh... ***HA, HA, HA!***
NOW THAT ***IS*** FUNNY!
I'M OFF IN LIMBO GETTING TORTURED AND SUPES TAKES IT AS A SIGN I FINALLY BECAME A RATIONAL ADULT!

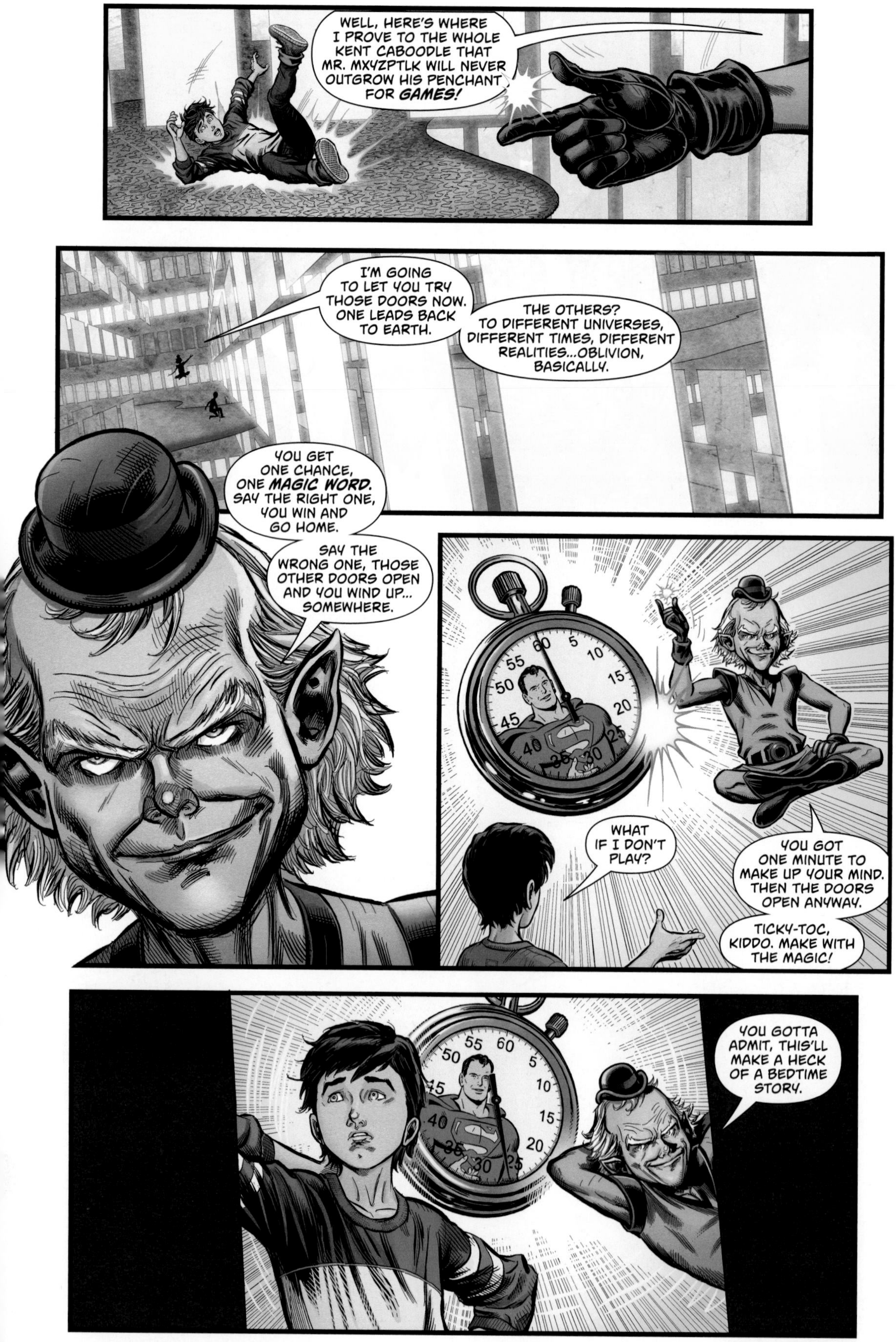
WELL, HERE'S WHERE I PROVE TO THE WHOLE KENT CABOODLE THAT MR. MXYZPTLK WILL NEVER OUTGROW HIS PENCHANT FOR GAMES!
I'M GOING TO LET YOU TRY THOSE DOORS NOW. ONE LEADS BACK TO EARTH.
THE OTHERS? TO DIFFERENT UNIVERSES, DIFFERENT TIMES, DIFFERENT REALITIES...OBLIVION, BASICALLY.
YOU GET ONE CHANCE, ONE MAGIC WORD. SAY THE RIGHT ONE, YOU WIN AND GO HOME.
SAY THE WRONG ONE, THOSE OTHER DOORS OPEN AND YOU WIND UP... SOMEWHERE.
WHAT IF I DON'T PLAY?
YOU GOT ONE MINUTE TO MAKE UP YOUR MIND. THEN THE DOORS OPEN ANYWAY.
TICKY-TOC, KIDDO. MAKE WITH THE MAGIC!
YOU GOTTA ADMIT, THIS'LL MAKE A HECK OF A BEDTIME STORY.

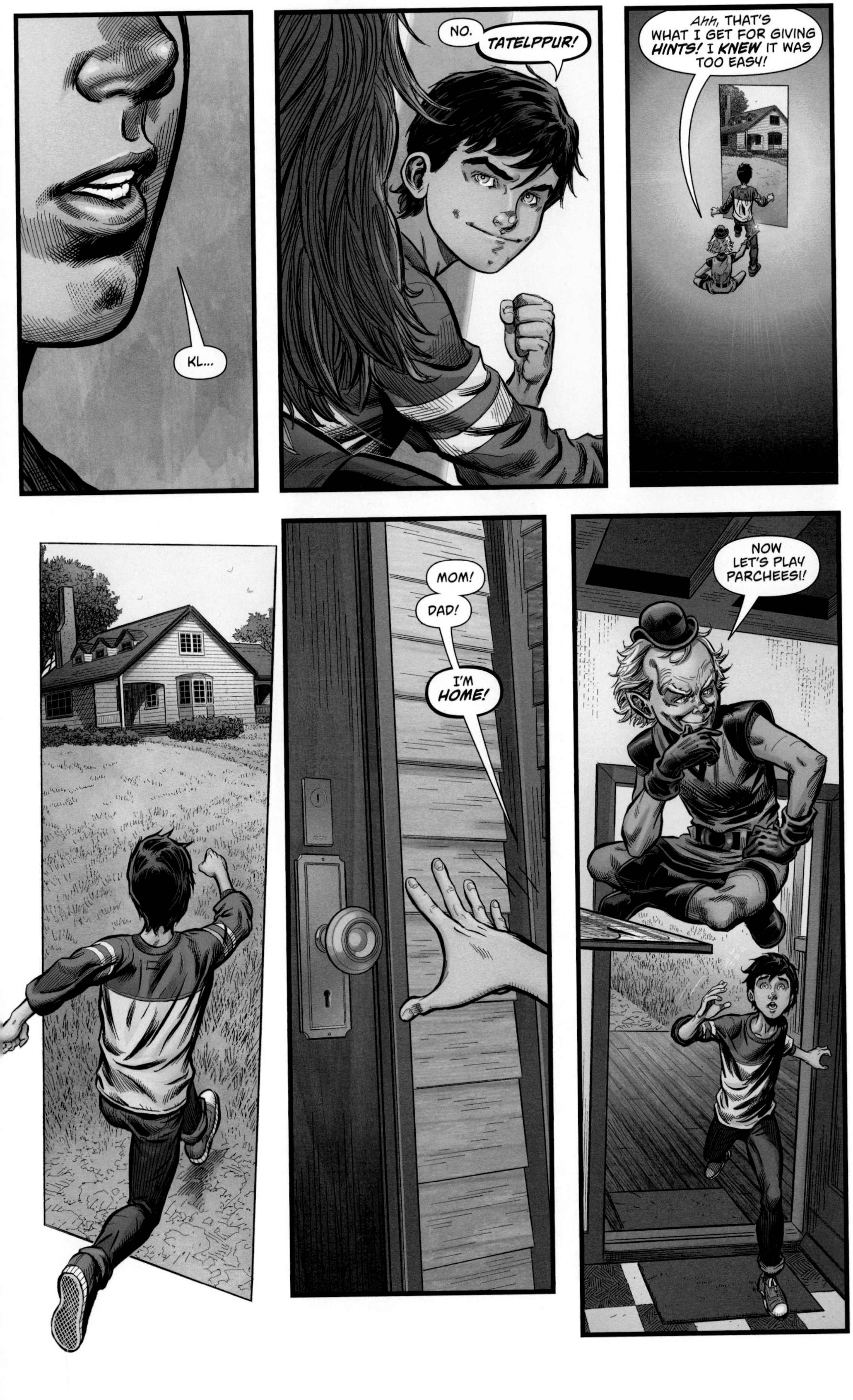
KL...
NO.
TATELPPUR!
Ahh, THAT'S WHAT I GET FOR GIVING HINTS! I KNEW IT WAS TOO EASY!
MOM!
DAD!
I'M HOME!
NOW LET'S PLAY PARCHEESI!

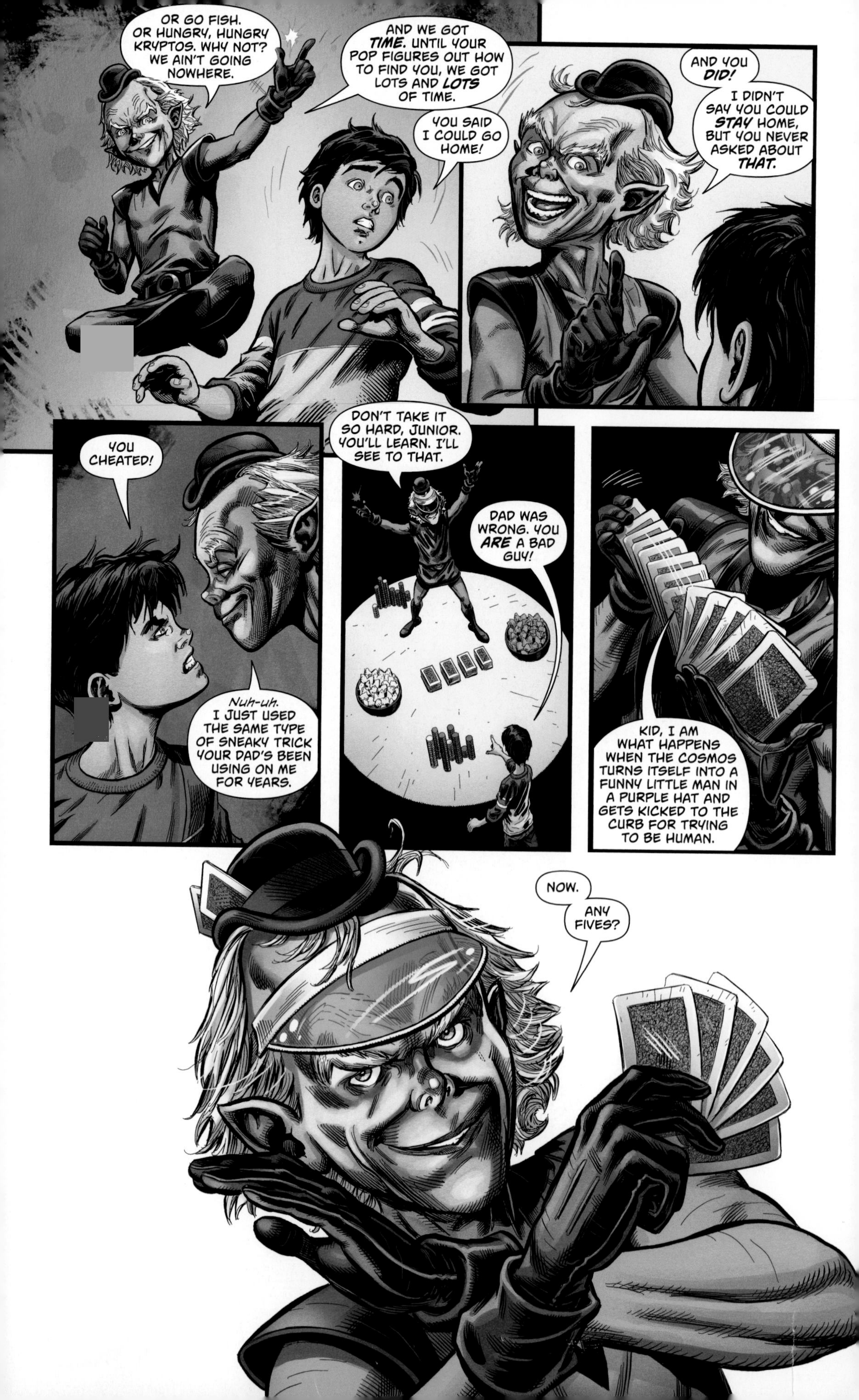
OR GO FISH. OR HUNGRY, HUNGRY KRYPTOS. WHY NOT? WE AIN'T GOING NOWHERE.
AND WE GOT TIME. UNTIL YOUR POP FIGURES OUT HOW TO FIND YOU, WE GOT LOTS AND LOTS OF TIME.
YOU SAID I COULD GO HOME!
AND YOU DID!
I DIDN'T SAY YOU COULD STAY HOME, BUT YOU NEVER ASKED ABOUT THAT.
YOU CHEATED!
Nuh-uh. I JUST USED THE SAME TYPE OF SNEAKY TRICK YOUR DAD'S BEEN USING ON ME FOR YEARS.
DON'T TAKE IT SO HARD, JUNIOR. YOU'LL LEARN. I'LL SEE TO THAT.
DAD WAS WRONG. YOU ARE A BAD GUY!
KID, I AM WHAT HAPPENS WHEN THE COSMOS TURNS ITSELF INTO A FUNNY LITTLE MAN IN A PURPLE HAT AND GETS KICKED TO THE CURB FOR TRYING TO BE HUMAN.
NOW.
ANY FIVES?

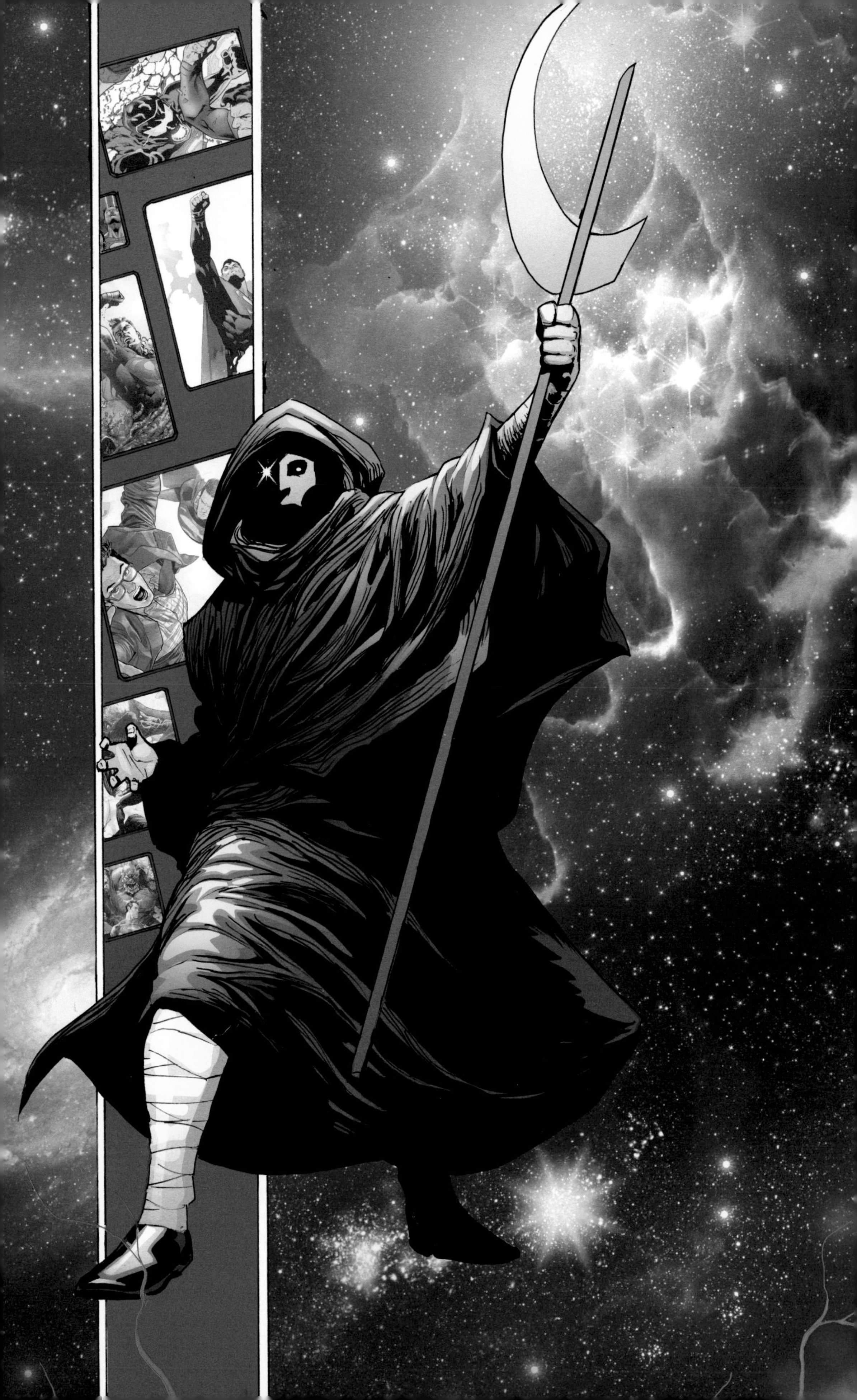

SUPERMAN: REBORN part three

PETER J. TOMASI & PATRICK GLEASON writer * PATRICK GLEASON penciller
MICK GRAY inker * JOHN KALISZ colorist
PATRICK GLEASON & JOHN KALISZ cover art

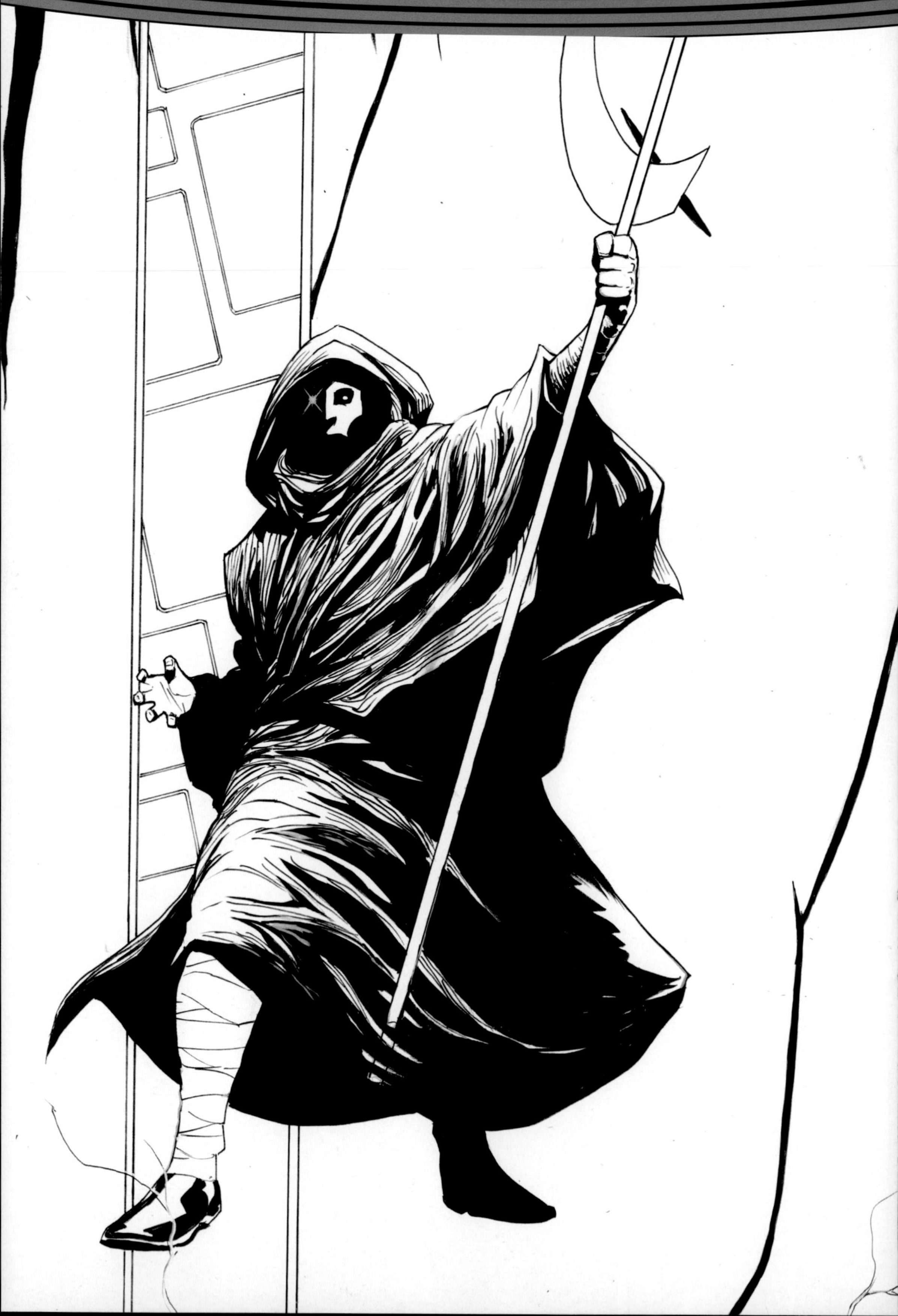

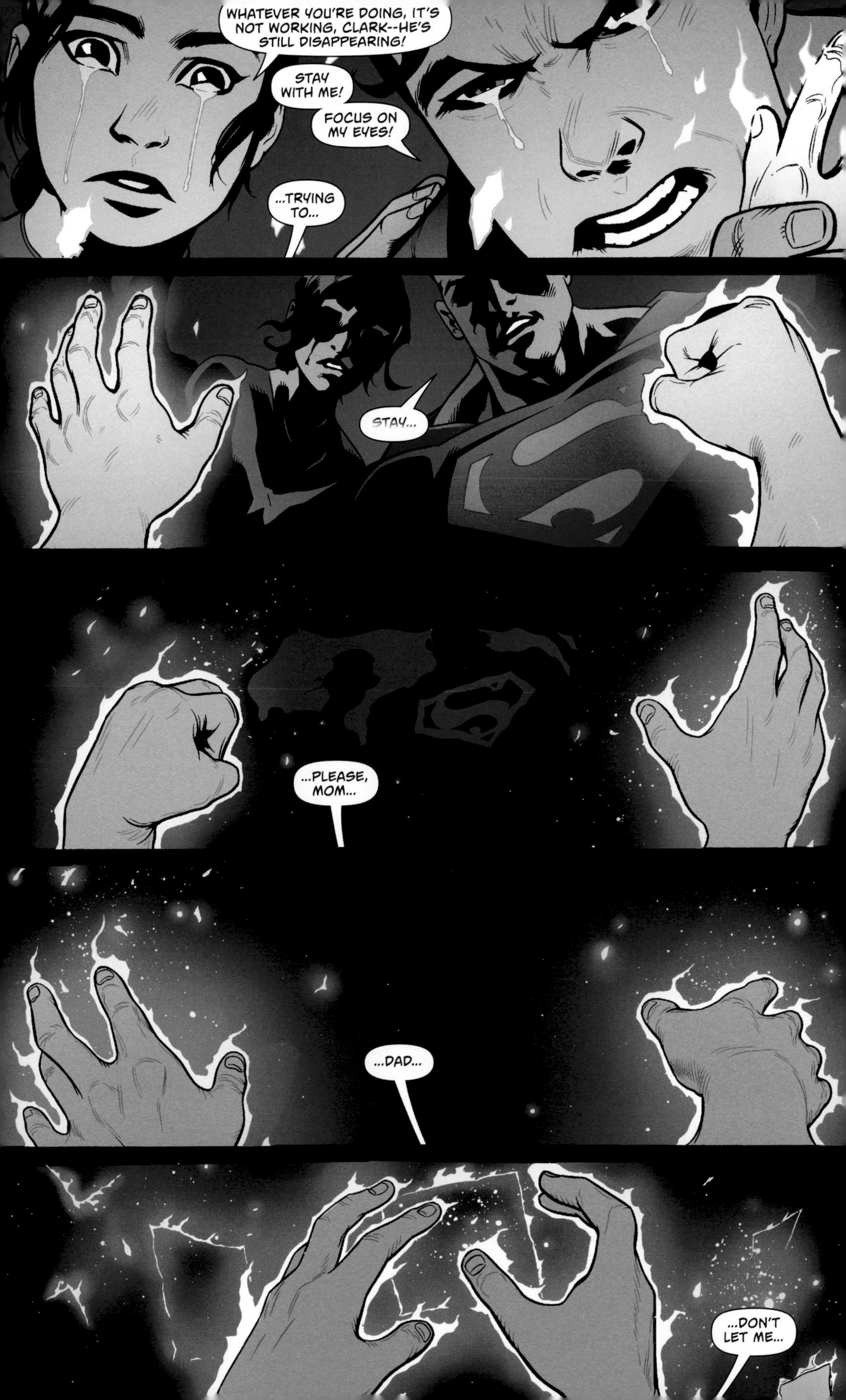
WHATEVER YOU'RE DOING, IT'S NOT WORKING, CLARK--HE'S STILL DISAPPEARING!
STAY WITH ME!
FOCUS ON MY EYES!
...TRYING TO...
STAY...
...PLEASE, MOM...
...DAD...
...DON'T LET ME...

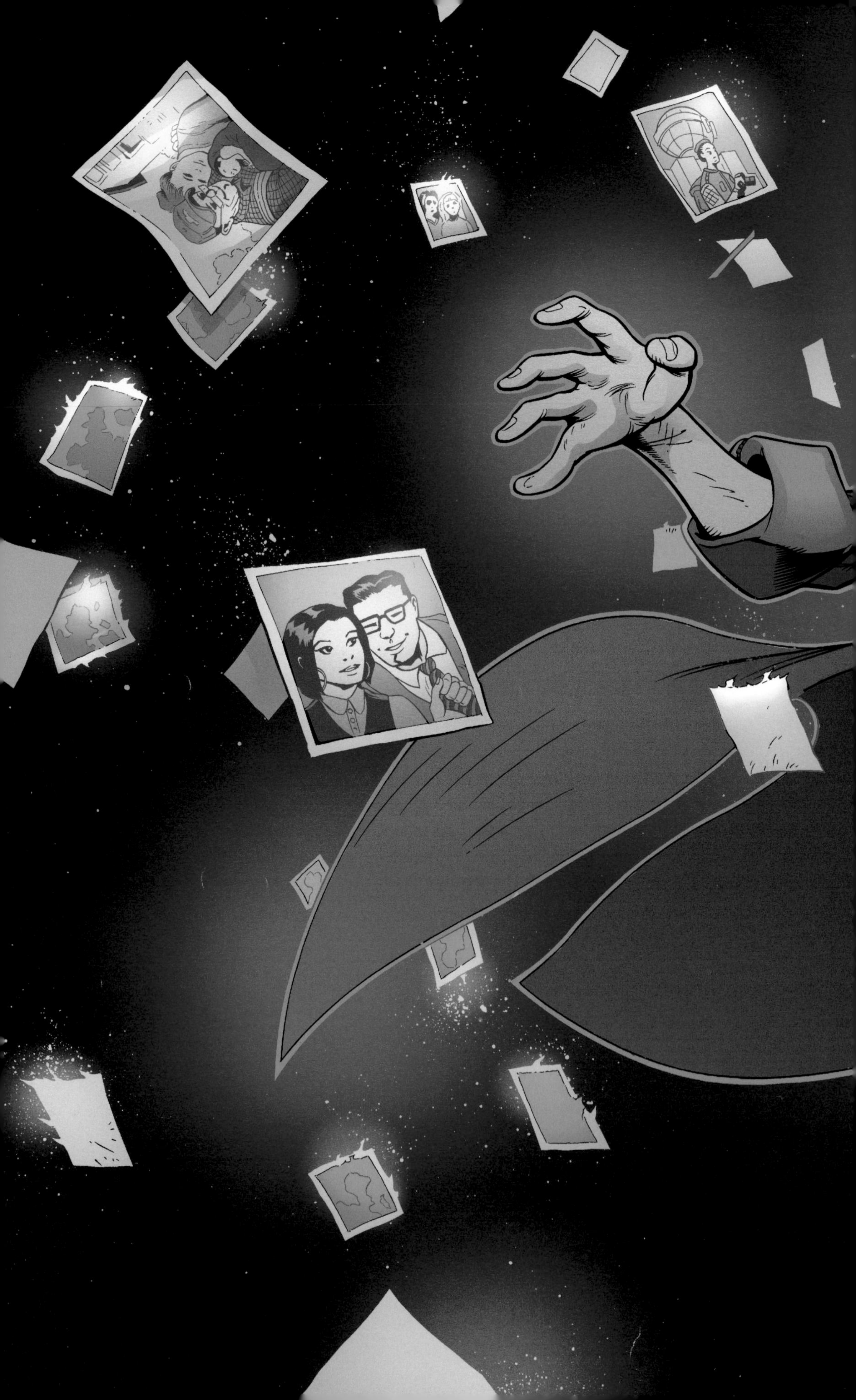

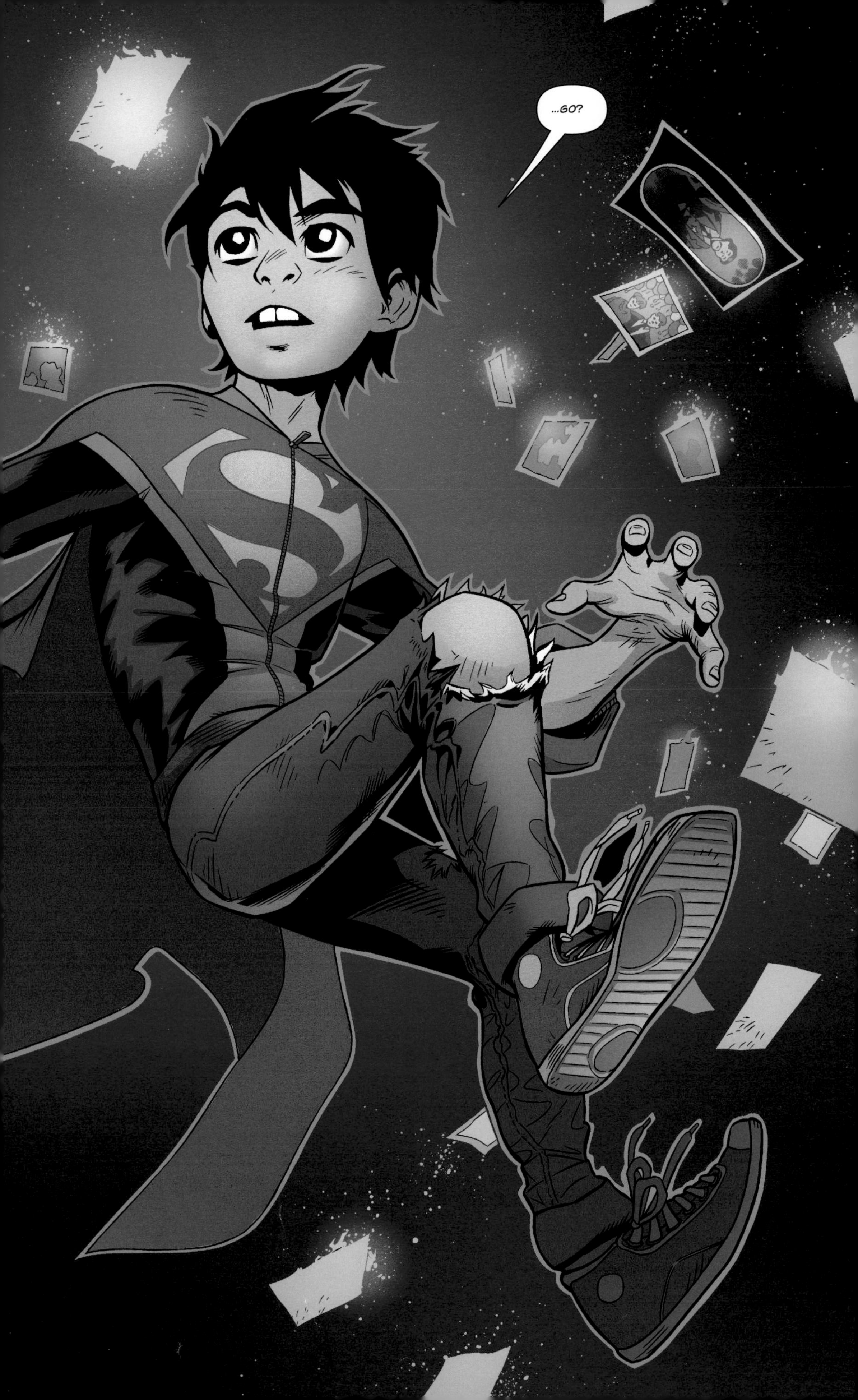
...GO?

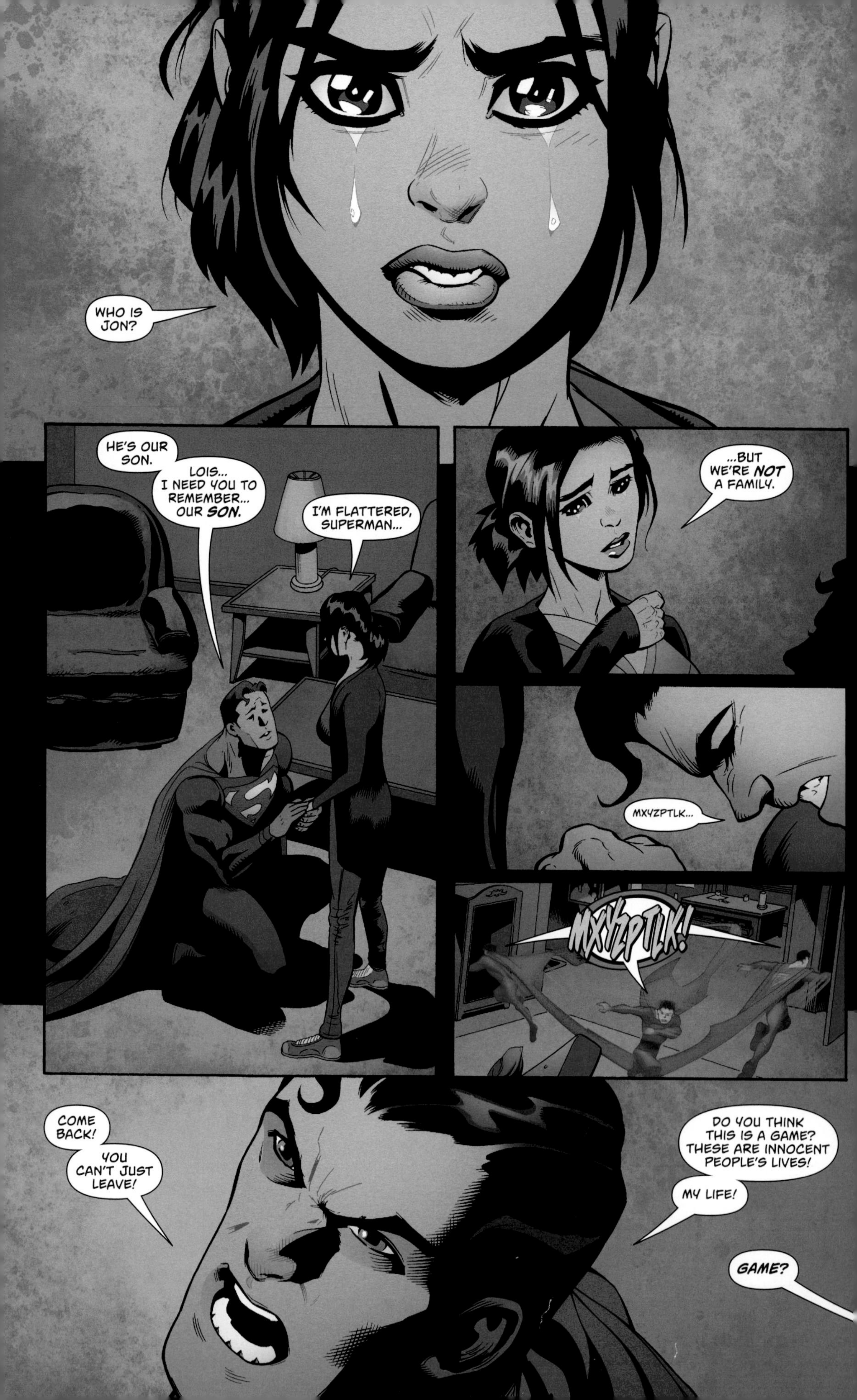
WHO IS JON?
HE'S OUR SON.
LOIS... I NEED YOU TO REMEMBER... OUR SON.
I'M FLATTERED, SUPERMAN...
...BUT WE'RE NOT A FAMILY.
MXYZPTLK...
MXYZPTLK!
COME BACK!
YOU CAN'T JUST LEAVE!
DO YOU THINK THIS IS A GAME? THESE ARE INNOCENT PEOPLE'S LIVES!
MY LIFE!
GAME?

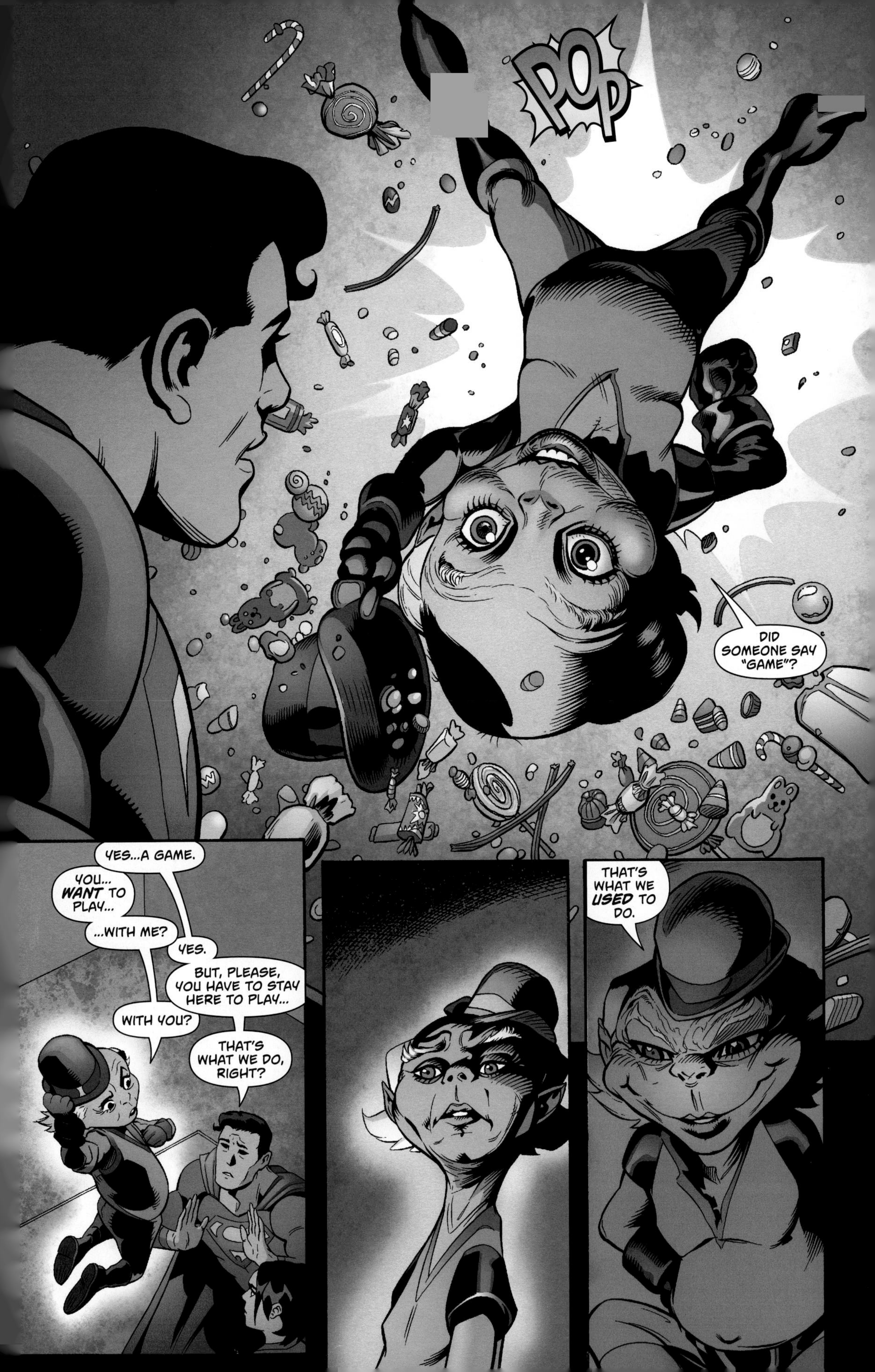
POP
DID SOMEONE SAY "GAME"?
YES...A GAME.
YOU... **WANT** TO PLAY...
...WITH ME?
YES.
BUT, PLEASE, YOU HAVE TO STAY HERE TO PLAY...
WITH YOU?
THAT'S WHAT WE DO, RIGHT?
THAT'S WHAT WE **USED** TO DO.

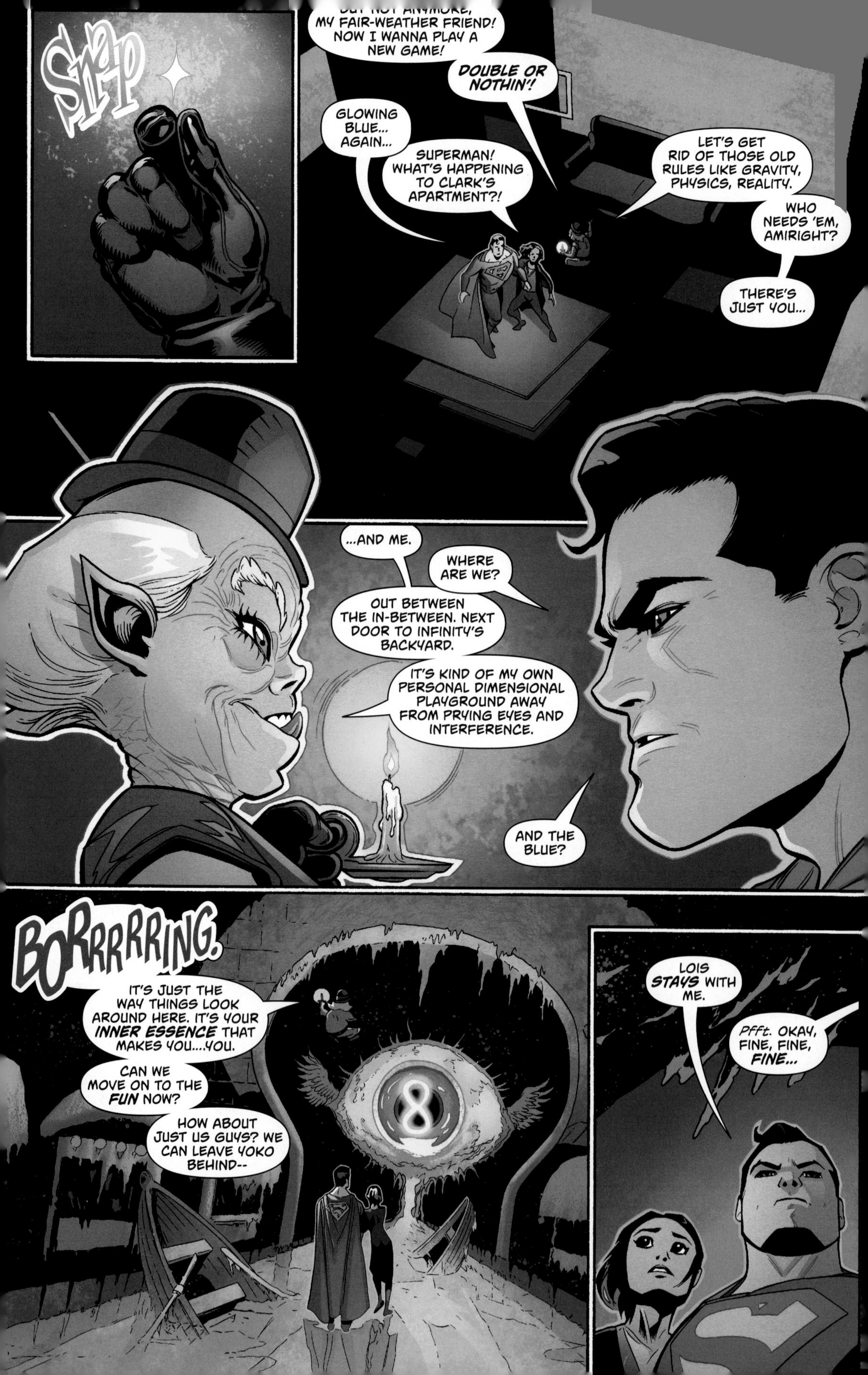
SNAP
MY FAIR-WEATHER FRIEND! NOW I WANNA PLAY A NEW GAME!
DOUBLE OR NOTHIN'!
GLOWING BLUE... AGAIN...
SUPERMAN! WHAT'S HAPPENING TO CLARK'S APARTMENT?!
LET'S GET RID OF THOSE OLD RULES LIKE GRAVITY, PHYSICS, REALITY.
WHO NEEDS 'EM, AMIRIGHT?
THERE'S JUST YOU...
...AND ME.
WHERE ARE WE?
OUT BETWEEN THE IN-BETWEEN. NEXT DOOR TO INFINITY'S BACKYARD.
IT'S KIND OF MY OWN PERSONAL DIMENSIONAL PLAYGROUND AWAY FROM PRYING EYES AND INTERFERENCE.
AND THE BLUE?
BORRRRRING.
IT'S JUST THE WAY THINGS LOOK AROUND HERE. IT'S YOUR INNER ESSENCE THAT MAKES YOU....YOU.
CAN WE MOVE ON TO THE FUN NOW?
HOW ABOUT JUST US GUYS? WE CAN LEAVE YOKO BEHIND--
LOIS STAYS WITH ME.
Pfft. OKAY, FINE, FINE, FINE...

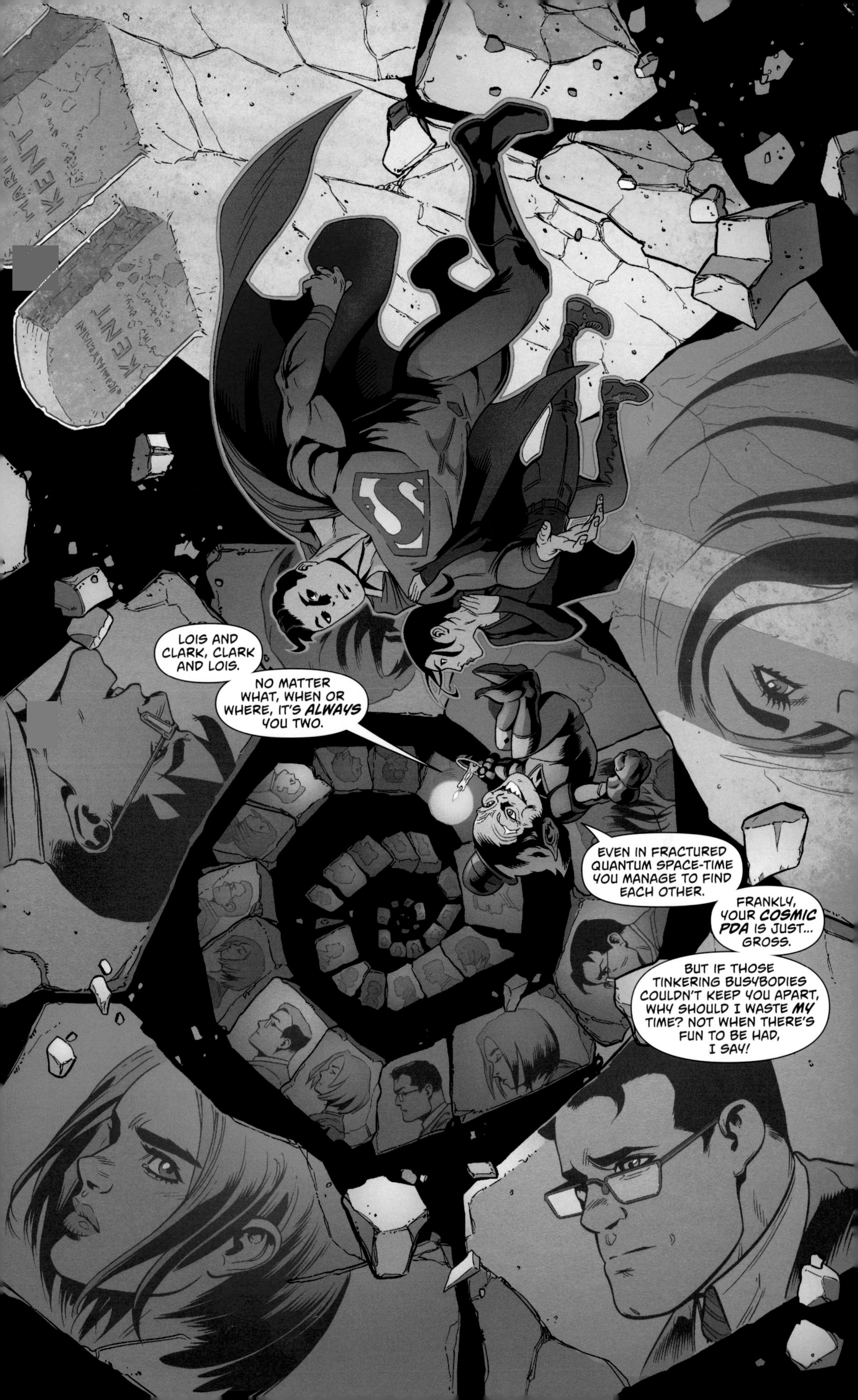
LOIS AND CLARK, CLARK AND LOIS.
NO MATTER WHAT, WHEN OR WHERE, IT'S *ALWAYS* YOU TWO.
EVEN IN FRACTURED QUANTUM SPACE-TIME YOU MANAGE TO FIND EACH OTHER.
FRANKLY, YOUR ***COSMIC PDA*** IS JUST... GROSS.
BUT IF THOSE TINKERING BUSYBODIES COULDN'T KEEP YOU APART, WHY SHOULD I WASTE *MY* TIME? NOT WHEN THERE'S FUN TO BE HAD, I SAY!

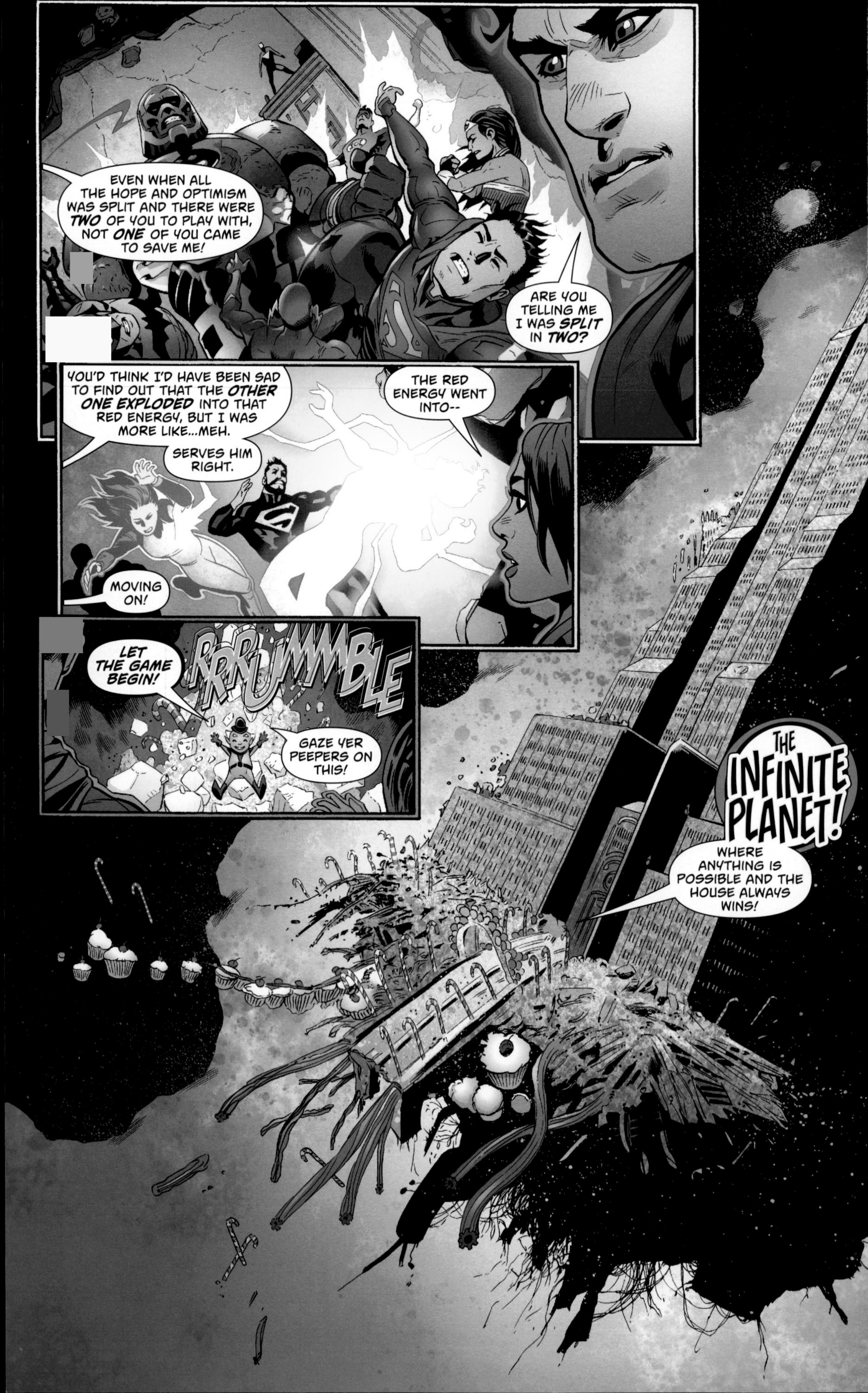
EVEN WHEN ALL THE HOPE AND OPTIMISM WAS SPLIT AND THERE WERE TWO OF YOU TO PLAY WITH, NOT ONE OF YOU CAME TO SAVE ME!
ARE YOU TELLING ME I WAS SPLIT IN TWO?
YOU'D THINK I'D HAVE BEEN SAD TO FIND OUT THAT THE OTHER ONE EXPLODED INTO THAT RED ENERGY, BUT I WAS MORE LIKE...MEH.
SERVES HIM RIGHT.
THE RED ENERGY WENT INTO--
MOVING ON!
LET THE GAME BEGIN!
RRRUMMMBLE
GAZE YER PEEPERS ON THIS!
THE INFINITE PLANET!
WHERE ANYTHING IS POSSIBLE AND THE HOUSE ALWAYS WINS!

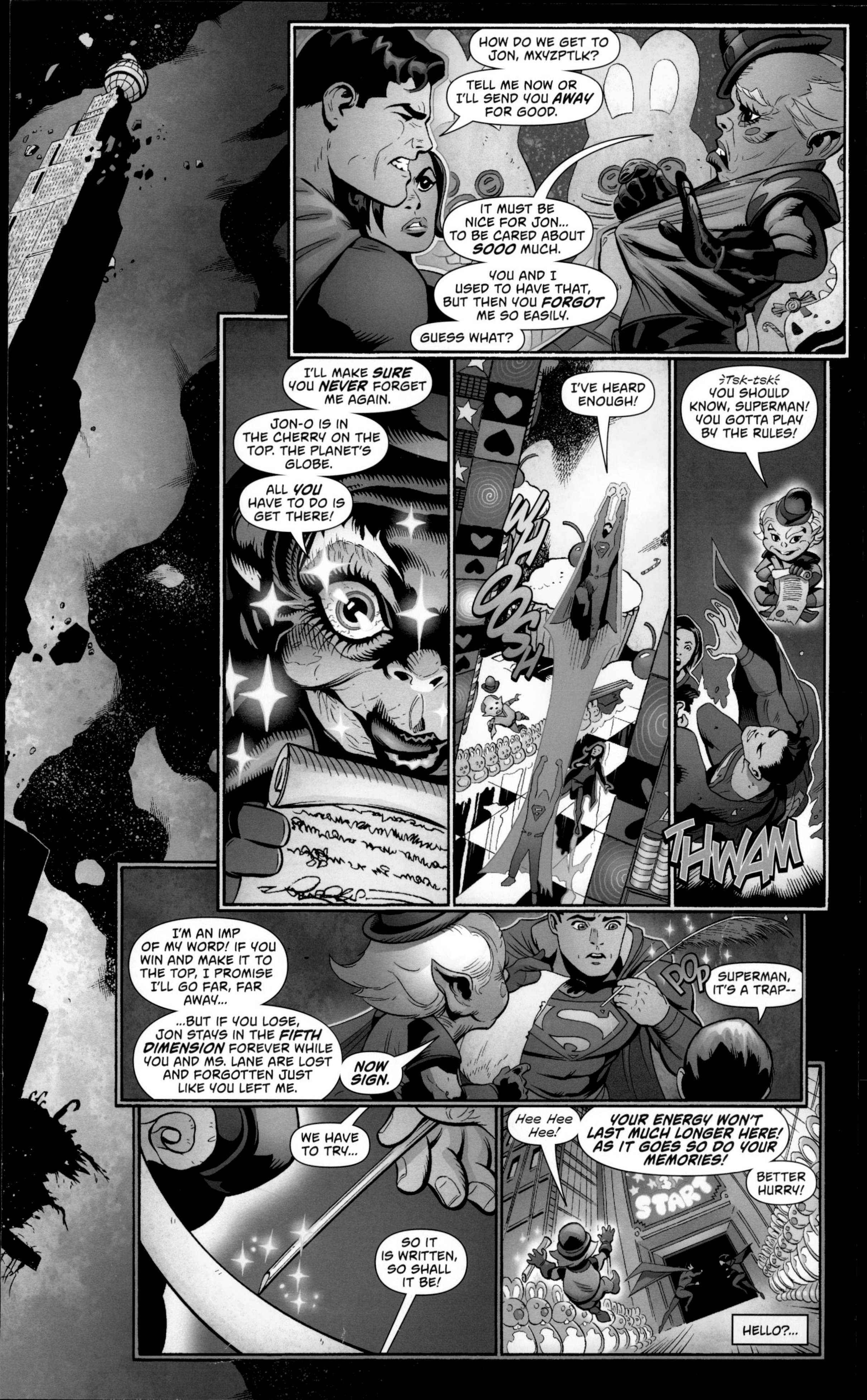
HOW DO WE GET TO JON, MXYZPTLK?
TELL ME NOW OR I'LL SEND YOU AWAY FOR GOOD.
IT MUST BE NICE FOR JON... TO BE CARED ABOUT SOOO MUCH.
YOU AND I USED TO HAVE THAT, BUT THEN YOU FORGOT ME SO EASILY.
GUESS WHAT?
I'LL MAKE SURE YOU NEVER FORGET ME AGAIN.
JON-O IS IN THE CHERRY ON THE TOP. THE PLANET'S GLOBE.
ALL YOU HAVE TO DO IS GET THERE!
I'VE HEARD ENOUGH!
WHOOOSH
Tsk-tsk
YOU SHOULD KNOW, SUPERMAN! YOU GOTTA PLAY BY THE RULES!
THWAM
I'M AN IMP OF MY WORD! IF YOU WIN AND MAKE IT TO THE TOP, I PROMISE I'LL GO FAR, FAR AWAY...
...BUT IF YOU LOSE, JON STAYS IN THE FIFTH DIMENSION FOREVER WHILE YOU AND MS. LANE ARE LOST AND FORGOTTEN JUST LIKE YOU LEFT ME.
NOW SIGN.
POP
SUPERMAN, IT'S A TRAP--
WE HAVE TO TRY...
SO IT IS WRITTEN, SO SHALL IT BE!
Hee Hee Hee!
YOUR ENERGY WON'T LAST MUCH LONGER HERE! AS IT GOES SO DO YOUR MEMORIES!
BETTER HURRY!
START
HELLO?...

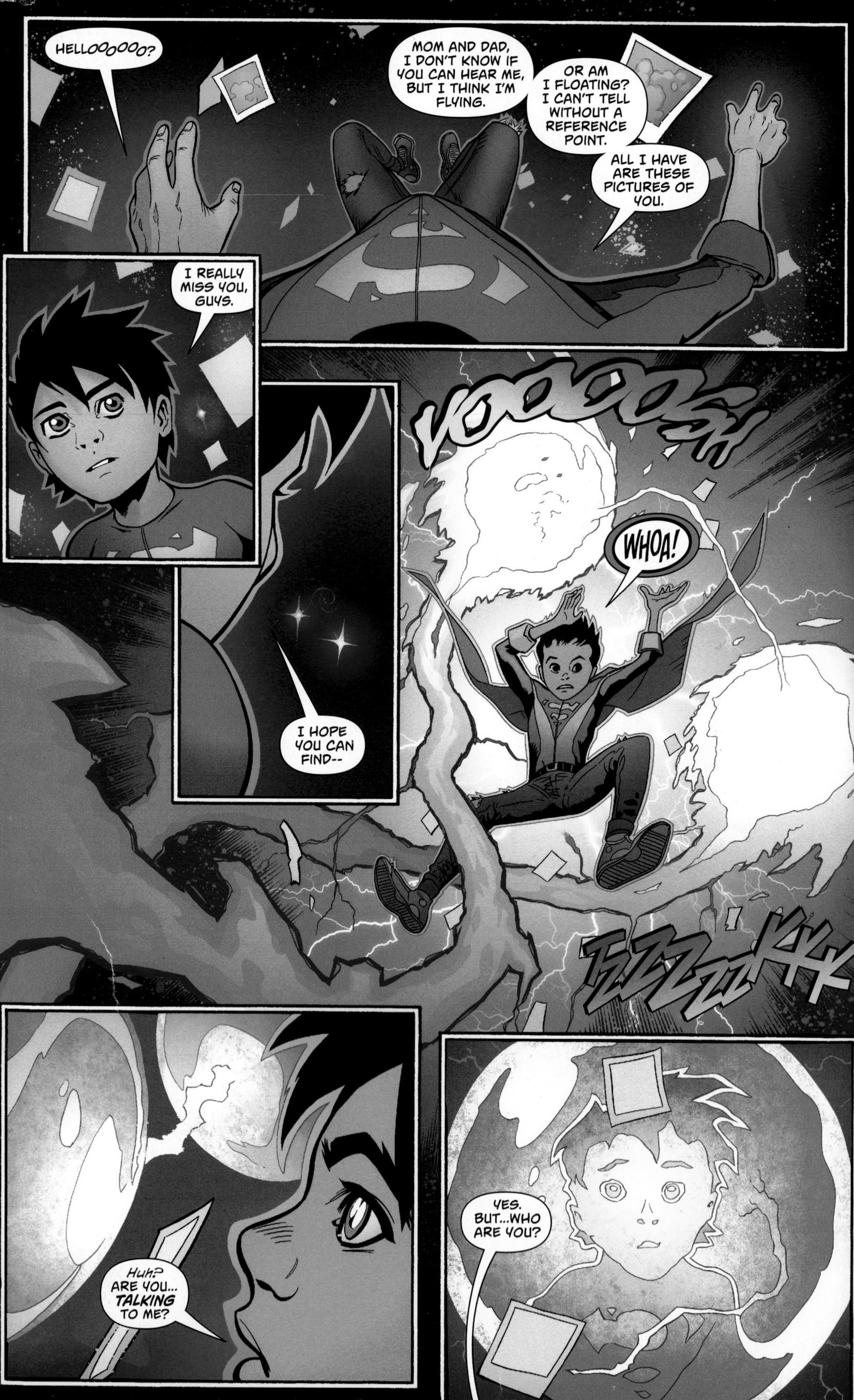
HELLOOOOOO?
MOM AND DAD, I DON'T KNOW IF YOU CAN HEAR ME, BUT I THINK I'M FLYING.
OR AM I FLOATING? I CAN'T TELL WITHOUT A REFERENCE POINT.
ALL I HAVE ARE THESE PICTURES OF YOU.
I REALLY MISS YOU, GUYS.
I HOPE YOU CAN FIND--
VOOOOSH
WHOA!
FZZZZzzKKK
Huh? ARE YOU... TALKING TO ME?
YES. BUT...WHO ARE YOU?

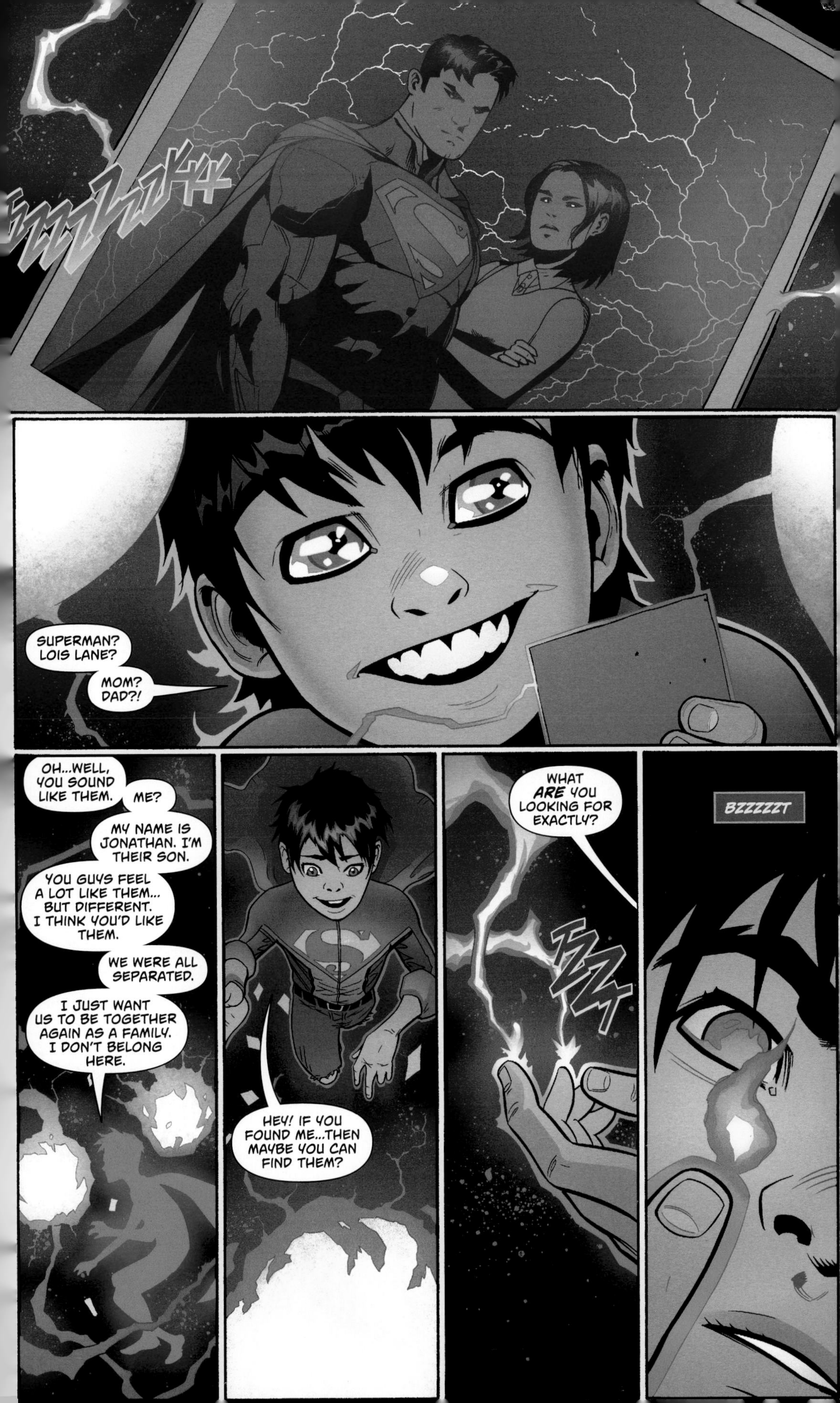
BZZZZZZAKKK
SUPERMAN? LOIS LANE?
MOM? DAD?!
OH...WELL, YOU SOUND LIKE THEM.
ME?
MY NAME IS JONATHAN. I'M THEIR SON.
YOU GUYS FEEL A LOT LIKE THEM... BUT DIFFERENT. I THINK YOU'D LIKE THEM.
WE WERE ALL SEPARATED.
I JUST WANT US TO BE TOGETHER AGAIN AS A FAMILY. I DON'T BELONG HERE.
HEY! IF YOU FOUND ME...THEN MAYBE YOU CAN FIND THEM?
WHAT ARE YOU LOOKING FOR EXACTLY?
BZZZZZT

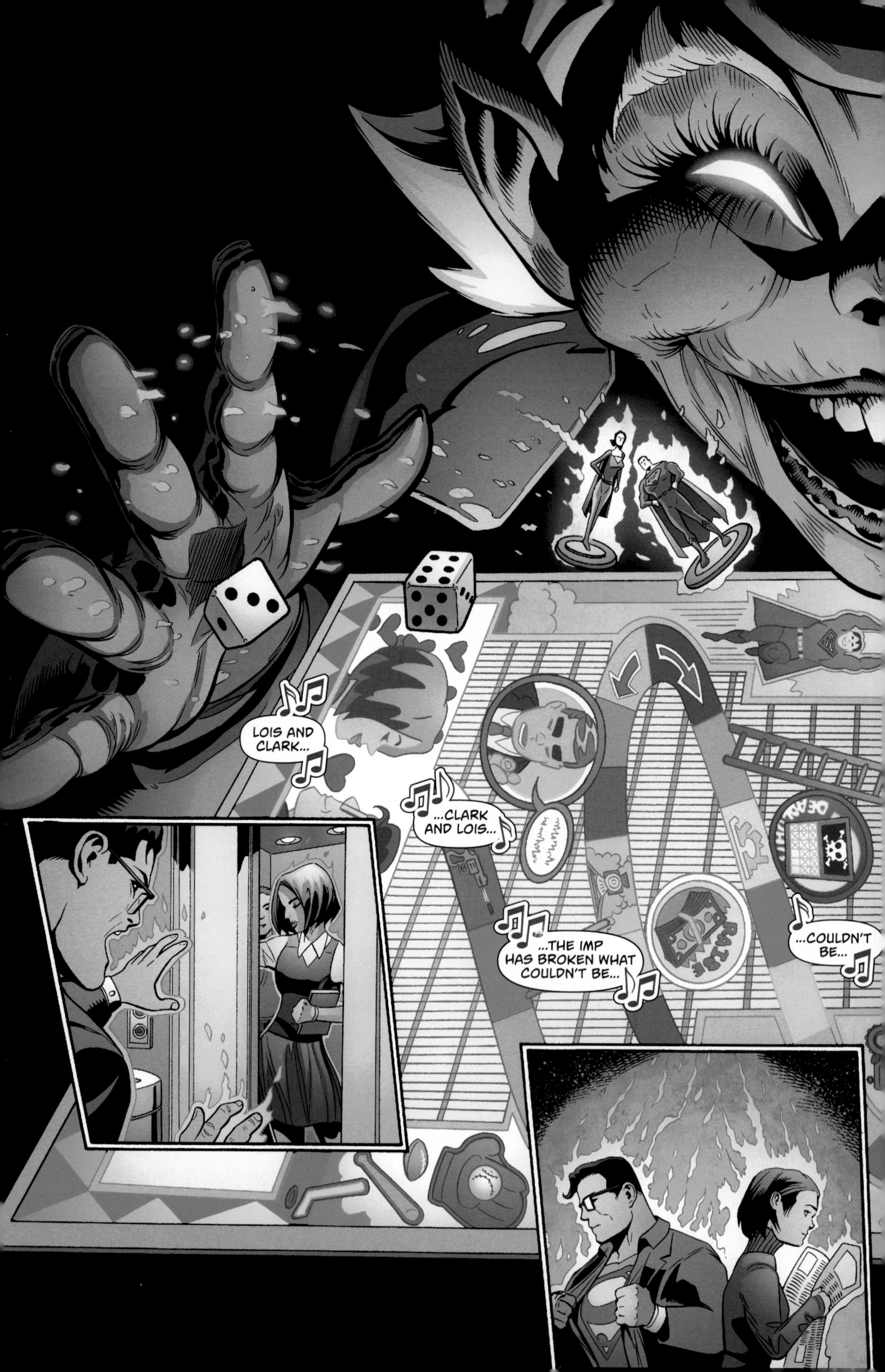
LOIS AND CLARK...
...CLARK AND LOIS...
...THE IMP HAS BROKEN WHAT COULDN'T BE...
...COULDN'T BE...
RAISE

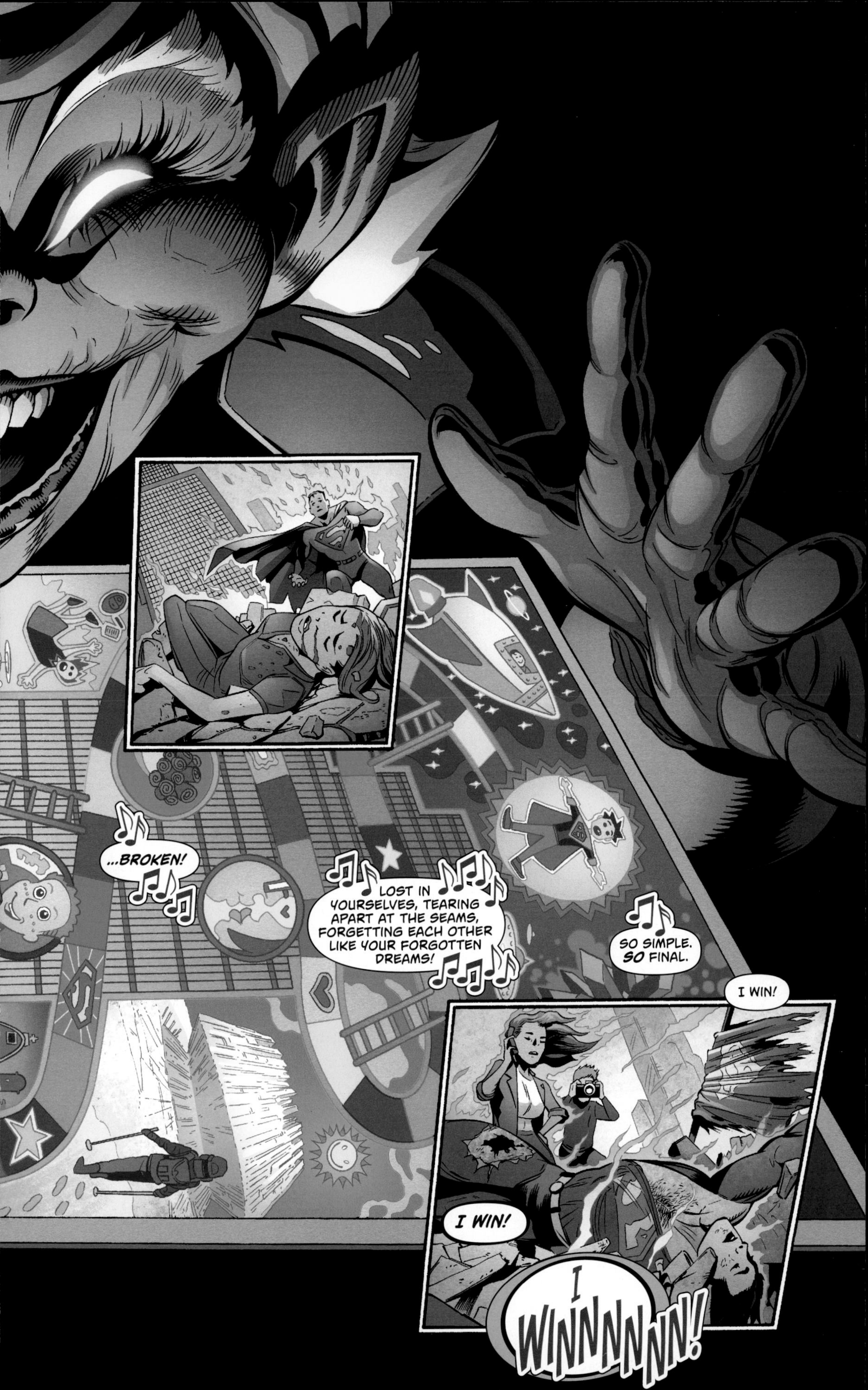
...BROKEN!
LOST IN YOURSELVES, TEARING APART AT THE SEAMS, FORGETTING EACH OTHER LIKE YOUR FORGOTTEN DREAMS!
SO SIMPLE. SO FINAL.
I WIN!
I WIN!
I WINNNNNN!

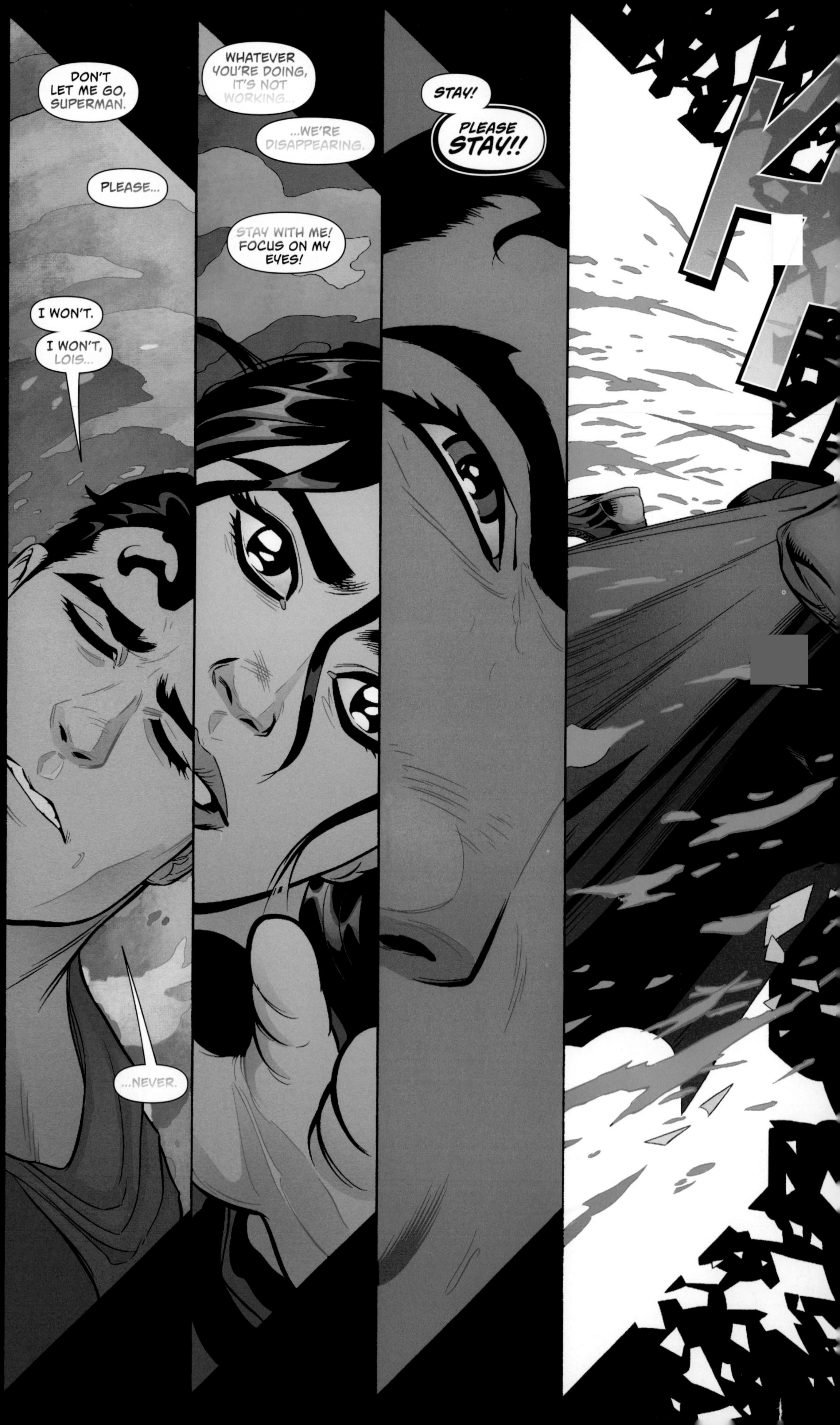
DON'T LET ME GO, SUPERMAN.
PLEASE...
I WON'T.
I WON'T, LOIS...
...NEVER.
WHATEVER YOU'RE DOING, IT'S NOT WORKING...
...WE'RE DISAPPEARING.
STAY WITH ME! FOCUS ON MY EYES!
STAY!
PLEASE STAY!!

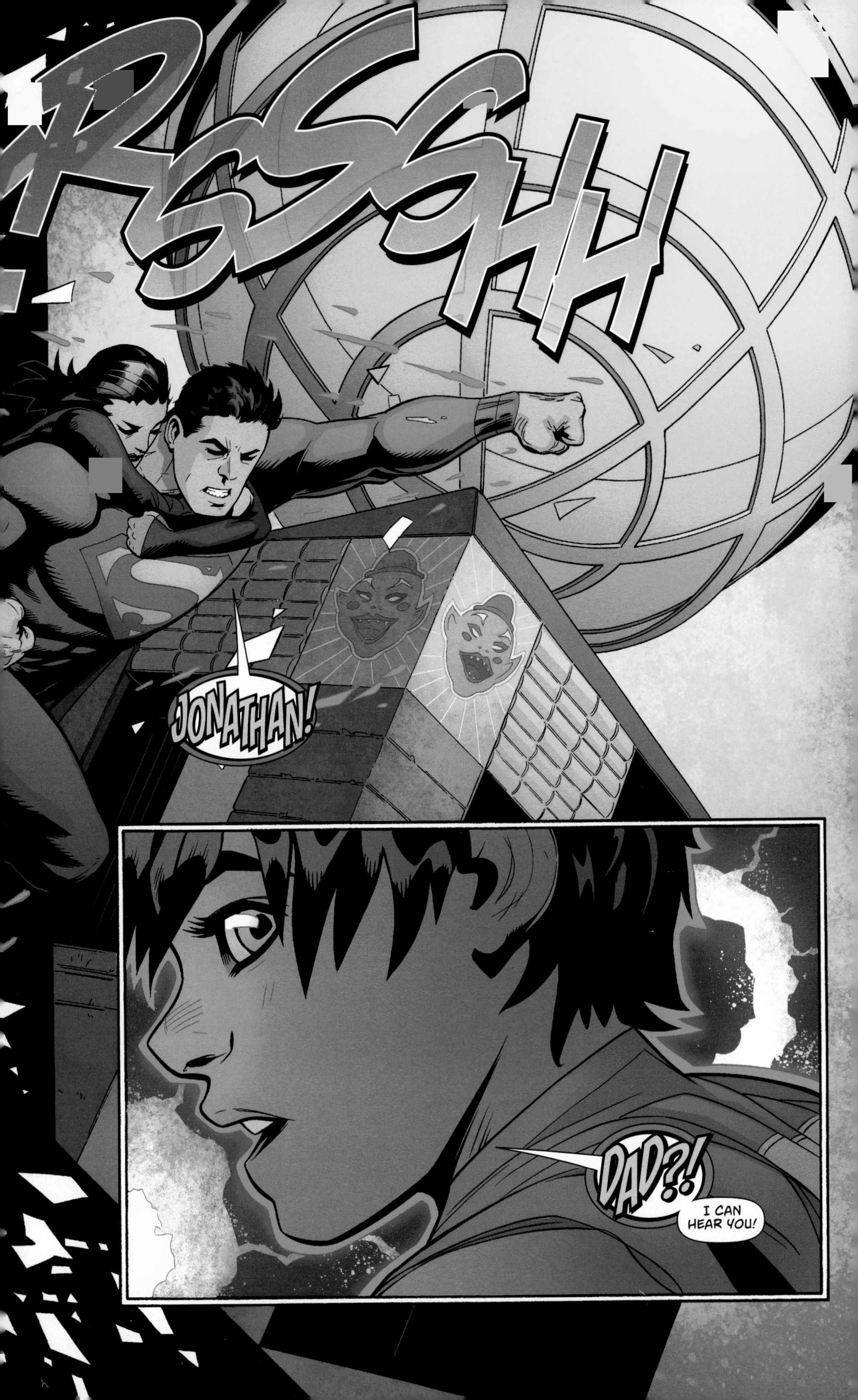
RSSHH
JONATHAN!
DAD?!
I CAN HEAR YOU!

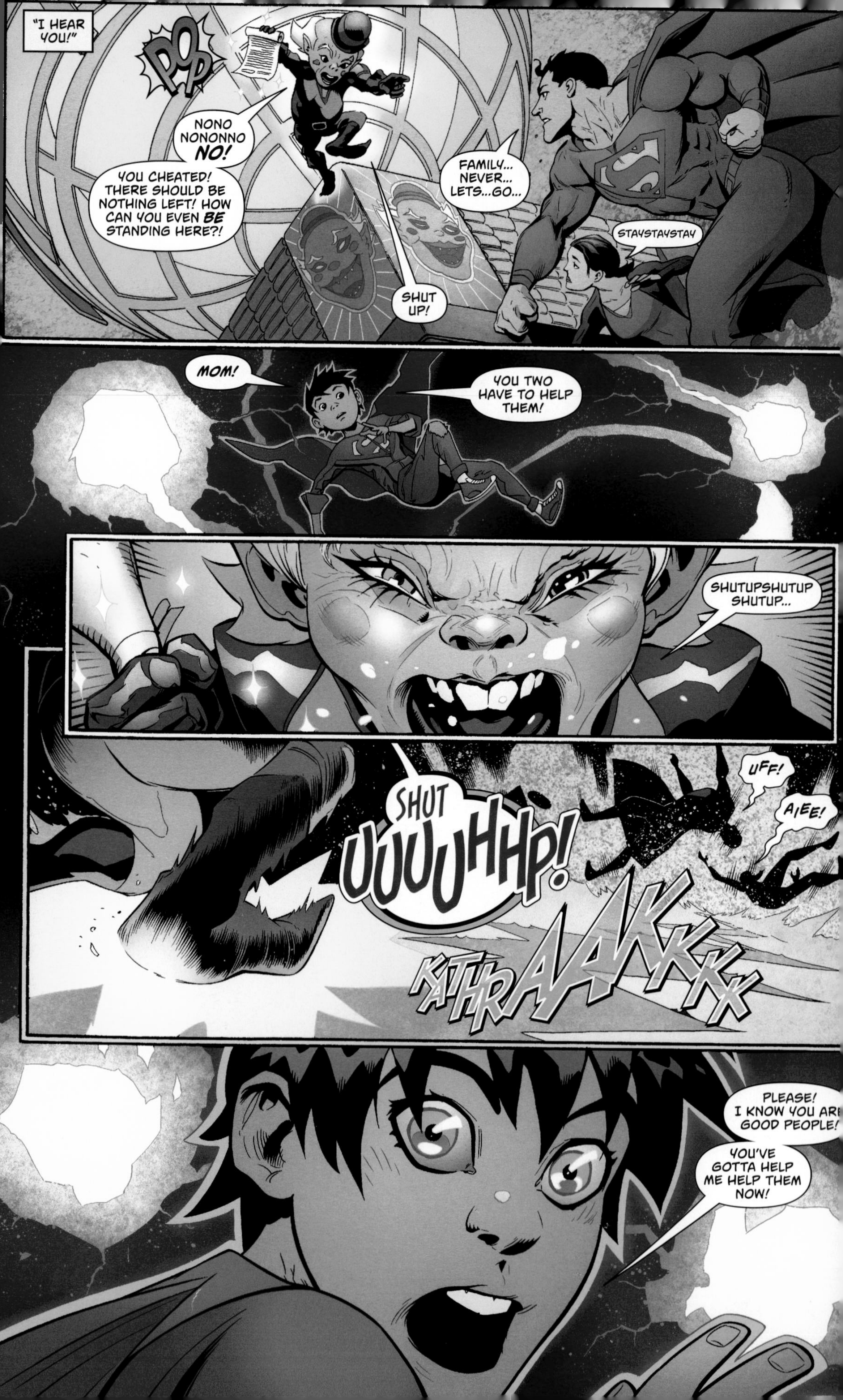
"I HEAR YOU!"
POP
NONO NONONNO NO!
YOU CHEATED! THERE SHOULD BE NOTHING LEFT! HOW CAN YOU EVEN BE STANDING HERE?!
FAMILY... NEVER... LETS...GO...
SHUT UP!
STAYSTAYSTAY
MOM!
YOU TWO HAVE TO HELP THEM!
SHUTUPSHUTUP SHUTUP...
SHUT UUUUHHP!
UFF!
AIEE!
KATHRAAAKKKK
PLEASE! I KNOW YOU AR GOOD PEOPLE!
YOU'VE GOTTA HELP ME HELP THEM NOW!

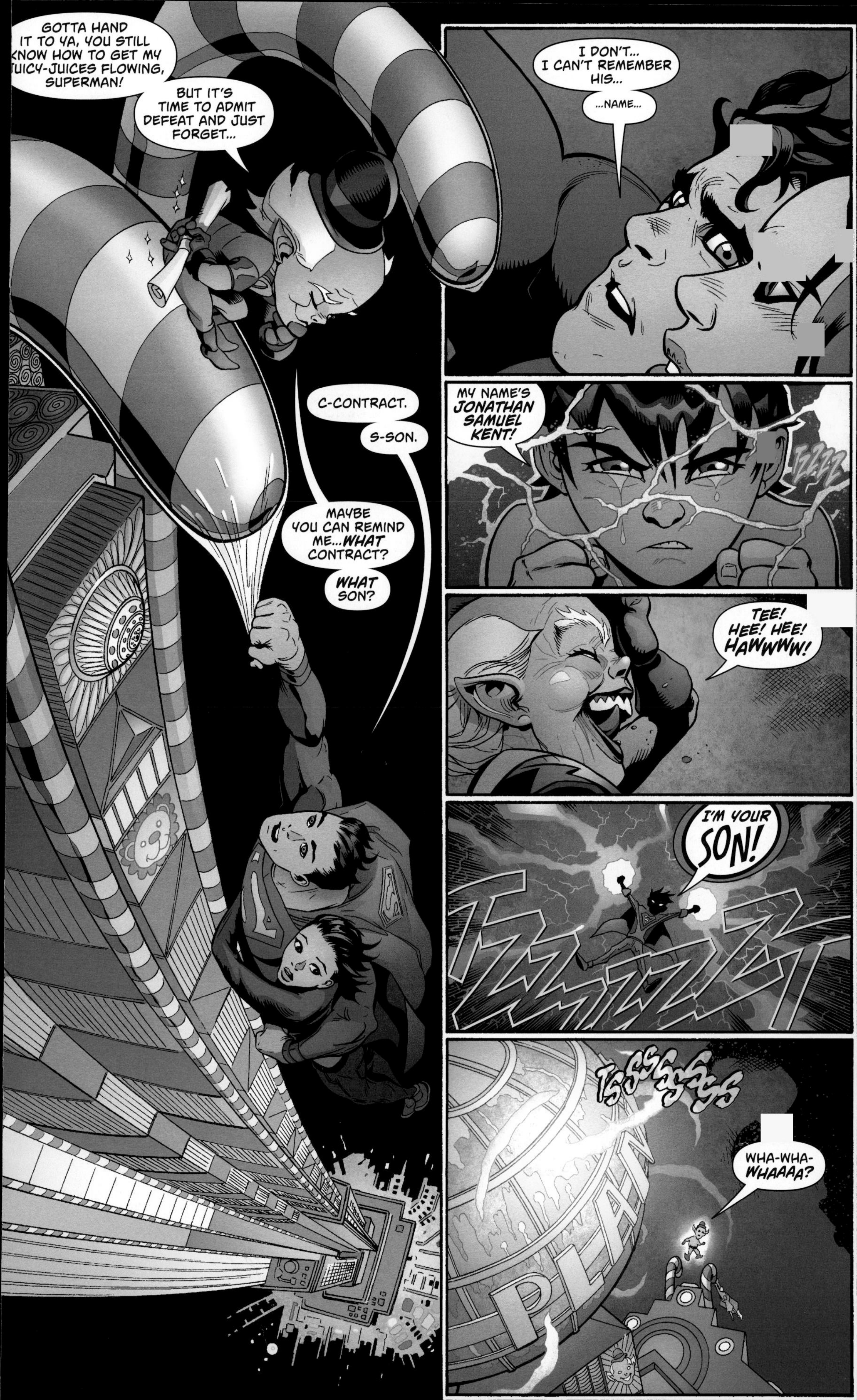
GOTTA HAND IT TO YA, YOU STILL KNOW HOW TO GET MY JUICY-JUICES FLOWING, SUPERMAN!
BUT IT'S TIME TO ADMIT DEFEAT AND JUST FORGET...
C-CONTRACT.
S-SON.
MAYBE YOU CAN REMIND ME...WHAT CONTRACT?
WHAT SON?
I DON'T... I CAN'T REMEMBER HIS...
...NAME...
MY NAME'S JONATHAN SAMUEL KENT!
TEE! HEE! HEE! HAWWWW!
I'M YOUR SON!
TSSSSSSS
WHA-WHA-WHAAAA?

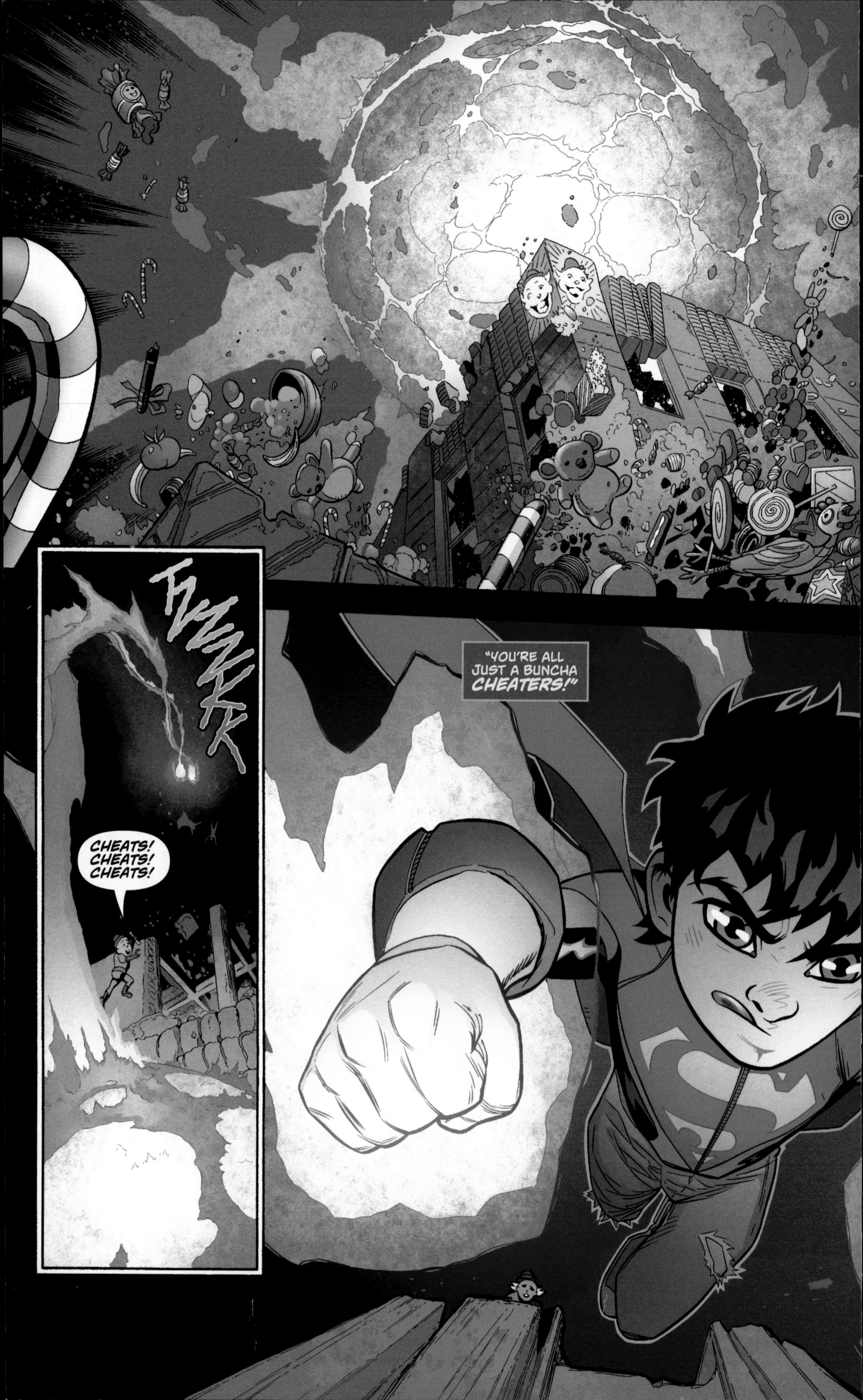
FZZZKK
CHEATS! CHEATS! CHEATS!
"YOU'RE ALL JUST A BUNCHA CHEATERS!"

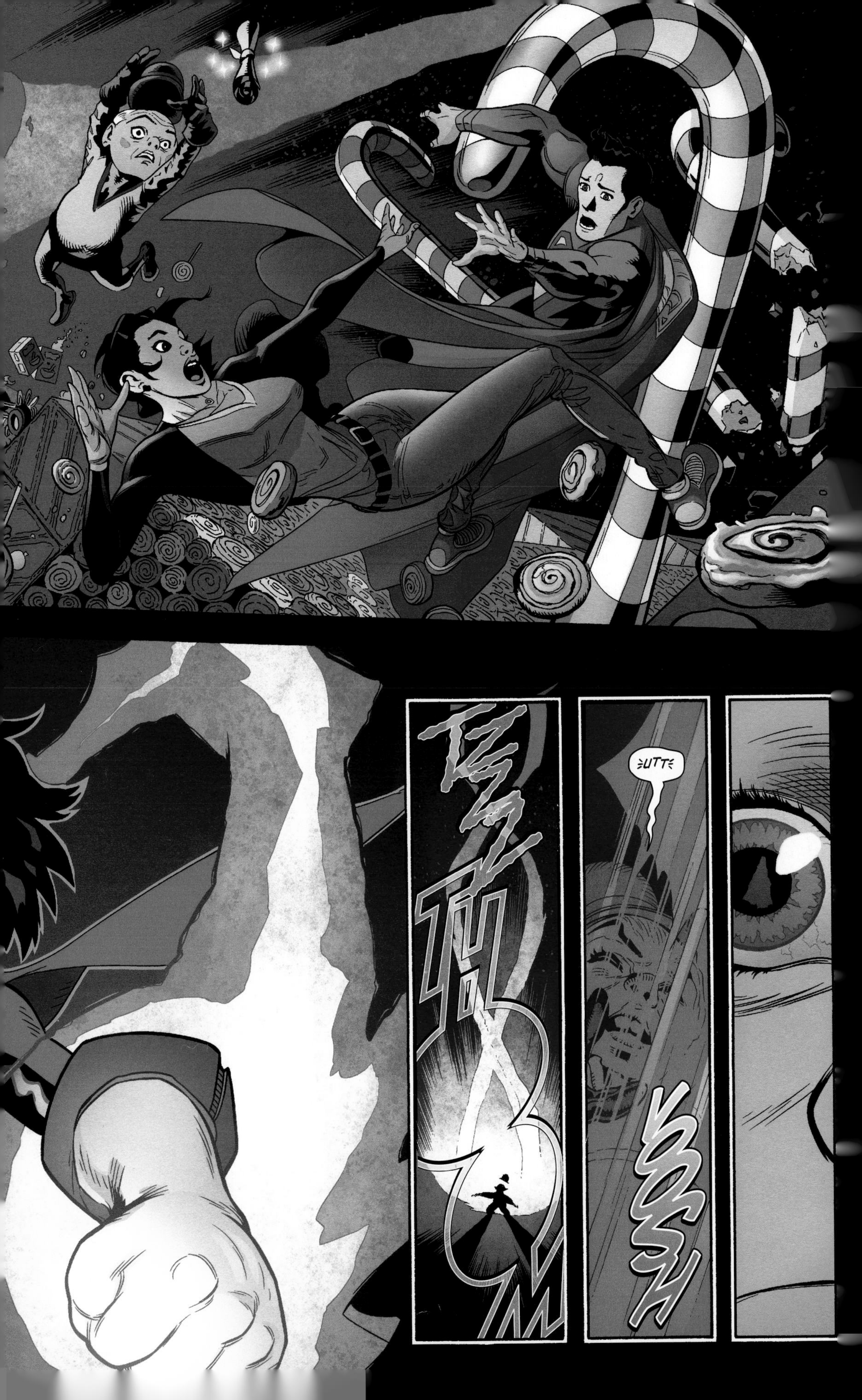
UTT
VOOSH

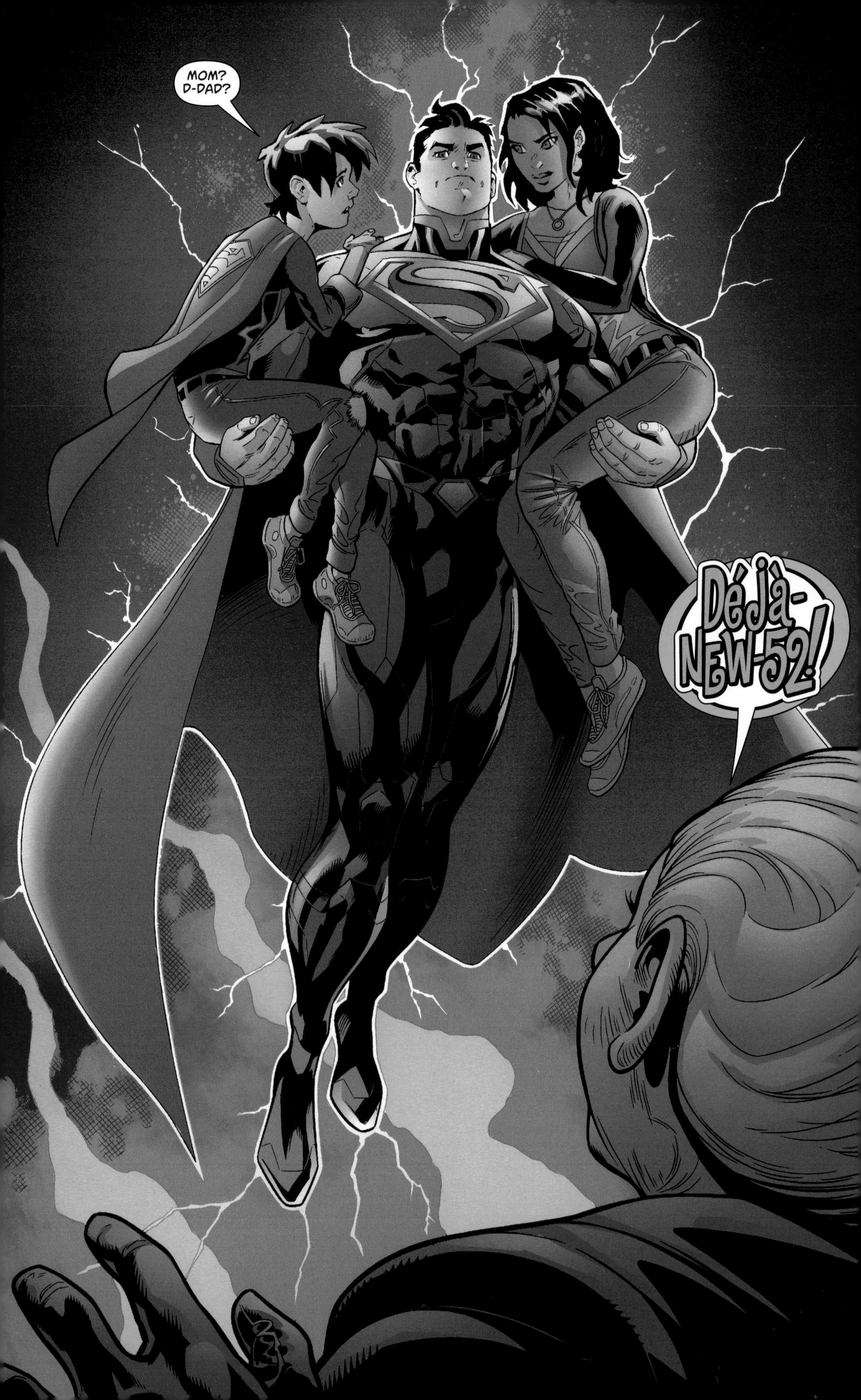
MOM?
D-DAD?
DÉJÀ-NEW-52!

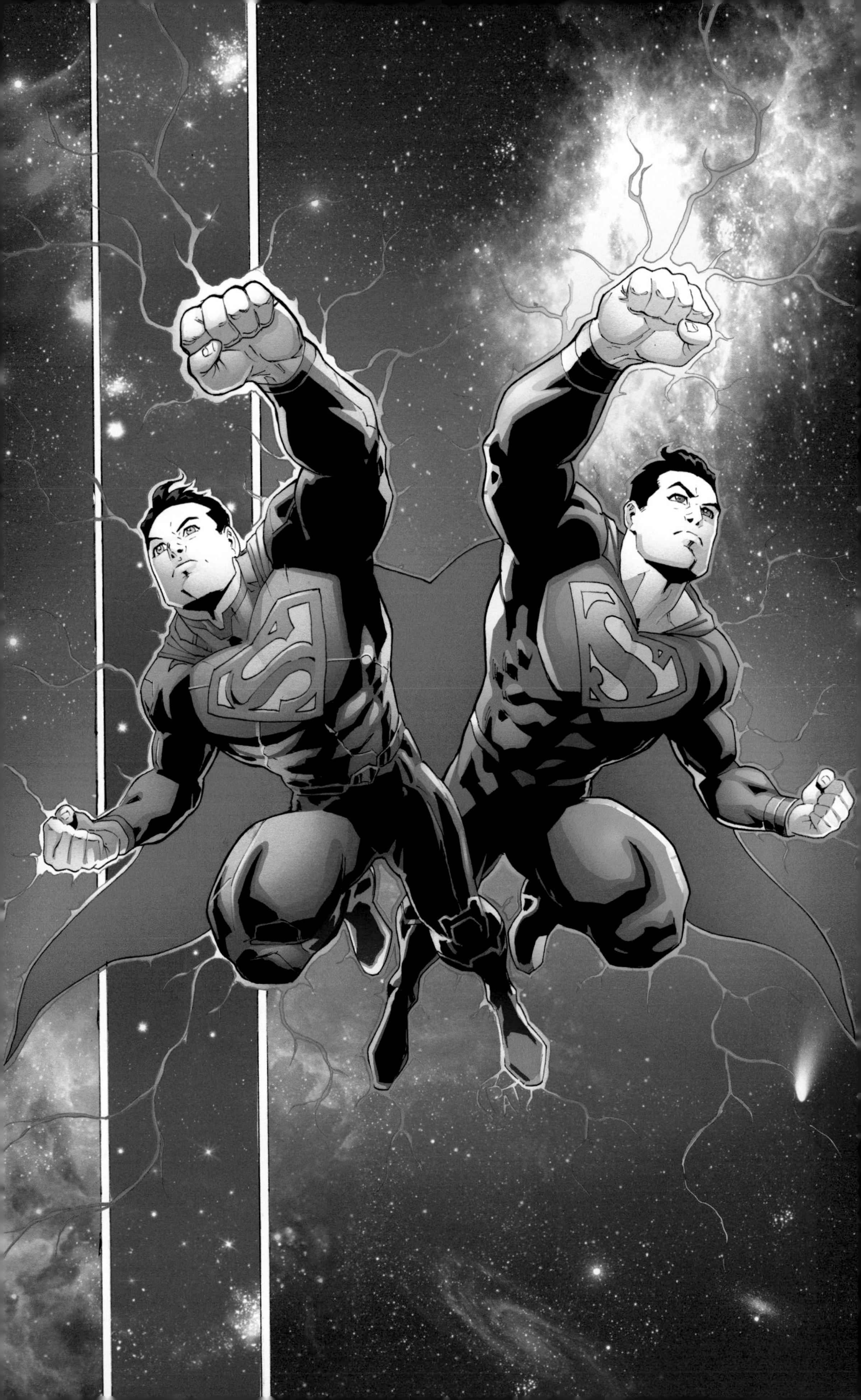

SUPERMAN REBORN part four

DAN JURGENS writer * DOUG MAHNKE penciller

JAIME MENDOZA, CHRISTIAN ALAMY & TREVOR SCOTT inkers

WIL QUINTANA colorist * PATRICK GLEASON & JOHN KALISZ cover art

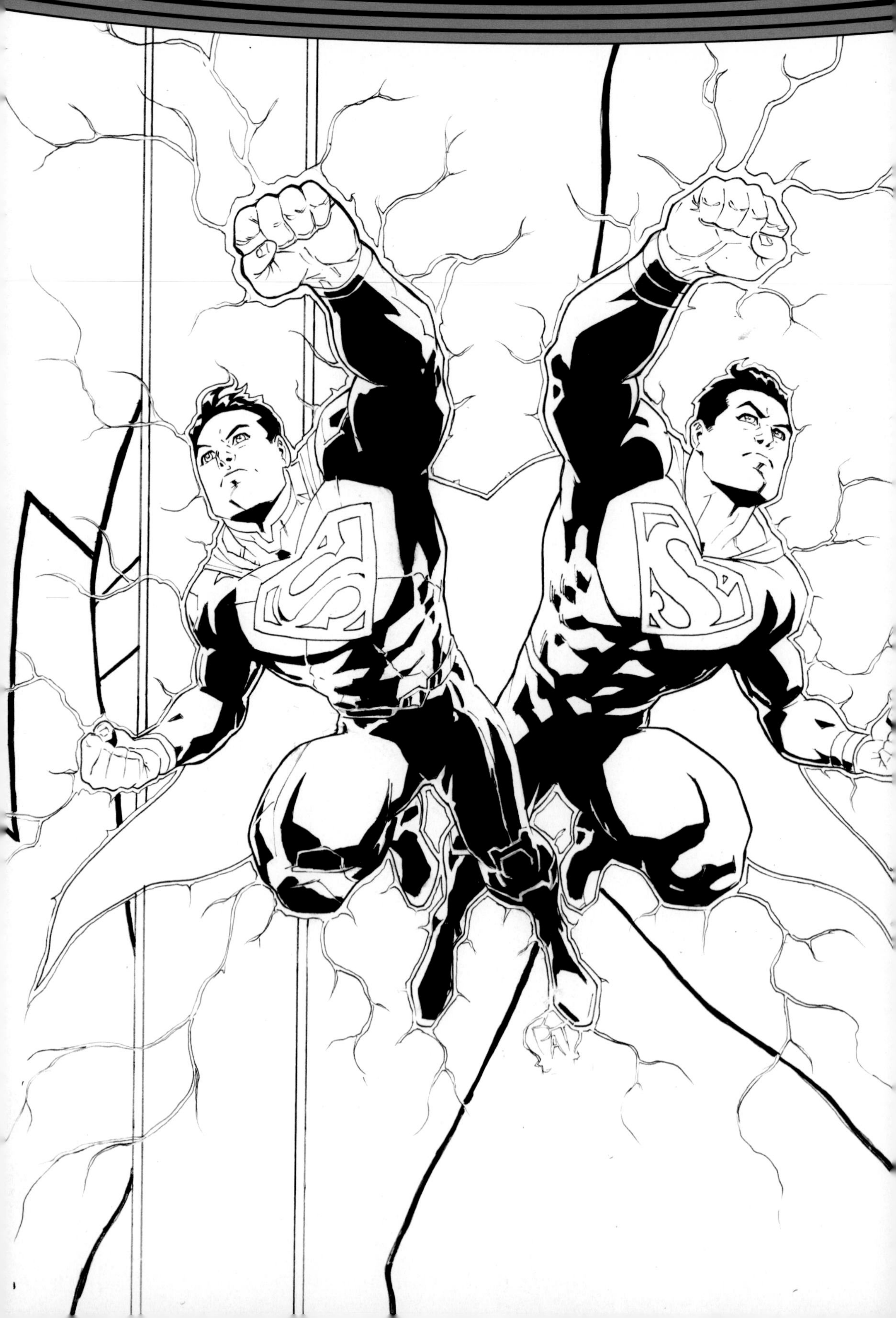

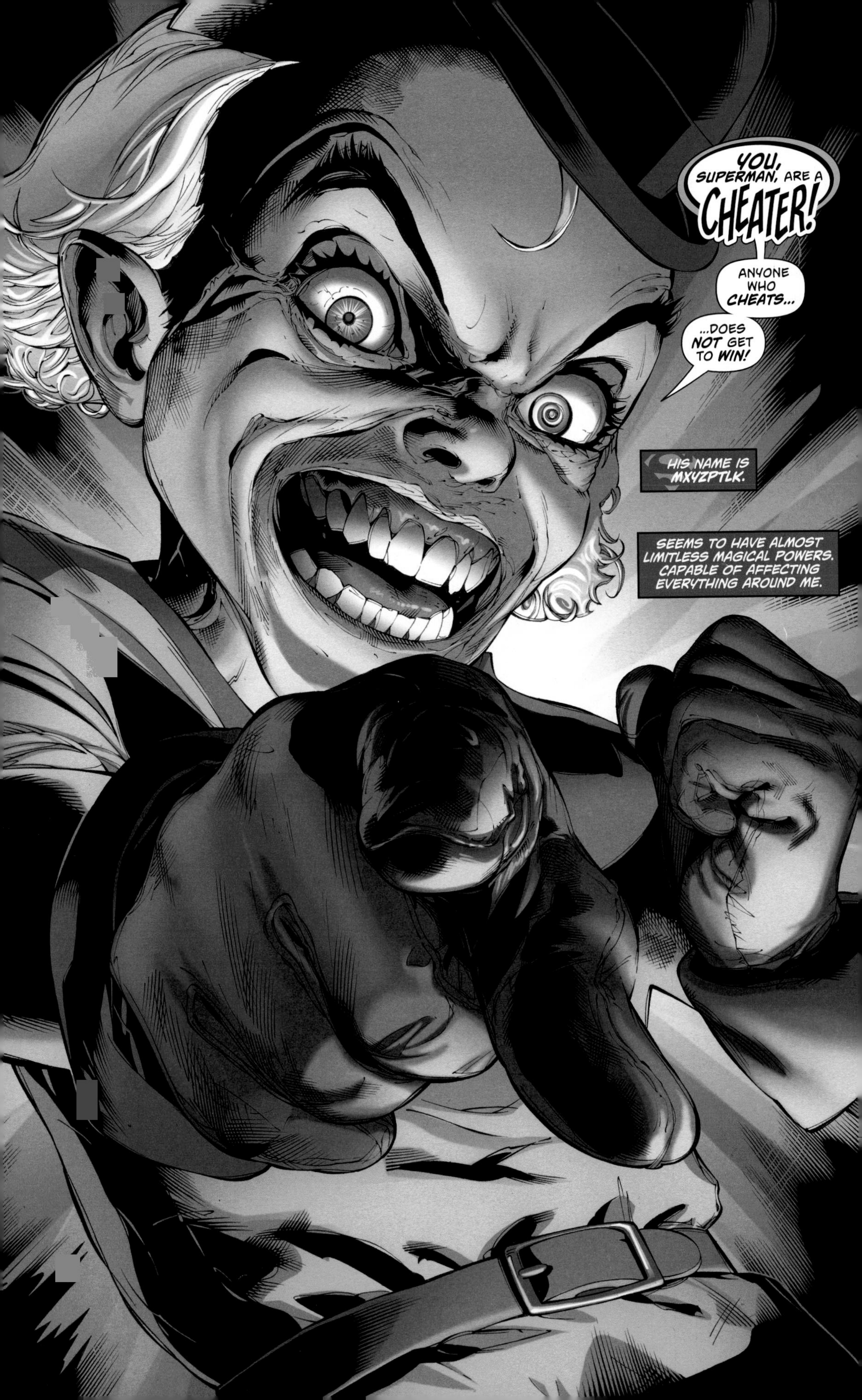
YOU, SUPERMAN, ARE A CHEATER!
ANYONE WHO CHEATS...
...DOES NOT GET TO WIN!
HIS NAME IS MXYZPTLK.
SEEMS TO HAVE ALMOST LIMITLESS MAGICAL POWERS. CAPABLE OF AFFECTING EVERYTHING AROUND ME.

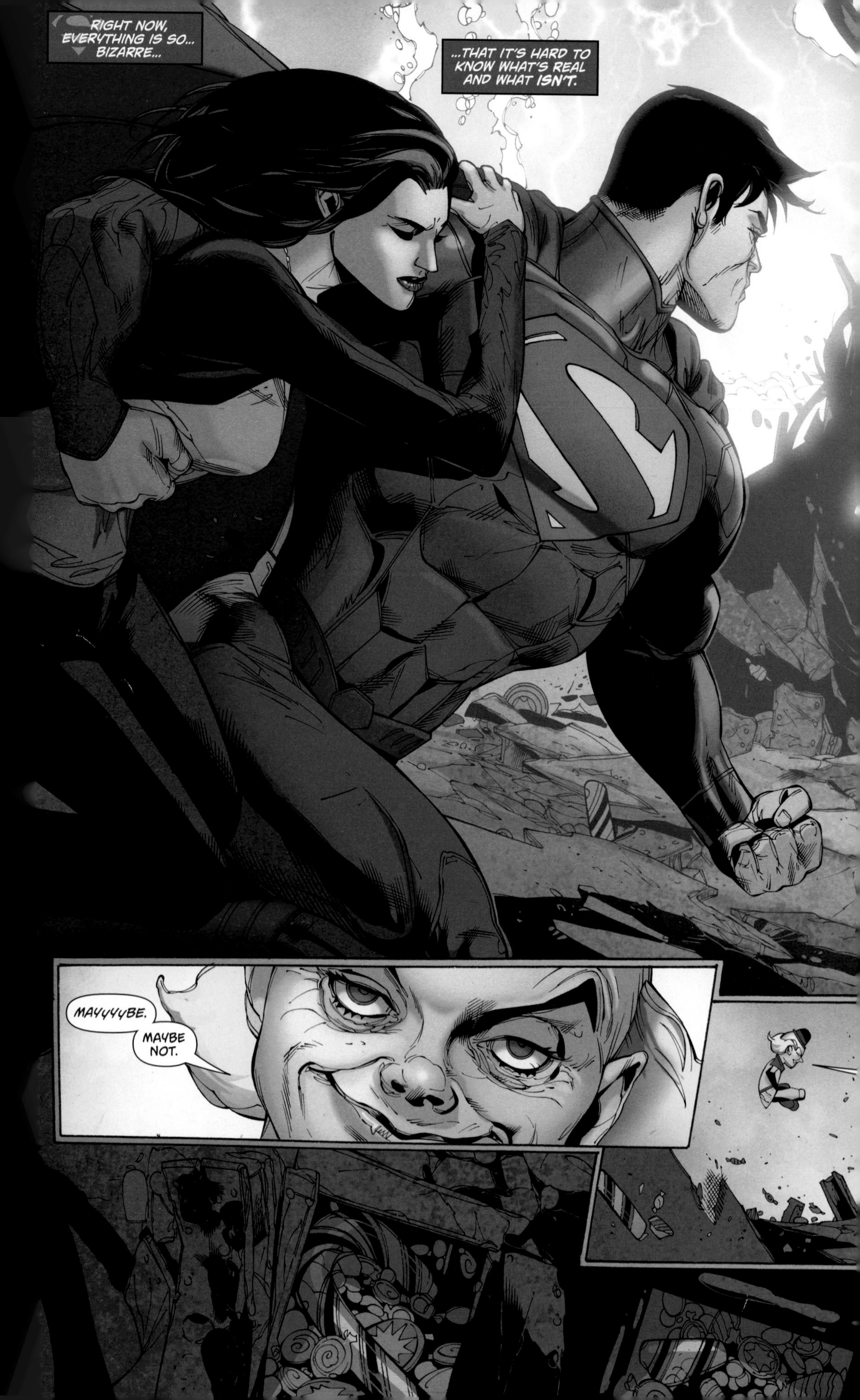
RIGHT NOW, EVERYTHING IS SO... BIZARRE...
...THAT IT'S HARD TO KNOW WHAT'S REAL AND WHAT ISN'T.
MAYYYYBE.
MAYBE NOT.

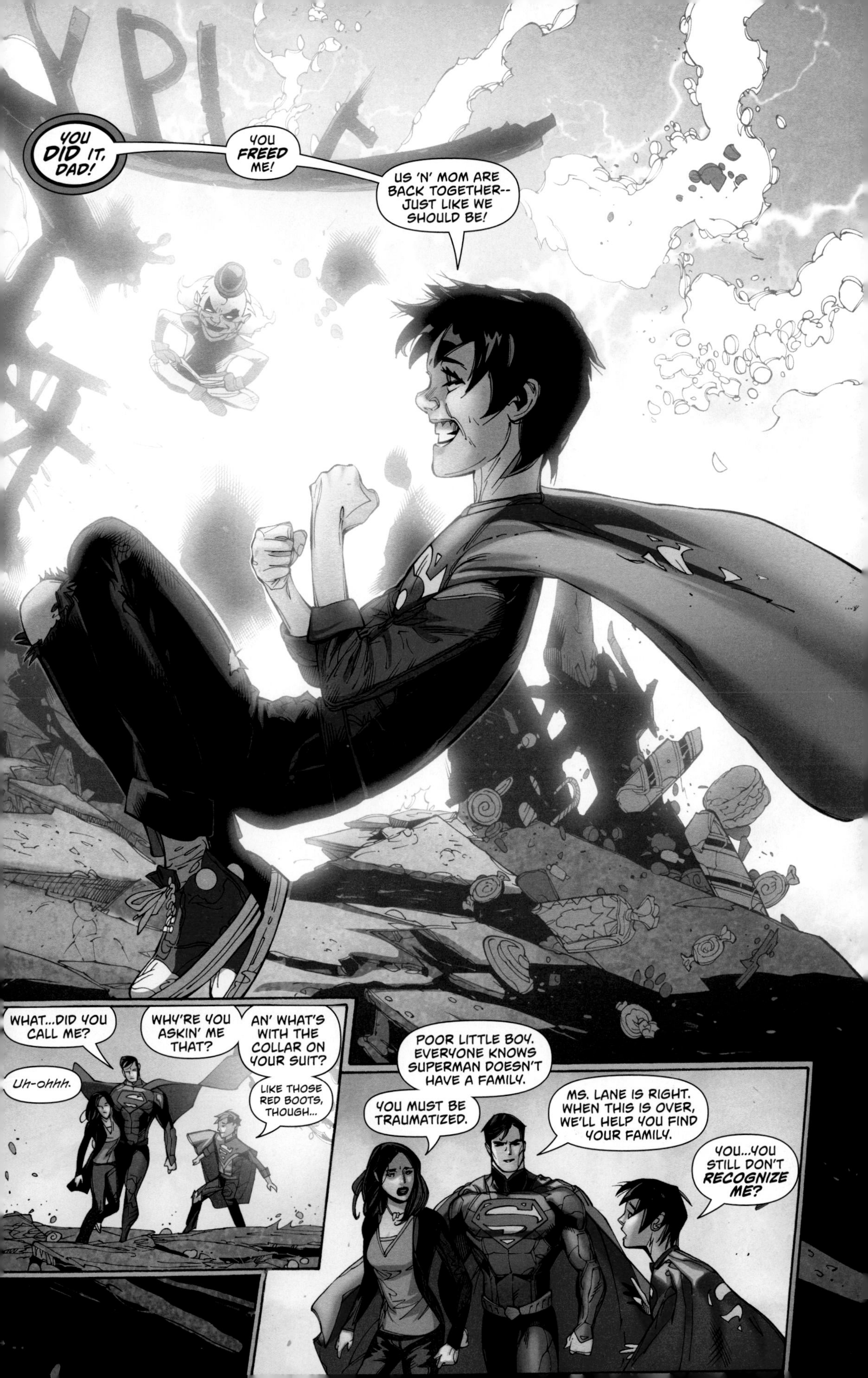
YOU DID IT, DAD!
YOU FREED ME!
US 'N' MOM ARE BACK TOGETHER-- JUST LIKE WE SHOULD BE!
WHAT...DID YOU CALL ME?
Uh-ohhh.
WHY'RE YOU ASKIN' ME THAT?
AN' WHAT'S WITH THE COLLAR ON YOUR SUIT?
LIKE THOSE RED BOOTS, THOUGH...
POOR LITTLE BOY. EVERYONE KNOWS SUPERMAN DOESN'T HAVE A FAMILY.
YOU MUST BE TRAUMATIZED.
MS. LANE IS RIGHT. WHEN THIS IS OVER, WE'LL HELP YOU FIND YOUR FAMILY.
YOU...YOU STILL DON'T RECOGNIZE ME?

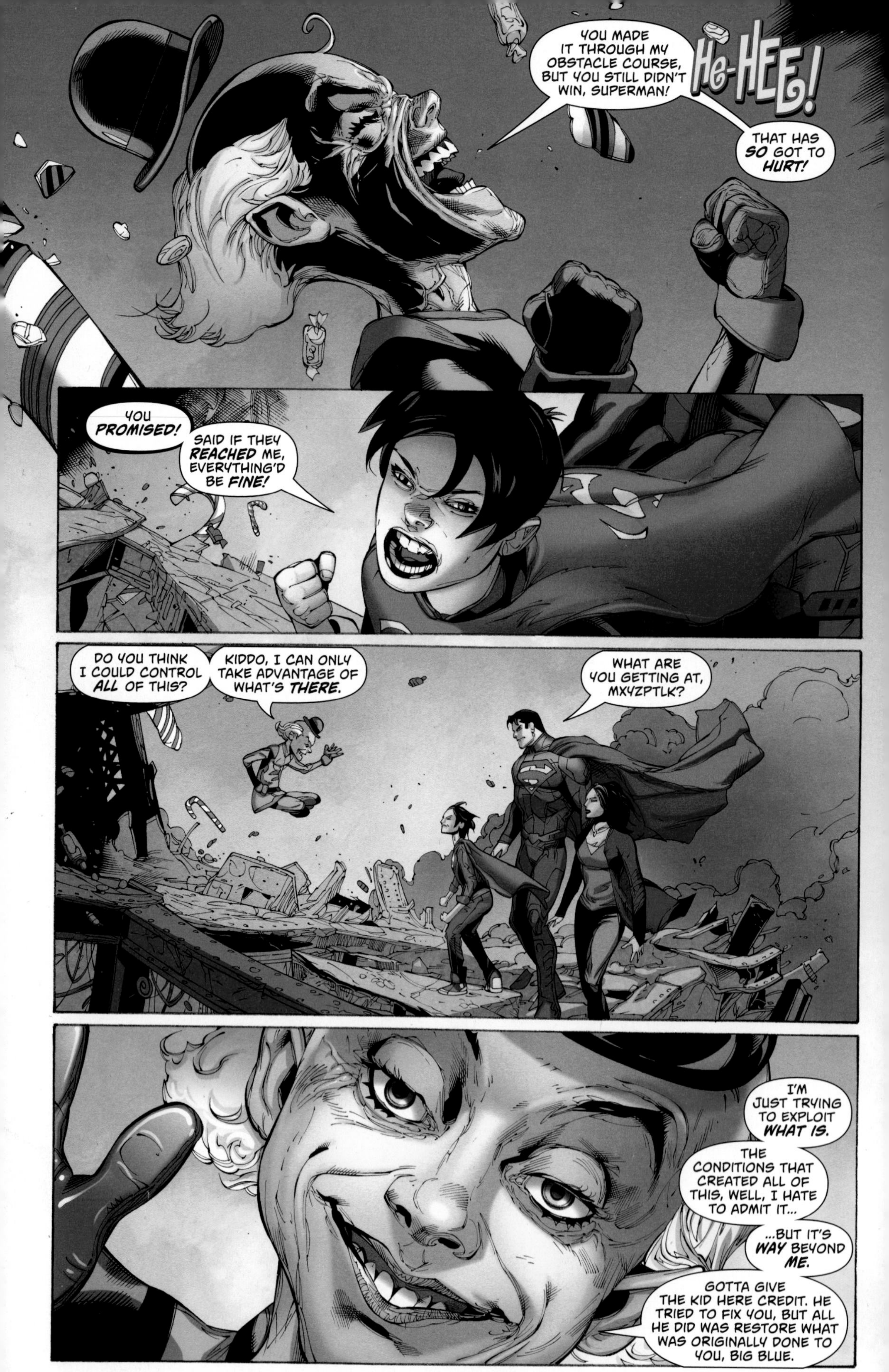
YOU MADE IT THROUGH MY OBSTACLE COURSE, BUT YOU STILL DIDN'T WIN, SUPERMAN!
HE-HEE!
THAT HAS *SO* GOT TO *HURT!*
YOU *PROMISED!*
SAID IF THEY *REACHED* ME, EVERYTHING'D BE *FINE!*
DO YOU THINK I COULD CONTROL *ALL* OF THIS?
KIDDO, I CAN ONLY TAKE ADVANTAGE OF WHAT'S *THERE.*
WHAT ARE YOU GETTING AT, MXYZPTLK?
I'M JUST TRYING TO EXPLOIT *WHAT IS.*
THE CONDITIONS THAT CREATED ALL OF THIS, WELL, I HATE TO ADMIT IT...
...BUT IT'S *WAY* BEYOND *ME.*
GOTTA GIVE THE KID HERE CREDIT. HE TRIED TO FIX YOU, BUT ALL HE DID WAS RESTORE WHAT WAS ORIGINALLY DONE TO YOU, BIG BLUE.

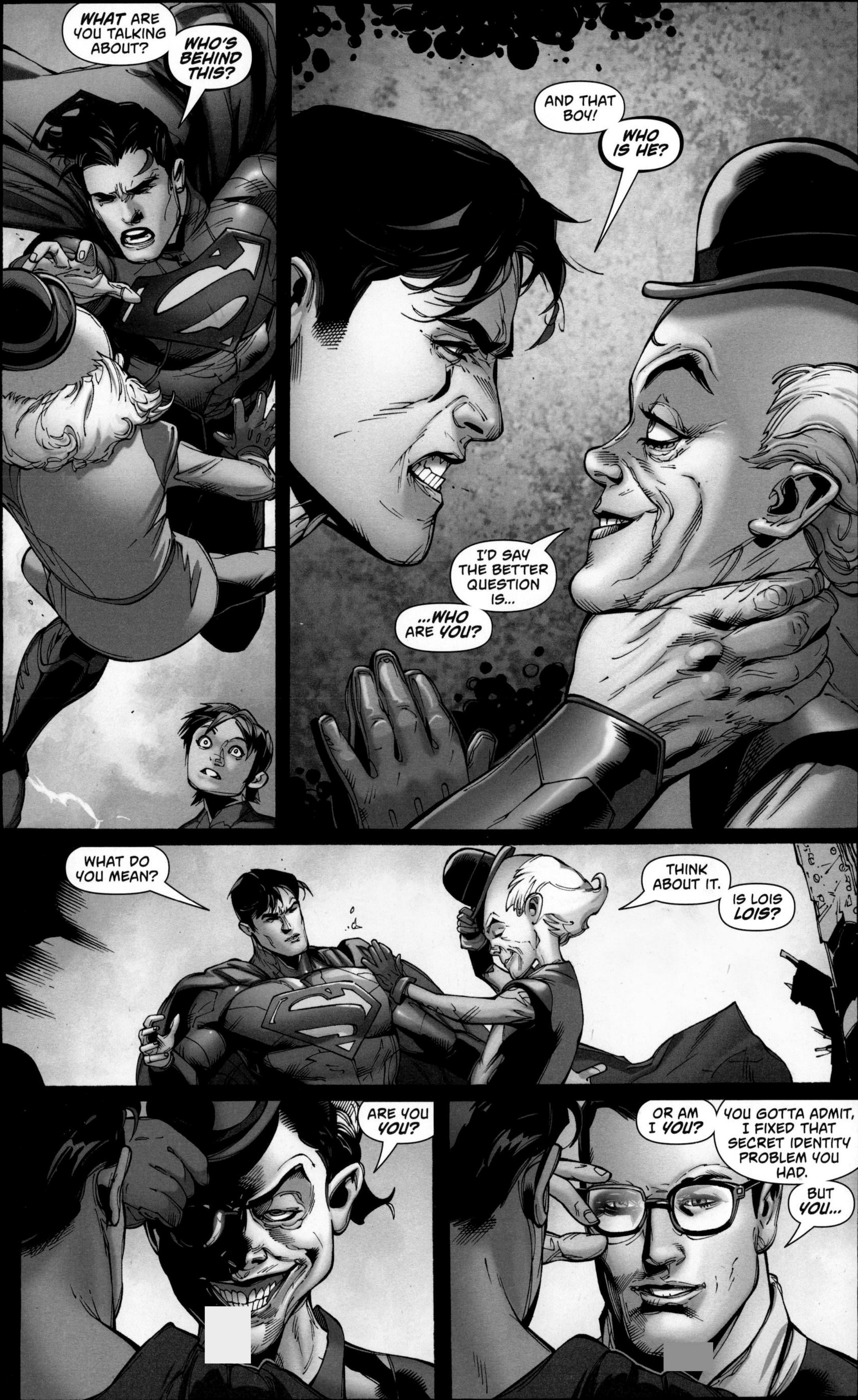
WHAT ARE YOU TALKING ABOUT?
WHO'S BEHIND THIS?
AND THAT BOY!
WHO IS HE?
I'D SAY THE BETTER QUESTION IS...
...WHO ARE YOU?
WHAT DO YOU MEAN?
THINK ABOUT IT.
IS LOIS LOIS?
ARE YOU YOU?
OR AM I YOU?
YOU GOTTA ADMIT, I FIXED THAT SECRET IDENTITY PROBLEM YOU HAD.
BUT YOU...

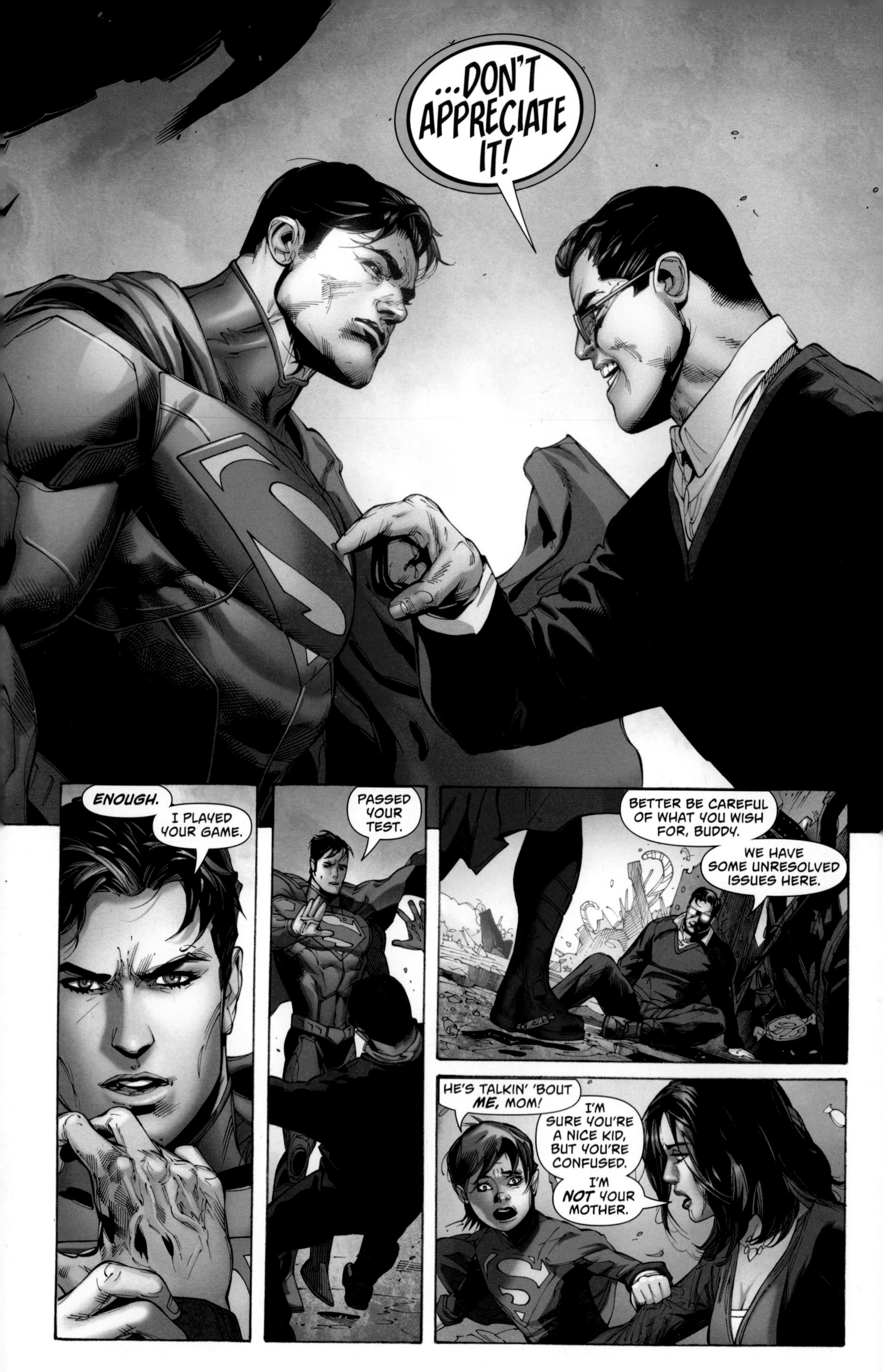
...DON'T APPRECIATE IT!
ENOUGH.
I PLAYED YOUR GAME.
PASSED YOUR TEST.
BETTER BE CAREFUL OF WHAT YOU WISH FOR, BUDDY.
WE HAVE SOME UNRESOLVED ISSUES HERE.
HE'S TALKIN' 'BOUT ME, MOM!
I'M SURE YOU'RE A NICE KID, BUT YOU'RE CONFUSED.
I'M NOT YOUR MOTHER.

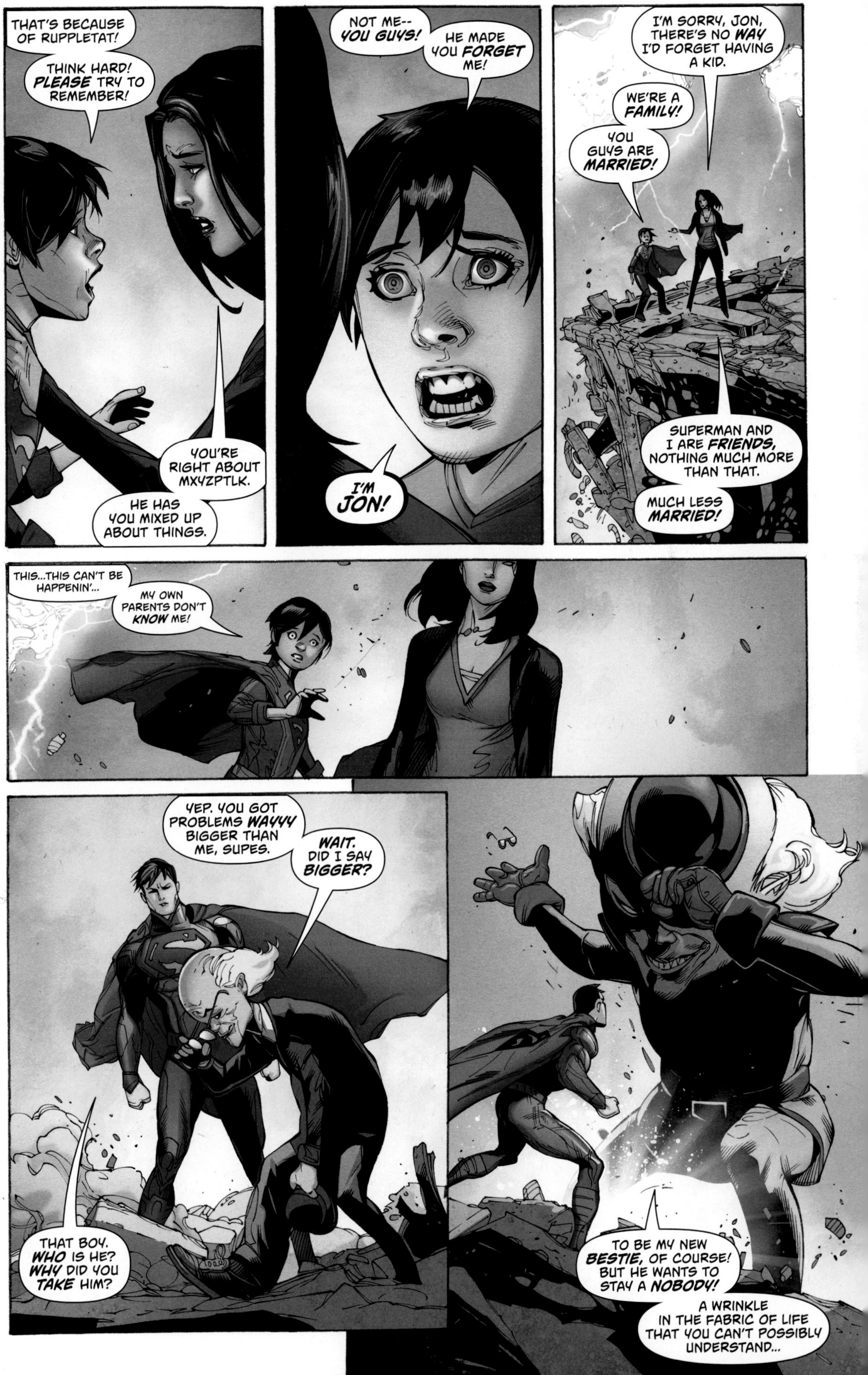
THAT'S BECAUSE OF RUPPLETAT!
THINK HARD! PLEASE TRY TO REMEMBER!
YOU'RE RIGHT ABOUT MXYZPTLK.
HE HAS YOU MIXED UP ABOUT THINGS.
NOT ME-- YOU GUYS!
HE MADE YOU FORGET ME!
I'M JON!
I'M SORRY, JON, THERE'S NO WAY I'D FORGET HAVING A KID.
WE'RE A FAMILY!
YOU GUYS ARE MARRIED!
SUPERMAN AND I ARE FRIENDS, NOTHING MUCH MORE THAN THAT.
MUCH LESS MARRIED!
THIS...THIS CAN'T BE HAPPENIN'...
MY OWN PARENTS DON'T KNOW ME!
YEP. YOU GOT PROBLEMS WAYYY BIGGER THAN ME, SUPES.
WAIT. DID I SAY BIGGER?
THAT BOY. WHO IS HE? WHY DID YOU TAKE HIM?
TO BE MY NEW BESTIE, OF COURSE! BUT HE WANTS TO STAY A NOBODY!
A WRINKLE IN THE FABRIC OF LIFE THAT YOU CAN'T POSSIBLY UNDERSTAND...

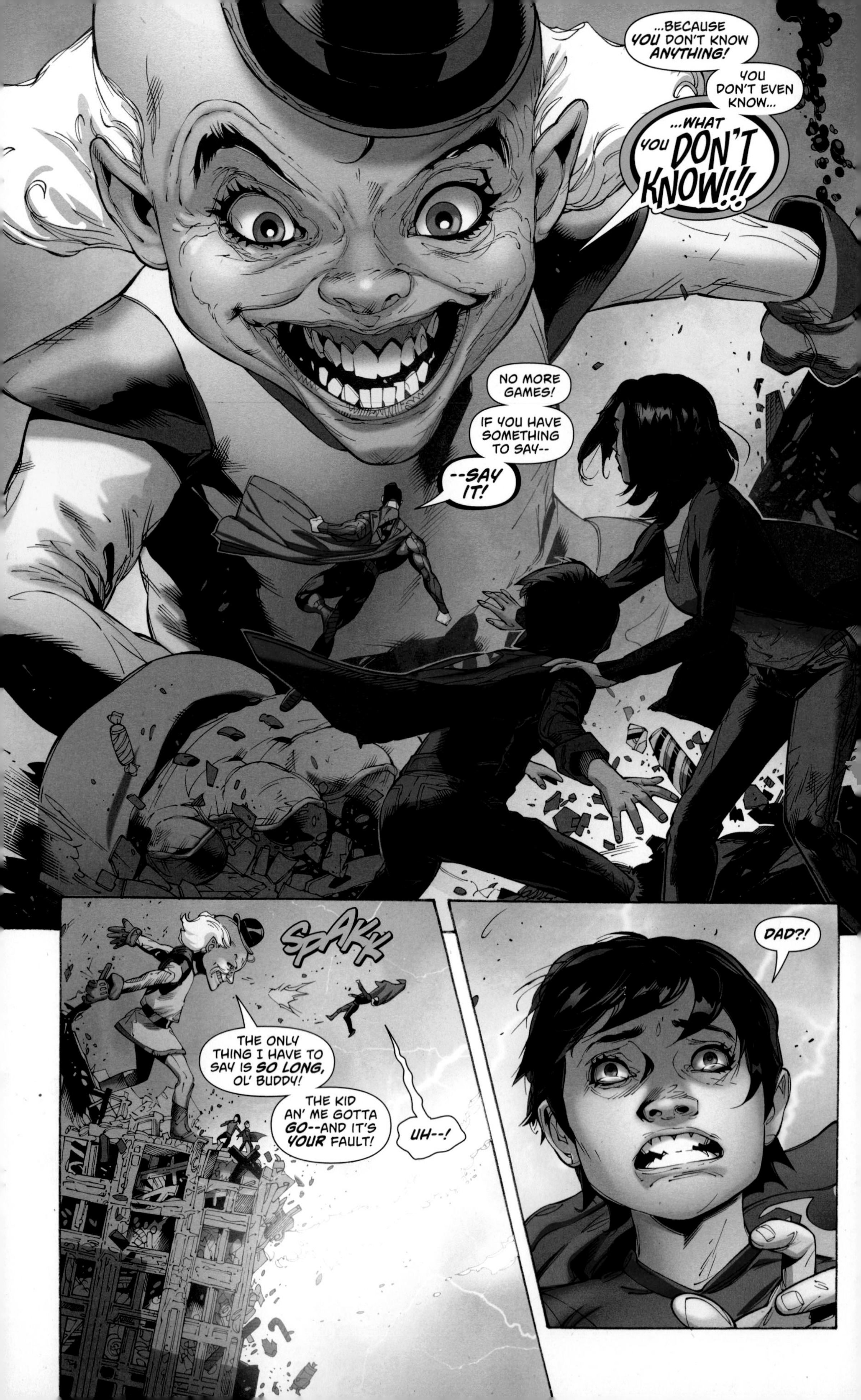
...BECAUSE YOU DON'T KNOW ANYTHING!
YOU DON'T EVEN KNOW...
...WHAT YOU DON'T KNOW!!!
NO MORE GAMES!
IF YOU HAVE SOMETHING TO SAY--
--SAY IT!
SPAK!
THE ONLY THING I HAVE TO SAY IS SO LONG, OL' BUDDY!
THE KID AN' ME GOTTA GO--AND IT'S YOUR FAULT!
UH--!
DAD?!

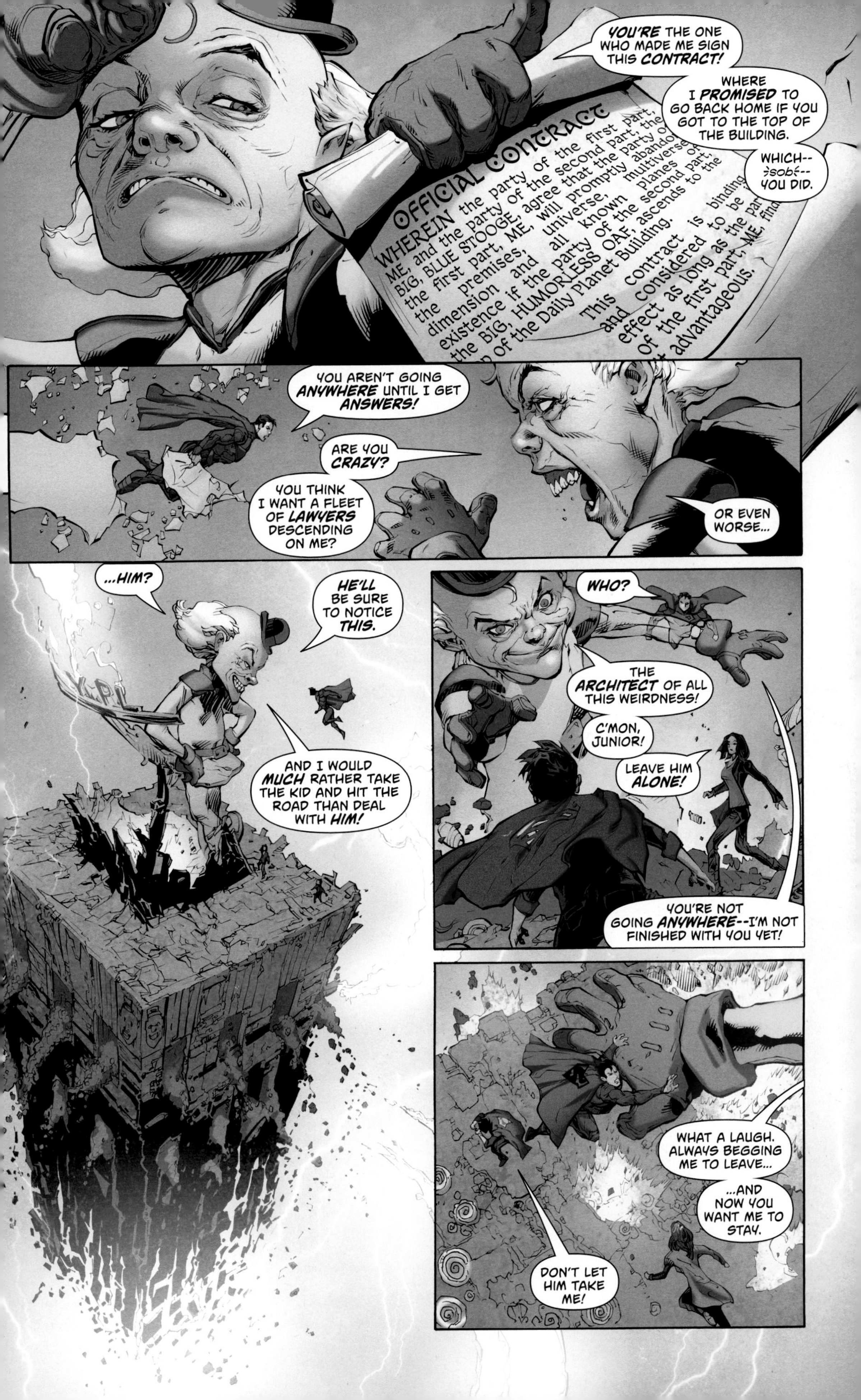
OFFICIAL CONTRACT
WHEREIN the party of the first part,
ME, and the party of the second part, the
BIG, BLUE STOOGE, agree that the party of
the first part, ME, will promptly abando
the premises, universe, multiverse
dimension and all known planes of
existence if the party of the second part,
the BIG, HUMORLESS OAF, ascends to the
p of the Daily Planet Building.
This contract is binding
and considered to be i
effect as long as the par
of the first part, ME, find
t advantageous.
YOU'RE THE ONE WHO MADE ME SIGN THIS CONTRACT!
WHERE I PROMISED TO GO BACK HOME IF YOU GOT TO THE TOP OF THE BUILDING.
WHICH-- sob-- YOU DID.
YOU AREN'T GOING ANYWHERE UNTIL I GET ANSWERS!
ARE YOU CRAZY?
YOU THINK I WANT A FLEET OF LAWYERS DESCENDING ON ME?
OR EVEN WORSE...
...HIM?
HE'LL BE SURE TO NOTICE THIS.
AND I WOULD MUCH RATHER TAKE THE KID AND HIT THE ROAD THAN DEAL WITH HIM!
WHO?
THE ARCHITECT OF ALL THIS WEIRDNESS!
C'MON, JUNIOR!
LEAVE HIM ALONE!
YOU'RE NOT GOING ANYWHERE--I'M NOT FINISHED WITH YOU YET!
WHAT A LAUGH. ALWAYS BEGGING ME TO LEAVE...
...AND NOW YOU WANT ME TO STAY.
DON'T LET HIM TAKE ME!

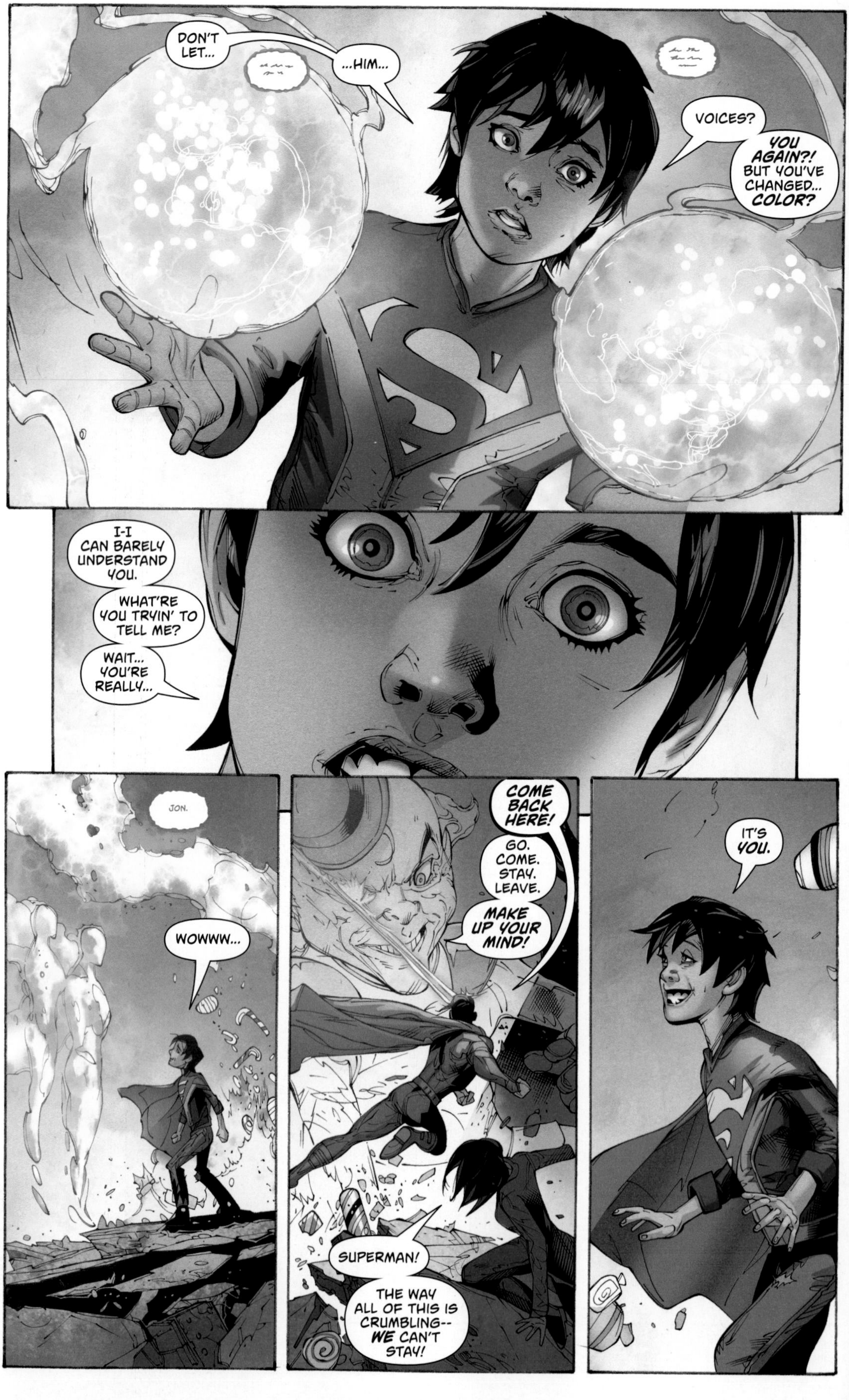

DON'T LET...
...HIM...
VOICES?
YOU AGAIN?! BUT YOU'VE CHANGED... COLOR?
I-I CAN BARELY UNDERSTAND YOU.
WHAT'RE YOU TRYIN' TO TELL ME?
WAIT... YOU'RE REALLY...
JON.
WOWWW...
COME BACK HERE!
GO. COME. STAY. LEAVE.
MAKE UP YOUR MIND!
SUPERMAN!
THE WAY ALL OF THIS IS CRUMBLING-- WE CAN'T STAY!
IT'S YOU.

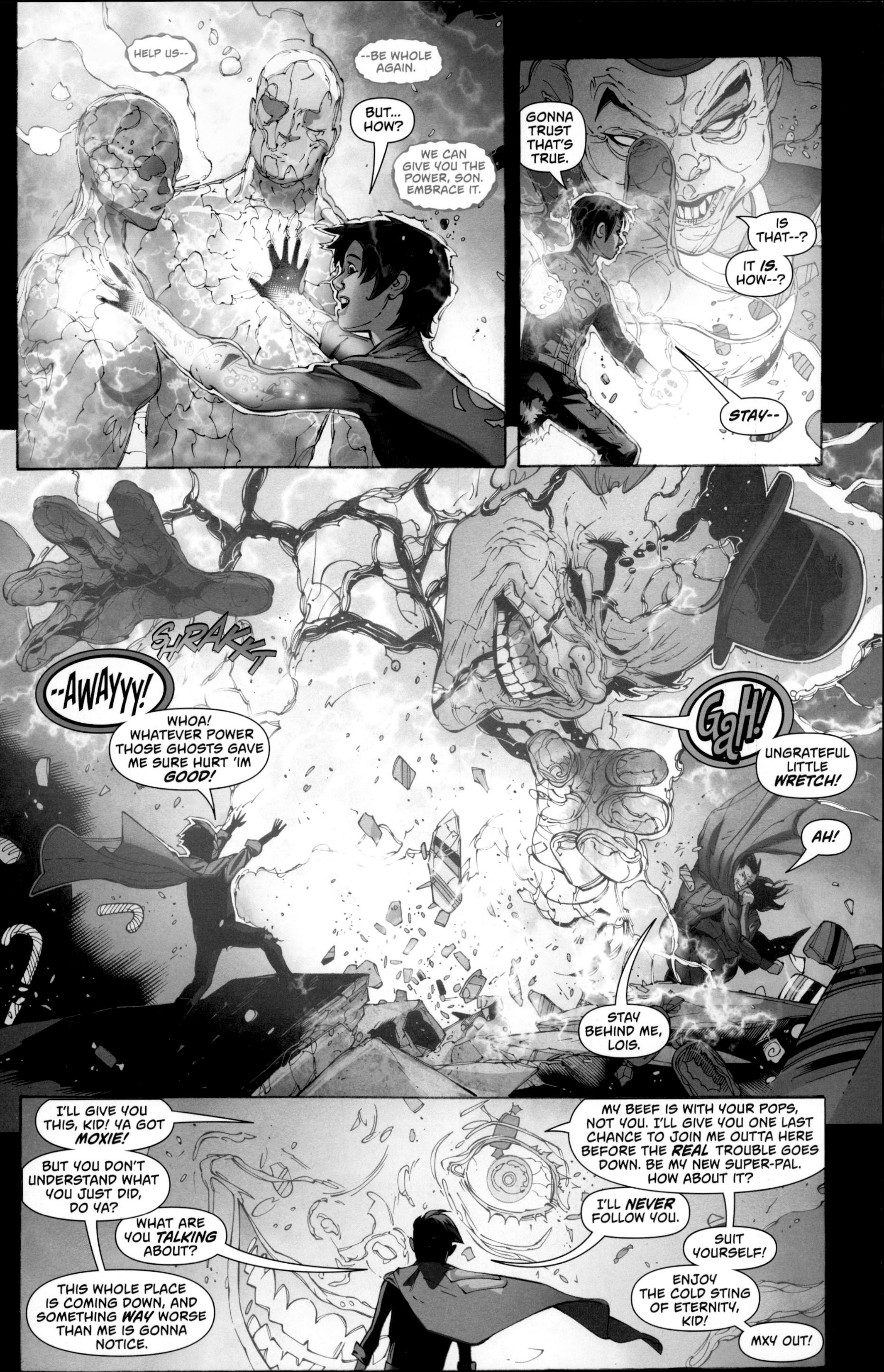
HELP US--
--BE WHOLE AGAIN.
BUT... HOW?
WE CAN GIVE YOU THE POWER, SON. EMBRACE IT.
GONNA TRUST THAT'S TRUE.
IS THAT--?
IT IS. HOW--?
STAY--
SHRAKKT
--AWAYYY!
WHOA! WHATEVER POWER THOSE GHOSTS GAVE ME SURE HURT 'IM GOOD!
GAH!
UNGRATEFUL LITTLE WRETCH!
AH!
STAY BEHIND ME, LOIS.
I'LL GIVE YOU THIS, KID! YA GOT MOXIE!
BUT YOU DON'T UNDERSTAND WHAT YOU JUST DID, DO YA?
WHAT ARE YOU TALKING ABOUT?
THIS WHOLE PLACE IS COMING DOWN, AND SOMETHING WAY WORSE THAN ME IS GONNA NOTICE.
MY BEEF IS WITH YOUR POPS, NOT YOU. I'LL GIVE YOU ONE LAST CHANCE TO JOIN ME OUTTA HERE BEFORE THE REAL TROUBLE GOES DOWN. BE MY NEW SUPER-PAL. HOW ABOUT IT?
I'LL NEVER FOLLOW YOU.
SUIT YOURSELF!
ENJOY THE COLD STING OF ETERNITY, KID!
MXY OUT!

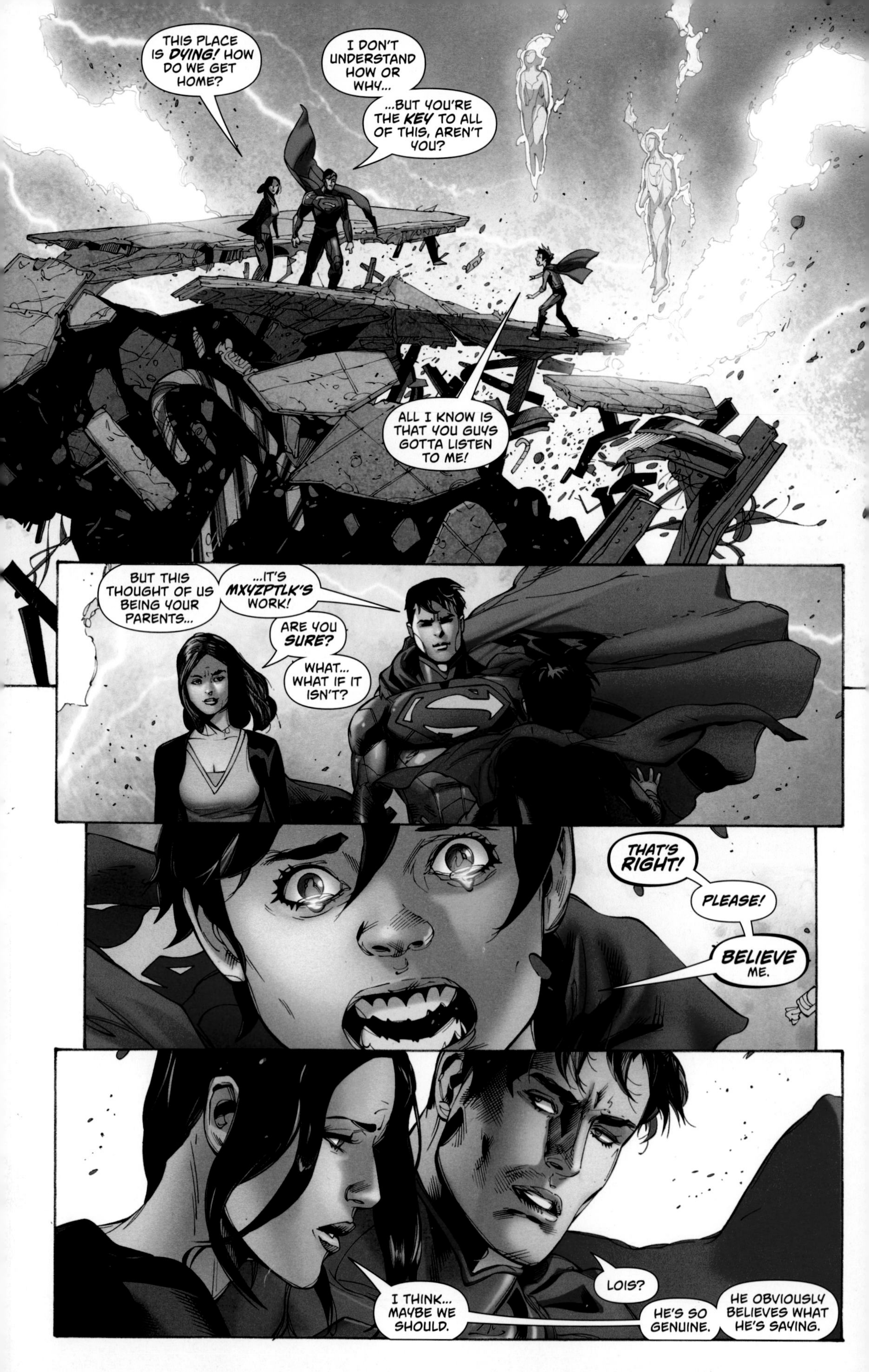
THIS PLACE IS DYING! HOW DO WE GET HOME?
I DON'T UNDERSTAND HOW OR WHY...
...BUT YOU'RE THE KEY TO ALL OF THIS, AREN'T YOU?
ALL I KNOW IS THAT YOU GUYS GOTTA LISTEN TO ME!
BUT THIS THOUGHT OF US BEING YOUR PARENTS...
...IT'S MXYZPTLK'S WORK!
ARE YOU SURE?
WHAT... WHAT IF IT ISN'T?
THAT'S RIGHT!
PLEASE!
BELIEVE ME.
LOIS?
I THINK... MAYBE WE SHOULD.
HE'S SO GENUINE.
HE OBVIOUSLY BELIEVES WHAT HE'S SAYING.

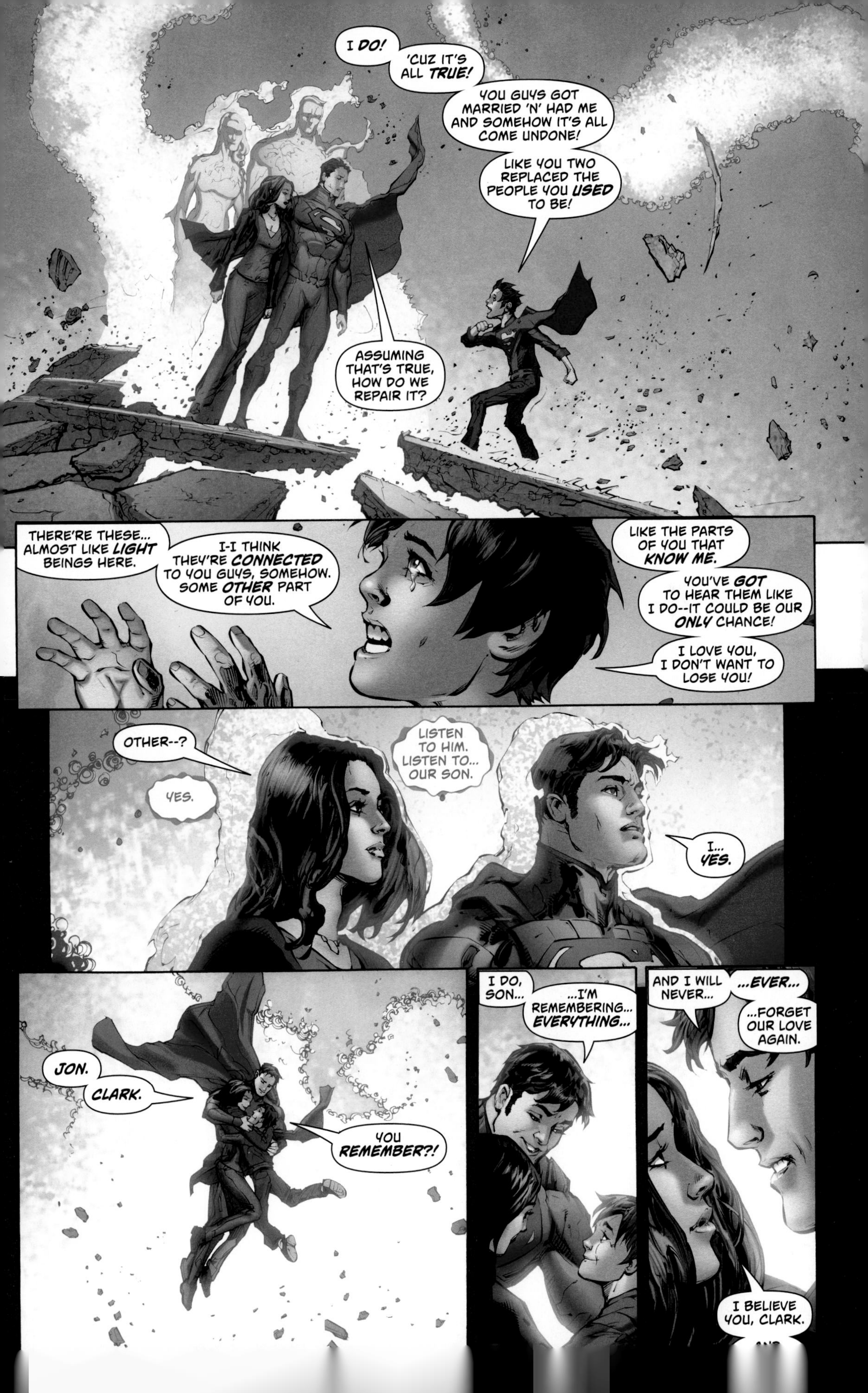
I DO!
'CUZ IT'S ALL TRUE!
YOU GUYS GOT MARRIED 'N' HAD ME AND SOMEHOW IT'S ALL COME UNDONE!
LIKE YOU TWO REPLACED THE PEOPLE YOU USED TO BE!
ASSUMING THAT'S TRUE, HOW DO WE REPAIR IT?
THERE'RE THESE... ALMOST LIKE LIGHT BEINGS HERE.
I-I THINK THEY'RE CONNECTED TO YOU GUYS, SOMEHOW. SOME OTHER PART OF YOU.
LIKE THE PARTS OF YOU THAT KNOW ME.
YOU'VE GOT TO HEAR THEM LIKE I DO--IT COULD BE OUR ONLY CHANCE!
I LOVE YOU, I DON'T WANT TO LOSE YOU!
OTHER--?
YES.
LISTEN TO HIM. LISTEN TO... OUR SON.
I... YES.
JON.
CLARK.
YOU REMEMBER?!
I DO, SON...
...I'M REMEMBERING... EVERYTHING...
AND I WILL NEVER...
...EVER...
...FORGET OUR LOVE AGAIN.
I BELIEVE YOU, CLARK.

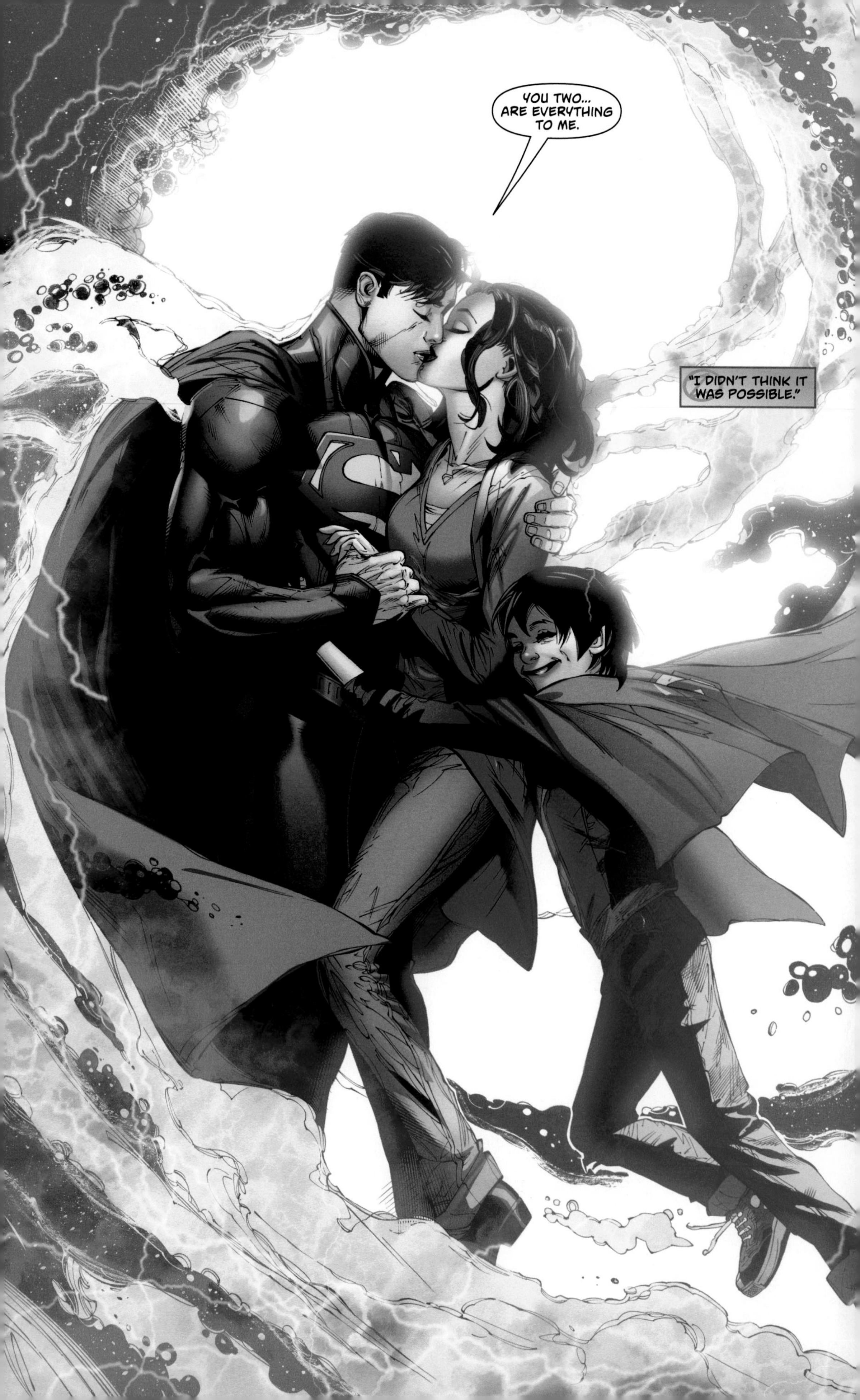

YOU TWO... ARE EVERYTHING TO ME.
"I DIDN'T THINK IT WAS POSSIBLE."

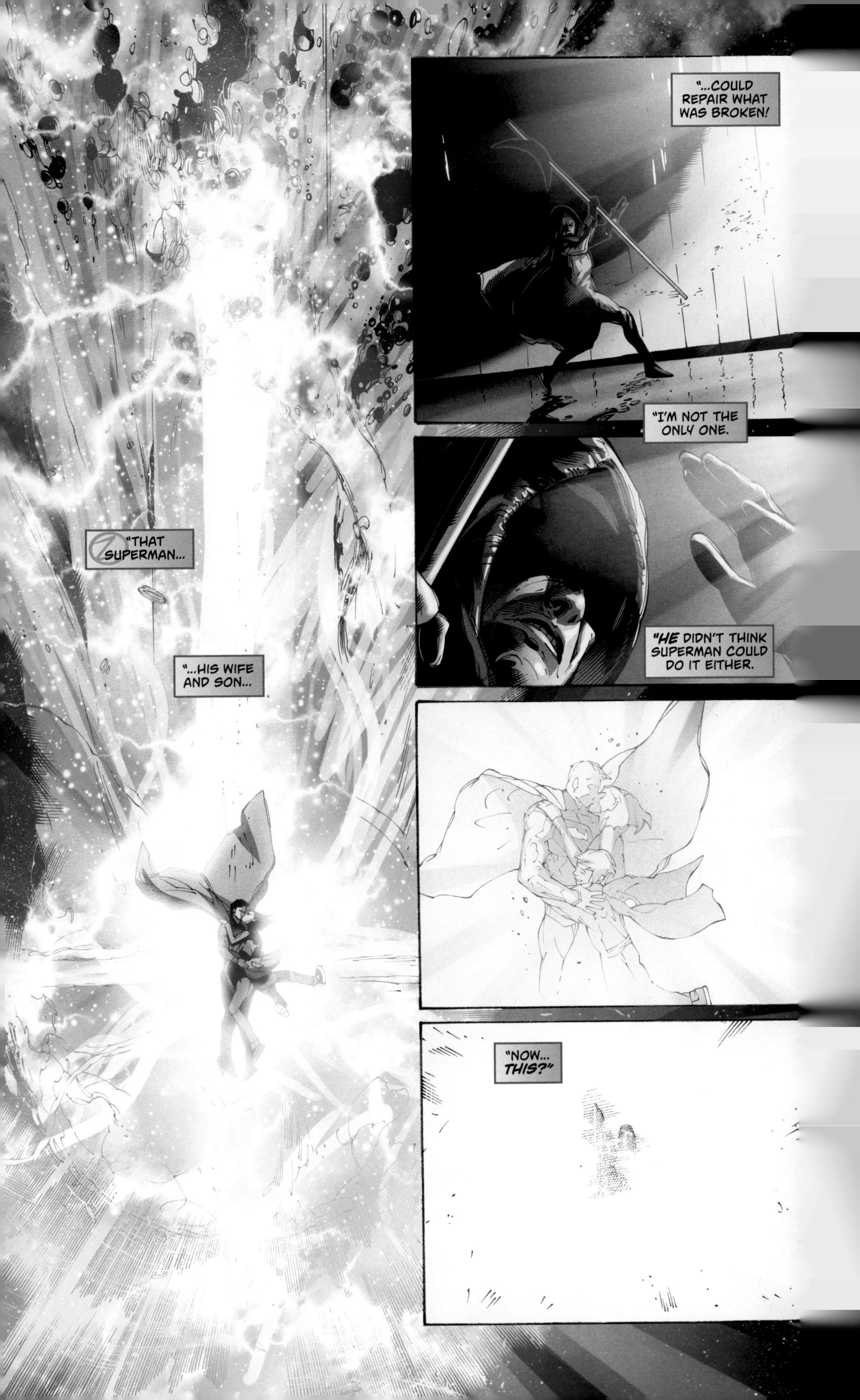
"...COULD REPAIR WHAT WAS BROKEN!
"I'M NOT THE ONLY ONE.
"HE DIDN'T THINK SUPERMAN COULD DO IT EITHER.
"THAT SUPERMAN...
"...HIS WIFE AND SON...
"NOW... THIS?"

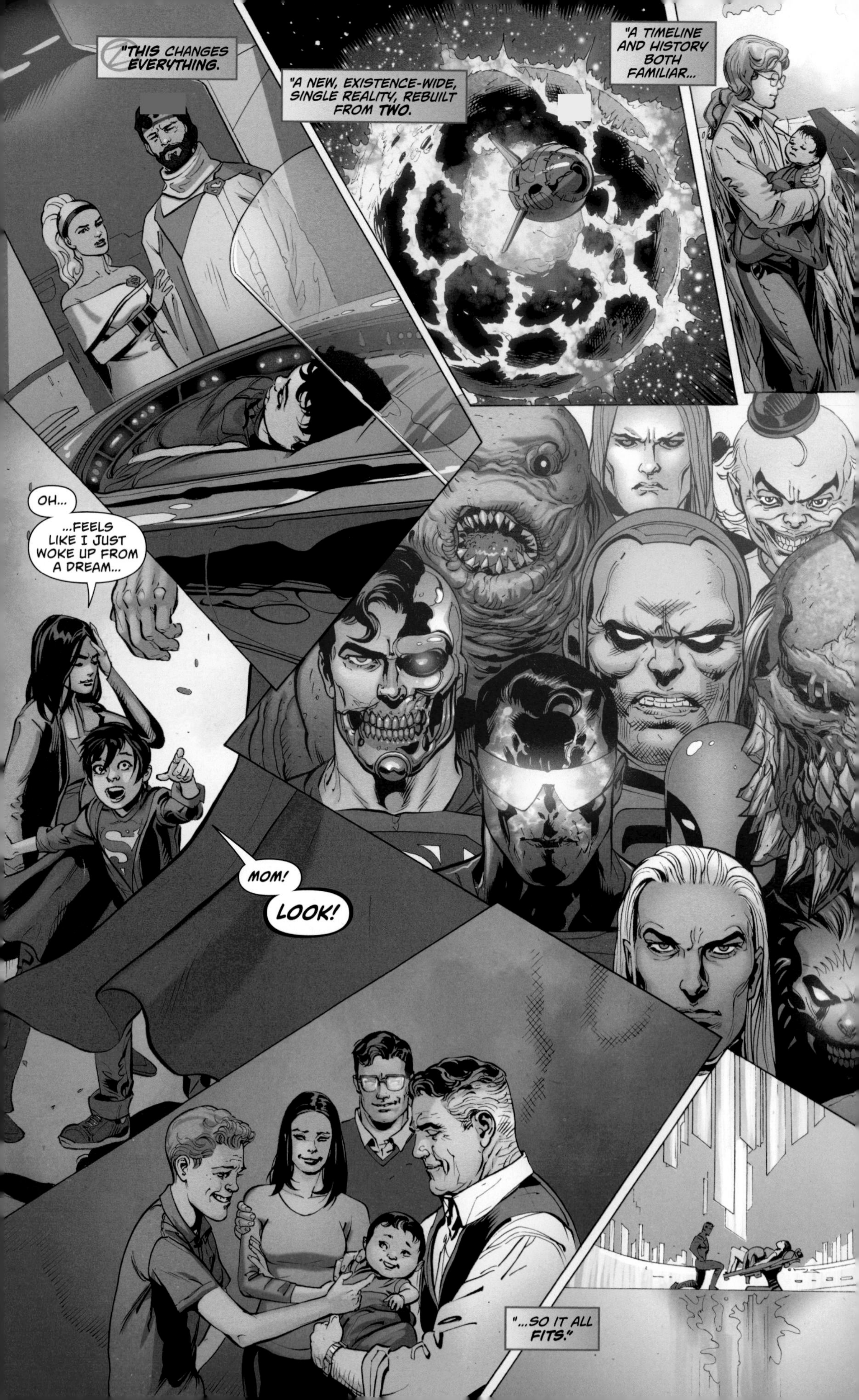
"THIS CHANGES EVERYTHING.
"A NEW, EXISTENCE-WIDE, SINGLE REALITY, REBUILT FROM TWO.
"A TIMELINE AND HISTORY BOTH FAMILIAR...
OH...
...FEELS LIKE I JUST WOKE UP FROM A DREAM...
MOM!
LOOK!
"...SO IT ALL FITS."

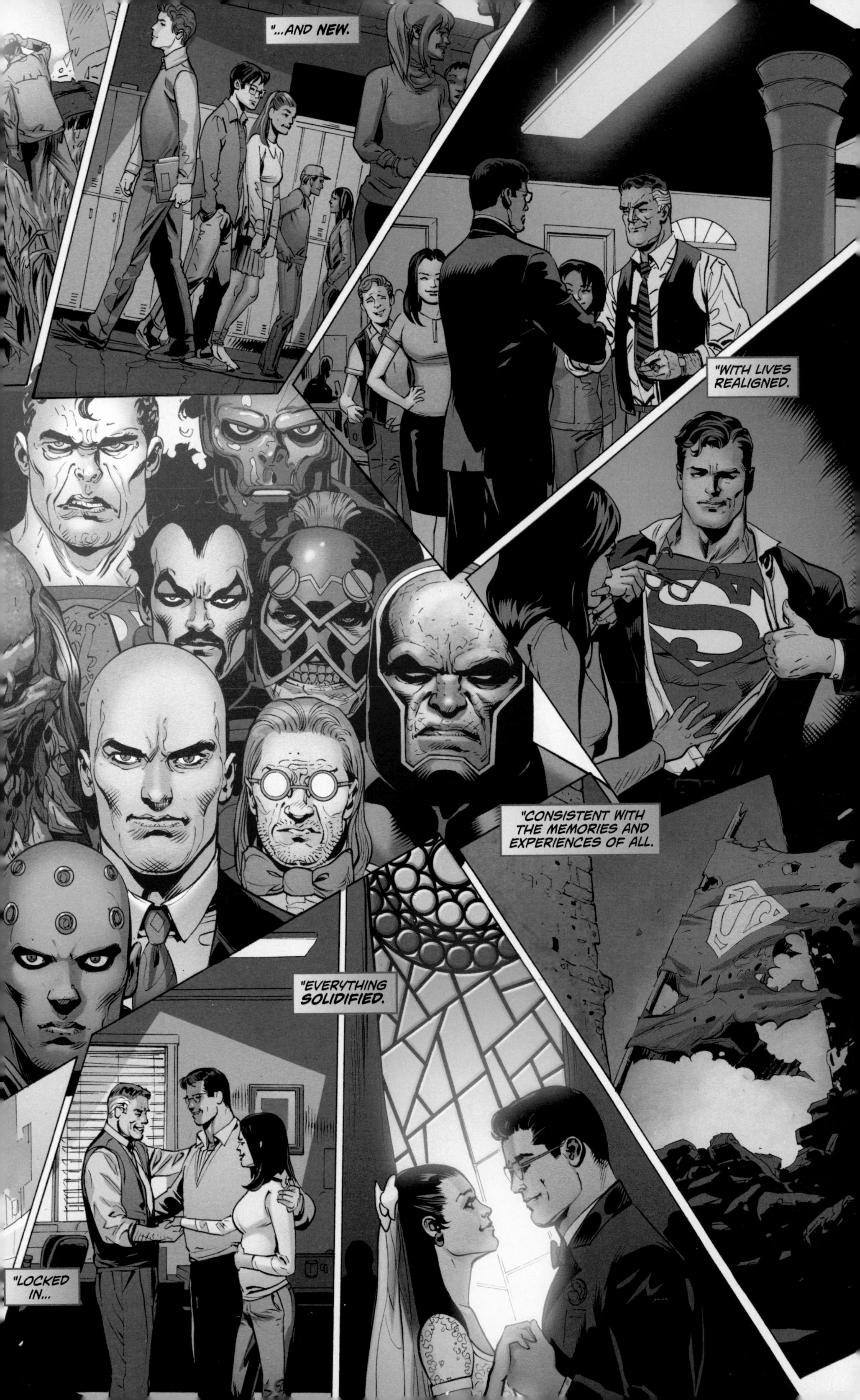
"...AND NEW.
"WITH LIVES REALIGNED.
"CONSISTENT WITH THE MEMORIES AND EXPERIENCES OF ALL.
"EVERYTHING SOLIDIFIED.
"LOCKED IN...

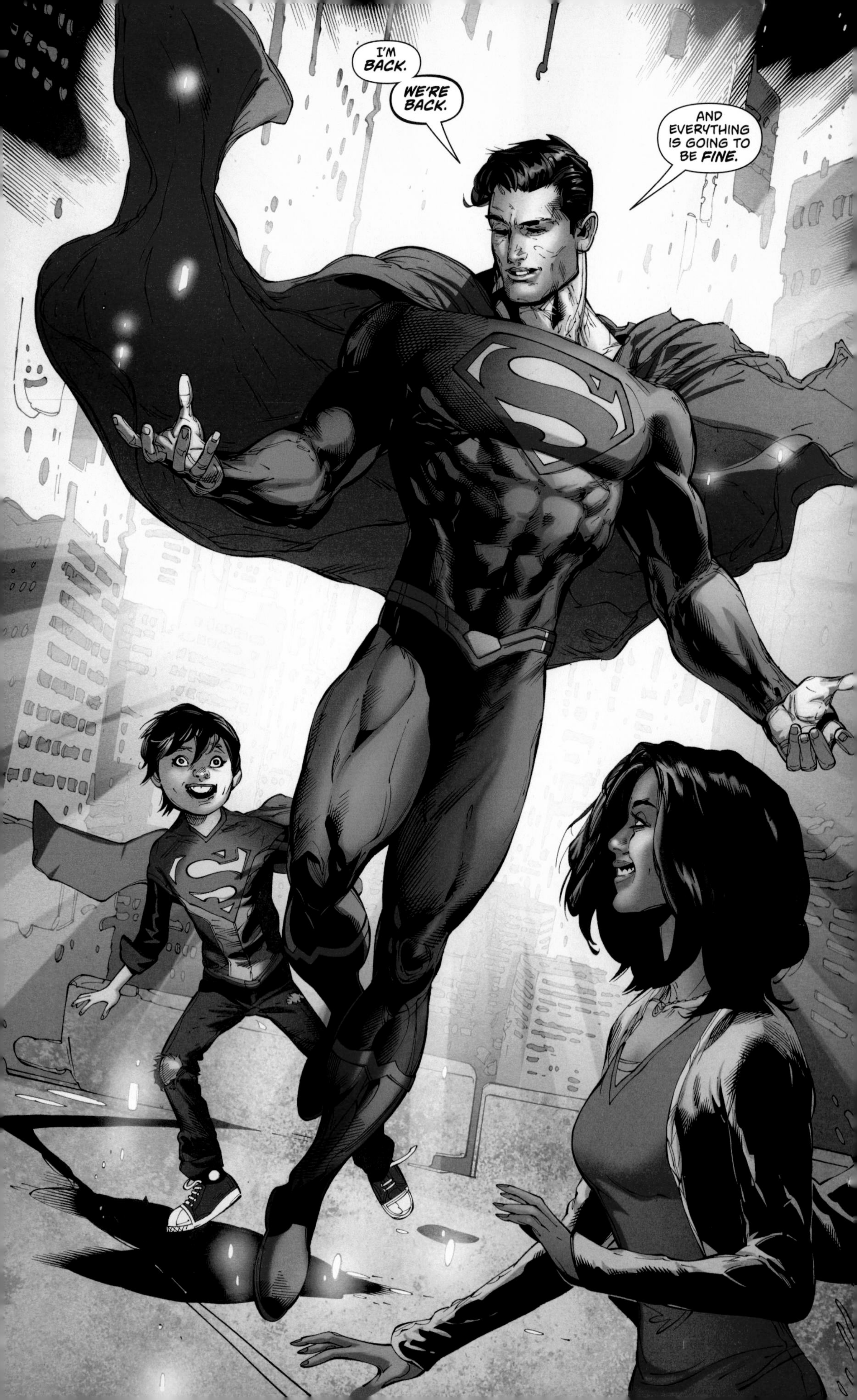
I'M BACK.
WE'RE BACK.
AND EVERYTHING IS GOING TO BE FINE.

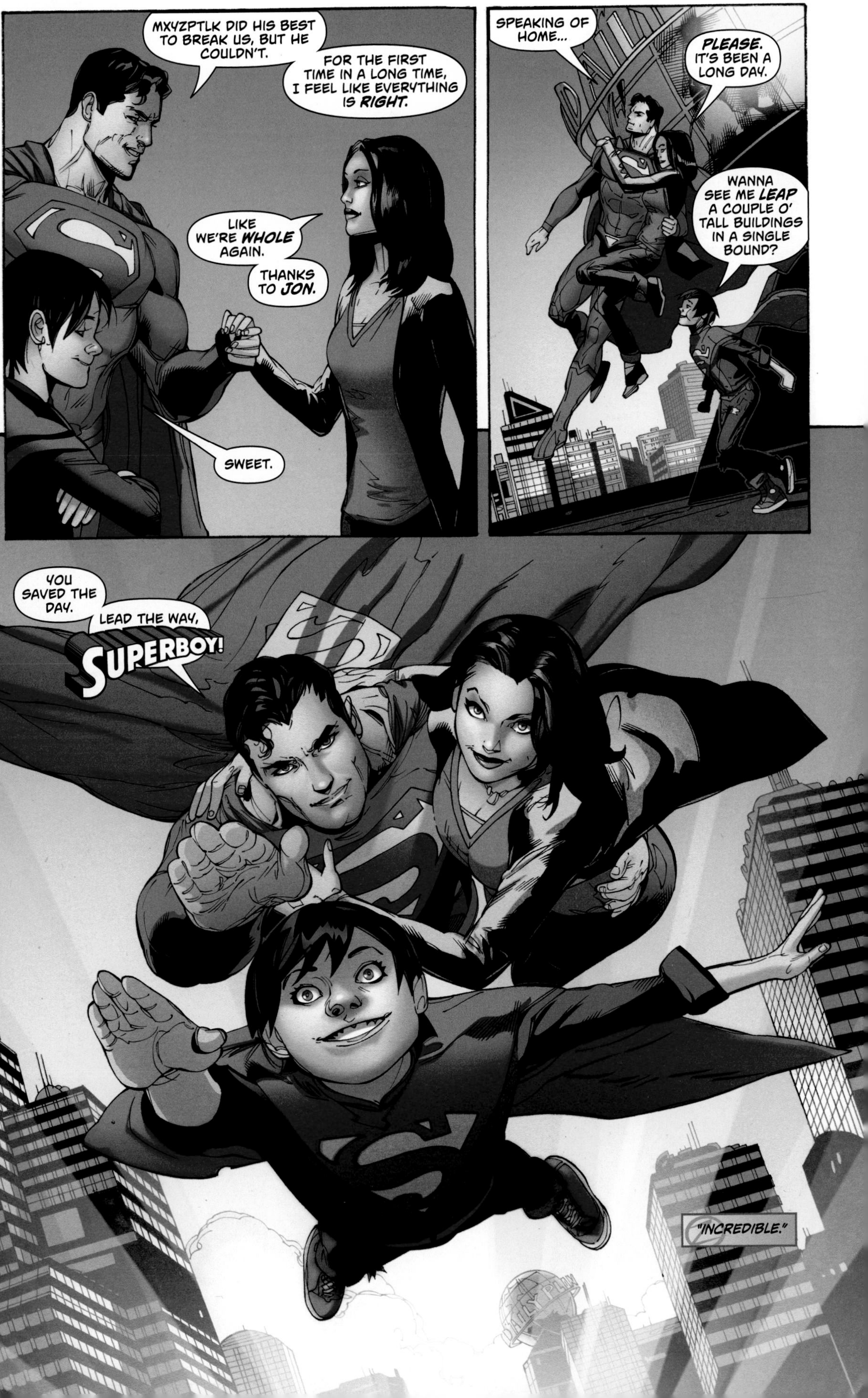
MXYZPTLK DID HIS BEST TO BREAK US, BUT HE COULDN'T.
FOR THE FIRST TIME IN A LONG TIME, I FEEL LIKE EVERYTHING IS RIGHT.
LIKE WE'RE WHOLE AGAIN.
THANKS TO JON.
SWEET.
SPEAKING OF HOME...
PLEASE. IT'S BEEN A LONG DAY.
WANNA SEE ME LEAP A COUPLE O' TALL BUILDINGS IN A SINGLE BOUND?
YOU SAVED THE DAY.
LEAD THE WAY,
SUPERBOY!
"INCREDIBLE."

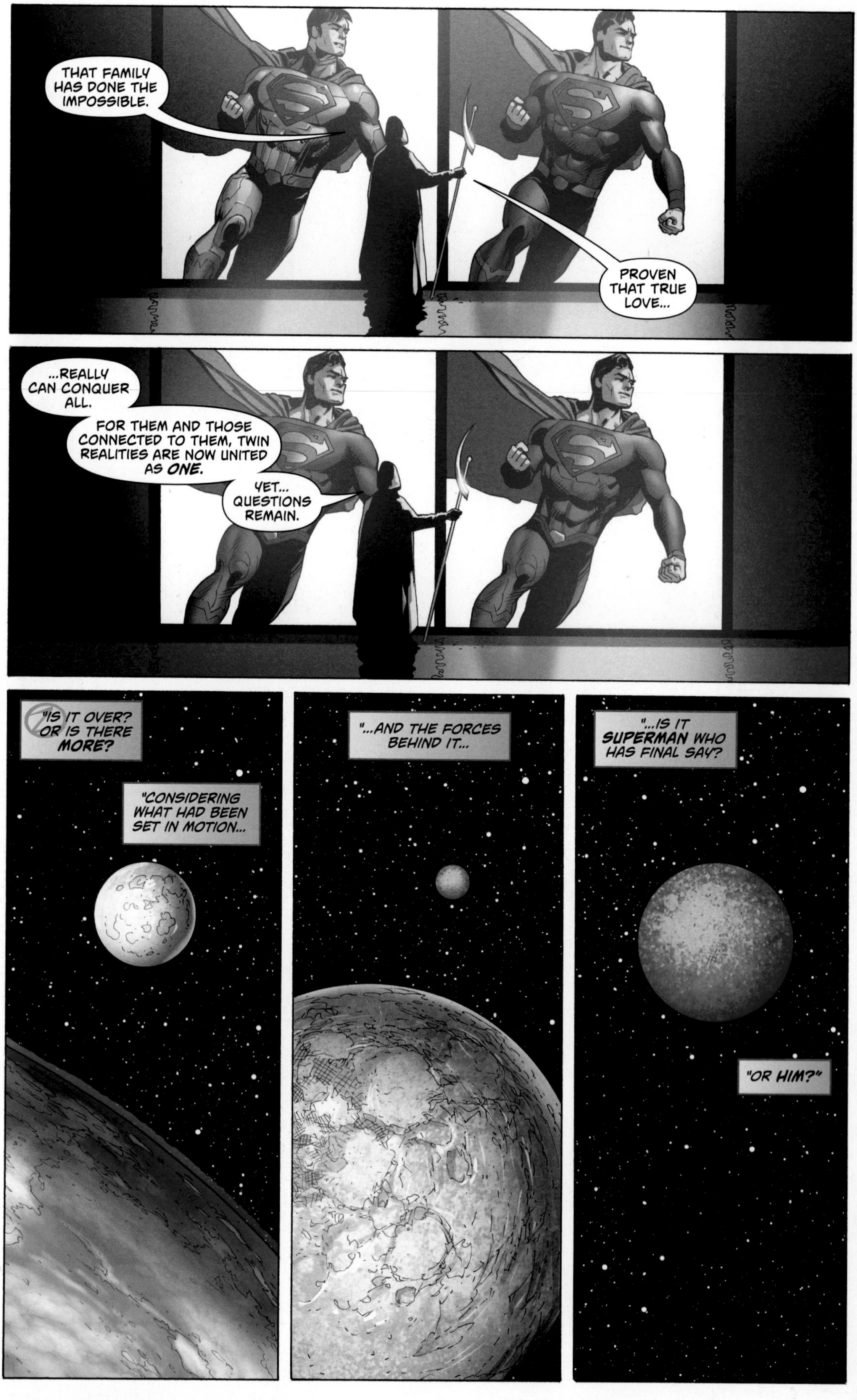
THAT FAMILY HAS DONE THE IMPOSSIBLE.
PROVEN THAT TRUE LOVE...
...REALLY CAN CONQUER ALL.
FOR THEM AND THOSE CONNECTED TO THEM, TWIN REALITIES ARE NOW UNITED AS *ONE*.
YET... QUESTIONS REMAIN.
"IS IT OVER? OR IS THERE *MORE*?
"CONSIDERING WHAT HAD BEEN SET IN MOTION...
"...AND THE FORCES BEHIND IT...
"...IS IT *SUPERMAN* WHO HAS FINAL SAY?
"OR *HIM*?"

SUPERMAN REBORN

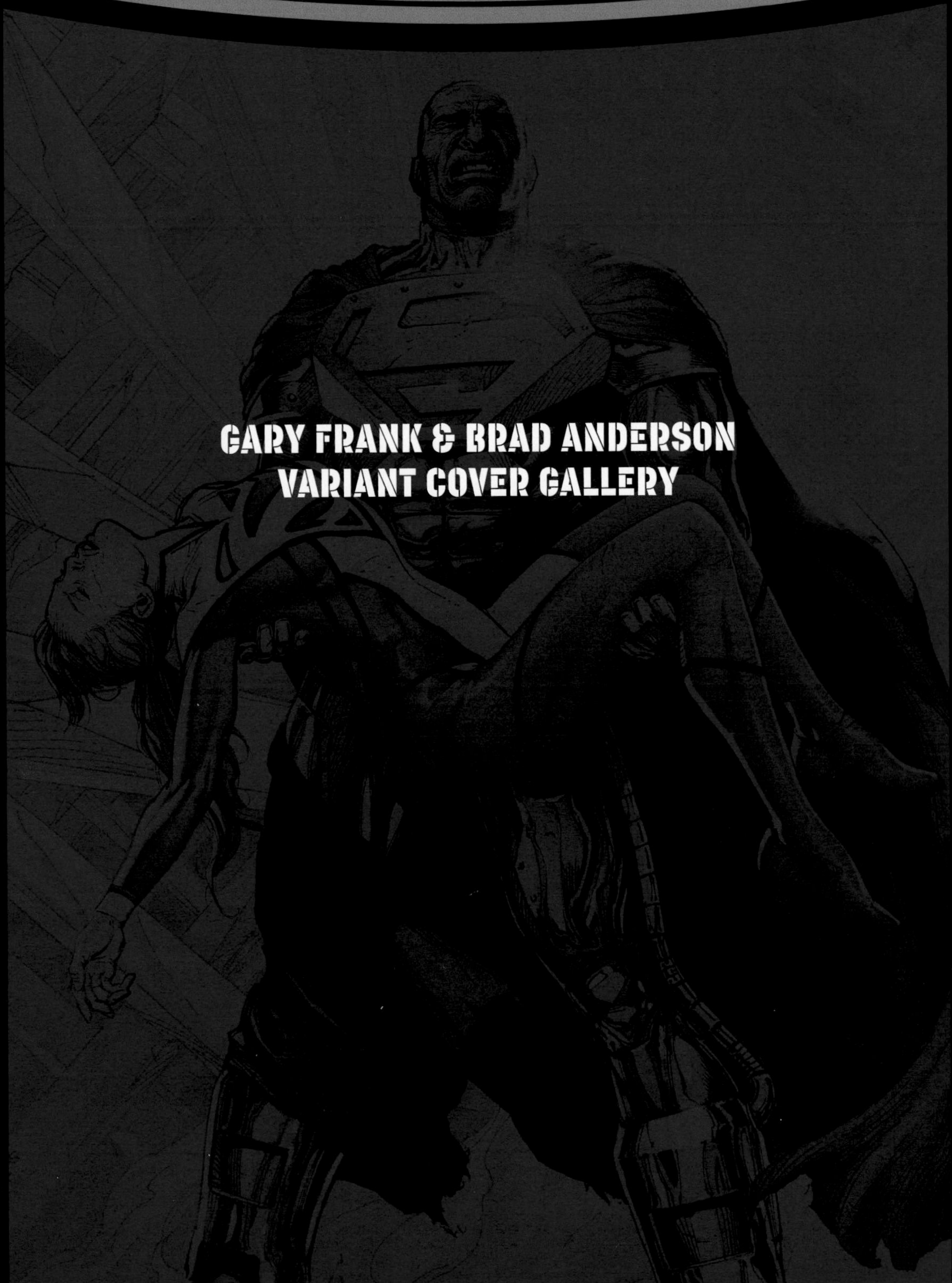

GARY FRANK & BRAD ANDERSON
VARIANT COVER GALLERY

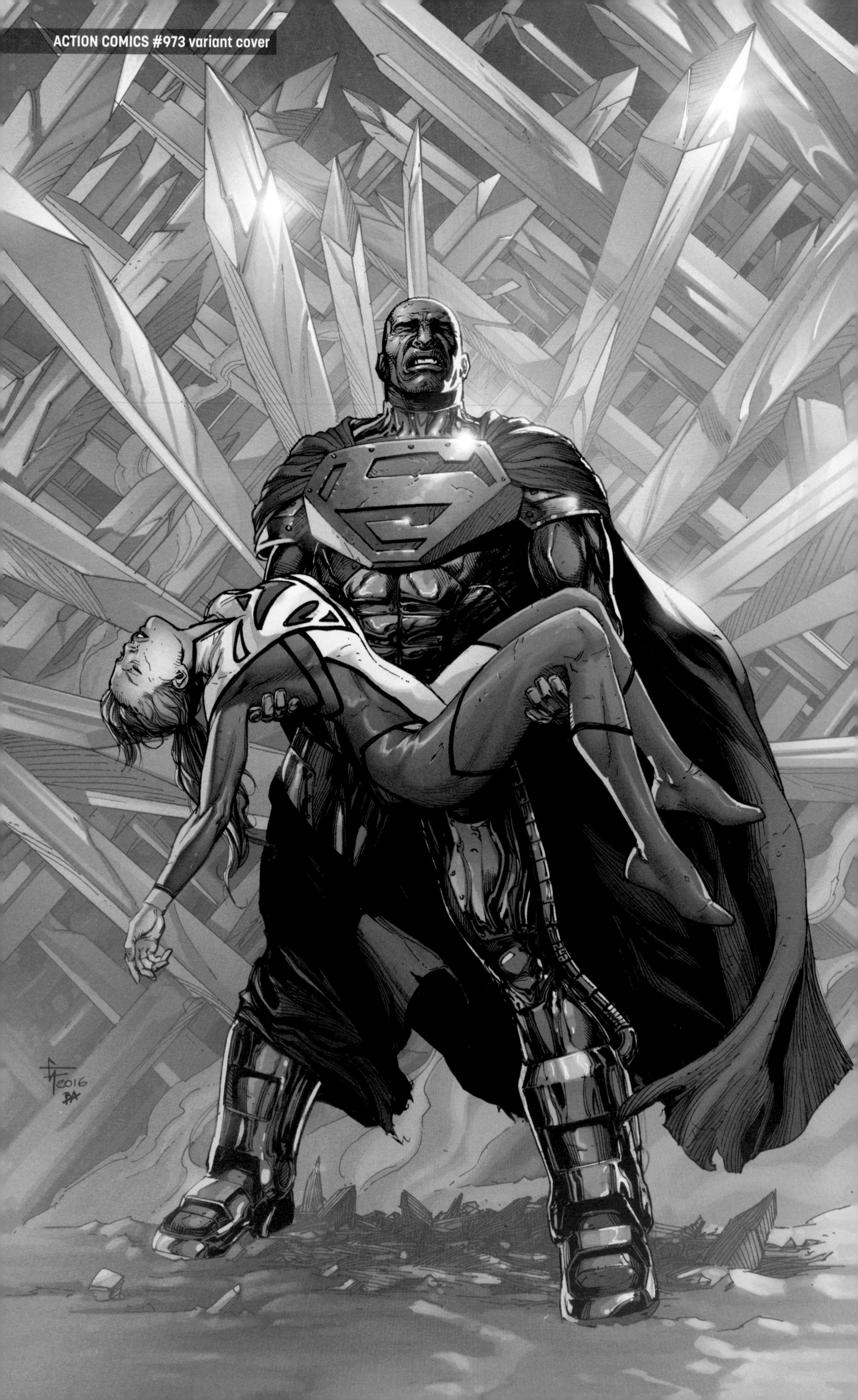

ACTION COMICS #973 variant cover

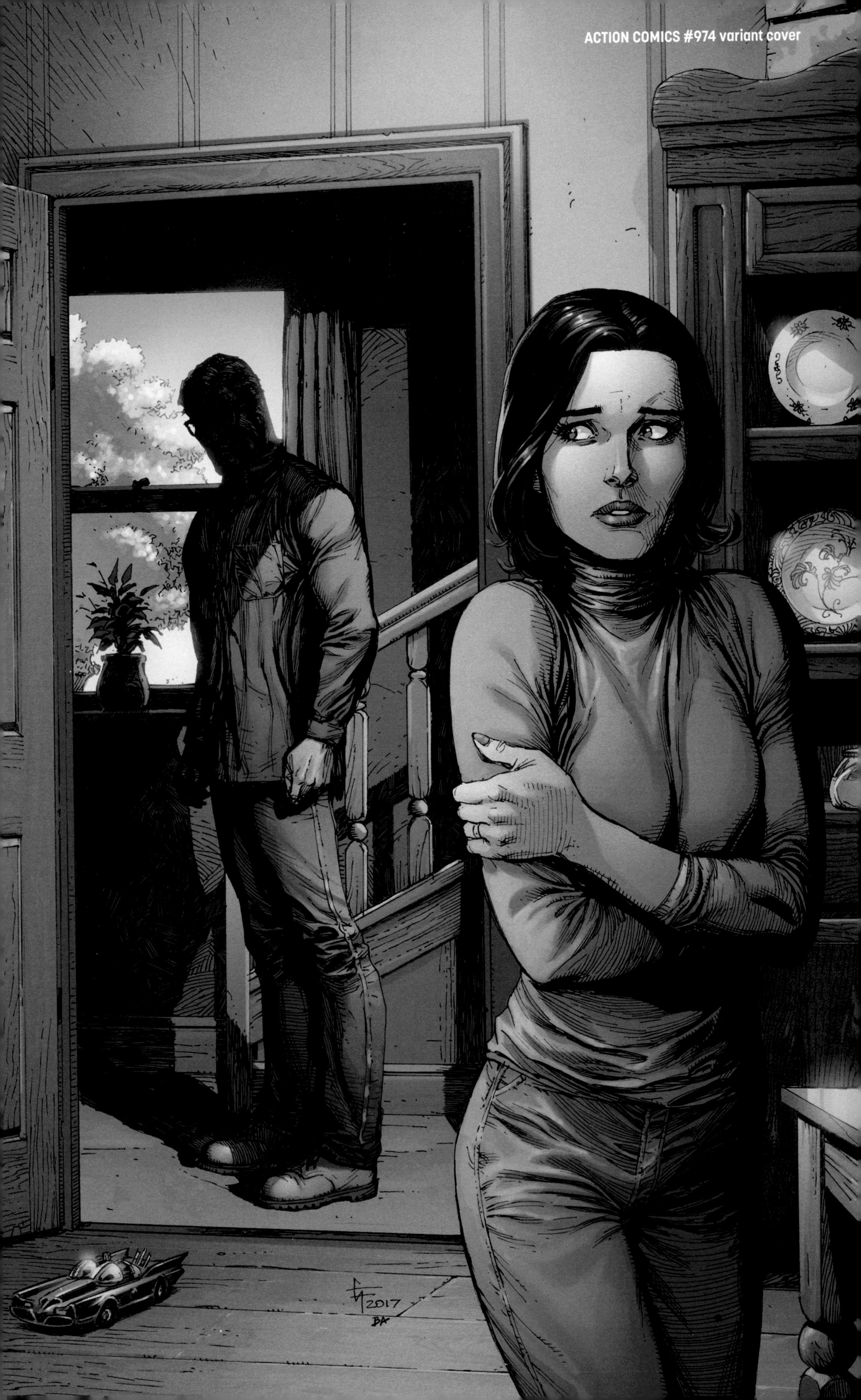

ACTION COMICS #974 variant cover

SUPERMAN #18 variant cover

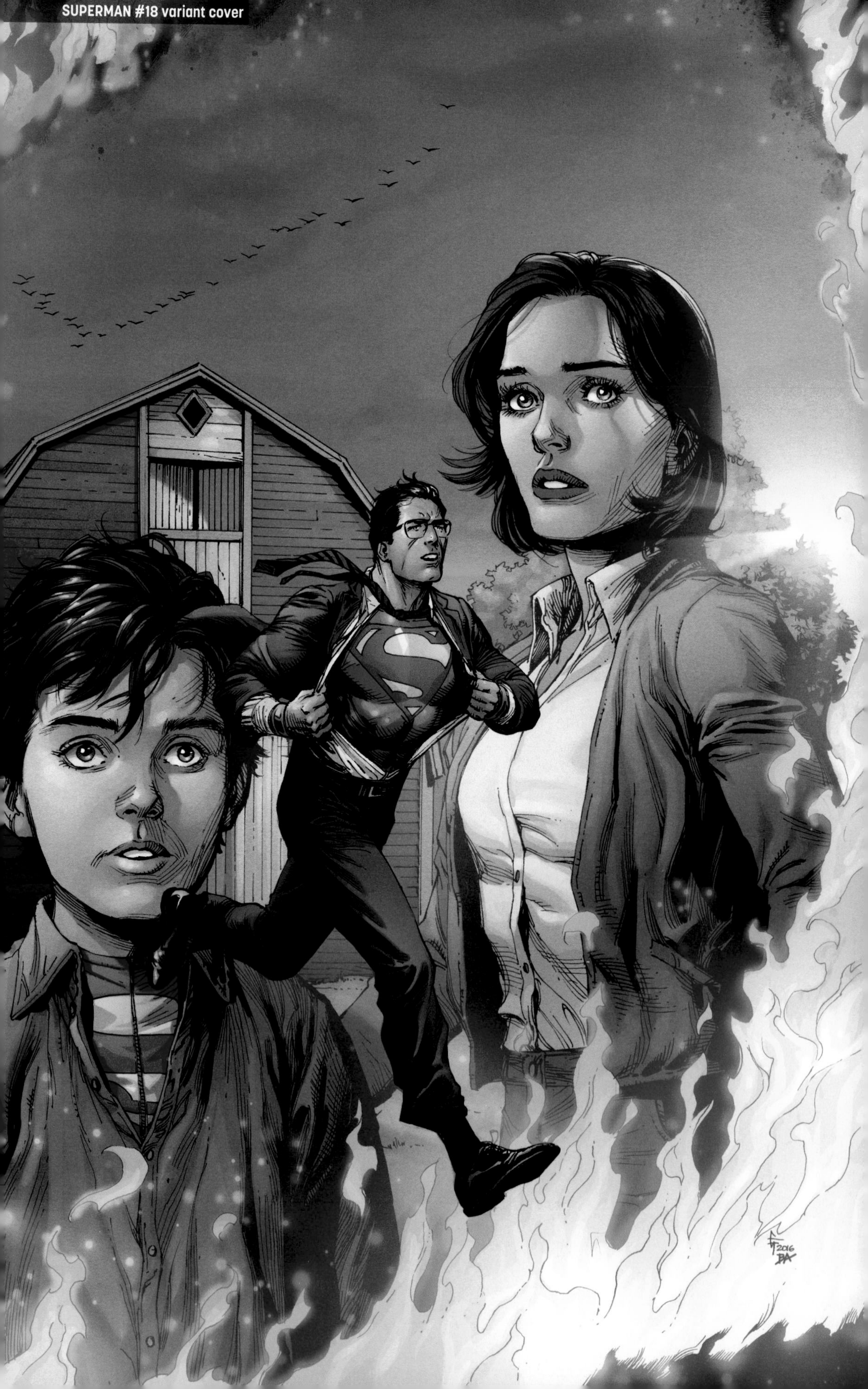

ACTION COMICS #975 variant cover

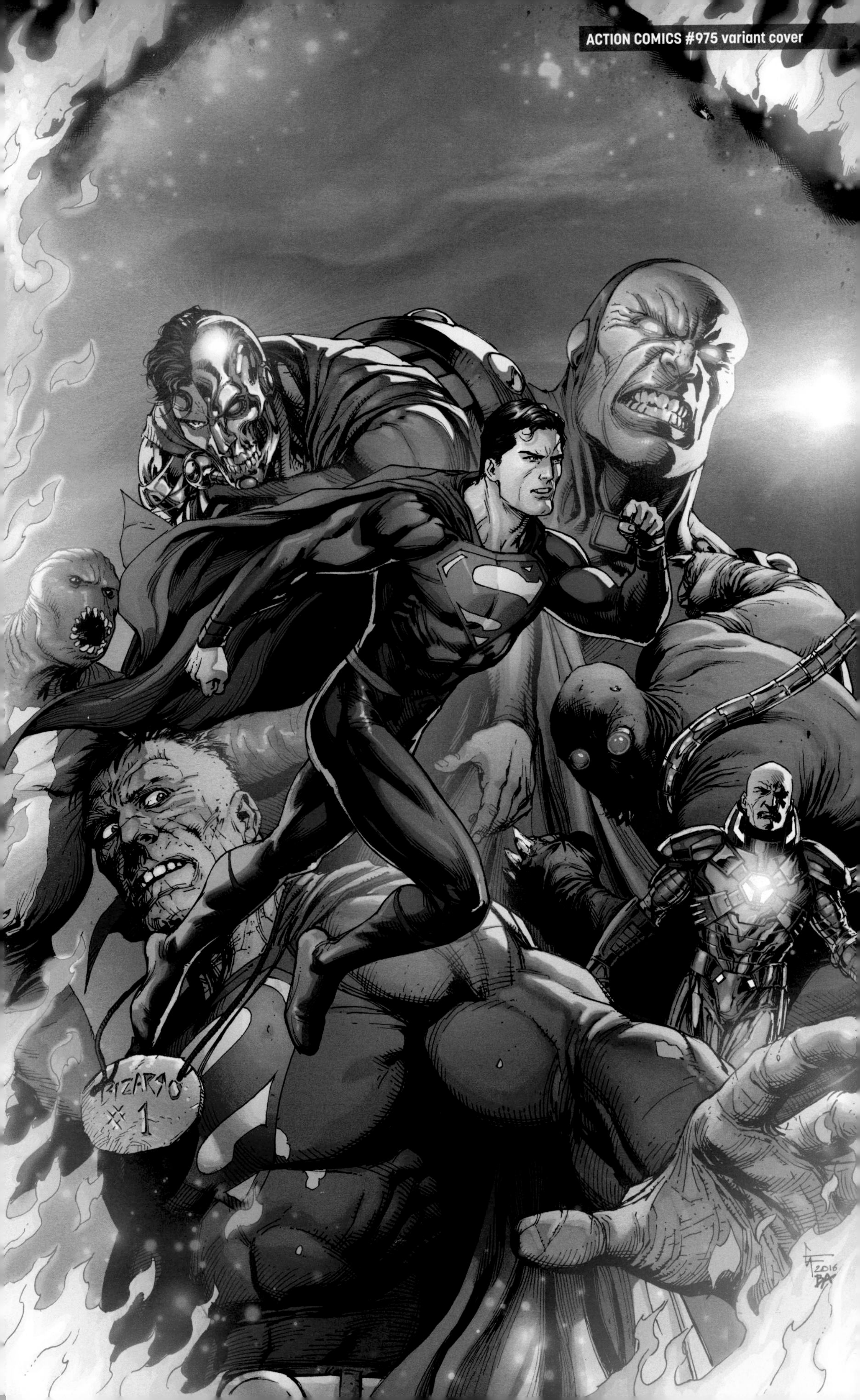

SUPERMAN #19 variant cover

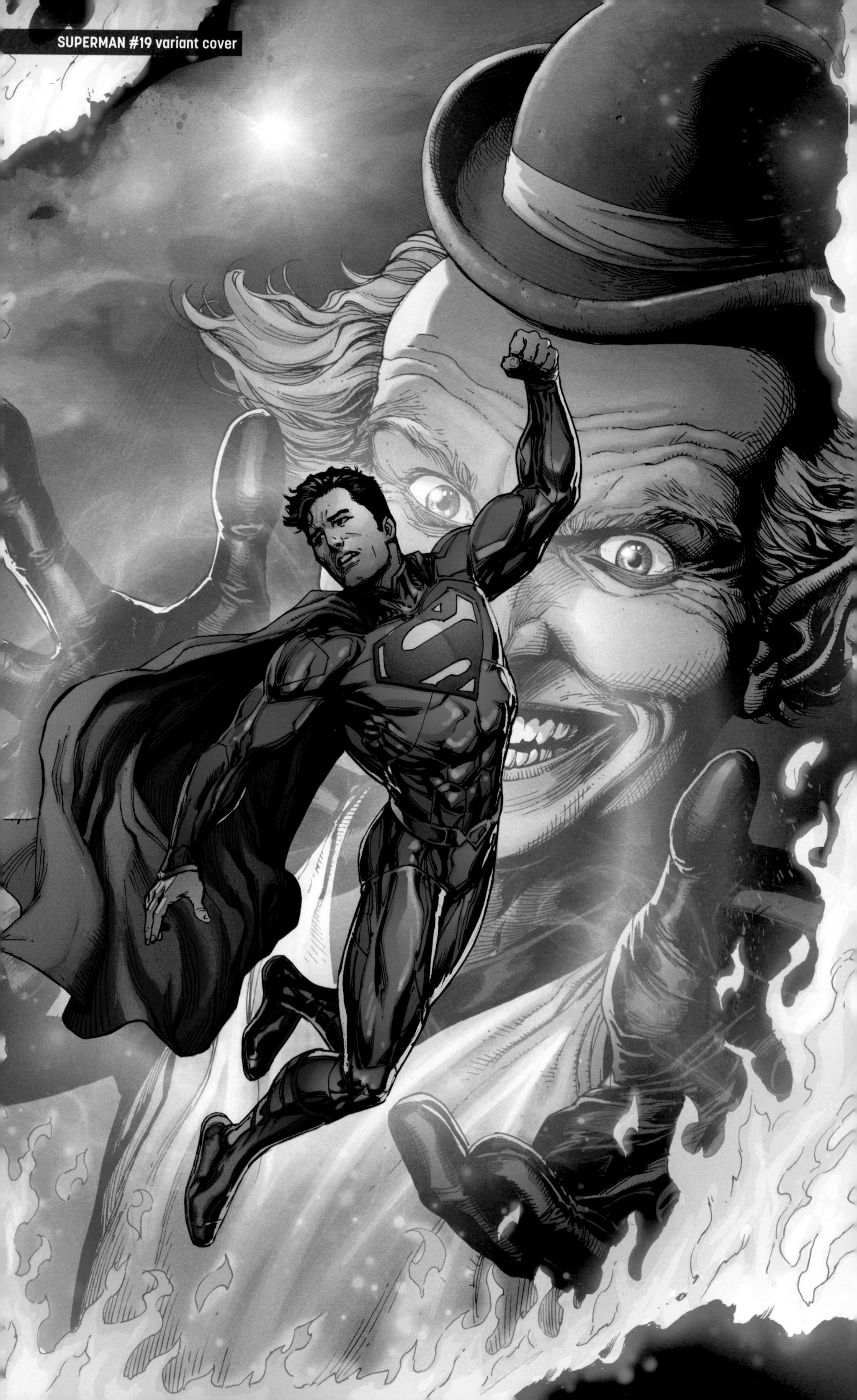

ACTION COMICS #976 variant cover

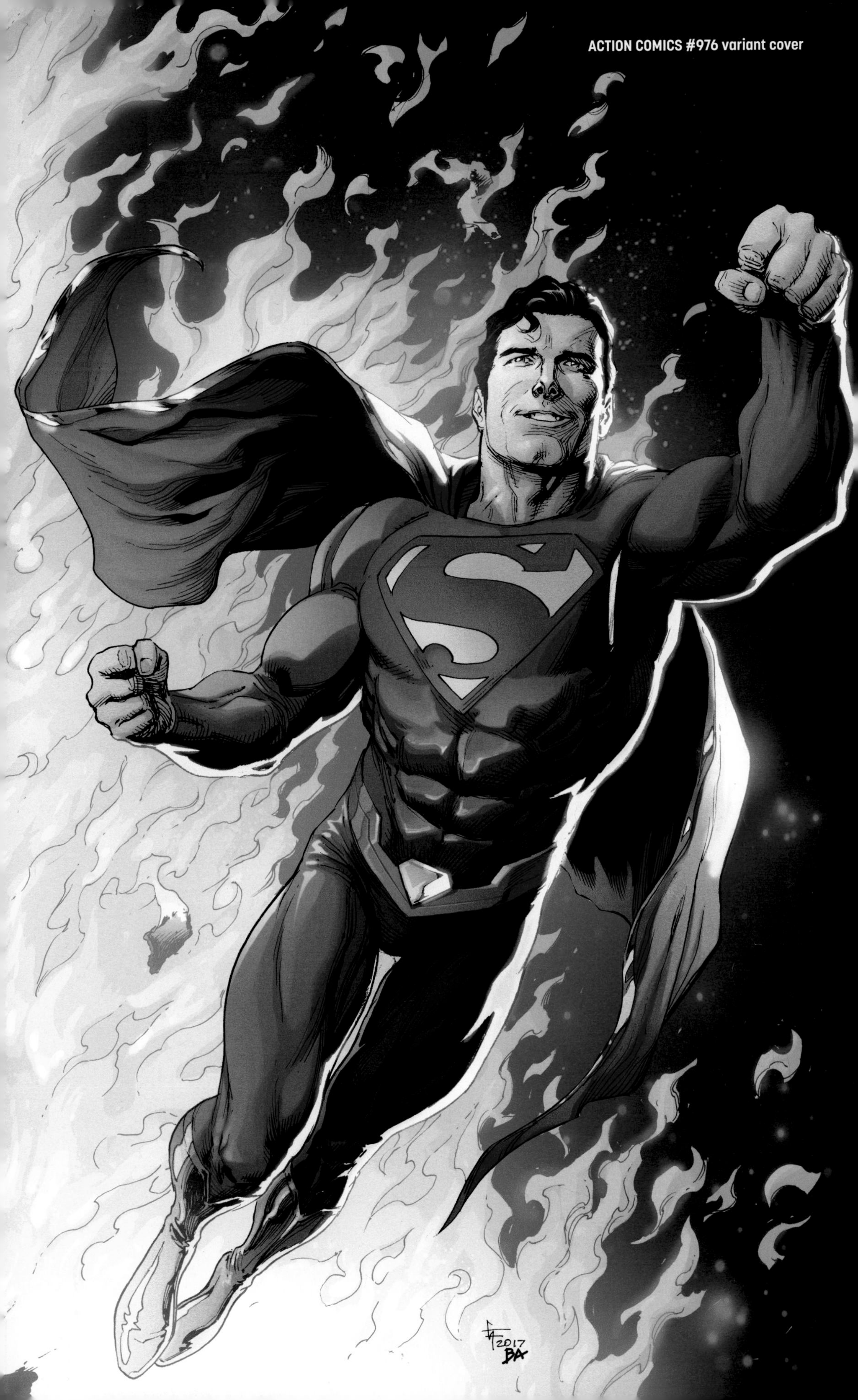

SUPERMAN REBORN COSTUME DESIGN BY PATRICK GLEASON

ART BY TOM DERRENICK

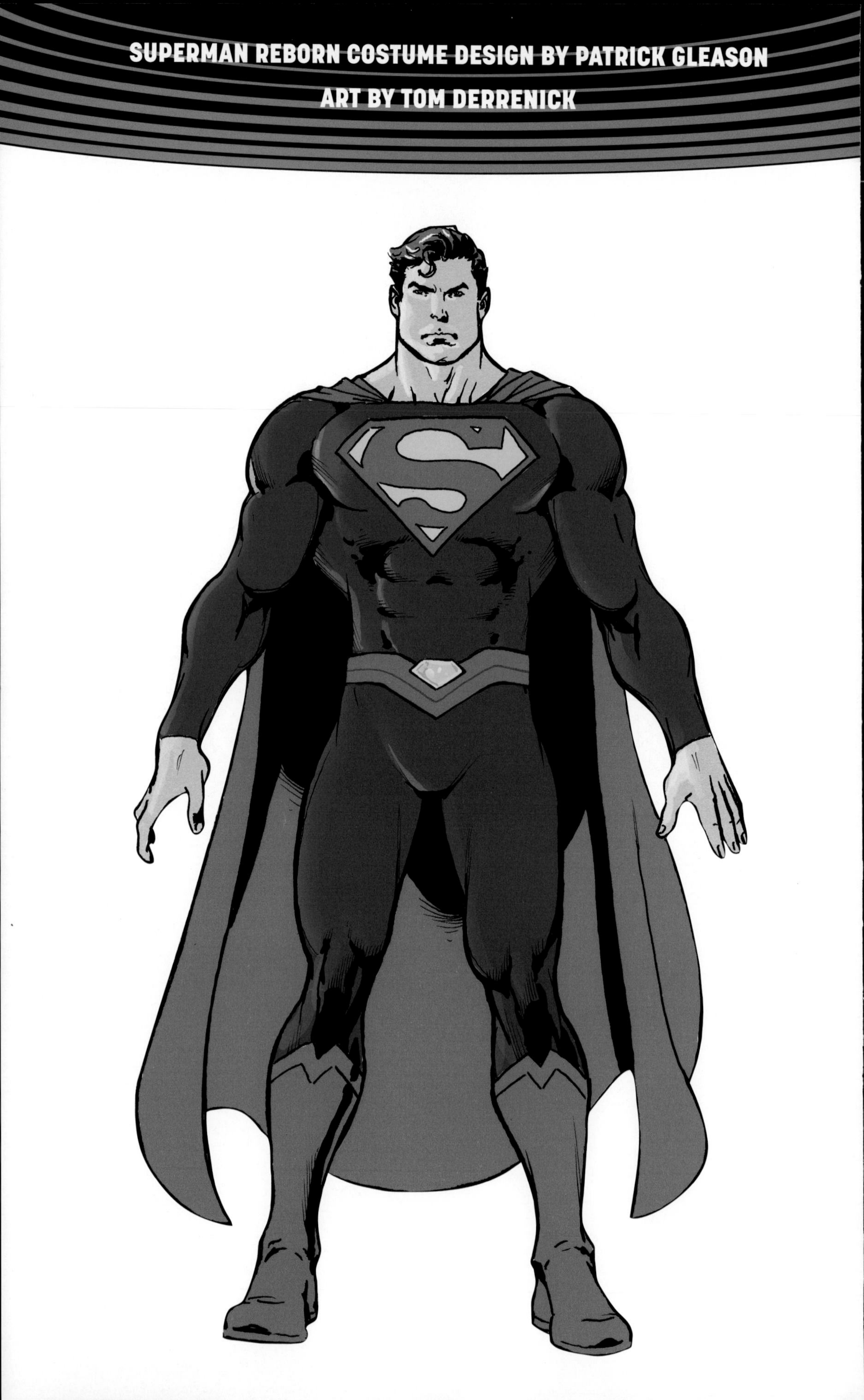

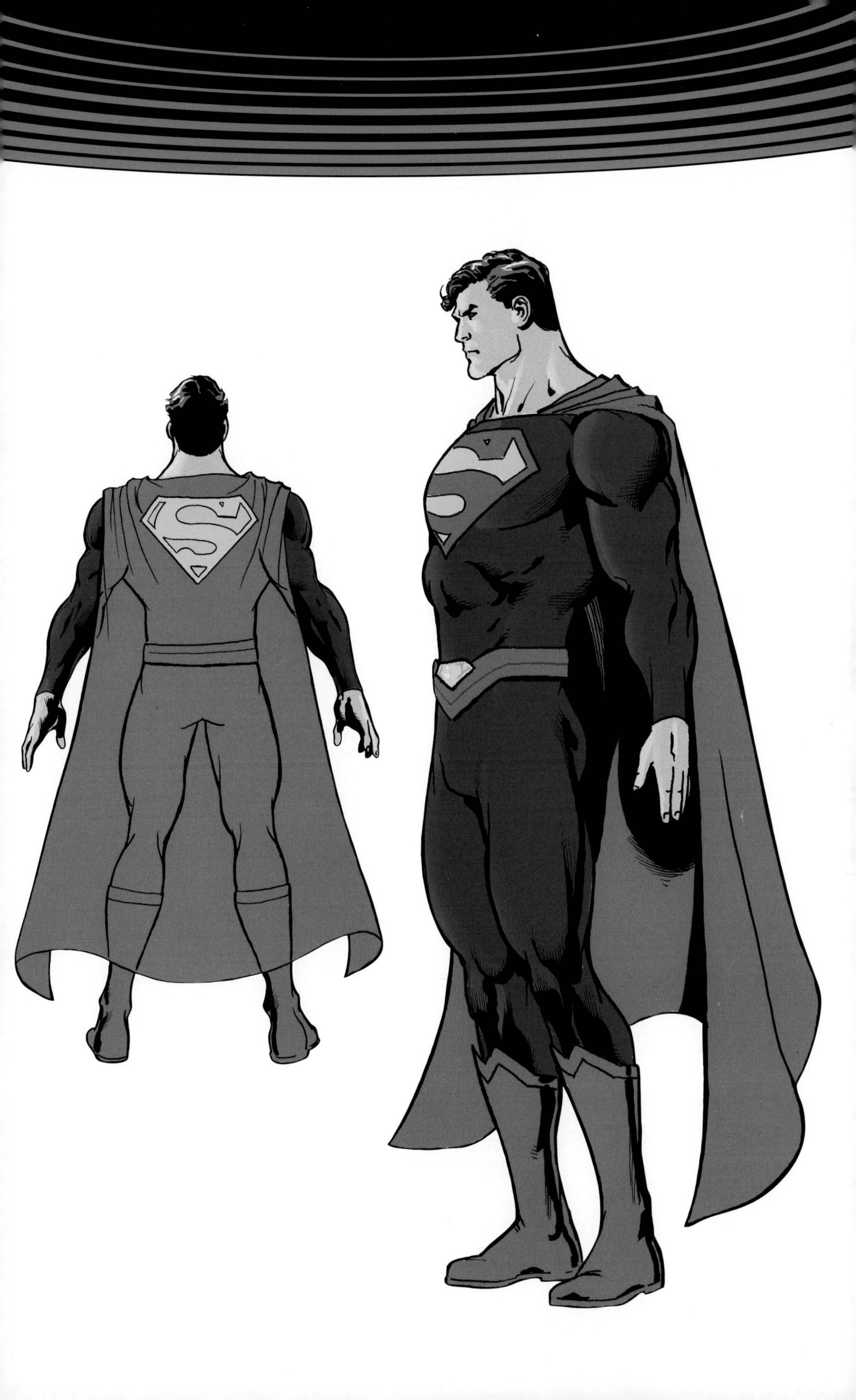

ORIGINAL SUPERMAN REBORN VARIANT IMAGE
BY GARY FRANK AND BRAD ANDERSON

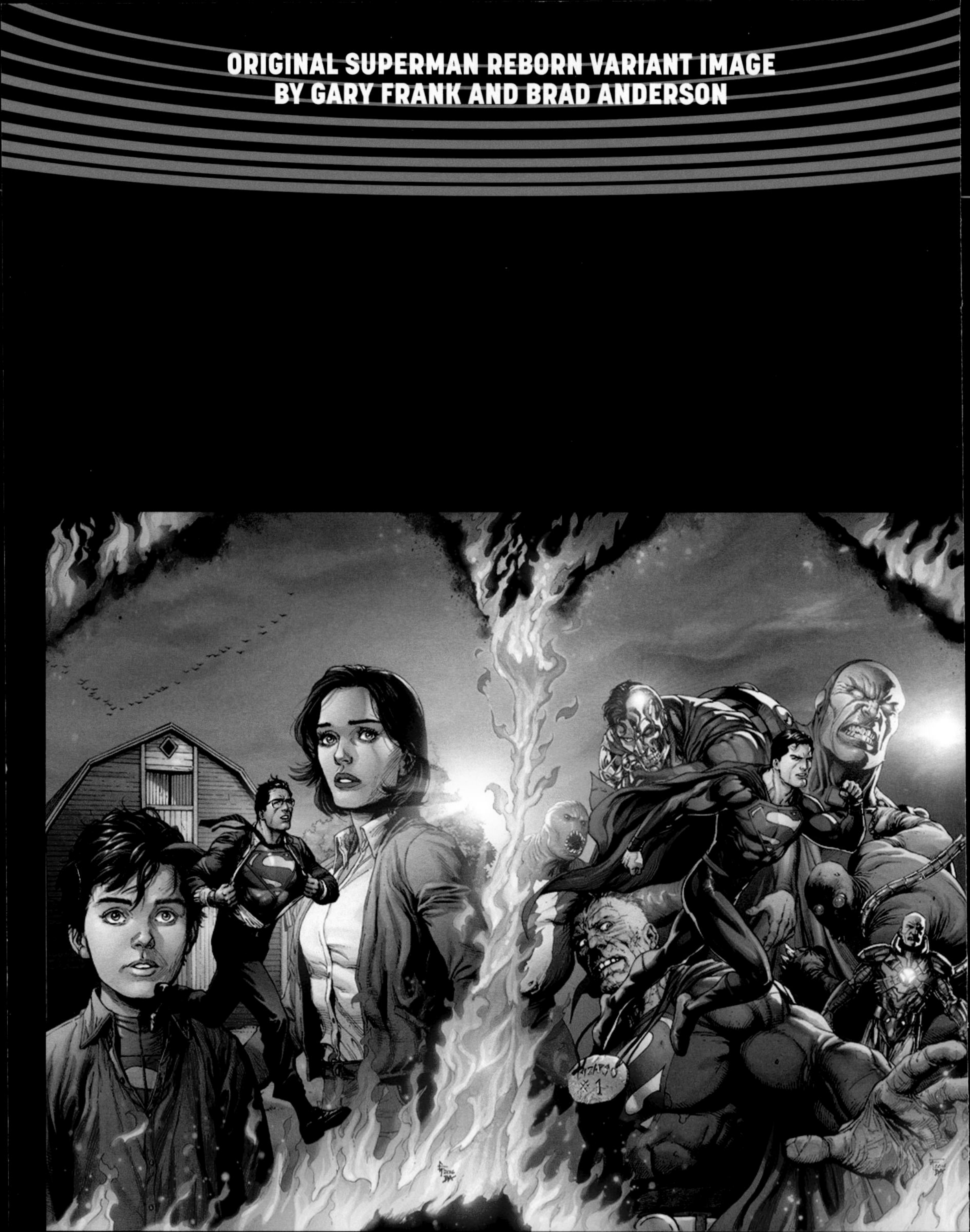

SUPERMAN REBORN CONNECTION SKETCH & COVERS BY PATRICK GLEASON

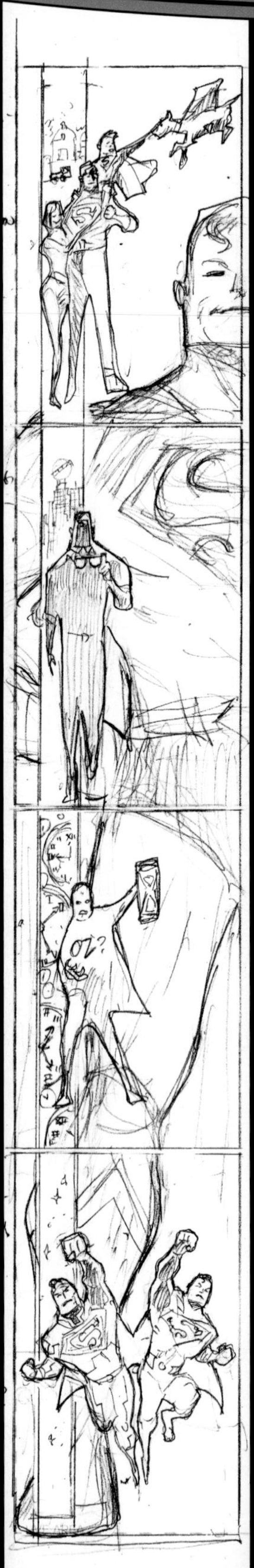
OZ?

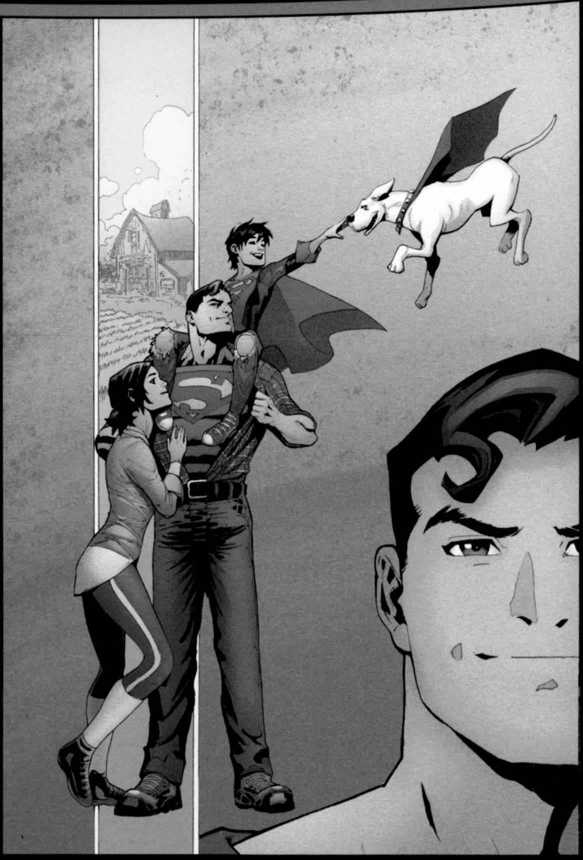

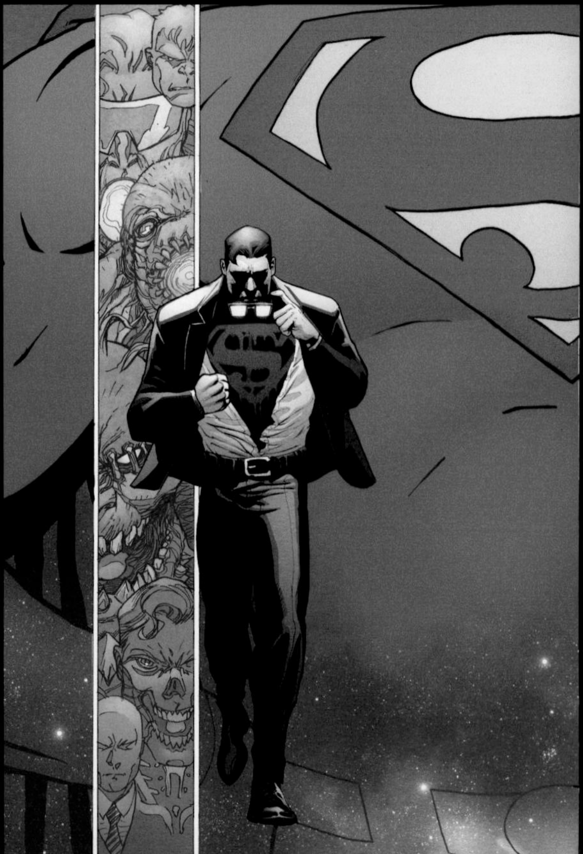

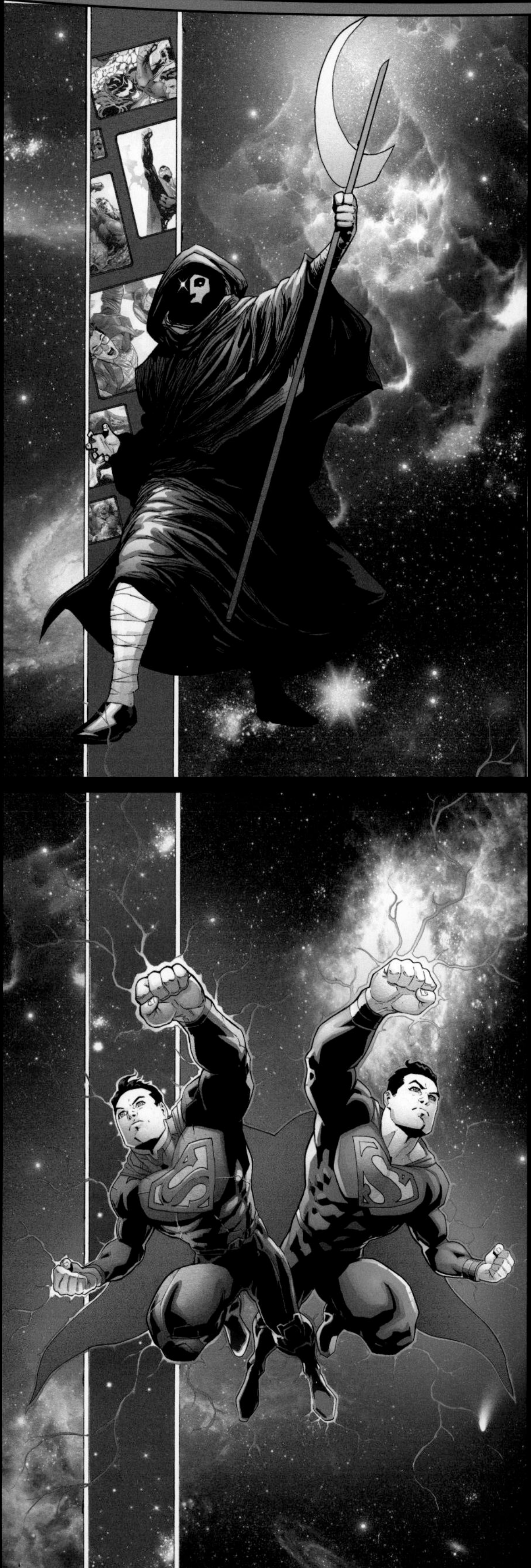
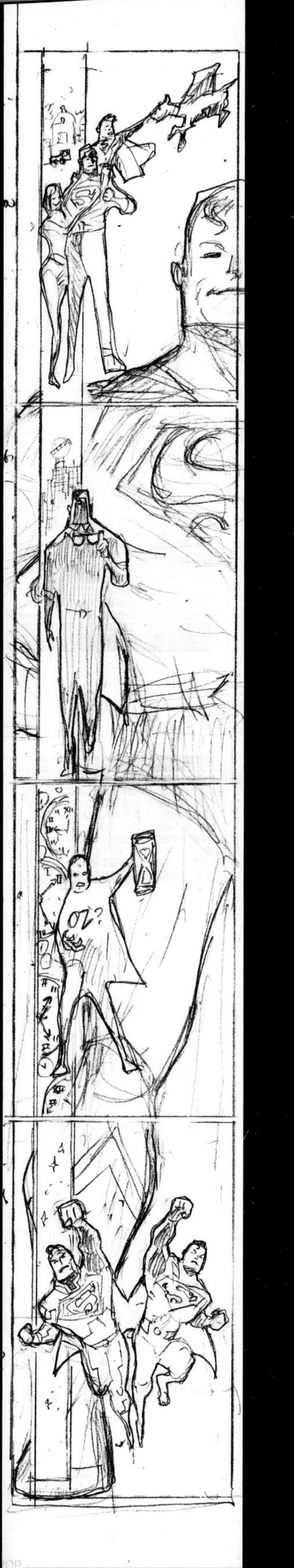

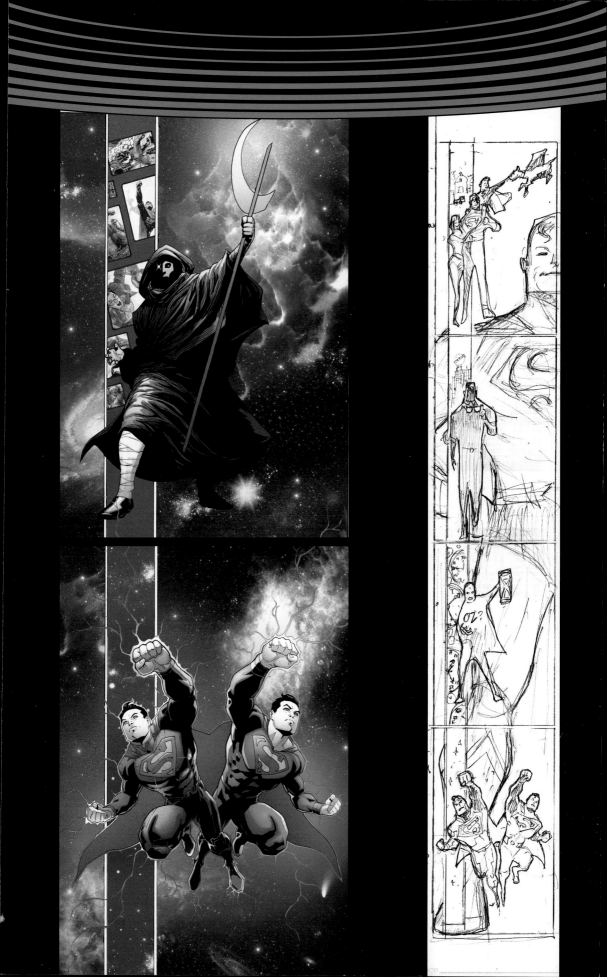

UNUSED SUPERMAN COVER BY PATRICK GLEASON

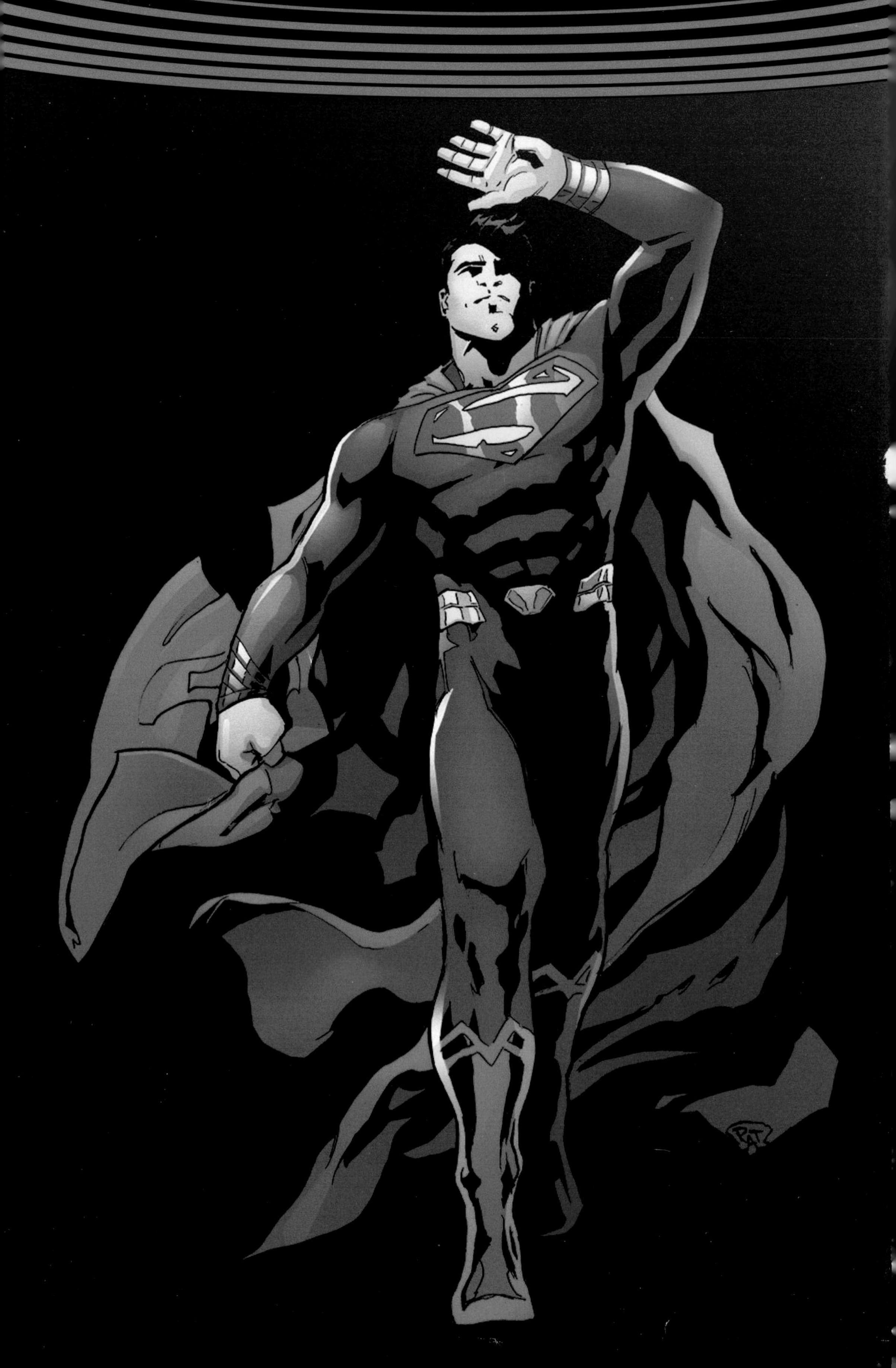
PAT